T0375443

CHINA'S ONE BELT ONE ROAD INITIATIVE

CHINA'S ONE BELT ONE ROAD INITIATIVE

LIM Tai Wei
East Asian Institute, NUS, Singapore

Henry CHAN Hing Lee
Singapore Management University

Katherine TSENG Hui-Yi
East Asian Institute, NUS, Singapore

LIM Wen Xin
East Asian Institute, NUS, Singapore

ICP

Imperial College Press

Published by

Imperial College Press
57 Shelton Street
Covent Garden
London WC2H 9HE

Distributed by

World Scientific Publishing Co. Pte. Ltd.
5 Toh Tuck Link, Singapore 596224
USA office: 27 Warren Street, Suite 401-402, Hackensack, NJ 07601
UK office: 57 Shelton Street, Covent Garden, London WC2H 9HE

Library of Congress Cataloging-in-Publication Data
Names: Lim, Tai-Wei, author.
Title: China's One Belt One Road Initiative / Tai Wei Lim (East Asian Institute, NUS, Singapore), Henry Chan (Singapore Management University, Singapore), Katherine Tseng (East Asian Institute, NUS, Singapore) & Wen Xin Lim (East Asian Institute, NUS, Singapore).
Description: New Jersey : Imperial College Press, [2016]
Identifiers: LCCN 2016000976 | ISBN 9781783269297 (hc : alk. paper)
Subjects: LCSH: China--Foreign economic relations--Eurasia. | Eurasia--Foreign economic relations--China. | China--Commerce--Eurasia. | Eurasia--Commerce--China. | Trade routes--Eurasia. | China--Commercial policy. | China--Economic policy.
Classification: LCC HF1604.Z4 E8355 2016 | DDC 337.5105--dc23
LC record available at http://lccn.loc.gov/2016000976

British Library Cataloguing-in-Publication Data
A catalogue record for this book is available from the British Library.

Desk Editors: Chandrima Maitra/Lixi Dong

Typeset by Stallion Press
Email: enquiries@stallionpress.com

Printed in Singapore

Contents

Foreword

In 2013, the Chinese government announced that it has the intention to revive the ancient trade routes famously known as the Silk Road. The world later learns that the intention, which came to be known as the Silk Road Economic Belt and the 21st Century Maritime Silk Road or One Belt One Road initiative, is actually an ambitious development strategy aiming to allow China to build stronger relationships with its neighbors, and *vice versa*, through sharing of resources.

Nevertheless, the professed scale of the One Belt One Road initiative is so impressive to the extent of making it a project unprecedented in history. This could be the reason which makes the initiative instead be greeted with caution, by the intended stakeholders.

Will the One Belt One Road initiative ultimately create a coprosperity sphere never before experienced by China and its neighbors in Southeast Asia and the Eurasian landmass? It remains to be seen. But one would agree that for a project of this scale, it requires collective wisdoms and efforts of all stakeholders to manage the risks and to meet the challenges that will come along. The Confucius Institute of the NANYANG TECHNOLOGICAL UNIVERSITY (CI-NTU) hopes that it could make a humble contribution in this direction. Thus, on 19 December 2015, CI-NTU jointly organized a seminar entitled: "One Belt One Road: Prospects and Possibilities" with the International Zheng He Society. The two organizations are extremely privileged to have Dr Tan Ta Sen as opening guest speaker and Mr Henry Chan Hing Lee, Dr Kong Tuan Yuen, Dr Lim Tai Wei, Miss Lim Wen Xin, Dr Tai Yew Seng, and Dr Katherine Tseng Hui Yi, to present their analyses on the dynamics of the One Belt One Road initiative, from a Southeast Asian perspective.

It is extremely encouraging to see that the insights which the scholars had shared with the participants of the seminar are now published as this volume. This would enable their research to go beyond the physical space of a lecture room through readership.

I would like to congratulate Henry, Tuan Yuen, Tai Wei, Wen Xin, Yew Seng and Katherine, for their accomplishments.

Dr Peng-fu NEO
Director, Confucius Institute
NANYANG TECHNOLOGICAL UNIVERSITY

About the Contributors

Henry CHAN Hing Lee 陳興利 is a PhD candidate (General Management), Singapore Management University. He has extensive working experience in business prior to taking the PhD program after retirement in 2012. He occupied senior management positions in agriculture, banking, flour milling, hotel, power generation, real estate business of La Filipina Uygongco Corporation, a mini-conglomerate based in Manila, Philippines. Chinese economic growth is his favourite research topic and he feels the traditional growth theory is not explaining it well. He is looking into aspects of political economy, strategy, innovation, industry policy and culture aside from traditional growth theory to better explain the Chinese growth phenomenon. He is also curious at the emerging post-Bretton Woods world economic order with the rise of China. He can be contacted at henry.chan.2012@phdgm.smu.edu.sg. His articles include: "Noble Peace Price for 2012", published by Economics Club of SMU in 2012; "What Happened to Indian Economy?" published by Economics Club of SMU in 2012; "新加坡精英政治的困局", unpublished paper "阿里巴巴上市讓世界看到中國的變化" published by *Lianhe Zaobao* in October, 2014.

Winglok HUNG is now studying his PhD in International Relations at Tsinghua University, China. He started his PhD at the City University of Hong Kong in August 2014 before moving to Tsinghua University in August 2015. He graduated from the Chinese University of Hong Kong in Government and Public Administration in 2009 and completed his MPhil in African Studies at the University of Cambridge in 2012. Previously he worked for Hong Kong Institute of Asia-Pacific Studies, the Chinese

University of Hong Kong as a research assistant. He has been writing commentaries for a local newspaper *Takungpao* since 2014.

KONG Tuan Yuen (康端严) is Visiting Research Fellow at East Asian Institute (EAI), National University of Singapore (NUS). He received his PhD in Industrial Economics from the National Central University, Taiwan. He had taken part in Taiwan's economic research projects during his postdoctoral fellowship at the Research Centre for Taiwan Economic Development, and joined Epson in turn, a Japanese multinational enterprise in Malaysia, to conduct business management as well as financial and planning analysis. During his service with Epson, he was sent to Japan to investigate on Toyota's production system and manufacturing automation. His current research interests include China's industry development, especially strategic emerging industries, corporate strategy and China–Malaysia relations. He can be reached at eaikty@nus.edu.sg.

LIM Tai Wei is a Senior Lecturer at SIM University of Singapore and Research Fellow Adjunct at the East Asian Institute (EAI) National University of Singapore (NUS). His teaching interests include East Asian History, World History and Japanese popular culture-related courses. His research interests include energy and environmental histories of contemporary Japan and China. He is an area study specialist (on contemporary China and Japan) and a historian by training.

LIM Wen Xin is a Research Assistant at East Asian Institute, National University of Singapore. She obtained her Bachelor's Degree of Social Science (Hons) in Economics and Chinese Studies from National University of Singapore. She was a reporter in *Sin Chew Daily* (2011) and has been actively involved in translation work. Her research interests include China–ASEAN relations, Chinese foreign policy and China's industrial development.

TAI Yew Seng (DAI Rouxing 戴柔星) holds a Bachelor's (Honours) and Master's degrees in Chinese Studies from the National University of Singapore. He graduated in 2012 with a PhD in Ceramic Archaeology from Peking University. Tai has published several articles on Chinese ceramic and coauthored two books on ancient maritime trade road. Tai has published several articles including "Ming Gap and the Revival of Commercial Production of

Blue and White Porcelain in China" (journals.lib.washington.edu/index.php/BIPPA/article/viewFile/9437/11882) and "The Ceramic Interregnum and the Ming Gap of the Ming Dynasty" ("*Proceedings of the International Symposium: Chinese Export Ceramics in the 16th and 17th Centuries and the Spread of Material Civilisation*" edited by Cheng Pei-kai, pp. 345–352, City University of Hong Kong, 2012). He has participated in archaeological excavations including in the Old Malindi City site in Kenya; the Xing kiln site in Lincheng, Hebei; Ge Type kiln site in Longquan, Zhejiang; Jingdezhen Imperial Kiln Site, Jiangxi; and, the Empress Place site Singapore. In the Empress Place excavation, Chinese porcelain expert Tai Yew Seng, who had been digging nearby that area, recognized the fragments as imperial-grade ceramics produced between 1368 and 1398. See more at: http://news.asiaone.com/news/singapore/racing-against-time-salvage-old-singapore#sthash.DZCCZVGv.dpuf. Tai Yew Seng is presently a part-time lecturer at the Confucius Institute, Nanyang Technological University, Singapore.

TAN Ta Sen is President, International Zheng He Society and Owner of Cheng Ho Cultural Museum, Melaka. Dr Tan Ta Sen was born in Singapore in 1936 and is basically a Chinese educated, graduated from Nanyang University in 1960 in History and Geography. Upon graduation he was offered an Indonesian scholarship to pursue Malay and Indonesian Studies in the University of Indonesia in Jakarta. He graduated with BA, Drs in Indonesian Studies and PhD in History. He is multilingual, proficient in Malay, Indonesian, Chinese and English. He has many publications in the above languages.

Katherine TSENG Hui-Yi is a Research Associate in East Asian Institute. After her Master's degree in Cambridge and New York University (NYU), she attended the World Trade Organization (WTO) negotiation team for Taiwan Government. After obtaining her doctorate degree with UW-Wisconsin, Madison, she went to Beijing, China, and spent some time with The Beijing Arbitration Committee (2010, Spring), studying arbitration issues in current China. She then joined the Singapore International Arbitration Centre (2010, Autumn), and had a good chance of looking at how states and private sectors worked to resolve their disputes. Subsequently, she joined the East Asian Institute around the end of 2010. She eyes the thriving events that rapidly change the political landscapes in the world map. She can be contacted at eaithy@nus.edu.sg.

ZHANG Huang is a Lecturer at NUDT of China. His research interests include national security and technology strategy. **LI Jie** is a research assistant in NUS of Singapore. Her research interests include relationships between China and Japan.

Section A
Introduction

Chapter 1
Introduction

LIM Tai Wei

The One Belt One Road (OBOR) is an ambitious economic diplomacy initiative from China with two components, one via the overland route from Asia to Europe and the other through the maritime route between Asia and Europe. President Xi Jinping declared that OBOR will be his one and only major foreign policy initiative during his administration. The initiative serves a number of functions for Chinese diplomacy. First, it consumes the overproduction, overcapacity and excess products and commodities from China, especially with the specter of an economic slowdown in the Chinese economy. OBOR is supported by newfound Chinese economic muscles, including the Asian Infrastructure Investment Bank (AIIB) which is initially funded at US$40 billion dollars and eventually raised to US$450 billion (in the future it may go up to US$100 billion). The BRICS Bank is also initially funded with US$50 billion and major contributors include India and China. The Silk Road Fund is provided with US$40 billion dollars for its coffers.

Second, it is seen as a foreign policy initiative to extend China's influence into other regions. The de-Sovietization of Central Asia offers an opportunity for China to link up with the Central Asian region economically. Moreover, Western sanctions on Russia mean that the latter is more receptive to the idea of looking eastwards for trade and business with China and other East Asian states to lower their economic dependence on Europe. Third, the OBOR is also seen as an opportunity to create alternative funding agencies that reflect China's growing economic strengths. Institutions that are going to fund OBOR's initiatives like AIIB, Silk Road Fund, BRICS Bank are seen as vehicles to address China's lower voting rights in World Bank (WB), International Monetary Fund (IMF) and Asian Development Bank (ADB).

If the Chinese national interests are clear (as detailed earlier), then what are those of the other states? Many developing economies are keen to apply for funding their infrastructure developmental needs. The current financial institutions added together are unable to fund those needs. With the advent of the AIIB and other OBOR-related funding agencies, economies in need of infrastructure construction have alternative sources of funding. They also have access to funding agencies that may have different sets of prerequisites or lower standards/criteria for infrastructure projects. Huang Yukon, former Country Director and current advisor for China at the WB and advisor to the ADB, provided some points related to possible operational philosophies behind AIIB: "Certain projects have higher environmental risks, others do not. So the right standard is developing what you need to do in line with the real risk of the project, rather than just having standards that you legally apply in everything".[1]

According to the ADB, Asia will need US$8.22 trillion of infrastructure investments for this decade.[2] In yearly terms, ADB calculates that Asia needs US$750 billion annually until 2020.[3] In addition, lower and middle-income countries in the developed regions of the world like parts of Central and Eastern Europe can also benefit from AIIB's funding facilities. Infrastructure developmental funding can also help to stimulate economic development in underperforming economies. Central Asia which has fallen into the backwaters of the global economy and is highly dependent on commodities trading is trying to develop its manufacturing sector. It is a good example of a regional economy that is trying to industrialize and avoid falling into the commodity supplies trap.

The conceptual idea of OBOR is based on a historical narrative. A German traveler in the 1800s coined the phrase "Silk Road" to describe the route through which camels plied to bring goods from China to Europe through a series of intermediaries along the route (including the Persians,

---

[1] Huang, Yukon, Demystifying the Asian Infrastructure Investment Bank, dated 21 April 2015 in the *Carnegie Endowment* website [downloaded on 15 December 2015] available at http://carnegieendowment.org/2015/04/21/demystifying-asian-infrastructure-investment-bank.

[2] Tan, Christine and See Kit Tang, Is AIIB the Answer to Asia's Infrastructure Needs? dated 25 June 2015 in CNBC.com [downloaded on 26 June 2015], available at http://www.cnbc.com/2015/06/25/is-aiib-the-answer-to-asias-infrastructure-needs.html.

[3] Orlik, Tom and Fielding Chen, One Belt, One Road — China's Modern Marco Polos Bring No Novelties Westward, dated 2 July 2015 in *Bloomberg Brief*, 2015, 2.

Arabs, Central Asians, etc.). Replacing the camels with high-speed rails (HSRs), the contemporary Silk Route is modernized and brought up to date. (In this publication, one of our contributors and editor, Henry Chan Hing Lee, will be detailing the development of these HSRs in OBOR.) Eventually, the railway lines may be followed by pipeline projects. Even the Maritime Silk Road (MSR) that was plied by Zheng He (Cheng Ho)'s ships and followed up by Vasco Da Gama's Portuguese ships is updated in the OBOR as well. According to sources from Xinhua and United Nations Educational, Scientific and Cultural Organization (UNESCO), the farthest sources of the overland route end in Germany, Netherlands and Italy while the maritime route is almost identical with Zheng He's seven maritime voyages. Since 2011, experimental trains have been initiated to bring goods and products from China to Europe, ending its journeys in Germany and Spain. The starting points of such journeys in the current and future contexts are likely to be trading centers like Yiwu and also cities in the western regions of China like Chongqing. The comparative advantage of using an overland route is that travel time is shorter although ships appear to be able to carry more cargo. The fact that ships were able to carry more cargo was a contributing reason why the overland route was historically declined in the first place. The idea therefore is to fill up the rail cargo with higher value-added items like luxury cars and time-sensitive products that need just-in-time delivery like smartphones so that feasibility is dependent on value-addedness of products rather than volume.

Operationally, China appears to be keen on initiating the Overland Silk Road (OSR) first, supplying aid to Pakistan to develop its infrastructure and also seems ready to build the infrastructure in Central Asia. (When President Xi announced the OBOR plan, he made a public address in Indonesia for the MSR and gave the public announcement for the OSR at Kazakhstan. The switch to economic diplomacy is an evolution of the charm offensive designed to manage the rise of China in the world. Initially dispensing loans that have no preconditions like environmental conditions and human rights, China began to realize that those loans and aids were easily brushed aside, reneged or ignored when national interests change or when ruling regimes are replaced. Therefore, the AIIB provides Chinese funding and dispenses aids and loans with some market-friendly mechanisms and meeting some environmental preconditions although not as onerous as those offered by Western institutions.

Huang Yukon, former Country Director and current advisor for China at the WB and advisor to the ADB, argued that AIIB "will focus on specific projects, building a road, a bridge or a power plant. It will not get into program loans or balance of payment loans, which are designed to support certain policy changes".[4] This feature appears to distinguish AIIB from the activities of the existing international funding agencies like WB, IMF and ADB. Huang goes on to state that "The weight of the shares of the AIIB will be determined by the size of the economy, so China will have a large share, but not a veto share. Asian countries as a whole will have majority voting rights".[5] This argument is used as a defense and justification against the possibility of Chinese dominance. Huang also hinted at the management structure of the AIIB: "the AIIB is trying to go for a structure where the board meets periodically, like in most corporations..., the board usually establishes the rules, the policies that give the president guidance. But afterwards they let the management run the organization. The AIIB is looking for a similar structure where the board is less active and less intrusive on a daily basis."[6]

But the OBOR has its inherent challenges, the most important of which are geopolitical challenges. Central Asia which is a focal point for the OBOR is the traditional backyard of Russian geopolitical influence. China must therefore be careful not to antagonize Russian national interests. China therefore is trying to concentrate mostly on economic cooperation and not forge political ties with Central Asian states while embracing Russia as a close partner geopolitically. This is especially important since Russia has a competing economic union with the Central Asian states, one that China is not involved in. Currently, the Chinese OBOR and AIIB are in a much stronger economic position than Russian regionalism initiatives, particularly at the time of this writing when oil prices stay low, hovering at around US$50 per barrel. European Union (EU) and Brussels are also watching Chinese forays into Eastern and Central European states carefully.

Many states in the Asian region are also wary of having to pick sides between Beijing and its initiative vs. Washington and its institutions. Some

[4] *Ibid.*
[5] *Ibid.*
[6] *Ibid.*

countries are trying to hedge Beijing's economic strength against Washington's strong geopolitical influence. Even high-speed train projects become politicized as East Asian states pick the competing proposals offered by the two countries as their system of preference. Another theater for picking choices occurred in the formative stage of AIIB when countries carefully considered joining the AIIB only after they were convinced they would not hurt relations with the West. The tipping point came when UK and other close American allies became members of AIIB.

Other countries are also worried about the influx of cheap Chinese products and labor that will follow Chinese infrastructure development. The African experience with some Chinese state companies accentuate this fear although Chinese competitiveness is not universally feared. There are also worries of neo-colonialism of resources, afraid that the Chinese are going for raw materials as the main purpose of the infrastructure construction. Then there are worries about the future that as Chinese commercial and business intertwines with those of the OBOR region, China will meddle in local and regional politics. These worries and fears are not usually shared to the same degree, but they remain as challenges for China as it embarks on this major economic diplomacy initiative.

In the realm of maritime disputes, the major challenge is again geopolitics. China is experiencing maritime disputes with many of its neighboring coastal states. In the East China Sea, it is experiencing disputes with Japan over the Senkaku/Diaoyu islands. In South China Sea, it is facing disputes with claimants of the disputed islands in that region. China claims much of the maritime territories of South China Sea through a nine-dash line map that marks out those territories and have completed three airstrips in the Nansha islands that are decried by other major powers and claimants. Of all the claimants, the Philippines and Vietnam have courted the help of other big powers like the US and Japan which are traditionally active in the East Asian region. The maritime situation appears to be more complicated than the OSR, given that China has better relations with the traditional power in OSR with Russia. In other words, a major challenge for China remains national interests that are defined by geopolitical priorities.

If OBOR and AIIB matures, it is possible that there are significant opportunities for these institutions to cooperate with existing international financial institutions like the WB. Platforms for coordination may develop to manage and handle such projects. Some aspects of convergence may even happen in the distant future. This edited volume covers the different perspectives of OBOR by including different aspects of the complex and complicated entity that is OBOR. It does not pretend to be comprehensive but tries to include as many different components of OBOR as possible.

The Belt and Road Initiative is comparable to the analogy of choice offering based on individual assessment of national interests at this moment. The ultimate adjudicating factor is in the details, how each individual economy or state will assess the national interests according to conditionalities, geopolitical priorities, domestic political situations, external factors and national resources and how the Belt and Road initiative + AIIB + BRICS Bank *vis-à-vis* current existing established institutions like ADB best serve their needs. The equilibrium or balance between overland and maritime trade routes in Chinese initiatives has already been highlighted in the international media narratives. They argued that such a prospect if not properly explained or managed may put maritime trading nations on their toes.

Organization of this edited review volume

This multidisciplinary publication brought together a large number of stakeholders interested in the historical Silk Road, the MSR and the OBOR initiative. These stakeholders include academics, businessmen, curators, graduate students, economists and researchers from China, Hong Kong, Malaysia, the Philippines, Singapore and Taiwan. Our volume covers three major aspects of the OBOR — the historical perspective, a business angle to railway technologies crucial to the central OBOR concept of connectivity and the maritime perspective on disputes, prospects and dangers. Chronologically, we began with the historical narrative. This publication is divided into six sections: A–F. Section A which contains this introduction is an overview of the publication's contents. It provides a brief background behind the OBOR initiative but does not pretend to be comprehensive. It also orientates the reader with regard to the organization of topics in the complex OBOR initiative. Section B is written by a world-renowned scholar Dr **Tan Ta Sen** on Admiral Zheng He (Cheng Ho) and the establishment of the historical MSR. It also discusses the origins of the OSR. Using his deep knowledge on the subject matter and his practitioner's experience as the curator of the Silk Road artefacts, this section sets the context for Section C which brings the discussion up to date to the contemporary MSR component of the OBOR initiative proposed by the Chinese President Xi Jinping and the Chinese leadership.

Historically, Dr Tan also pointed out that, apart from silk and tea, the most important Chinese export was ceramics which was traded in large quantities. The elegant porcelains have long been China's major export commodity. By the Ming dynasty, due to the development of the private kilns, the quantity and quality of ceramic production were enhanced remarkably, where large quantities of cheap and good export ceramics were shipped to the world including the European, African, East Asian, Southeast Asian, South Asian and Central Asian markets. The global demand for Chinese ceramics then became huge. The elegant ceramics became a social status symbol and ceramics were also items to be buried together with the deceased. In the 12th century, China exported through Southeast Asia a great deal of celadon wares to Central Asia and India. Before the 17th century, Asia was Chinese ceramics' biggest market.

Before Dr Tan's discussion on Zheng He and his activities related to maritime trade and tributary system, archaeologist Dr **Tai Yew Seng** will discuss the Yuan dynasty system of Official Capital Ship and how the imperial authorities tried to regulate trade before the advent of Zheng He's attempts to establish the tributary system and maritime trade during the Ming dynasty. This discussion sets the context for discussing Ming maritime trade and Zheng He's role in this maritime system. Dr Tai basically argues that there was already a precedent for official trade immediately before the establishment of the Yuan dynasty but also highlights the differences between the two. This then leads on to Dr Tan's in-depth discussion of Zheng He's activities and their significance.

In Section C, **Lim Tai Wei** examines media narratives on OBOR as it progresses through different stages of maturity. Some of these narratives may be perceptions, but perceptions are sometimes equally as important as concrete developments in issues related to international relations, geopolitics and economic competition. For most countries, the Chinese vision and more established developmental paths of the developed economies are not mutually exclusive, there are overlaps between these two choices. It provides more diversity of choices for funding and infrastructure development. For the critics, the problems they see with this range from challenging the status quo of the prevailing world order of trade and politics to accusations of neo-Colonialism in resource extraction.

A major question arose as to how China will disperse its funds. The key word that is mentioned in the international media, top leaders and policy makers' statements as well as the scholarly conference and seminars that I attended was "connectivity" — how to link up the entire belt of countries along both OSR and MSR so that trade can be stimulated. Up till December 2014, details were not forthcoming from Chinese sources on how their Silk Road-related budget will be utilized. Along with observers and the international media, this began to cause some countries located along both the OSR as well as the MSR to seek more details about the initiative.

In seeking this reaction from the Chinese government, the immediate response can be divided into three ways: (1) to use official and track II channels to ask for more details so that states in the designated regions of the Silk Road initiative can react accordingly to maximize their economic benefits from the scheme; (2) to preempt any issues incompatible with national interests by first opposing the institutions associated (or perceived to be associated) with the scheme such as opposition to the AIIB; (3) regardless of the shape and form of the Silk Road initiative which is expected to be organic and dynamic both in implementation and development, to persuade Beijing to be more transparent and conform to international norms by integrating with the international community, e.g. early persuasion by various countries to Beijing to locate the headquarters of the AIIB in their own capitals like Seoul, Singapore, Jakarta and perhaps even the semi-autonomous Hong Kong rather than Shanghai or Beijing.

These questions are pondered internally within China as well, between an internationalist faction keen to see the Silk Road initiatives as part of China's opening up with greater transparency and harmonization with international norms vs. those keen to construct an international trade and commerce system with firmer Beijing control. Lim, a historian, examines contemporary media narratives related to the OBOR initiative. Through these narratives, his research objective is to find out how contemporary commentators appropriate narratives about historical events related to the MSR to interpret current policy agendas and legitimize diplomatic or economic exchanges. In Section C on the MSR, Lim Tai Wei's chapter focuses on the historical background of the MSR.

Admiral Zheng He (Cheng Ho in Wades Giles spelling) made seven voyages to the known maritime trading world on behalf of the Chinese Ming dynasty during the reign of Emperor Yongle. His accomplishments in navigational history is universally recognized by many scholars. The tangible and intangible legacies that he left behind are shaped by various interpretations to fit different historical narratives. Historically, imageries of Ma took multiple forms, from fearsome gigantic explorer to a testicle-less eunuch. Added to these sets of images, in Southeast Asia, he was deified and became a Taoist God with his own following of worshippers.

In the revived talk on a contemporary "Maritime Silk Road (MSR)", narratives of Zheng He may become part of the current discourse on Chinese plans to revive the MSR which covers the span of trading cities from Fuzhou to Italy (the "one road" component of the "one belt one road" concept known as Belt and Roads initiative in official Chinese terminology). Other interpretations see the MSR ending in Antwerp, Belgium, at the European end of the MSR. Regardless of the shape of the contemporary and future MSR, Zheng He's legend will be continually molded and shaped by the Chinese government and other stakeholders to support the OBOR initiative.

Following the chapter on Lim's historical background on the MSR, to reflect the diversity and spectrum of opinions, **Lim Wen Xin** surveyed secondary sources of textual materials related to the OBOR policy. W. X. Lim's literature review chapter gathers, consolidates and reviews the current level of information, presenting the readers with different interpretations of the OBOR, the economic and political implications of the plan, and possible challenges that it would encounter including the internal challenges and external factors. It is an important survey of existing literatures and debates on the OBOR initiative. In her literature review, Wen Xin Lim argues that the ultimate adjudicating factor for the success of OBOR is in the details of the initiative itself and the viability of the newly-established institutions such as the AIIB and the Silk Road Fund. It also depends on how China is able to overcome the deficit of trust and suspicions among countries, convincing each individual countries that the OBOR is genuinely a sincere plan for joint economic development and a win–win approach for all sovereign states. Therefore, to address a spectrum of opinions in this aspect, Lim's literature review gathers, consolidates and reviews the current level of information, presenting the readers with different interpretations of the OBOR, the economic and political implications of the plan, and possible challenges that it would encounter including the internal challenges and external factors.

In the maritime arena, one such challenge to OBOR is discussed in **Katherine Tseng Hui-Yi**'s chapter which details the revival of Beijing's interest in the MSR that problematizes any overly optimistic and uncritical ideas and narratives of the implementation of a revived MSR. Nearer to China, adopting a Taiwanese perspective, Tseng argues that contesting legal developments combined with tensed geopolitical events in the South China Sea since 1973 have increased to certain levels such that territorial quarrels among China and ASEAN claimants are in fact interrupting, or at least, hindering the amicability necessary for inter-state cooperation in many aspects. The lack of effective cooperation mechanisms in a variety of issues, such as fishing regulation and maritime environmental administration, is unfortunately one direct outcome of these territorial disagreements. All claimant parties need to start tackling the ongoing urgent issues of depletion of fishing resources, increasing costs of maritime traffic and loss of lives on the sea. Tseng's chapter ends Section C on the MSR.

In Section D, the fourth major section of this publication zooms in on the OSR. **Lim Tai Wei**'s chapter samples different media narratives about the OBOR policy. In terms of implementation priorities, some argue that China's main target is Central Asia and eventually proliferate to other regions that will not only include train infrastructure but also ports and at some point energy pipelines.[7] Connectivity in the OSR will be dependent on high-speed and medium-speed railways. Infrastructure connectivity is a priority in the implementation of the OBOR initiative. Observers are focused on the rail connectivity in the OBOR Initiative. The unprecedented speed and scale that China has set up its passenger HSR system, from virtually 0 to 19,000 km in less than a decade's time at a significantly lower cost that even a lower middle income country with per capita of US$3,000 can afford, has attracted many neighboring countries to take a second look at using rail as a viable land transport backbone for moving passengers. Such attention

[7] Escobar, Pepe, China is Building a New Silk Road to Europe, and it's Leaving America Behind, dated 16 December 2014 in *Mother Jones* website [downloaded on 18 December 2014], available at http://www.motherjones.com/politics/2014/12/chinas-new-silk-road-europe-will-leave-america-behind.

focused on railway tracks may be visualized as going against the general developmental trend of post-WWII transport networks which typically consists of highways and airports.

To fund these projects, **Henry Chan Hing Lee** examines the issue of multilateral funding agencies like AIIB. Given that funding is an important aspect of OBOR, complementing China's effort to develop the Silk Road economic belt, it initiated the setting up of AIIB to finance the infrastructure projects of member countries. This is China's second major initiative after BRICS Bank to set up an alternative multilateral development funding institutions different from the traditional post-war Bretton Woods setup of the WB and its associated institution in 1966, the ADB. This move is perceived by some observers as an expression of Chinese response to the shareholding, voting and operations of the existing institutions.

China faces several important roadblocks in making AIIB a viable multilateral infrastructure development institution, foremost of which is the shareholding structure of the bank. In both WB and ADB, the most important shareholder holds less than 16% of the bank, control of US and Japan in the two institutions were exercised through soft management control and the joint unwritten voting bloc arrangements of US, European countries and Japan. China's initial shareholding of 50% in AIIB negated the multilateral nature of the institutions. There are many other issues facing the smooth start up and operations of a multilateral development bank, and China must work out these issues one by one. China had not worked on these problems before and there will be a steep learning curve.

Aside from the symbolic ideological and geopolitical victory, if China can make this alternative developmental model in the form of a China-centric South–South Bank work, it will free China from the burden of bilateral financing to push its cost-effective infrastructure technology abroad. The enjoyment of "privileged lender" legal status of AIIB means China's overseas infrastructure loan push is credit-wise safe. The section on multilateral funding agencies will examine the issues facing AIIB and the approaches that China can take to make AIIB work.

In terms of railway infrastructure construction (one of the important recipients of OBOR funding), **Henry Chan Hing Lee** studies the issue of the HSR in the section on transportation and logistics. Senior Chinese government officials led by President Xi Jinping and Premier Li Keqiang have been actively promoting the export of railway technologies since the third quarter of 2013 in what observers called "rail diplomacy". Chinese press had dubbed Premier Li as the super salesman of Chinese rail technology and China had placed rail system export as one of the priority Silk Road infrastructure projects. Chinese leaders' confidence in pushing "rail diplomacy" lies in the success of its recently-developed HSR and upgraded combo cargo/passenger conventional rail network that had contributed meaningfully to its economic development. China had built the world's most extensive and cost-effective rail-based land transport system.

At the same time, China skilfully leveraged its economies of scale and commanding cost advantage in the construction of rail system. Many developing countries had taken note of it and they expressed interest to acquire the Chinese system. China had indicated its willingness to offer generous bilateral financing to the export of rail system. Chinese offers are often the best on the table. However, China's efforts to export rail system had not been successful in many cases. Domestic politics and geopolitical factors often derail China's efforts. Henry's chapters will analyze the strengths and weaknesses of the Chinese rail industry at present, contextualize them in terms of current opportunities and threats facing China's rail export, and analyze the prospects of China's rail diplomacy.

Also, on the railway topic but looking at it from the perspective of marketing technologies and managing complex international relations, **Zhang Huang and Li Jie**'s important chapter is written from the Chinese perspective. He highlighted that Chinese high-speed railway system's selling points include mature technology, high performance price ratio and abundant operation experience. However, he argues that these advantages may not be enough to offset the importance of unimpeded access to the sale of high-speed railways to overseas customers. Two setbacks Chinese companies encountered in the Mexico market reflects the strategic nature of Chinese high-speed railways from the perspective of its destination countries' national interests. These case studies become the subject of his analysis in his chapter on marketing railways to other countries.

Section E in the volume includes several country-specific chapters, it is the comparative studies segment of this publication project. **Winglok Hung**'s chapter aims to explain OBOR with the use of Professor Yan Xuetong's analytical framework of international order system. The central question of this chapter is, "Why is Europe more important than other regions in China's OBOR economic strategy?" In this first part, Hung explains his conception and understanding of OBOR. OBOR is a new economic strategy. In the remaining three parts, Hung continues to examine China's economic strategies and relations with Europe under the framework of OBOR. As OBOR is fundamentally different from an American-led private investment and trade liberalization since the Second World War, China's OBOR attempts to construct a new international system after the global financial crisis in 2008. In the conclusion, Hung returns to the same puzzle of why Europe is important in China's OBOR strategy to establish a new international order.

After looking at railway systems, maritime networks and funding agencies, Section E of the publication updates the readership in region-specific development. **Lim Tai Wei**'s chapters on Central and South Asian regions are discussed as case studies in the third section of the publication. Both Central Asia and South Asia are important regions for China's OSR outreach. Lim looks at South and Central Asian regions as important components of the OBOR, which is the latest major policy initiative by Chinese President Xi Jinping to tap into the Eurasian region and beyond. To lend economic resources to the OBOR initiative, the Chinese government has started to fund institutions like the Silk Road Fund, AIIB and the BRICS Bank. Central Asia is one of the most important regions for Chinese OBOR initiative. The region wants to industrialize and depend less on commodities export for its economic development. To modernize, the region needs to encourage the growth of mass education, infrastructure investments, industrialization, skills and management training, etc. These are items that China can offer. Steel and coal resources are also important for the industrialization process. The intention to industrialize occurs at an opportune time when China is facing overcapacity in these two commodities.

Lim Tai Wei also noted that China has singled out Pakistan, an old and reliable ironclad ally, for extending assistance. It has promised to pump US$46 billion to aid Pakistan's economic development. China wants to increase the number of coal-fired power plants in Pakistan and increase electricity supply to its people. Even India, at times a geopolitical rival to China, is interested in applying for AIIB funding to build coal-fired power plants as it has difficulties securing such loans from the WB which rejects funding of such projects unless under very exceptional circumstances. Like the European

Coal and Steel Community, Beijing's OBOR initiative to provide such commodities for Central and South Asian development may eventually become regional energy grids that not only provide conduits for steel and coal but also oil, gas and hydropower. The caveat is China must tread carefully in Central and South Asia as there are existing dominant powers in these two regions, including Russia in Central Asia and India in South Asia. Beijing would do well to avoid a head-on clash with the other major powers' traditional national interests in these regions.

Besides the traditional Soviet backyard of Central Asia, one of the major targets for railway connectivity and OBOR funding in South Asia is China's ally, Pakistan, with whom it has a special relationship. In South Asia, China reached out to Pakistan with developmental funds of US$46 billion, the single largest sum of funding for China's *youhao* friendship partners. The projects that China was building and funding in Pakistan were mainly infrastructure. The guiding philosophy was also declared to be market friendly, a targeted economic initiative. The Chinese–Pakistani cooperation can help to contain or mitigate religious extremism originating either from or passing through Pakistan. China's strategic partnership is aimed at promoting bilateral relations or solving common problems between or among states. For China, there is no true alliance as the very term implies a working relationship between a senior and junior partner. To the Chinese, an alliance is often targeted at the third party and it has to have a common enemy. With an eye for egalitarianism and non-alignment, China is sensitive to entering a relationship where it becomes a senior partner. Chinese-style strategic partnership focuses on inclusiveness, while an alliance is exclusive. On the other hand, Chinese major power status in the future is likely to exhibit inclusiveness, development-focused orientation, friend and not enemy-seeking, military-free content in partnership and emphasis on common-goods approach.

Away from the OSR, developments are also taking place in Southeast and East Asia. In maritime Southeast Asia, **Kong Tuan Yuen** argues that Malaysia could benefit from China's OBOR initiatives. First, through the OBOR, China could provide infrastructure investment fund for developing industrial park such as Malaysia–China Kuantan Industrial Park (MCKIP) and reconstructing seaports like Port Klang and Port Malacca. Second, the process of technology transfer will occur from China to Malaysia, especially in the field of infrastructure construction. Third, Malaysia can easily access

Chinese market and bring Chinese *halal* food and Muslims commodities in Muslim world to Chinese consumers.

However, Malaysia will also meet challenges including the instability of Malaysia's political and economic situations and a festering ethnic issue in domestic politics. There are also other external factors affecting Malaysia like the impact of the economic slowdown of China, geopolitics in the South China Sea and US perception of Malaysia. These factors may impede or redirect attention away from developing China–Malaysia economic cooperation in terms of OBOR initiatives. Malaysia will keep a two-pronged strategy to maximize its economic interests which are in turn subjected to political impact from domestic affairs to international events. In terms of economic perspectives, Malaysia will fully support China's OBOR initiatives by offering more bilateral collaborative project opportunities and deepening their trade partnership. But in political terms, Malaysia will continue to pay attention to concerns from the domestic ethnic Malays majority and external perceptions of this relationship by other ASEAN countries and the US.

Another important neighboring East Asian country to China is Japan. Both countries have a long historical exchange, and are simultaneously longtime economic partners as well as strategic rivals. **Lim Tai Wei** provided an update to Japan's own outreach into Central Asia and Southeast Asia in end 2015. As the other major economy in Northeast Asia, Japan is also tapping into the economic potential of the region with Prime Minister Shinzo Abe's one-week official tour of the region in late October 2015 that took him through Mongolia, Turkmenistan, Tajikistan, Uzbekistan, Kyrgyzstan and Kazakhstan (in that order). Japan is playing catch-up with Russia and China that have been present in the region for much longer durations. Distinguishing its approach from others, Japan's marketing tack focuses on good quality infrastructure and high value-added industrial processing technologies (e.g. gas, oil, uranium processing plants and chemical fertilizer plants). In other words, Central Asian leaders are keen to process their raw materials in addition to obtaining funding for infrastructure and logistical equipment that transport them. For the purpose of providing high quality equipment, Mr Abe brought 50 leading business sector leaders with him. Besides the OSR, Japan is also active in the MSR. In fact the term "Maritime Silk Road" was coined by a Japanese researcher to describe the maritime ceramics trade from Jingdezhen. Given that Japan is an island nation, it is active in keeping up relationship-building in Southeast Asia. 2015 marks an end to a year experiencing a flurry of ASEAN diplomacy for all major powers in the East Asian region, including Japan.

Finally, the publication will end off by summarizing the main points of the volume and discussing the prospects for the implementation of the OBOR initiative.

Bibliography

Orlik, Tom and Fielding Chen, One Belt, One Road — China's Modern Marco Polos Bring No Novelties Westward, dated 2 July 2015 in *Bloomberg Brief*, 2015.

Tan, Christine and See Kit Tang, Is AIIB the Answer to Asia's Infrastructure Needs? dated 25 June 2015 in CNBC.com [downloaded on 26 June 2015], available at http://www.cnbc.com/2015/06/25/is-aiib-the-answer-to-asias-infrastructure-needs.html.

The Economist Intelligence Unit, Prospects and Challenges on China's "One Belt, One Road": A Risk Assessment Report in *The Economist* [downloaded on 15 December 2015], available at http://www.eiu.com/Handlers/WhitepaperHandler.ashx?fi=One-Belt-One-Road-report-EngVersion.pdf&mode=wp&campaignid=OneBeltOneRoad.

Section B

The History of Zheng He (Cheng Ho) and the Maritime Silk Road

Chapter 2

Introduction of the Overland Silk Road and Maritime Silk Road

TAN Ta Sen

In September and October of 2013, the President of China, Xi Jinping, spelt out his vision of rebuilding economic belts along two ancient Silk Roads, the Northern Silk Road and the Southern Maritime Silk Road. In the context of the Maritime Silk Road, President Xi also mentioned the legendary voyages made by Cheng Ho (Zheng He in Hanyu Pinyin pronunciation) from China to East Africa in the 15th century. This prologue to the edited volume first brings you through an interesting historical journey of the two Silk Roads setting a stage for the appearance of the Ming dynasty Admiral Cheng Ho. His historic seven voyages fill the pages of the last part of this prologue giving the readers insights into the man himself, his voyages and its historical and contemporary significance in relation to today's business opportunities and international relations.

Zhang Qian's expeditions to Central Asia

Zhang Qian, who was credited for opening up the Silk Road, was an official during the reign of Emperor Wu of the China's Han Dynasty (206 BC–AD 220).

During the Han dynasty, the Inner Asian steppe in Central Asia to the west of China known as the Western Regions by the Chinese, was dominated by nomadic Xiongnu tribes. In the late 3rd century, Xiongnu formed the first great confederation of nomadic tribes along China's north and northwest borders. The Great Wall was built by Emperor Qin (Qinshi Huang) as a defense measure against them. However, Xiongnu continued to be a major threat to early Han emperors and prevented Han China from establishing economic relations with the Western Regions.

In 138 BC, Emperor Wudi sent a mission led by Zhang Qian to the Yuezhi in modern-day Tajikistan with an aim to form an alliance against the Xiongnu. While traveling south of the Kunlun Mountains and crossing Qinghai, the group was captured by the Xiongnu and was put to hard labor. The courageous and devoted diplomat Zhang Qian married a native wife who bore him a son just to gain the trust of the Xiongnu king. Taking advantage of the internal power struggle within the Xiongnu tribe when the old king died in 126 BC, Zhang Qian and his men escaped but only three (Zhang Qian, his Xiongnu wife and the Xiongnu member of the mission) made it to the capital Changan (now Xian, Shaanxi province). During these 13 years abroad, he held on to his imperial insignia.

In 115 BC, Zhang Qian was ordered to lead another mission to the Western regions. After he reached Wusun at the southeastern part of Issyk Kul Lake in southeast Uzbekistan, he dispatched his deputies to forge ties with Dayueshi, Afghanistan, Iran, India and other native states which led to trade between Han China and Persia.

Caravan traders

The Silk Route started from China's Changan to Istanbul, the capital of the Eastern Roman Empire linking up along the way with the trade routes of Central Asia, South Asia and Western Asia to reach Europe and North Africa. The Silk Route served as the principal highway for trade and cultural exchange between the East and the West till the 13th century AD.

The Silk Road was roughly divided into three major sections: (1) Eastern section beginning in Changan, and running along the northern and southern borders of the Taklamakan Desert to the Pamir Mountains; (2) Central Asian section crossing the Pamirs and the Central Asian region of Samarkand and (3) Western section that runs through Persia to the Mediterranean.

Trade between Changan and the Mediterranean was through a chain with each trader and segment of the above three trade sections representing a crucial link in the trade. Goods passed from one trade section to another in short segments.

To illustrate, along the eastern section of the Silk Road, the Chinese produced silk to trade or sell to the Central Asian traders and merchants in exchange for their herbal medicines and pieces of jade from Khotan. These Central Asian traders would then transport the silk by caravan through the oasis towns of Central Asia.

In the oasis town markets, the traders would exchange their silk for other goods from traders from the other side of the Pamir Mountains, who would then transport the silk through the region of Samarkand. Other Persian, Armenian and Jewish traders handled the silk trade through Persia to the Mediterranean regions, where the silks were finally purchased with gold from Rome.

The caravan traders often traveled in group in a caravan with a line of camels to trade goods moving from one trading center to another, from market to market. The caravan would usually make stopover at two popular trade centers, Bactria and Samarkand, which were filled with bustling bazaars. Traders from many different regions would barter and sell their goods there. Local merchants would exchange goods with the caravan traders, who would buy goods to sell further along the Silk Road. At the trade centers, Caravan traders would put up at the caravanserai where they would eat, drink and socialize with one another.

Cultural Cross-fertilization

Syncretism: Buddhism, Confucianism and Daoism

Buddhism spread to China through the Silk Route around the 1st century during the reign of Eastern or Later Han Emperor Mingdi (57–75). The advent of Buddhism to China imparted a tremendous impact and influence on Chinese religion, philosophy and arts. But the most marvelous achievement is its transformation from an alien religion in China into Chinese Buddhism. An Shigao, Dharmaranya and Kumarajiva came from India to China between the 2nd and 4th centuries. These three important pioneer foreign Buddhist scholars and priests translated Buddhist sacred texts into Chinese. On the other hand, pioneer Chinese monks like Faxian and Xuanzhang traveled to India via the Silk Road to collect more Buddhist scripts in the 5th and 7th centuries, respectively. To facilitate preaching in

China, Buddhist monks borrowed Daoist (Taoist) and Confucian words and terms to express Buddhist doctrines in translating Buddhist scriptures. As a consequence, Buddhism became fully Sinicized and an integral part of Chinese culture.

A dialogue between Islam and Confucianism

The contact between China with the Islamic Arab world could be traced back as early as the 7th century during the Tang dynasty soon after Islam was founded by Prophet Muhammad in the Middle East. In contrast to the proactive and assertive approach in the Arab world and in Central Asia, Islam's coming to China was a byproduct of trade and diplomatic ties between China and Arab during the Tang and Song dynasties (618–1279). There were no concerted efforts on the part of the missionaries and Arab rulers like Caliphates.

Islamic scholars and Chinese Muslim scholars seem to accept arbitrarily the year 651 when Caliph Uthman sent an envoy to Changan as the beginning of Islam's spread to China. The Annals of the Old Tang Dynasty recorded that the state of Da Si (the name of Arab Kingdom in Chinese dynastic history) dispatched a tributary mission to the court in the second year during the reign of Tang Emperor Gaozong (651).

Islam spread to China as early as the Tang dynasty in the 7th century by Arab and Persian Muslim traders following the Overland Silk Road and Maritime Silk Road. From the Tang to Song dynasties, they were sojourners doing businesses in a foreign lands.

Some of them settled down in China. They were known as *hushang* (foreign Merchants like the Central Asian Hu people), *fanke* (foreigners or sojourners) and they were restricted to live in *fanfang* (living quarters or settlements) in coastal port cities of Guangzhou, Yangzhou, Quanzhou, Hangzhou, Mingzhou and Changan. Intermarriage with locals was not allowed and interaction with locals not encouraged. They lived in their own ethnic enclaves and preserved their own social and religious life. There was no preaching activity and few Chinese were converted to Islam. The spread of Islam in China was slow during the Tang to Song dynasties.

Islam expanded rapidly during the Mongol rule in China from 1271 to 1368. The influx of Muslims from Central and Western Asia to China had brought changes to the political and social landscapes in China as well as the outlook of the closed and inward-looking Muslim minority group. Under the Mongolian rulers' political patronage, Muslims' social status was enhanced to become the ally of the ruling Mongols. Muslims were acknowledged as subjects of China, paving the way for the evolution of the Hui communities in China. In addition to Quanzhou, Guangzhou, Yangzhou, Hangzhou, Mingzhou (Ningbo) and Xian (Changan), new Muslim settlements were formed in the north-western and south-western provinces of China such as Shaanxi, Gansu, Ningxia, Xinjiang, Shanxi, Henan, Qinghai, Shandong, Hebei, Yunnan and Beijing during the Yuan Dynasty. They were no longer foreigners but subjects of Yuan China. Many Muslims from Central and Western Asia held senior posts in government's military and civil administration. The Hui communities began to take shape. During the Yuan Dynasty, mosques were built in Guangzhou, Quanzhou, Hangzhou, Kunming, Changan, Beijing, Yangzhou, Ningbo, Ningxia, Dali, Dingzhou and elsewhere. These Islamic icons became the landmarks of the Hui communities which established and cultivated strong ties between Muslims in China and the lands of Islam in Central and Western Asia. Mosques were also the focal points where Muslims organized their religious and social life. The ethnicity of the Hui Huis was generally preserved during the Yuan dynasty. The

Figure 1: The Huay Shang Mosque of tiered roof built in Tang Dynasty in Guangzhou

enhanced social status and localized subjects identity given to the Hui Hui Muslims began to change the outlook of the Muslims. Towards the end of the Yuan Dynasty, they became more self-confident and outward-looking. There was also increased interaction with the Han Chinese in cultural, social, economic and political activities. They began to re-orientate themselves to fit into the larger Chinese society.

The Mongols and Hui Hui from Central and Western Asia also introduced advanced Islamic science and technology to China. Kublai Khan formed an Institute of Muslim Astronomy in 1271. Muslim medicine became popular in China during the Yuan Dynasty. Sayid Ajall Shamsuddin used Islamic hydraulic engineering technology to build the irrigation system in Yunnan. In addition, the Islamic calendar, mathematics, architecture, etc. were also imported to China. These advanced Islamic science and technology had greatly enriched Chinese culture.

In the 16th and 17th centuries during the Ming Dynasty (1368–1644), significant changes took place in the Muslim Hui Hui community. The *Madrasa* educational system using the mosque as an educational center was institutionalized. *Madrasa* schools provided Muslims children with a formal religious education based on the orthodox doctrines of the Sunni school of Islam and trained potential *imams* for mosques which were growing in number at a fast pace.

In addition, the Islamic revival movement which commenced in the 17th century also focused on translating and writing Islamic scriptures in Chinese to meet the increasing demand of such publications by the Sinicized Hui Hui Muslims, and to introduce Islamic doctrines to the Chinese masses and literati. These learned Islamic writers and translators were also well versed in Confucianism, Buddhism and Daoism. They made an enterprising attempt to strike a dialogue between Islam and Chinese traditional culture, particularly, Confucianism. They tried in their works to make a systematic reconciliation between Islam and Confucianism by interpreting Islamic doctrines in the light of neo-Confucian teachings. As such, they hoped to introduce and promote Islam to the Chinese gentry and literati in their own Confucian language. The movement of annotating and translating Islamic texts into Chinese with Confucian terminology reflected two characteristics: Confucianized Islamic values and Islamized Confucian ideas. The Confucian

Muslim scholars primarily used Confucian ideas to expound and disseminate Islam in order to advance Islam's cause. On the other hand, sometimes they reinterpreted some Confucian concepts with Islamic ideas. For example, the Confucian Five Constant Regulations (*wuchang*) were likened to Five Islamic Pillars (*wugong*). In so doing, they Islamized certain Confucian ideology to put forward their arguments.

In short, the ancient Chinese mosques with traditional Chinese pagoda design and architectural layout reflect the physical Chineseness of Chinese Islam. Following Cheng Ho's historic voyages to the Western Ocean in the 15th century, these Chinese style mosques were common in Southeast Asia.

Maritime Silk Road

China also has a long history of maritime trade. The Maritime Silk Road was another East–West ancient trade route which can be traced to the period of the Three Kingdoms in the 3rd Century when Sun Quan dispatched Zhu Ying and Kang Tai to sail to Southeast Asia. By the Tang Dynasty (618–907), Chinese maritime trade was already well established involving large numbers of Arab traders who came to trade, and some to settle, in Guangzhou and Quanzhou. Chinese maritime traders also showed up in the Persian Gulf. The Maritime Silk Road stretched from Guangzhou and Quanzhou across the Malay Archipelago to the Persian Gulf and was flourishing during the Tang and Song dynasties (618–1279). Fleet of ships carrying Southeast Asian tributary missions, Chinese, Indian and Arab traders were shuttling along the Maritime Silk Road.

Arab traders in Tang China

The Arab and Persian Muslim traders first came to China approximately in the 7th century via the Overland Silk Route in northern China and the Maritime Silk Road in the south. Since the 6th century, the Arab and Persian traders monopolized the East–West international trade in silks, pepper, spices, which were highly in demand in the West, as they controlled all movement of ships in the Persian Gulf and the Red Sea. The geopolitics along the Silk Route from China via Central Asia to Persia dictated the specific role played by each stakeholder in the profitable East–West trade. Sassanid Persia as middleman merchants and Tang China as producer were the two great political and economic powers at either end of the Silk Road. China exported silk, tea, spices like pepper and Chinese medicinal herbs to the consumer markets in the West such as the Byzantine Empire in Europe through Indian and Arab traders. Persian merchants controlled the ports where the Indian traders made their stopover and virtually bought all shipments of the goods brought by them. In addition, Arab and Persian merchants and ships traveled everywhere from India to China. Consumers and traders of the Western countries had no choice but to buy these goods from the Arab middlemen. It gradually expanded to absorb half of the Turkish kingdoms in Central Asia. It effectively blocked the Byzantine Empire to deal directly with the sources of supply including India, and China and the West remained a mere customer of the Arabs.

Tang and Song governments adopted an open foreign trade policy to attract foreign traders to trade with China. To facilitate and promote foreign trade, a special department, Office of Foreign Trade, was set up at Guangzhou to administer foreign trade as well as the affairs of tributary missions in 714. The Foreign Trade official enforced shipping and foreign trade rules and regulations and collected customs duties. The organization of the Foreign Trade Office was strengthened and expanded into the Office of the Commissioner of Foreign Trade during the Song dynasty. Besides Guangzhou, the Office of the Commissioner of Foreign Trade was also established in Quanzhou, Mingzhou and Hangzhou. It provided management and services for the outgoing and incoming cargo ships such as issuing of exit permits for Chinese cargo ships, port and customs clearance, import duties, reception of envoys and foreign traders, etc.

Initially, Arab Muslim traders came to the capital Changan through the Silk Route. However, after the mid-Tang period, the Overland Silk Road was disrupted by the Turks and as a consequence, the Arab traders arrived in increasing numbers via the maritime Ceramic Road to major southern Chinese ports like Guangzhou, Yangzhou, Mingzhou, Quanzhou and so on. Guangzhou and Yangzhou were the two most important *entrepot* centers during the Tang Dynasty. But following the Song government shifting its political powerbase and economic centers to the south, Quanzhou overtook Guangzhou as the number one sea port.

Maritime Silk Road: A case for renaming

Apart from silk and tea, the most important Chinese export was ceramics which was traded in large quantities. The elegant porcelains have long been China's major export commodity. By the Ming dynasty, due to the development of the private kilns, the quantity and quality of ceramic production were enhanced remarkably, where large quantities of cheap and good export ceramics were shipped to the world including the European, African, East Asian, Southeast Asian, South Asian and Central Asian markets. The global demand for Chinese ceramics then became huge. The elegant ceramics became a social status symbol and ceramics were also items to be buried together with the deceased. In the 12th century, China exported through Southeast Asia a great deal of celadon wares to Central Asia and India. Before the 17th century, Asia was Chinese ceramics biggest market. In the next chapter, Dr Tai Yew Seng will discuss the Yuan dynasty system of Official Capital Ship and how the imperial authorities tried to regulate trade before the advent of Zheng He's attempts to establish the tributary system and maritime trade during the Ming dynasty.

However, by the 17th century, European traders began to ship large quantities of celadon wares to Europe enabling it to overtake Asia as the Chinese ceramics largest market. From 1602 to 1682, China exported through the Dutch East India Company a total of 16 million pieces of porcelains over a span of 80 years. Besides the Dutch East India Company, China also exported ceramics via Chinese, Arab, British, Japanese, Indian, Portuguese and Southeast Asian trading groups.

Chapter 3

The Official Capital Ship of Yuan Dynasty and Yang Shu: Chinese Navigation in the Indian Ocean Before Zheng He

TAI Yew Seng

The Mongolians from northern China defeated the Song Dynasty (960–1278) of southern China in 1279. According to the *History of Yuan Dynasty*, Kublai Khan (忽必烈 1215–1294) implemented the "Official Capital Ship" (官本船) policy in 1284:

> (至元) 二十一年, 设市舶都转运司于杭、泉二州, 官自具船、给本, 选人入蕃, 贸易诸货。其所获之息, 以十分为率, 官取其七, 所易人得其三。.... 延祐元年 (1314), 复立市舶提举司, 仍禁人下蕃, 官自发船贸易, 回帆之日, 细物十分抽二, 粗物十五分抽二。七年 (1320), 以下蕃之人将丝银细物易于外国, 又并提举司罢之。(《元史·食货志》卷九十四 "市舶")
>
> In the 21st year of Zhiyuan reign (1284), the Shipping Superintendent Offices in Hangzhou and Quanzhou were set up. Officials build the ships, provide capital, and select people to sail to foreign countries to barter trade. The officials have 70% of the profit and the traders have 30%.... In the first year of Yanyou reign (1314), re-established the Shipping Superintendent Offices, but still banned the seafaring, only send official ships for trading.... In the 7th year of Yanyou reign (1320).... banned the official ships and removed the Shipping Superintendent Offices.[1]

[1] Lian Song, *The Yuan Dynasty History*, Vol. 94. Beijing: Zhonghua Publishing, 1976, 2402. (《元史》)

One thing to take note, the records of *Yuan Dynasty History* did not mention the policy was terminated shortly 6 months after in 1285. Instead, the source mentioned sending the Official Capital Ship again in 1314. It looks like the Official Capital Ship policy was abolished only in 1320, that is over 36 years of implementation. In fact, it was implemented for only a very short period of time in early Yuan Dynasty, and lasted 14 years in total. This policy was proposed by a Han Chinese Lu Shirong (卢世荣 ?–1285) who was advisor to the Mongolian emperor in 1284:

> (至元二十一年十一月，卢世荣) 又奏: "于泉、杭二州立市舶都转运司,造船给本,令人商贩,官有其利七,商有其三。禁私泛海者,拘其先所蓄宝货,官买之;匿者,许告,没其财,半给告者。" (《元史·卢世荣传》)
>
> *Appoint a Shipping Superintendent at the ports of Quanzhou and Hangzhou, build the ships and provide the capital needed, and appoint merchants to trade. Official takes 70% of the profit and the merchants have 30%. Prohibits private trading, arrest the offenders, confiscate their cargoes and sell the cargoes officially. Those who hide, their properties will be confiscated. Informer will get half of the confiscated property.*[2]

It is a form of state monopolization of trade. But we need to take into consideration that during Yuan Dynasty, craftsmen worked for the country and the status of craftsmen passed on from father to son. It is natural that merchants work for the country too. The fact that merchants who traded on ships were not liable to perform labor service as a form of duty indicated that they were "public servants" like craftsmen.

Lu Shirong's proposal was accepted by the Kublai Khan (忽必烈 1215–1294), but Lu was executed a few months later due to political struggle and his policy was terminated in 1285:

> (至元二十二年六月二十九日) "官司做买卖的罢了,百姓做买卖的每市舶的勾当做者，依着在先体例里要课程抽分者。" (《元典章·户部》"市舶")

[2] Lian Song, *The Yuan Dynasty History*, Vol. 205. Beijing: Zhonghua Publishing, 1976, 4566. (《元史》)

(6th month 22nd year of Reign of Zhiyuan) Terminate official trading, Superintendents collect the customs duties from the people who traded according to law.[3]

After the Official Capital Ship policy was terminated, the collection of the customs duties of cargoes on board was as before. In 1293, Kublai Khan once again tried to improve the management of ports and trading activities. He issued a decree titled "The 23 Customs Regulations" that detailed the duties of Superintendents, customs duties, customs procedures and management on ships. It allowed private trading until the succeeding Emperor Chengzong (成宗 1265–1307) partially terminated it in 1296:

(元贞) 二年，禁海商以细货于马八兒、呗喃、梵答剌亦纳三蕃国交易，别出钞五万锭，令沙不丁等议规运之法。(《元史·食货志》卷九十四"市舶")

Second year (of the Yuanzhen reign, 1296), ban maritime merchants trading fine goods with Malabar, Kollam and Calicut. Issued 50,000 tales of cash (as capital) and ordered Shahbuddin to discuss and plan for shipping.... This year (1298), re-established the Zhiyong Department. On the 7th year (of Dade reign, 1303), closed the department because of sea ban.[4]

After the new emperor banned the trade of fine goods with the Indian Ocean kingdoms in 1296, he ordered to find a new way to trade. He re-established the Zhiyong Department in 1298, but imposed sea ban and abolished the department 6 years later. There is no mention of Official Capital Ship in this record, but the epitaph of the Sea Transport Battalion Commander Yang Shu (杨枢 1283–1331) stated that:

大德五年 (1301)，君年甫十九，致用院俾以官本船浮海至西洋，遇亲王合赞遣使臣那怀等如京师，遂载之以来。(黄溍《松江嘉定等处海运千户杨君墓志铭》)

---

[3]Anon *Compendium of Statutes and Sub statutes of the Yuan Dynasty*, Vol. 22. Beijing: China Radio and Television Publishing House, 1998, 943. (《大元圣政国朝典章》)

[4]Song Lian, *The Yuan Dynasty History*, Vol. 94. Beijing: Zhonghua Publishing, 1976, 1593.

In the 5th year of the reign of Dade (1301 A.D.), at the age of 19, he sailed to the Indian Ocean in the Official Capital Ship allocated by the Zhiyong Department. He met the envoy of Sultan Ghazan on the way to the capital (of China).[5]

According to the epitaph, Yang Shu sailed to the Persian Gulf in 1301 at the age of 19 using the Official Capital Ship issued by the Zhiyong Department. It means that during the reign of Chengzong Emperor, the policy of Official Capital Ship was re-implemented with the re-establishment of Zhiyong Department. The epitaph of Yang Shu is significant as it also proved that Chinese officials sailed to the Persian Gulf directly from China in 1301. When Yang Shu set sail again in the eighth year of Dade reign (1304) to send the envoy back to his homeland, a sea ban on maritime trading was imposed the year before and the Official Capital Ship was scraped. But, it did not bring about the end of the Official Capital Ship as yet.

延祐元年(1314),复立市舶提举司,仍禁人下蕃,官自发船贸易,回帆之日,细物十分抽二,粗物十五分抽二。七年(1320),以下蕃之人将丝银细物易于外国,又并提举司罢之。(《元史·食货志》卷九十四"市舶")

In the first year of Yanyou reign (1314), reinstatement of the Superintendent offices, but still imposes the sea ban on the people. The official will sent ships for trading. When they return, impose 20% tax on the fine goods and 13.33% on the coarse goods. In the 7th year (1320), abolished it together with the Superintendent offices due to the traders traded the fine goods likes silk and silver wares with the foreign countries.[6]

The emperor Renzong (仁宗 1285–1320) re-established the Official Capital Ship system in 1314, but eventually abolished it together with the Superintendent Offices 7 years later. This was formally the end of the Official Capital Ship policy in Yuan Dynasty.

---

[5]Huang Jin, The Epitaph of Songjiang, Jiading and etc. areas' sea transport battalion commander Yang Shu (《松江嘉定等处海运千户杨君墓志铭》), in *Selected Works of Huang Jin* (《金华黄先生文集》), Vol. 35, 15–17, in *Continuation Series of the Complete Collection of the Imperial Library* (《续修四库全书》), Vol. 1323,. Shanghai: Shanghai Guji Publishing, 2002, 452–453.

[6]*Ibid.*, 2403.

In short, the Official Capital Ship policy was implemented from 1284 to 1285 (6 months), 1298 to 1303 (6 years) and 1314 to 1320 (7 years). It lasted 14 years in total over three periods with intervals in between. The next section will discuss briefly the man behind the Official Capital Ship.

Yang Shu (1283–1331)

Yang Shu came from a family involved in maritime trade. His grandfather Yang Fa surrendered to Yuan Dynasty and become a high-ranking official in Yuan Dynasty.

> 于是至元十四年....立市舶司三于庆元、上海、澉浦，令福建安抚使杨发督之。每岁招集舶商，于蕃邦博易珠翠香货等物。及次年回帆，依例抽解，然后听其货卖。(《元史·食货志》卷九十四 "市舶")
>
> Therefore, in 14th year of Zhiyuan reign (1277).... established three Shipping Superintendent Offices at Qingyaun (Ningbo, Zhejiang), Shanghai and Ganpu (Haiyan, Zhejiang), and ordered Pacification Commissioner of Fujian, Yang Fa, to be the person in-charge. (The Shipping Superintendents) recruit merchants to barter trade for pearls, gem stones, incense and etc. goods from foreign countries. (The merchants) return the next year, (the cargoes will be) taxed accordingly and permitted to be sold.[7]

Yang Fa was the Pacification Commissioner of Fujian, therefore he was put in charge of running the three ports in early Yuan dynasty. His family members probably started to get involved in the shipping business from this time onwards.

His son Yang Zi was the Pacification Commissioner of Java, he was involved in the campaigns against Java in 1292.

> 至元二十九年二月，诏福建行省除史弼、亦黑迷失、高兴平章政事，征爪哇。.... 三十年正月，至构栏山议方略。二月，亦黑迷失、孙参政先领本省幕官并招谕爪哇等处宣慰司官曲出海牙、杨梓、全忠祖，万户张塔剌赤等五百余人，船十艘，先往招谕之。(《元史·爪哇传》卷二百一十)

[7] *Ibid.*, 2401.

> The 2nd month in 29th year of Zheyuan reign, (the Mongolian emperor) ordered Fujian's Manager of Governmental Affairs Shi Bi, Yi Hei Mi Shi, Gao Xing to conquer Java[8].... In the first month in 30th year (of Zhiyuan rcign), (the navy fleets) called at Pulau Gelasa to plan for a strategy. In the second month, Yi Hei Mi Shi and Assistant Grand Councilor Sun led their Ancillaries and Pacification Commissioners of Java and other regions, Qu Chu Hai Ya, Yang Zi, Quan Zhongzu and Brigade Commander Zhang Talachi, totalling about 500 people in ten ships as the advance party to declare war (on Java).[9]

After the Java campaign, Yang Zi was promoted to Pacification Commissioner-in-chief. However, in another persona of this Pacific Commissioner, he was actually an artist more than an officer. He invented the Haiyan Opera (海盐腔) and trained hundreds of servants under his charge to perform this art form at home.

Yang Shu is the second son of Yang Zi. He sailed to the Persian Gulf at the age of 18 in 1301. According to his epitaph:

> 大德五年，君年甫十九,致用院俾以官本船浮海至西洋,遇亲王合赞遣使臣那怀等如京师,遂载之以来。那怀等朝贡事毕,请仍以君护送西还。丞相哈剌哈孙答剌罕如其请，奏授君忠显校尉、海运副千户，佩金符，与俱行。以八年发京师，十一年乃至。其登陆处，曰忽鲁模思。是役也，君往来长风巨浪中，历五星霜。凡舟楫糗粮物器之须，一出于君，不以烦有司。既又用私钱市其土物白马、黑犬、琥珀、蒲萄酒、蕃盐之属以进，平章政事察那等引见宸庆殿而退。方议旌擢,以酬其劳,而君以前在海上感瘴毒,疾作而归,至大二年也。(黄溍《松江嘉定等处海运千户杨君墓志铭》,《全元文》卷九七四)
>
> *In the 5th year of the reign of Dade (1301 A.D.), at the age of 19, he sailed to the Indian Ocean with the Official Capital Ship allocated by the Zhiyong Department. He met the envoy of Sultan Ghazan on the way to the capital (of China). After paying tribute, the envoy requested to be sent back by Yang*

---

[8]The Javanese disrespected the Chinese envoy to Java, therefore the Mongolian emperor ordered the attack.

[9]Song Lian, *The Yuan Dynasty History*, Vol. 94. Beijing: Zhonghua Publishing, 1976, Vol. 210, 4665.

Shu. The Prime Minister agreed. Yang Shu was promoted to Deputy Sea Transport Battalion Commander to escort the envoy. They left the capital in 1304, and reached the destination in 1307. The port called is Ormuz (Hormuz). In this voyage, Yang Shu sailed for 5 years on the sea. All supplies were provided by Yang Shu's offices, without troubling the central authorities. On the other hand, he bought white horses, black fur dogs, amber, grape wine and foreign salt with his own money to pay tribute. The Manager of Governmental Affairs Cha Han received him in the Hall of Chenqing. There was discussion of promoting him for his hard work, but he became sick on the sea and return home in 1309.[10]

He met the envoy of Ilkhanate (1256–1335) and escorted him back to the capital of China. He cultivated good relationship with the envoy. When the envoy returned to the Ilkhanate, Yang was specially requested to be the escort of choice. According to Yuan dynasty law, the escort of foreign mission must be at least rank five and above. But Yang Shu was not senior enough (he was just 18 year-old!) at that time. And so the imperial court promoted him to Transport Battalion Deputy Commander (Rank 5b) to qualify him for the mission. The voyage took him 5 years. This was his second trip to the Persian Gulf, and his final. He did not sail after this voyage, not only because he was sick, but Yuan Dynasty banned all seafaring from 1303 to 1314, including the deployment of the Official Capital Ship. He was out of work for the next 20 years before he was recalled to be the Sea Transport Battalion Deputy Commander of the Changshu, Jiangyin and other regions in 1327, in charge of transporting grains to the imperial capital. He was later promoted to the Sea Transport Battalion Commander of Songjiang, Jiading and other regions but he passed away on 16 September 1331, at the age of 48, before receiving his promotion.

Conclusion

In the Yuan Dynasty, private trading in overseas was allowed from 1323. Private maritime trading flourished until the late 14th century in the early

---

[10] Huang Jin, "The Epitaph of Songjiang, Jiading and etc. areas' sea transport battalion commander Yang Shu (《松江嘉定等处海运千户杨君墓志铭》)" in *Selected Works of Huang Jin* 《金华黄先生文集》), Vol. 35, 15–17, in *Continuation Series of the Complete Collection of the Imperial Library* (《续修四库全书》), Shanghai: Shanghai Guji Publishing, 1323, 2002, 452–453.

Ming Dynasty when the famous Ming Ban stopped all private maritime trading again. The difference between the sea bans of the Yuan and Ming dynasties is: the Yuan dynasty emperors used the sea ban and Official Capital Ships to monopolize maritime trade and maximize profits for the imperial coffers, but Ming dynasty emperors used the sea ban on maritime trading and the tributary system to manage and fend off neighboring countries involved in piracy. During the Ming Ban, Zheng He's (郑和 1371–1433) expeditions to East Africa can be considered as the natural progression of Yang Shu's voyages to Persian Gulf.

Chapter 4

Cheng Ho's Legacy: Business Opportunities and World Dream

TAN Ta Sen

The magnitude and duration of the state-organized expeditions led by Cheng Ho from 1405 to 1433 are unprecedented. Cheng Ho has left a lasting impact on cross-continental cultural exchange between the East and the West. The expeditions had widened and deepened inter- as well as intra-regional culture contact in the Afro-Asian world.

Under normal circumstances, events are unfolding recently which may suggest that history sometimes does repeat itself. Nearly 2,000 years after the opening up of the Land Silk Road, 1,400 years after the Maritime Silk Road and over 600 years from Cheng Ho's voyages from China to East Africa, the Silk Roads and Cheng Ho stole the limelight again lately in world media in September and October 2013. It highlights the economic and political implications of the ancient trade routes as well as Cheng Ho's legacy in the Age of Globalization.

On 3 October 2013, referring to the Maritime Silk Road and Cheng Ho's voyages, President of China Xi Jinping in his speech to the Indonesian Parliament in Jakarta said, "Over the centuries, the vast oceans have served as the bond of friendship connecting the two peoples, not a barrier between them.... Vessels (of Cheng Ho) full of goods and passengers traveled across the sea, exchanging products and fostering friendship." He proposed to join efforts with countries in the region to build a new "Maritime Silk Road" to promote trade and military ties. He added that to build the new "Maritime Silk Road", China will have to strengthen maritime cooperation with ASEAN countries "to make good use of the China–ASEAN Maritime Cooperation Fund set up by the Chinese government".

Two days later, as if to respond to President Xi's proposal, Malaysia's former Prime Minister Dr Mahathir announced the formation of the Cheng Ho Multicultural, Friendship and Business Association in Kuala Lumpur after a meeting with President Xi earlier.

The Star Online dated 5 October 2013 reports:

"A body called the Cheng Ho Multicultural, Friendship and Business Association will be set up for Malaysian and Chinese businessmen to enhance cooperation between the two nations", said Tun Dr Mahathir Mohamad.

"The former Prime Minister announced this following a private meeting with China's President Xi Jinping, whose maiden state visit ends Saturday".

"The name of the association is in remembrance of the contributions of the Admiral Cheng Ho," he said, referring to the famous Ming Dynasty Muslim admiral who docked at Malacca at least five times during his seven voyages and established the first link between China and Malaysia.

"Dr Mahathir said Xi had expressed support for the association's inception".

"He added that he would like to see more Chinese investments here, noting that at the moment, Malaysian investments in China far outweighed the former".

"Xi, in his keynote address Friday, encouraged Chinese companies to actively participate in Malaysian development projects".

A month earlier on 7 September 2013, President Xi Jinping while making a speech titled "Promote People-to-People Friendship and Create a Better Future" at Kazakhstan's Nazarbayev University, expressed that more than 2,100 years ago, during China's Western Han Dynasty (206 BC–AD 24), imperial envoy Zhang Qian was sent to Central Asia twice to open the door to friendly contacts between China and Central Asian countries as well as the transcontinental Silk Road linking East and West, Asia and Europe. Thus, he proposed to build a Silk Road economic belt with Central Asian countries to boost trade and transport links and strengthen regional policy coordination from the Pacific to the Baltic Sea.

Simon Denyer in *The Washington Post* of 1 November 2013 observed, "Armed with tens of billions of dollars in investment deals and romantic tales of ancient explorers, Chinese President Xi Jinping spent much of September and October promoting his vision of two new "Silk Roads" to connect his country to the West and secure its energy supplies — one by land and another by sea".

All these developments signify the dawn of new business opportunities brought about by the Legacy of the Silk Roads and Cheng Ho's voyages, especially in the tourism and leisure industry as well as maritime trade.

Implications of new Maritime Silk Road

To explore the opportunities (especially business opportunities) brought about by these developments, we propose to focus on four platforms: cultural exchange, maritime trade, tourism and international relations.

Cultural exchange

There is room for development in the Cheng Ho studies. Cheng Ho left distinct footprints from Nanjing to Malindi, for example, legends, relics (heritage sites, artefacts, shipwrecks), navigation and boat budding, architectural style, traditional Chinese medicine, trade (ceramics, spices), and art and culture. These are fertile untapped sources for the study of Cheng Ho's legacy and it provides good opportunity for international cooperation among research institutes and researchers in joint inter-disciplinary research projects. In 2010, the National Museum of China, School of Archeology of the Peking University and the Kenyan National Museum embarked on joint terrestrial and underwater archeological exploration to find the shipwreck in and around Lamu islands, where one of the Chinese navigators Cheng Ho's ships is believed to have sunk in the 15th century.

In addition, the value and application of Cheng Ho's Art of Collaboration in contemporary international politics, business management and practice as well as human relationship are worthy topics for serious research.

For the study of Cheng Ho's legacy, we would like to see more international conferences, joint research projects, joint exhibitions and exchange program for scholars taking place in the future.

Maritime trade

The establishment of new land and sea Silk Road economic belts will bring closer economic ties between China and Central Asian countries in the north and Afro-Asian countries especially the developing countries in the south.

The Maritime Silk Road formed the basis of the plans to enhance trade between China and developing countries, including the ASEAN countries in the south. The Maritime Silk Road formed the basis of the plans to enhance trade between China and ASEAN countries during the current visit of Chinese President Xi Jinping to Indonesia and Malaysia where he stated that the Maritime Silk Road would help turn the "Golden Decade" between China and the region into "Diamond Decade". Currently, China is ASEAN's largest trading partner, with the two-way trade exceeding US$400 billion last year in 2012, a six-fold increase since a decade ago. In 2010, China and ASEAN commenced free trade area. The Maritime Silk Road economic belt will build a free trade zone in the Asia-Pacific and Indian Ocean regions covering countries from China to East Africa.

Unique Cheng Ho branding tourism

From Nanjing to Malindi, Cheng Ho left distinct footprints which are fertile untapped resources for Cheng Ho theme tour routes. Along the Maritime Silk Road, there are plenty of legends, relics (heritage sites, artefacts, shipwrecks), navigation and boat building, traditional Chinese medicine, trade (ceramics, spices), and art and culture in connection with Cheng Ho's expeditions.

Traces of Cheng Ho's legacy are still visible in most of the places visited by Cheng Ho. Fishermen in Cochin, Calicut and Quilon are still using Chinese fishing nets which the locals call "cheenavala" (China net) for fishing. Chinese cooking utensils like Chinese "wok", which they called "cheenachatti" and urns for storing food are common in Kerala state. In Kenya (Malindi) Siyu village on Pete Island, a journalist of Beijing-based *People's Daily* found a native Kenyan man practicing Chinese medicine to treat patients. Legend has it that one of Cheng Ho's ships, shipwrecked off in Lamu Island. Some surviving crew members were rescued by the locals and they settled down and married native women. Since 2010, archeologists from China and Kenya conducted both terrestrial and underwater archeology to find the shipwreck. Chinese-style wooden doors and a fort in Chinese architectural style, and ancient Chinese tombs and the graves inlaid with Chinese porcelain were also found. The wall at the entrance of the graveyard of Wali Bonang in Surabaya is embedded with Ming porcelain plates. Apart from embedding antique porcelain plates on walls, numerous big and small Ming jars and urns are used by mosques as holy-water containers.

Sam Poo Kong temples, which revered Cheng Ho are found in Semarang, Surabaya, Ancor, Ayutthaya, Bangkok, Penang, Malacca, Kuala Lumpur and Trengganu. A mosque (Masjid Muhammad Cheng Ho) in Surabaya was named after Cheng Ho in 2003. In Malacca, there is Sam Poo Kong Hill (Bukit Cina) where the Sam Poo Kong Temple and Perigi Raja (related to Ming princess Hang Li Po legend) are located. A Cheng Ho Cultural Museum was also built in 2005 on the original site where Cheng Ho built his *guanchang* (official warehouse complex). Other Cheng Ho heritage sites and relics include Sanbao Pagoda and Sanbao Harbor in Bangkok, temple and tomb of one of Cheng Ho's commanders *Poontaokong* in Sulu; Ong Sum Ping Road in Burma's capital named after Wang Jinghong, Cheng Ho's tri-lingual stone inscription in Sri Lanka. There are legends associated with Cheng Ho, such as the legend of Hang Li Po where a Ming princess married Sultan Mansor Shah of Malacca as recorded in the *Sejarah Melayu.* The Semarang Chronicle documents the development of the Chinese Muslim community in Java in the 15th and 16th centuries. Loan vocabulary in Indonesian and Malay showing Chinese origin include, for example, *Tofu*, *Tokua*, *top*, *tohui*, *toki*, *teh*, *tekoh*, etc.

According to Kwan Hwie Liong, one of Cheng Ho's captains by the name of Bi Nang Un migrated from Champa to Lasem, Java, in 1413, together with his wife Na Li Ni, son Bi Nang Na, daughter Bi Nang Ti and other relatives. His wife and daughter were said to be pioneers in making *batik* cloth in Lasem as they were good *batik* cloth makers. Until today, special Chinese auspicious motifs such as phoenix, dragon, *qilin,* butterfly, fish and flora and fauna like chrysanthemum, peony, etc. are still popular in *batik* production in Java. Lasem's architecture shows a dynamic cross-cultural interaction, with traditional Chinese-style house roof with a crown at its gable top, Paladian windows, as well as 17th century Mediterranean balcony. Its complex house plan also evolves from the Sino-Javanese traditional house concept.

The *Malay Annals of Semarang and Cirebon* stated that Cheng Ho had built mosques in Java's Semarang, Sembung, Sarindil, Talang, Ancol, Lasem, Tuban, Gresik and Jiaotung. Though these ancient mosques built by Cheng Ho in Java might have been destroyed or renovated, his pioneering works

Figure 1: Chinese PM Mr Li Keqiang and his wife, Dr Tan Ta Sen and Chief Minister of Melaka, Mr Idris Hj. Haron looking at Cheng Ho Fleet diorama at Cheng Ho Cultural Museum on 22 November 2015

would certainly have influenced subsequent designers and builders. Hence, marks of Chinese architectural influence, such as multitiered roof, pagoda-shaped minaret, curved roof edges and woodcarving, in local religious buildings in places visited by Cheng Ho are still visible.

Theme tour routes

Lu Tianyun, formerly the head of the Kunming Municipal Office, in a paper "Conceptualizing International Zheng He's Journey of Peace Tour Routes" gives an in-depth analysis of the subject. Based on the history of the voyages as well as Cheng Ho spirit, he argues that Cheng Ho being a prominent historical figure, like celebrity, is a good resource for cultural tourism and a valuable product of tourism. He uses the method of value analysis to make qualitative and quantitative analytical evaluations of the value of Cheng Ho's tourism resources. Supported by theoretical and statistical analysis as well as the development theory of theme park property development, he concludes that through the joint efforts of the regional tourism authorities and corporations, the international Cheng Ho's Journey of Peace Tour Routes will be ideal "golden" tour routes. However, local authorities and tourism sectors have to play their part in taking good care and preservation of the heritage sites.

To begin with, there are basically two types of Cheng Ho tour routes, general and specific, as outlined:

1. General Cultural Tour Route: Kunyang (Cheng Ho's home village in Yunnan), Nanjing, Quanzhou, Changle, Qui Nhon (Champa), Ayuthaya (Thailand), Melaka, Palembang, Semarang, Gale (Sri Lanka), Cochin and Calicut, Hormuz, Muscat, Aden, Mogadishu, Brava, Malindi and Lamu.
2. Spice Trade Route: Palembang, Samudra, Majapahit, Tuban, Gresik, Surabaya, Semarang, Ceribon, Demak and Moluccas.

Well defined and diverse tour routes will be designed for various tour groups. For instance, tourists can opt for general cultural tour route which can be further broken up into a few shorter sub-routes to suit individual needs. One can also join specific theme tour routes like spice trade route and so on.

Multilingual informative tour guide materials have to be made available. For serious tourists and school groups, educational guidebook is a must to assist students to explore commerce, navigation, communication, cultural exchange, handicraft and culture when traveling the Maritime Ceramic Road.

Theme resorts and attractions

Cheng Ho's legacy has opened up another window for big-ticket investment in developing Cheng Ho theme parks, resorts and attractions along the Maritime Silk Road. For the time being, Melaka seems to be taking a lead in this direction.

A multifunction mega commercial project to build a seaside resort (Cheng Ho City) in Melaka is in the planning stage by a private business group Cheng Ho City Sdn Bhd.

Figure 2: Woodcarving showing Cheng Ho's fleet and Mazu and other deities protecting the voyages (relics found in Cheng Ho Cultural Museum)

Termed as the Jewel of the East, Cheng Ho City sits on 900 acres of reclaimed land in Melaka's Klebang. It is a mixed development blending tourism, commercial and residential projects with prime seafront vantages. Apart from international convention center, shopping plaza, luxury hotels, food court and recreation center, there will also be a Cheng Ho Treasure Museum, Cheng Ho monument, Cheng Ho Treasure Fleet and world cultural village and world cultural theme park and so on.

In the meantime, *The Star Online* dated 3 September 2013 reported that Melaka will become the first city outside China to stage the 10th production in a series of outdoor musical shows titled "Impressions" produced by acclaimed Chinese filmmaker Zhang Yimou. The "Impression Melaka" show has been endorsed as the latest entry point project within Malaysia's Tourism National Key Economic Area. "Impression Melaka" is a project between PTS Impression Sdn Bhd and China Impression Wonders Art Development Co. Ltd. The stage for "Impression Melaka" will be performed on a gigantic stage built to resemble Admiral Cheng Ho's Treasure Ship with a revolving seating area in the middle. The story will reflect Melaka's vibrant cosmopolitan history and heritage.

Cheng Ho's legacy and world dream

World Order Now and Then Unilateral Power Diplomacy

From the 16th century to the modern age, in an age of colonialism and imperialism, Western powers armed with excellent and advanced weapons began to show their mighty hard power in harnessing natural resources in Asia and Africa. In the Cold War, Soviet Union and the United States of America became superpowers due to the possession of nuclear weapon. They dominated the world and divided the world into two camps, communist and democratic nations. Since the end of the Cold War, as a result of the disintegration of the Soviet Union, the US has since become the world's sole superpower. Thus, the US pursued global justice and promoted western democracy, capitalist economic development and individualistic western lifestyle. The last decade of the 20th century and the first decade of the 21st century have enjoyed peace and yet the world has been full of smoke from gunpowder, conflicts and endless suicidal bomb explosions due to the ideological differences, struggles between major powers and clash of interests. Nowadays, international relations are still dominated by realist power politics and diplomacy.

Chapter 5
Cheng Ho and His Voyages

TAN Ta Sen

Cheng Ho

Cheng Ho was a great navigator, a global explorer, a diplomat, a warrior, an East–West trading network builder, a cultural disseminator, an adventurer and a Muslim eunuch in the Ming court. From 1405 to 1433, he led a huge fleet of ships to venture into the Western Ocean seven times, across the South China Sea, Indian Ocean and Persian Gulf. He visited more than 30 countries. The seven historic voyages were unprecedented.

Cheng Ho was born in a respectable Muslim family in 1371 at He Dai village in Kunyang province, Yunnan. The family name was Ma. His ancestors, who were noblemen in Uzbek bordering Xinjiang, migrated to China in 1070 during the Song dynasty. One of his great-great-grandfathers became a high-ranking official during the Yuan dynasty and was a member of a Mongol garrison situated in Yunnan. Both his grandfather and father had made pilgrimages to Mecca.

Cheng Ho's childhood was a memorable one, with love and happiness. When the Ming forces invaded Yunnan, he was only 10 years old. The war had destroyed his dream and ruined his family. His father died in the war and he was captured and castrated. He became a captive. It was the greatest tragedy in his life and the first turning point in his life too.

Cheng Ho was brought to Beijing. He was hardworking, courteous, alert and quick-witted. He stood out among all the young slaves. He was soon given basic military training and fought in several battles at a very young age. He grew up in the army and became a tough, strong and tall young man with a loud voice. When he was about 20 years of age, he was transferred to serve Prince Yan Zhu Di, as a result of the restructuring of the Ming armed forces.

The transfer was another defining moment in his life. He soon caught the attention of Prince Yan who made him his trusted bodyguard.

After Emperor Zhu Yuanzhang passed away in 1398, a court revolt broke out in the following year. Cheng Ho fought fiercely beside Zhu Di and gave him critical support. Zhu Di came out a victor in the court revolt and ascended to the throne and became Emperor Yongle. For Cheng Ho's meritorious service, Emperor Yongle rewarded him by promoting him to be the Principal Eunuch of the interior department and conferred on him a family name Cheng. Ma Ho's name was hence changed to Cheng Ho since then.

Cheng Ho's fleet

In 1405, Emperor Yongle sent Cheng Ho to visit native states in the South China Sea, Indian Ocean and Persian Gulf to expand Ming's political and economic influence in the region, and to spearhead Ming's foreign trade with these native states. From 1405 to 1433, he led a huge fleet of ships to venture into the Western Ocean seven times and visited more than 30 countries.

The fleet led by Cheng Ho was the largest in the world in the 15th century. The well-organized fleet comprised more than 200 ocean-going ships, big and small. According to their specification and use, there were six types of ships:

(1) Treasure ship: Being the flagship of the fleet, it was the largest vessel. Each treasure ship usually had nine masts with nine sails.
(2) Horse ship was also called speed ship. It functioned as a supplies ship.
(3) Grain carrier ship had seven masts, 302 ft. by 130 ft. for storing food supplies.
(4) Water storage ship's function was to store fresh water. This was the first in maritime history that a water tanker was specially provided for storing fresh water throughout the journey. It had the same measurements as the grain carrier ship.
(5) The Command ship also called battleship had six masts and measured 259 ft. by 102 ft. Military personnel, e.g. soldiers and commanders, occupied it, very much like an army camp on land. It was also the operation center during crises.

(6) The War ship with five masts measured 194 ft. by 73 ft, was light and handy being fully equipped with advanced arms and weapons such as gun powder, iron canons, cannon balls, flaming arrows, pikes, brass, exploding shells, etc. to protect the fleet.

Cheng Ho's fleet was the world's largest ocean-going fleet at that time. For every expedition, Cheng Ho mobilized more than a 100 types of ships, with 62 or 63 large and medium treasure ships forming the main body of the fleet. The first expedition in 1405 was the grandest. Cheng Ho mobilized more than 200 ships and 25,700 men.

Cheng Ho's crew was organized into four major functional groups:

1. Command Center comprising chief envoys, deputy envoys, lesser eunuchs and eunuchs. This was the nerve center of the fleet responsible for policy matters and decision making on foreign affairs, trade, navigation and war.
2. Navigation Affairs Department comprising navigators, compass-men, ship captains, meteorological officers, technicians, etc. was responsible for the safety of the voyage.
3. Foreign Affairs and Supplies Department comprising foreign affairs officers, foreign trade officers, protocol officers, interpreters, financial officers and supplies officers and medical officers responsible for food and water supply, diplomacy and foreign trade, tributary affairs, health, etc.
4. Military and Defence Department comprising brigadiers, captains, soldiers and other military officers responsible for the armada's safe passage and security.

Navigational technology

The fleet was also guided by contemporary navigational manual which traced the routes followed by Chinese ships and convoys. The most cited manual of the time was a series of Cheng Ho's nautical maps showing the Indian Ocean with the openings of the Persian Gulf and the Red Sea. The notes include indications of half-tide rocks and shoals as well as all ports and havens. Routes are given for inner and outer passages of islands, sometimes with preferences if outward- or homeward-bound. In addition to Cheng Ho's nautical maps, there are two or three more typical rutters or navigational compendia, for example, the *Shunfeng Xiangsong* (Fair Winds for Escort), *Hanghai Zhinan*, (Navigational manual) and *Zhinan Zhengfa* (The navigational guidebook).

Cheng Ho also used compasses and navigational diagrams to determine the course to steer. The Chinese compass has 24 directional points and uses the magnetic needle to show the direction accurately.

The four navigational diagrams as shown in the nautical charts were based on a navigational method known as Kamal, first invented by the Arabs to calculate the ship's longitude by studying the stars. The so-called star observation across oceans technique was to use an ivory-made square block of 6 cm, together with 12 square wooden blocks of various sizes, ranging from 24 cm to 2 cm, every block being smaller by 2 cm than the earlier one. The four corners of the ivory-made block were cut off. The method was fairly complicated. Cheng Ho's crew also measured the distance traveled using hour-glasses of sand. One hour-glass equaled two and a half hours, the length of one watch for the seamen on duty.

The movement of Cheng Ho's armada was dictated by the monsoons. He sailed westward between October and March (northeast monsoon) and eastward between April and September (southwest monsoon). Due to the monsoons, each expedition took between 1½ and 2 years.

The seven expeditions could be divided into three phases. The first three expeditions from 1405 to 1411 were confined to nearby Southeast Asia and South Asia. The fleet did not go beyond Calicut in India. At Calicut, Cheng Ho learned of Hormuz being the international trading center for West Asia, Europe and Africa. Therefore, he made an effort to call at Hormuz in his fourth expedition from 1412 to 1415. At the age of 60, he was ordered by Emperor Xuanzhou to make the seventh voyage from 1431 to 1433 which brought the fleet further to East Africa. However, he never returned because he fell sick and passed away in Calicut.

Provisions supply of the fleet

Provisions were fundamental and critical for sustaining the long voyages at sea. Cheng Ho built trading bases at Malacca, Samudra, Calicut and Hormuz and these bases were also used as provisions supply stations along the long journeys. The staple foods — grain, rice, oat and wheat, millet and rice — were carried in separate supply ships, enabling a fleet to stay at sea for several months without replenishing supplies. Supply ships were used for storing food supplies. The water ship's function was to store fresh water. An imperial edict issued by Emperor Yongle, in 1421, orders that the accompanying eunuchs be given salt, sauce, tea leaves, wine, cooking oil, candles and so forth in accordance with the crew ration. These were drinks and ingredients for food seasoning. A famous Arab traveler Ibn Battuta boarded a Chinese large vessel in Calicut in the 1330s. He wrote in his book *The Travels of Ibn Battuta* that the sailors cultivated green stuffs, vegetables and ginger in wooden tanks. Cheng Ho's fleet also raised chickens and goats and cultivated vegetables, bean, onions, gingers, carrots, etc. on board. They also bought fresh meats, vegetables and fruits in each port of call during the voyages. In addition, they brought along preserved or salted fish, vegetables, fruits and salted and century eggs, salted crabs and prawns, preserved meats such as waxed ducks and sausage, bean-curd, spices like peppers, nutmegs, cloves, etc. These preserved and salted foods were stored in barrels, and often had to last for months on the sea that were spent out of sight of land.

Art of collaboration

The magnitude and duration of the state-organized expeditions led by Cheng Ho from 1405 to 1433 is unprecedented. Cheng Ho has left a lasting impact on cross-continental cultural exchange between the East and the West. The expeditions had widened and deepened inter- as well as intra-regional culture contact in the Afro-Asian world.

Cheng Ho's overseas missions were carried out with an art of collaboration which was characterized by a set of strategy and code of conduct aimed to implement the policy set out by the Ming founding emperor Zhu Yuanzhang to promote national prestige and cherish relations with native states from afar. Zhu Yuanzhang after ascending to the throne adopted a diplomacy of peace. He advocated a foreign policy of non intervention, peace and friendliness. He instructed his descendants not to invade neighboring states and designated 15 states including Japan, Korea, Ryukyu, Annam, Champa, Zhenla, Siam, Srivijaya, Java, Pahang, Samudra and

Brunei as countries not to be invaded. Subsequently, Emperor Yongle continued the diplomacy of peace and ordered Cheng Ho to sail to the Western Ocean on a mission of peace. Throughout his seven voyages, Cheng Ho acted as an envoy of peace, a patron of international trade and promoter of Chinese culture to create a harmonious and collaborative atmosphere or environment in international relations.

As envoy of peace

Cheng Ho fostered good relationships with foreign states, emphasized peaceful coexistence and provided dignified protocol etiquette accorded to visiting missions. As a supreme maritime power, Ming China sent out mighty fleets but it harbored no ambition to occupy native states visited by the fleet but to maintain regional peace and safeguard security of maritime trade routes.

Cheng Ho upheld the principle of harmonious world order and valued peace and harmony in international relations amid diverse political systems. He warned Siam not to invade Melaka. Whenever Siam was about to take military action against Melaka, a timely warning was given to Siam by the Ming court. Ming China helped Melaka maintain its sovereignty. Consequently, without the threat of foreign invasion, Melaka eventually grew to become a powerful regional political, economic and religious center in the Strait of Malacca.

Patron of international trade

To play an effective role of a patron of international trade, Cheng Ho's first task was to be a law and order enforcer to maintain regional peace and safeguard the security of maritime trade routes. After Majapahit's invasion in the 14th century, Palembang was transformed into a Chinese pirate haven. Notorious Chinese pirates like Chen Zuyi and Liang Daoming from China's Guangdong province controlled Palembang and ruled over the Straits of Malacca and the Spice Road in the Malay Archipelago to prey on traders and trading ships. The rebellious pirate activities in Palembang posed threat to Ming state-run trading activities under the tributary system. Foreign tribute missions and traders were at times attacked and robbed of their goods by them. In 1407, Chen Zuyi pretended to surrender but plotted to rob Cheng

Ho's ships. Consequently, Zuyi was captured and brought to the court and executed. After Chen Zuyi's pirate-style operation was crushed by Cheng Ho, the sea-routes in the Malay Archipelago had become safe and secure.

Along this wide and long maritime trade routes spreading from the Malay Archipelago to East Africa, Cheng Ho's fleets called at major ports to trade Chinese silk, tea and porcelain for local produce such as spices, medicinal herbs, etc. with traders from all over the world. As each overseas operation was a major one involving more than 200 ships and 25,700 men and with large stock of provisions, water, imperial gifts, tributes, arms and weapons, gold and silver, silk, tea and porcelain for export and local produce and products a board, Cheng Ho had to set up strategic bases along the long journey ranging from months and even years to serve as mid-way houses while awaiting fair monsoon winds for home-bound voyages. Apparently, Cheng Ho divided his overseas business operation into four zones: Malay Peninsula, Indonesia Archipelago, South Asia and Arabia. He had also identified four key ports of call within each zone as his administrative centers: Malacca, Samudra, Calicut and Hormuz. These administrative centers were selected for their being regional commercial hubs which could facilitate carrying out his two vital diplomatic and foreign trade missions. Cheng Ho engaged in trade with international traders at these bases selling Chinese silk, porcelain and tea and buying local products. Meanwhile, his staff also collected in these market places useful political and economic information like trade methods, local products, local currency, knowledge of local political systems and market demand for Chinese goods and the like. He built heavily guarded official warehouses (*Guanchang*) in Malacca, Samudra, Calicut and Hormuz to store treasures and goods.

Promoter of cultural exchange

Cheng Ho promoted Chinese culture abroad. Wherever he visited, he introduced Chinese culture, technology and skills of production as well as Chinese lifestyles to the native ruler and people. These included gifts like Chinese calendar, almanac, books, costumes, customs, food culture, tea, silk, porcelain, architectural designs and construction methods, medicine, tea planting, agriculture, fishery, ceramic manufacturing, shipbuilding, metallurgy and weaving techniques. Through cultural exchange and transfer of technology Cheng Ho had enriched local culture and raised the standard of living of the native people.

On the other hand, trade conducted under the state-organized foreign trade as well as under the tribute mission framework saw local products and produce of Middle East, East Africa, South and Southeast Asia exported to China. These local products and produce consisted mainly of medicinal herbs, spices, jewellery and exotic animals, as follows:

1. Medicinal herbs: aloes, myrrh, dragon's blood, nutmegs, cardamoms, sappan wood, putchuck (*radix dulcis*), cubebs, asafoetida, liquid storax, etc.
2. Spices: pepper, camphor, frankincense, lakawood, dammar, benzoin, rose water, garu wood, Huang-shou-xiang gharu wood, sandal wood, cloves, musk wood, ambergris, bees wax, sweet benzoin, gardenia flowers, wugu tree, cherry apple, etc.
3. Jewellery: coral, opaque glass, cat's eye, pearls, ivory, rhinoceros horns, kingfishers' feathers, tortoiseshell, etc.
4. Animals: parrots, giraffe, zebra, tiger, ostrich, camel, elephant, flamingo, turkey, etc.

These local products greatly enriched Chinese lifestyle and broadened Chinese horizons. Many foreign herbs, plants and animals have enriched Chinese classification of herbs, animals and plants. Cheng Ho's seven grand voyages brought about an era of political stability, economic prosperity and cultural harmony from China to East Africa. It gives a stark contrast to the war-torn region under the rules of Western colonial powers from the 16th to 20th centuries.

Chapter 6

Cheng Ho Spirit and World Dream

TAN Ta Sen

Ming China in the 15th century was arguably the major naval power in the world. Despite Cheng Ho being instructed clearly by Emperor Zhu Di to promote national prestige and cherishing native states, he did not use bullying tactics in conducting international relations. Cheng Ho, in pursuing peaceful diplomacy based on Confucian humanism, aimed to establish a harmonious international order. Cheng Ho's voyages to the Western Ocean showed such features of Confucian ethics as humanism, benevolence, righteousness, forgiveness, morality, harmonious interpersonal relationships, as well as a stable social order. He incorporated Confucian ethics into his foreign policy as a form of the "Art of Collaboration". The spirit of Cheng Ho as demonstrated by his "Art of Collaboration" is the most appropriate illustration of his diplomacy of peace implemented during his voyages with the following salient features:

1. Good neighborliness, friendliness and coexistence (diplomacy) — Ming China's foreign relations with Afro-Asian states were based on non-intervention and aimed to establish a harmonious world. Whenever Cheng Ho visited a native state, he would call on the ruler first and present him with valuable gifts and perhaps a Mandarin royal hat, seal and robe to acknowledge and respect his high position. Ming China's foreign relations with Afro-Asian states were based on non-intervention and aimed to establish a harmonious world.
2. Valuing peace and harmony in international relations amid diverse political systems (politics) — Cheng Ho provided assistance to the weak, upheld justice, and maintained harmonious world order, peace and stability. He actively assisted weaker native states against foreign invasion,

for instance, intervening to protect the Malacca kingdom from Siam's attacks. In addition, Ming government took steps to remove undesirable forces threatening stable world order, harmonious society and safe passage of trade routes such as notorious Overseas Chinese pirates in Palembang.

3. Bestowing valuable gifts worth more than what is received and valuing righteousness above material gain (economy) — In carrying out diplomatic activities and foreign trade within the tributary system, the Ming court was altruistic. It was obligatory for vassal states to send regular tribute of local produce to the Ming court. Likewise, Ming emperors would return them with generous and more valuable gifts. Foreign envoys or rulers made their tributary trips to the Ming court with such local produce and rare and exotic animals like peacock and crane from Brunei, elephant and ivory from Champa, elephant, coral and pepper from Siam, and giraffe, lion and pearls from Hormuz and Malindi. In return, the Ming court bestowed them with gifts including tens of bales of silk, thousands of porcelain, silver and gold.
4. Benevolence and conciliation to win the hearts of native peoples (as a form of culture) — Humanism is the essence of Chinese culture. Confucian teachings aimed to build an orderly society and a government ruled by virtue. In the international stage, Cheng Ho fostered tolerant international relations with humanistic spirit of benevolence and racial equality so as to pacify the world. He was merciful towards friends but strict with self. For instance, the pirate Chen Zuyi was severely dealt with but the Javanese West king who killed his crew by mistake and the Sri Lankan king who attacked his fleet were leniently handed over to the Ming court for judgment.

World dream of universal harmony, peace and prosperity

Cheng He's Art of Collaboration is certainly relevant and practical in today's international relations and politics. Confucian teachings aimed to build an orderly society, a government ruled by virtue and a harmonious world order. In the international stage, Cheng Ho fostered tolerant international relations with humanistic spirit of benevolence and racial equality so as to achieve a great unity among nations on win–win footing. Therefore, this

Cheng Ho spirit could be a model for contemporary international relations and foreign relations. Reliving Cheng Ho's spirit in international relations based on mutual respect, non-invasion, non-intervention and fostering good relationships with foreign states will result in the creation of a world order where multipolar powers are in a partnership to achieve world peace, universal harmony and equality.

Section C
The Maritime Silk Road

Chapter 7

Narratives Related to Zheng He: Explaining the Emergence of Ethnic Chinese Communities Overseas and the Rise of a Regional Trading Network

LIM Tai Wei

Admiral Zheng He (Cheng Ho in Wades–Giles spelling system) made seven voyages to the known maritime trading world on behalf of the Chinese Ming dynasty during the reign of Emperor Yongle. His accomplishments in navigational history are universally recognized by many scholars. The tangible and intangible legacies that he left behind are shaped by various interpretations to fit different historical narratives. This writing is interested in these narratives related to Zheng He and his legacy in Southeast Asia and Greater China. It pays special attention to how Zheng He's voyages are often narrated as the origins of bustling overseas Chinese trading communities in Southeast Asia and "Greater China" (a term sometimes referring to Hong Kong, Taiwan and Macau). It does not pretend to be comprehensive but rather offers a sampling of the various ways in which Zheng's voyages are interpreted today in Southeast Asia. In this writing, I am not interested in the authenticity or accuracy of Zheng He's account (which forms important research work for archaeologists and historians) but how his voyages are interpreted in contemporary narratives and representations.

Methodology. Related to the subject matter, I collected digital materials on the internet, collected printed articles related to Zheng He and, as part of my fieldwork, took photos in Indonesia's Batam Island in the Riau Archipelago as well as Singapore for my analysis. For my analysis, I carried out interpretive work on printed, photographed and narrated materials. I collected and utilized an eclectic variety of materials including monographs, media reports/commentaries, online materials in order to select and analyze representative examples of Zheng He-related materials published in various mediums. Many of these materials including contemporary physical artefacts reconstruct Zheng He and/or his voyages according to local imaginations, sentiments and nativist interpretations. I also spent time to comprehensively search for secondary literature related to this topic in the contemporary China section of the National University of Singapore (NUS) library. I am utilizing mainly English language materials because English is a major working language in much of the regions covered in this writing, they reach a wider audience globally compared to the many local languages found in East Asia and due to the author's familiarity with these materials. The intention is not to privilege these materials as the author recognizes the importance of analyzing non-English native language materials as the subject of a separate study.

It is also important to note that Zheng He's voyages as well as Chinese voyages before and after him were not only about trade. There were cultural and religious elements to the journeys. These are equally important narratives but for this writing due to word length, personal interests as well as the narratives that I have collected, I will focus on trade historical issues more closely. For Zheng He/Cheng Ho's impact on Islamic proselytization aspects, please refer to the important literature written by Tan Ta Sen (*Cheng Ho and Islam*), who established the linkage between the two in his comprehensive account which traces Chinese cultural, religious and trade exchanges between China and Southeast Asia from the Stone Age/Neolithic period through the Ming period and beyond.[1] I have visited some of the sites that Tan mentioned in his writing and found his arguments to be persuasive narratives[2] in some aspects. For example, Tan pointed out that Southeast Asian scholars highlighted the presence of Chinese cultural influence even before Ming, supporting John Wong's narrative discussed later. In terms of materials artefacts,

[1] Tan, Ta Sen, *Cheng Ho and Islam in Southeast Asia*. Singapore: Institute of Southeast Asian Studies, 2009.

[2] As mentioned before, I am more concerned with narratives than archaeological/documentary evidence and will leave the latter to their field experts.

Figure 1: Photo of Liu Rong Shi that the author took in Guangzhou during fieldwork visit on 1 April 2013

for example, Tan also pointed out that Liu Rong Shi (Shrine) in Guangzhou constructed in AD 573 showed *stupa*-like shapes and forms that showed commonalities with Southeast Asian buildings like the Kampung Kling Mosque in Malacca (location of Zheng He's warehousing facility in Malacca) and Javanese architecture.[3]

Literature review. In trade commercial publications, semi-mythical imageries of Zheng He can be located. Sterling Seagraves' trade commercial book success *Lords of the Rim* dedicated Chapter 7 to discussing the individual known as "Sanbao the Sailor":

> Of all the children of Yueh, one of the most extraordinary and one of the most influential in opening up the doors of the world to the Chinese, was the man known as Ma Sanbao. To start with, this Ming Dynasty admiral

[3]Tan, Ta Sen, *Cheng Ho and Islam in Southeast Asia.* Singapore: Institute of Southeast Asian Studies, 2009, 198–199.

> was over eight feet tall, and said to be five feet around the middle ... Most likely, he is also the real source of the legend of Sindbad the Sailor.[4]

This narrative may contain semi-mythical exaggerations but was indicative of half-fictional portrayal of the man himself. Beyond the man and his size itself, Ma's eunuch status is also discussed in the same publication:

> ... Ma of the 'Three Jewels'. The title was a wordgame of the sort Chinese love ... In vulgar circles, it referred to Ma's being a superb warrior despite having no testicles and penis ('Three Jewels' or Thrice Precious'). By giving him this title, the emperor figuratively made him whole again.[5]

Therefore, imageries of Ma took multiple forms, from fearsome gigantic explorer to a testicle-less eunuch. Added to these sets of images, in Southeast Asia, he was deified and became a Taoist God (see the following text) with his own following of worshippers. Regardless of his physical appearance, his exploits, however, tend to be more well-known as someone who navigated his ships to much of the known world at that point of history. While Zheng He's feats are well discussed, historians have continually revised or re-evaluated Zheng He's trips based on uncovered new findings and new understanding of evidence, materials and artefacts related to Zheng's trips. Geoff Wade's reassessment of Zheng He's voyages noted that eunuch-led voyages were made to the "Western Ocean" (the part of maritime Southeast Asia west of Borneo reaching out to the Indian Ocean) and other less prominent trips to the "Eastern Ocean (today's Philippines, Borneo and Eastern Indonesia)" as the third of the three-pronged southern expansion promulgated during Emperor Yongle's reign (1402–1424) in Ming dynasty.[6] There are a number of narratives and explanations related to Yongle's purpose in sending Zheng He to visit other countries. One possible explanation was his

---

[4] Seagrave, Sterling, *Lords of the Rim*. Great Britain: Bantam Press, 1995, 75.

[5] *Ibid.*, 78.

[6] Wade, Geoff, The Zheng He Voyages: A Reassessment dated October 2004 in the Asia Research Institute Working Paper Series No. 31. Singapore: National University of Singapore Asia Research Institute, 2004, 10.

desire to legitimize his succession to the throne[7] since he was not the first choice and deposed his nephew to rule China and one possible way to do this is to send impressive naval ships to other countries to pay tribute to the Chinese state. His military background was also narrated as another reason for military and naval swaggering to awe overseas states, despite his father's reservation about such overseas ventures.[8] The reasons behind the end of Zheng He's voyages are also analyzed by scholars. Wang's publication probably provided one of the most dominant explanations for stopping the voyages: tax burdens on the state for financing the voyages, attention needed to manage Mongols in northern China and other competing expensive projects like establishing the new capital city in Beijing.[9] There are others who see the geopolitical value of Ming expansion. Weng Eang Cheong's writing indicated that "For the early Ming rulers, the sea was the medium to launch a diplomatic offensive to spread the pacific word of an evenhanded Chinese world order".[10]

While some parts of his journeys were considered less prominent and far removed from Beijing's worldview, Zheng He's presence left important legacies in formerly peripheral areas of the Sino-centric universe. In this writing, due to limited word length, the nature of materials collected as well as location in which the research is carried out, I will restrict the scope mainly to maritime Southeast Asia (in particular, Indonesia and the Malay Peninsula) and parts of Greater China (especially with regard to post-Zheng He narratives on the formation of trading communities). I will explain my findings related to these two regions in the following section.

Tan Ta Sen quoted Fairbank's classification of Chinese foreign relations during the dynastic periods and, within this classification, narratives related to the "outer zone" that includes Southeast Asia[11] is the one that I am most interested in this writing. Because of my research location in Singapore,

---

[7] Wang, Gungwu, *China and the Chinese Overseas.* Singapore: Times Academic/Eastern Universities Press/Marshall Cavendish, 2007, 60 and 66.

[8] *Ibid.*, 66.

[9] *Ibid.*, 65.

[10] Cheong, Weng Eang, *The Hong Merchants of Canton Chinese Merchants in Sino-Western Trade.* Richmond Surrey Great Britain: Nordic Institute of Asian Studies, 1997, 4.

[11] Tan, Ta Sen, *Cheng Ho and Islam in Southeast Asia.* Singapore: Institute of Southeast Asian Studies, 2009, 167.

compared with other world regions, I can access materials found in this zone more easily. In addition, because Southeast Asia is located in the periphery (along with Europe, Japan and South Asia in the Sino-centric world), its location farthest away from the Chinese empire and civilization provides the freest possible narrative space for ideas to develop, away from the orbit of the Chinese Confucian civilization. Therefore, narratives in this zone (Southeast Asia which is the focus of this writing) have the greatest potential to develop independently away from Sino-centric official histories and historical writings. Besides this zone, I am also interested in narratives related to a constructed sphere known as "Greater China", a term that emerged much later in the late Qing and early Republican period onwards.

The narrative of Zheng He's voyage is also evident in overseas Chinese or Chinese diasporic literatures. Lynn Pan included a brief mention of Zheng's voyages in her edited volume *Encyclopedia of the Chinese Overseas* where she mentioned about archaeological evidence found in a Nanjing shipyard related to Zheng's ships and offered explanations of how the Chinese capitol's shift from Nanjing to Beijing signified priorities shifting to continental matters.[12] In fact, from the Ming dynasty onwards, China's attention decisively shifted to maintaining border integrity with non-Han people from north of China and, in Qing dynasty, energies were focused on Western overland territorial expansion.

Not all historical narratives acknowledge Zheng He's voyages as the major catalyst in developing the maritime trade route. In fact, veteran contemporary China economist John Wong argued that trading communities had started even before Zheng's trips.

> The Maritime Silk Road also originated in China. It started as the Chinese people ventured out to South-east Asia, traditionally called Nanyang (or South Seas) by the Chinese. By the Song Dynasty (960–1280), Imperial China had established tributary relations with many states in Nanyang. The tribute-bearing missions were, as observed by eminent Harvard historian John K. Fairbank, actually a convenient "cloak for trade". In fact, China already operated a lot of maritime activities along the China coast and in Nanyang

---

[12] Pan, Lynn (ed.), *The Encyclopedia of the Chinese Overseas*. Singapore: Chinese Heritage Center/Archipelago Press/Landmark Books, 1998, 69.

> well before Admiral Zheng He's expeditions (1405–1433). Subsequently, China's burgeoning relations with Nanyang were further boosted by successive waves of Chinese emigration, particularly in the 19th century.[13]

This quotation establishes the narrative that trading activities had begun even before Ming dynasty and that Chinese trading communities in the Southeast Asia ("Nanyang") were constantly reinforced by generations of traders coming out of China. Besides intellectuals, contemporary seasoned diplomats also observed the pre-Ming migration and trade presence of the Chinese people. According to Singapore's Ambassador to Indonesia Lee Khoon Choy, Chinese migration to Thailand started as early as the Northern Sung dynasty (960–1127, the Thai royalty also borrowed their institutional setups from the Chinese) and they built up Sino-Thai trade connections and by 1350, the population had grown to 1.5 million Chinese with Chinese junks parked in the river up to Sawangkalok (nearly 120 leagues from the river mouth).[14]

All these narratives indicated that Zheng He's voyages or the impact of those voyages was only one of the successive arrivals. This narrative acknowledges the importance of Zheng He's voyages but seeks not to privilege it as the dominant explanation for the emergence of an ethnic Chinese trading network in Southeast Asia or the Greater China interactions that emerged later. Tan Ta Sen's important scholarship on Admiral Cheng Ho agrees with this interpretation. He argues:

> From the tenth to fourteenth centuries during the Song and Yuan dynasties, China's maritime trade saw a period of boom. Tribute missions from Southeast Asian native states and Chinese and foreign traders were seen playing the Southeast maritime route ceaselessly.[15]

---

[13]Wong, John, Reviving the Ancient Silk Road: China's New Economic Diplomacy, dated 9 July 2014 in the *Straits Times* [downloaded on 26 November 2014], available at http://www.straitstimes.com/news/opinion/invitation/story/reviving-the-ancient-silk-road-chinas-new-economic-diplomacy-20140709.

[14]Lee, Khoon Choy, *Golden Dragon and Purple Phoenix*. Singapore: World Scientific, 2013, 1.

[15]Tan, Ta Sen, *Cheng Ho and Islam in Southeast Asia*. Singapore: Institute of Southeast Asian Studies, 2009, 51.

Like Wong, Tan Ta Sen also emphasized the presence of an existing trading network before the arrival of Zheng He. He even emphasized that a hierarchical Sino-centric order was set up through the tributary missions to regulate this trade. In order words, Zheng He inherited Chinese traditions of regulating trade and recognizing favored nation statuses and innovated and expanded them instead of re-inventing new systems of trade relations. Some writers like Lo Jung-pang (grandson of Kang Youwei) would even go as far as to argue the following:

> Indeed, during the three centuries from the Southern Song to the early Ming period, the maritime and overseas activities of the Chinese people were so great in extent and consequence that China then was more of a sea power than a land power. The China Seas were Chinese in fact as well as in name. They were a *mare clausum* over which the Chinese navy ranged unchallenged. Under the aegis of their naval power, the Chinese extended their political influence from Japan in the east to Ceylon in the west, from the Yellow Sea in the north to the Java Sea in the south.[16]

This narrative was probably the most extreme reading of Chinese maritime power in the Sung to Ming period. Many would argue about the limitations of Chinese maritime supremacy, for example, Mongol rule in Yuan dynasty and its failure to capture Japan through naval power, distractions from non-Han tribes from the north, the emphasis on trade and tributary missions rather than naval expansionism. On the last point, in many narratives related to Zheng He including Tan's, the imagery of the voyages is said to be relatively peaceful with little direct intervention in local affairs.

> For example, to wipe out pirate leader Chen Zuyi in the Straits of Malacca was for the sake of maritime traders as the move had kept the East–West maritime trade route safe. Although Javanese Western king killed his 170 crew members, Cheng Ho took no military action but settled the matter amicably.[17]

---

[16] Lo, Jung-pang, *China as a Sea Power 1127–1368*. Singapore: National University of Singapore and Hong Kong University Press, 2012, xiv–xv.

[17] Tan, Ta Sen, Cheng Ho Spirit and China's Soft Power in the *International Zheng He Society* website [downloaded on 7 December 2014], available at http://www.chengho.org/downloads/CH_spirit_China_soft_power_1.pdf, 5.

This narrative and other versions with some similarities to it have been appropriated by some scholars/observers/policy makers to argue that the rise of China follows past historical traditions of behaving as a non-interventionist peaceful large power. This narrative is controversial, contentious and still the subject of an intense ongoing debate.

Supporting the idea that trade between China and Southeast Asia pre-dated Ming, one of the most authoritative texts on early South China Seas Nanhai trade is written by Wang Gungwu whose classic *The Nanhai Trade* talks about this subject matter in detail. I refer readers who are interested in pre-Zheng He trade in the South China Sea to this publication, and will only briefly introduce this important book here by selecting materials most directly relevant to the subject matter. The publication began with coastal trade in China (Shang Dynasty to 5th century BC), before economically expanding southwards into the Nan Yueh territories (221–111 BC) and by AD 220–440, trade and missions were established with most Southeast Asian kingdoms.[18] The growth in Southern Chinese population, widening contact with South India and its domination of maritime Southeast Asia, rise in Buddhist artefacts trade alongside the spread of that religion characterized the period between 420 and 589 and in the next few decades (589–618), the port of Fuzhou became important as the Chinese started sending silk down to Southeast Asia with naval escorts and in turn received reciprocation of gifts and envoys from the native rulers.[19] The rise (increased consumption demand in new Southern Chinese markets and political stability offered by a strong China) and fall (trouble with Arab/Persian traders) saw the corresponding rise and decline in the Nanhai trade during the Tang dynasty (618–960) and this period slowly transited to a post-Tang middlemen-mediated trade conducted by the Arabs, Persians, Ceylonese and Indian ships.[20] And this was the situation before the rise of the Sung, Yuan and Ming trades described by Wong and Tan. A travel feature article (originally printed in *China Daily* and also appeared in Singapore's *My Paper* on 15 October 2014) that I spotted in *The Straits Times* on Quanzhou published on 23 December 2014 also mentioned the Maritime Silk Road during Tang, Song and Yuan dynasties:

[18] Wang, Gungwu, *The Nanhai Trade*. Singapore: Times Academic Press, 1998, 1–42.
[19] *Ibid.*, 43–68.
[20] *Ibid.*, 69–115.

> Radiating lovely historical charm, it [Quanzhou] is famous as the starting point for the Maritime Silk Road and as the largest port in Asia during the Song (960–1279) and Yuan (1271–1368) dynasties ... One important group of foreigners who came to Quanzhou via the Maritime Silk Road during the Tang Dynasty (618–907) were Muslim merchants.[21]

Like the narratives from the following mentioned Indonesian tourism authorities, historical stories about Quanzhou served the practical purpose of romantic and nostalgic recollections of its past roles, colored by testimonials of legendary travelers who recorded their diachronic observations of the trading city. This narrative also supported the earlier-stated points and arguments that maritime trade routes did not start with Zheng He since there was already an existing robust trading network starting from Tang dynasty. Just as maritime trade did not really begin with Zheng He's voyages, it also did not end when his ships were withdrawn by the court. Wang Gungwu's publication again is useful in highlighting the continuity of trade even in the absence of official support:

> But the fleets were withdrawn after 1435 and the ban on private foreign trade remained in force. For the 200 years from the late fourteenth to the second half of the sixteenth century, private trade overseas was forbidden. This ban did not, of course, stop private trade, it merely made it more dangerous.[22]

This passage indicated that, even in the most adverse situations compounded by an official isolationist policy and lack of state support, private trade with overseas nations continued by evading the authorities' attention.

In contrast to the emergence of trading communities in post-Zheng He Southeast Asia, waves of overseas Chinese migrations to Greater China occurred during the decline of the late Qing dynasty with the ceding of

---

[21] China Daily/Asia News Network, Discover Historic Gems Galore in Fujian's Cities, dated 23 December 2014 in *The Straits Times Classified.* 2014, C1.

[22] Wang, Gungwu, *China and the Chinese Overseas.* Singapore: Times Academic/Eastern Universities Press/Marshall Cavendish, 2007, 212.

Hong Kong to the British, Macau to the Portuguese and Taiwan to the Japanese. Hong Kong is a prominent example of a recipient of successive overseas Chinese migrations during this period. Between the founding of Hong Kong as a British colony and the start of World War II in 1939 with the fall of Poland, more than six million Chinese transited through Hong Kong to reach other countries.[23] Throughout the historical periods of declining late Qing dynasty, the warlordism of Republican China, the communist takeover of mainland China, Hong Kong received many traders, businessmen, entrepreneurial refugees, similar to Southeast Asia. In the immediate post-WWII period, overseas Chinese in Hong Kong remitted US$500–600 million annually back to their families on the mainland.[24] Most academic narratives conceptualize ethnic Chinese migrations as a cyclical rather than a deterministic process. They reflect events in mainland China and the contesting priorities of imperial regimes in maintaining the integrity of landed borders, secure maritime trade and political impulses of opening up or isolationism.

Chinese preoccupations with maritime and overland territorial issues. One reason for the cyclical nature of Chinese attention to maritime matters alternating with overland territorial issues is because of its semi-continental and semi-maritime (East and South China Seas) geographical make-up. A number of maps that I obtained digitally from university websites and databases indicate selectively Chinese attention paid to continental matters. Therefore, through interpretive work and extrapolation, it was possible to understand Chinese dilemma in dividing its time between continental and maritime affairs. Late pre-modern Chinese had its own idiosyncratic interpretive features in map designs. Map designs reflected the fluidity in which pre-modern Chinese conceptualized their territorial boundaries. PhD candidate Eric Vanden Bussche explained this in a *Stanford Report* when he examined how the Chinese negotiated with the British over the boundaries for Burma:

---

[23] Skeldon, Ronald, "The case of Hong Kong" in *The Encyclopedia of the Chinese Overseas* edited by Lynn Pan. Singapore: Chinese Heritage Center/Archipelago Press/Landmark Books, 1998, 67.

[24] Yahuda, Michael, *Hong Kong China's Challenge*. London and NY: Routledge, 1996, 23.

> A typical 19th century Chinese map shows regional hierarchies and landmarks, such as the prefecture seats depicted as walled compounds, the trade routes marked by passes, and the areas controlled by various chieftains. And unlike western maps, the Chinese maps themselves rarely contained distance measurements. Textual descriptions indicated distances between various landmarks. "The Chinese believed that maps could not adequately convey the geographical knowledge found in written sources."[25]

Given that distances are not accurately calibrated in two-dimensional terms proportionately and represented textually, this provides leeway to stretch, extend or minimize distances graphically on the maps. Therefore, it is not possible to gauge with precise measurements the extent and exact routes of Zheng He's voyages. But material artefacts like temples in Indonesia as well as stories of the communities that his followers left behind help in the process of tracing his journey. Throughout the Ming-Qing historical periods, like the westward expansion of China's boundaries, its maritime borders were also never really secured. J.A.C. Mackie described Ming maritime trade in the following:

> Outside the framework of tributary trade, Chinese and Japanese were fellow-freebooters in the endemically piratical, smuggler-ridden character of East Asian maritime commerce in the Ming dynasty (1368–1644). Relations between many of these extra-tributary traders were close, so close that the mid-16th century raids on the Chinese coasts were joint Chinese–Japanese endeavours. Chinese merchants had also to ally themselves with the Portuguese (who had established a base in Macao) to conduct trade in the teeth of Chinese imperial proscription.[26]

---

[25] Smith, Rachel, Stanford Historian Sees New Perspectives on Chinese Border Disputes in Declassified Qing Dynasty Maps, dated 29 May 2014 in *Stanford Report* [downloaded on 27 November 2014], available at http://news.stanford.edu/news/2014/may/declassified-chinese-maps-052914.html.

[26] Mackie, J.A.C., "Business relations with non-Chinese" in *The Encyclopedia of the Chinese Overseas* edited by Lynn Pan. Singapore: Chinese Heritage Center/Archipelago Press/Landmark Books, 1998, 126.

This narrative indicated unstable territorial markers in the periphery of Chinese trading maritime network. Trade was unregulated and sometimes depended on the protection of non-Chinese entities in some areas. In fact, even its coastal territories faced threats from maritime incursions from time to time. With constant threats and security issues, Chinese officialdom would have struggled between allocating budget, manpower, time and resources to cope with foreign intrusions at its maritime and landed borders. From this perspective, it may be possible that Zheng's voyages was a victim to such changing priorities in border defenses. In the Republican modern period of Chinese history, boundaries were eventually drawn more accurately and with greater consciousness of peripheral limits to the reach of Chinese sovereignty, effective control, power and influence *vis-à-vis* other states in the region.

Regardless of the reasons behind the end of Zheng He's voyages, and China's alternating priorities of maritime and overland trade reach, his historical exploits have become subjects of worship today. Sterling Seagraves's publication *Lords of the Rim* narrated how Admiral Zheng He is remembered today in Asia:

> Six images of the admiral are preserved in temples in the region. There is a Sanbao Harbor, a Sanbao Pagoda, a Sanbao Town. In Indonesia, Chinese go every year to Tajue Temple to pay homage on the anniversary of Cheng Ho's first visit. In Malacca the oldest well is called Sam Bao Kung. In Thailand incense is burned for him at San Pao Temple.[27]

Some of these temples are discussed is the following sections as case studies of how Zheng He is remembered today in Southeast Asia. Interestingly, one of the countries where I was able to locate information about Cheng Ho or Admiral Zheng He is in Indonesia. When I did a search online of the Admiral, I found number of sites mentioning Chinese restaurants in Indonesia with the name "Cheng Ho". In a blog, for example, I came across a discussion on a "Cheng Ho Restaurant" and how it served Southeast Asian and localized Islamic Chinese food with a critique of service quality at the

---

[27] Seagrave, Sterling, *Lords of the Rim.* US: Putnam's Sons, 1995, 90.

restaurant.[28] From these narratives, there seems to be a stereotypical association of Muslim Chinese food with the Admiral. Such imagined popular association with Zheng He is not only found in Indonesia but are also applicable to organizations like the military that want to appropriate the Zheng He symbolism for portraying certain images. For example, the Taiwanese military named one of their frigates after Cheng Ho, the ROCS Cheng Ho FFG-1103 (formerly the Oliver Hazard Perry class frigate in the US navy). This frigate is part of the December 2014 sale (approved by HR3470 house resolution) of four advanced frigates by the US to Taiwan under the Taiwan Relations Act (35th anniversary in 2014) which states that the US remains committed to the defense of Taiwan, a development that attracted strong criticisms from Beijing.[29] The exact historical background and decision-making process of utilizing the name "Cheng Ho" however is not as well-known and would be interesting research to uncover the origins of this name and the narrative behind it.

Online research also revealed that the Admiral's name can also be found in the official Indonesian tourism websites. For example, Palembang's ancient name Srivijaya was described in the following manner in an officially-authorized site for the Indonesian tourism industry:

> Monks from China, India and Java used to congregate here to learn and teach the lessons of Buddha. In AD 671 Chinese chronicles wrote that the famous Chinese Buddhist monk, I Ching sojourned in Palembang for six months on his way to India. I Ching wrote that there were more than 1,000 Buddhist monks in the city and advised Chinese monks to study Sanskrit in Palembang before proceeding to India. While the Srivijaya kings lived inland on shore, his subjects lived along the wide Musi river, manning the powerful fleet and busily trading in gold, spices, silks, ivories and ceramics with foreign merchants who sailed in from China, India and

[28] Vogue Mum, Restoran CHENG HO (AMY SEARCH) Will it be my Last Trip? dated 14 March 2009 in Voguemom Blog [downloaded on 23 December 2014], available at http://voguemom.blogspot.sg/2009/03/restoran-cheng-ho-amy-search-will-it-be.html.

[29] Panda, Ankit, US Finalizes Sale of Perry-class Frigates to Taiwan, dated 20 December 2014 in *The Diplomat* [downloaded on 8 January 2015], available at http://thediplomat.com/2014/12/us-finalizes-sale-of-perry-class-frigates-to-taiwan/.

Java ... Later, Chinese admiral Cheng Ho, emissary of the Chinese emperor visited Palembang in the 15th century.[30]

Three points are important from this narrative: (1) It indicated clearly that China was not the only source of visitors nor the first visitors to Indonesia. Others from India and kingdoms from within Indonesia traveled to Srivijaya; (2) Ming Chinese were also not the first to chronicle travels to Srivijaya. According to this narrative, Buddhist monks studied Sanskrit in Palembang enroute to India and traders were also active in the region before the appearance of Zheng He; (3) Zheng visited in 15th century, he was a relative latecomer when compared to Southern Indian empires' representatives and early Chinese monks and traders. Another official tourism site introduced the Zheng He temple at Semarang. I will discuss this website later in the section dedicated to this Semarang temple.

Background of Zheng He temples in Indonesia. In these maps and the narratives I collected, Indonesia located in the far periphery of the Sino-centric world had often briefer mention compared to Ming–Malacca relations in the historical narratives. The materials that I collected tended to emphasize Malacca's Parameswara's foresight in asking for the protection of Ming China symbolized Zheng He's ships in contesting the strength of the Majapahit Empire and the Kingdom of Siam. Eventually, after Zheng He's voyages stopped, Malacca grew into a great regional power. Viewed from the periphery's perspective, narratives related to Zheng He can still be found in local interpretations of his journeys.

Singapore Ambassador to Indonesia Lee Khoon Choy's important publication on overseas Chinese and their descendants also mentioned about Admiral Zheng He traveling to Southeast Asia with 63 treasure ships and left behind crews in the stopover ports.[31] According to Lee, during his tenure as Singapore's ambassador to Indonesia, he found out that half a millennium ago, most Chinese Peranakans were converted to Islam due to the arrival of Zheng He and nine religious figures Wali Songo (eight of them were Chinese)

[30]Tourism of Indonesia i Norsk, Tourism of Indonesia i Norsk, dated 29 December 2011 in the *Tourism of Indonesia i Norsk* website [downloaded on 23 December 2014], available at http://tourism-n.jazz.or.id/category/sumatra/page/3/.

[31]Lee, Khoon Choy, *Golden Dragon and Purple Phoenix*. Singapore: World Scientific, 2013, vii.

associated with his travels assisted in resisting and eventually overthrowing the Hindu kingdom of Majapahit.[32] Paralleling Lee's account, Robert W. Hefner, an expert on the subject matter of politics of multiculturalism, noted the significance of Chinese traders in conducting trade between the 15th and 17th centuries and an important legacy is that several of the Muslim "saints" (*wali*) were Chinese or half-Chinese.[33] In terms of material artefacts in Indonesia to support Zheng He and his followers' presence in the archipelago, there are temples dedicated to commemorate Admiral Zheng He. *The Jakarta Post* ran an article on 17 November 2000 highlighting the Klenteng Sampo constructed for Admiral Zheng He (1371–1435) in the following narrative:

> The people of Semarang believe that Zheng He and his fleet landed on the 30th day of the sixth month of the lunar year but in which year that actually was is unclear. The event is commemorated every year with a big procession — complete with dragon and lion dances accompanied by deafening music — from Tay Kak Sie, Semarang's other main temple, to Gedung Batu.[34]

The article noted the political nature of these celebrations, pointing out that Suharto's regime did not permit the festivities to go on and it was only in the year 2000 that the celebrations returned after the fall of the Suharto regime.[35] (An Asian financial crisis that occurred 3 years before this article,[35] contributed to the downfall of a strongman regime in Indonesia that ruled for decades.) The origins of the temple is attributed to Zheng He's followers. According to *The Jakarta Post*'s narrative, Zheng He's helmsman Wan Jin-Hong was sick and Zheng He let one of his ships remain in Indonesia

---

[32] Lee, Khoon Choy, *Golden Dragon and Purple Phoenix*. Singapore: World Scientific, 2013, xii–xiii.

[33] Hefner, Robert W, "Introduction: Multiculturalism and Citizenship in Malaysia, Singapore, and Indonesia" in *The Politics of Multiculturalism* edited by Robert W. Hefner. Honolulu: University of Hawaii Press, 2001, 18.

[34] *The Jakarta Post*, Semarang's Temple, A Tribute to Adm. Zheng He, dated 17 November 2000 in *The Jakarta Post* [downloaded on 26 November 2014], available at http://www.thejakarta-post.com/news/2000/11/17/semarang039s-temple-a-tribute-adm-zheng-he.html.

[35] *Ibid.*

and allocated 10 crew members to tend to Wan.[36] Known locally as Kyai Juru Mudi, Wan resided in Semarang where he was healed, grew crops and used a marine vessel to meander coastal areas for trade.[37] His followers married locals and this was the start of a community that expanded as the Muslim follower Wan spread the religion to the community in honor of Admiral Zheng He and even built a mosque at the cave where he was located before passing away at 87.[38] The mosque was rebuilt as a temple and became Klenteng Sampo.

The *Jakarta Post*'s information on the Semarang temple corroborated with the information that I located in the official Indonesian tourism site. The following narrative from the official Indonesian tourism website explained how the temple was restored a number of times, eventually becoming a fixture for Indonesian heritage tourism:

> The first and second restorations took place in 1879, financed by the wealthy Oei Tjie Sien, who took over possession from Yam Hoo Loo, and made the complex open to the public. The temple underwent further restorations in 1937 and new additions were added to the structure such as the gate, the sacred garden and the main lobby. In March 2011, a bronze statue of Admiral Cheng Ho was erected within the temple. The statue stands over 10 meters high and weighs nearly 4 tons, and is an icon of Semarang Tourism.[39]

The tourism caption is interesting as it mentioned how upkeep of the temple passed on from religious villagers and community-based leadership to wealthy Chinese merchants. Access to the site was then opened to the public realm and a gap in development of the temple grounds occurred during the long-reigning autocratic Suharto regime weary of Chinese cultural influence. After the collapse of this regime, with the introduction of democracy to Indonesia, ethnic Chinese once again installed large Cheng Ho statues and

---

[36] *Ibid.*

[37] *Ibid.*

[38] *Ibid.*

[39] Ministry of Tourism, Republic of Indonesia, The Sam Poo Kong Temple of Semarang: dedicated to Chinese Admiral Cheng Ho, dated 2013 in the *Wonderful Indonesia* website [downloaded on 23 December 2013], available at http://www.indonesia.travel/en/destination/560/the-sam-poo-kong-temple-of-semarang.

Figure 2: The local marketplace at Semarang. (Photo included here with the permission of Chia Lin Sien)

fixtures to the temple grounds. It is a story of multiple identities for a site that is nominally associated with Zheng He (built by his followers[40]) and then developed a hybridized identity with its mixed heritage of Chinese–Malay Muslim origins. It was eventually integrated into an ethnic Chinese Taoist facility funded by ethnic Chinese merchants. The same website also mentioned that a festival is held on the temple grounds to celebrate Zheng He's birthday on the 29th of Lak Gwee in the Chinese lunar calendar.[41] I am including some photos of the temple with the permission of their photographer, Chia Lin Sien.

Other than Jakarta, there are Zheng He-related intangible representations and physical heritage that I located in other parts of Indonesia, e.g. in

[40]The Ministry of Tourism's website mentioned that the foundations of the temple were built by Admiral Zheng He himself: "The temple foundations were first built by Admiral Cheng Ho, elsewhere better known as Admiral Zheng He — a Muslim explorer from Mainland China. He arrived in Java sometime between the years 1400 and 1416, although the exact year is disputed. Finding a small cave in a rocky hillside, Cheng Ho used the site for prayer and later built a small temple in its place." (*Source*: Ministry of Tourism, Republic of Indonesia, The Sam Poo Kong Temple of Semarang: Dedicated to Chinese Admiral Cheng Ho, dated 2013 in the *Wonderful Indonesia* website [downloaded on 23 December 2013], available at http://www.indonesia.travel/en/destination/560/the-sam-poo-kong-temple-of-semarang).

[41]Ministry of Tourism, Republic of Indonesia, The Sam Poo Kong Temple of Semarang: Dedicated to Chinese Admiral Cheng Ho, dated 2013 in the *Wonderful Indonesia* website [downloaded on 23 December 2013], available at http://www.indonesia.travel/en/destination/560/the-sam-poo-kong-temple-of-semarang.

Figure 3: Here, the large Zheng He statue is visible peering down on visitors to the entrance of the temple. (Photo included here with the permission of Chia Lin Sien)

Figure 4: A close-up of the Admiral Zheng He statue standing outside the temple. (Photo included here with the permission of Chia Lin Sien)

Figure 5: An Indonesian interpretation of a traditional Chinese gate with the name "Sam Poo Kong (The Three Treasures Admiral)" referring to Zheng He embossed on the gate-plate. (Photo included here with the permission of Chia Lin Sien)

Figure 6: A large sign with the words "Sam Poo Kong" installed above an open-air car park at the temple grounds. (Photo included here with the permission of Chia Lin Sien)

Figure 7: An imperial palace-like structure in the temple which seems to have been renovated relatively recently. (Photo included here with the permission of Chia Lin Sien)

the Riau Archipelago. Some of the photos that I captured are discussed in the following sections.

These temples may be part of what Tan Ta Sen described as the "… cult of Cheng Ho, which is a purely Overseas Chinese invention, very popular and widespread among the Chinese communities in Southeast Asia".[42] In addition, for fans to worship Zheng in a cult-like manner, it also requires the religion of Taoism to be flexible in accommodating the spirituality as well as theological grounds to deify the mortal admiral. Besides static display in a local temple, in 2012, the city of Batam organized the Chinese Peranakan Festival at Kepri Mall from 2 to 4 November 2012. The narrative of Admiral Zheng was weaved into the event:

> However, after the arrival of Admiral Zheng He (or better known in Indonesia as Admiral Cheng Ho), Chinese influence became more widespread and more immigrants came in Indonesia. Today, large communities of Chinese can be found in Singkawang in West Kalimantan, on the islands

[42]Tan, Ta Sen, *Cheng Ho and Islam in Southeast Asia*. Singapore: Institute of Southeast Asian Studies, 2009, 252.

Figure 8: In my fieldwork in Batam (September 2014), I came across large figurine representations of Zheng He, his followers and ship in a Tua Pek Kong and Confucius (The Klenteng Nabi Khong Hu Cu located at Block VI Lubuk Baja Batam) temples in Batam

Figure 9: This picture shows a comprehensive side view of the ship found in my fieldwork in Batam (September 2014)

of Bangka and Belitung, Palembang in South Sumatra, Medan, North Sumatra, in Jakarta, and along the north coast of Java.[43]

Like other materials that I found, a commonality amongst Zheng He narratives is that they appear to assume an ahistorical approach to his voyages, casting the journeys as a symbolic start to massive Chinese migration to a particular region (in this case, Indonesia). Experts lend historicity to their accounts in this area. Senior Curator of the Asian Civilisations Museum Singapore, Ms Heidi Tan pointed out the following:

> The Chinese were very keen on importing exotic products such as Kingfisher feathers, resin, bees wax and Kemenyang (aromatics such as benzoin or camphor) which they used for incense. So the Chinese communities settled early on, particularly after the voyages of Zheng He, the imperial eunuch, during 14th century. Zheng He had established tributary trading connections between local rulers and Chinese emperors. Peranakan origin can be traced to these early Chinese settlers.[44]

In this account, traded items as well as dates are added into the narrative. Outside museum and curatorial narratives, consciousness of the linkage between Zheng He and the Peranakan community in Southeast Asia is not strong although the latter's cultural heritage remains visible publicly, especially in Singapore, Malacca and Penang. In my fieldwork in Singapore, I visited locations and collected relics related to the Joo Chiat (an area where the Peranakan community in Singapore used to reside) heritage trail. Heritage related to Peranakan culture is rich, textured and colorful, playing an important part of the cherished multicultural narrative in Singapore.

---

43 Wonderful Indonesia Indonesia's Official Tourism Website, The Chinese "Peranakan" Cultural Festival in Batam, dated 4 November 2012 in the *Wonderful Indonesia* website [downloaded on 26 November 2014], available at http://www.indonesia.travel/en/event/detail/566/the-chinese-peranakan-cultural-festival-in-batam.

44 Lalwani, Bharti, Cross-cultural Influences Shape the Island of Sumatra, dated 2 November 2010 in Focus, Magazine Culture360.org website [downloaded on 26 November 2014], available at http://culture360.asef.org/magazine/cross-cultural-influences-shape-the-island-of-sumatra/#sthash.JbQiXkIY.dpuf.

Figure 10: This handcrafted mooncake mould was purchased in a shop in Joo Chiat that is listed as an outlet that still sell Peranakan traditional utensils and kitchenware (collected during author's fieldwork in November 2014)

Figure 11: Left photo: this is a picture of Peranakan houses that the author took during his fieldwork in Singapore's Koon Seng Road in November 2014. The photo on the right shows the Baba House, a former Peranakan residence that has been converted into a private museum owned by the NUS

Figure 12: These are some traditional Peranakan *kueh* pastries that the author acquired during his fieldwork in Singapore's Orchard Road in November 2014

Figure 13: Peranakan tiles on heritage buildings (from author's fieldwork in November 2014)

Another interesting indirect link between Peranakans and the Cheng Ho narrative can be found in Cheu Hock Tong's interesting thesis on Malay *keramats*. This thesis is made available online by the Faculty of Arts of the NUS. Cheu cited the character Sam Poh Neo Neo (known as Sanbao Niang-niang in Chinese, Datuk Puloh Besar in Malay, and the Granny of Pulau Besar in English) as evidence of this indirect connection (*Note*: Puloh Besar is an island off Malacca).[45] An artistic interpretation of this character is found in *Sam Poh Neo Neo Keramat* which features a basket prop on display in Sam Poh Neo Neo Temple that belonged Datuk Bakul (Basket Granny), a character possibly based on a Malay-Muslim consort of Sam Poh Kong.[46] The word Sanbao refers to Cheng Ho whose deified form is immortalized as Sam Poh Kong (Sanbao Gong) in Singapore, Malacca, Penang and Trengganu.[47] According to Cheu, the Ming-era (1368–1644) textual documents of *Dongxiyang Kao* (*Explorations of the Eastern and Western Oceans*) and the *Qiongzhoufu Zhi* (*Hainanese Records, Vol. 8*) support the idea of Chinese worshipping the Malay *keramat* with the Straits Chinese taking a lead in this aspect.[48] Cheu argues that Chinese worship of Malay *keramats* eventually gave rise to a Datuk Kong cult which was hybridization of traditional Chinese locality deities with Malay *keramat* culture and a balance between Chinese and Malay spiritual worlds.[49]

Outside some selected narratives that connect Peranakan history with Zheng He's voyages, most other Zheng He-related narratives are commercial in nature. Unrelated to the Peranakan heritage, in other parts of Singapore, there are some historical representations of Zheng He located in sites that reconstruct images or symbols of his voyages.

It is important to note that the Straits Settlements during the colonial period (Penang, Melaka and Singapore) should not be construed as the only nucleus of Peranakan traditions. Peranakan heritage and tradition is also very strong in Java — including Soerabaya, Semanang, Bintang and elsewhere in

---

[45] Cheu, Hock Tong, Malay Keramat, Chinese Worshippers: The Sinicization of Malay Keramats in Malaysia Academic Session 1996/97 [downloaded on 8 December 2014] in the Faculty of Arts National University of Singapore website. Singapore: Department of Malay Studies National University of Singapore, 1997, 17.

[46] *Ibid.*, 16.

[47] *Ibid.*, 17.

[48] *Ibid.*, 16.

[49] *Ibid.*, 15–16.

Figure 14: I took this photo of a Datuk Kong shrine located in Tiong Bahru in front of its reconstructed market complex on 8 December 2014

Java. Local conditions shaping the emergence of Peranakan cultures in these areas need to be studied here as well.

Zheng He or Cheng Ho's symbols, signifiers and representations appear to be closely related with commercial concerns. In Singapore's leisure industries, a private enterprise Singapore Tours borrows the name "Cheng Ho" for their cruise services. Unintended to be historically accurate, the program of the cruise read: "You will board on a duplicate of the ancient ship of Chengho which sailed from China to Europe."[50] The commercial flavor of this Zheng He/Cheng Ho narrative is visible. The statue donation arose from the commercial success of an entrepreneur while the tour narrative for the cruise promises an experience retracing Zheng's journey through an imagined recreation of that experience. Other tour operators affiliated with this tour were more conservative in their narration of the commercial tour:

> Sail through the Straits of Singapore on Chinese junks just as the original settlers did in the early days. Take your pick of the 'Morning Glory',

[50] Singapore Tours, Admiral Cheng Ho Cruise, dated 2010 in the Tours in Singapore.com website [downloaded on 30 November 2014], available at http://www.toursinsingapore.com/singapore-sightseeing/admiral-cheng-ho-cruise.html.

Figure 15: A Datuk Kong shrine found at Beo Crescent Singapore. I took this picture on 14 December 2014

> 'Dragon', 'High Tea' or 'Imperial Dinner' cruise on authentic replicas of original China vessels for two and a half hours either in the morning, afternoon or evening.[51]

In this quotation, the promise of an authentic historical journey and recreated vessel cannot be found. Instead, it relates the journey to the pioneering ethnic Chinese sojourners who came to Singapore although the "early days" phrase is not well-defined historically. It is probably referring to the late

[51] ComeSingapore.com, Cheng Ho Cruise, dated 2010–2011 in the ComeSingapore.com website [downloaded on 30 November 2014], available at http://comesingapore.com/tourist-directory/review/278/cheng-ho-cruise.

Figure 16: The statue of Zheng He stands in the Chinese garden in Singapore, donated by an entrepreneur who derived his wealth from manufacturing and selling *popiah* skin (a popular rolled product in Singapore). From author's fieldwork collection in Singapore in October 2014

Qing period. In other words, the experience is probably related to a traditional Chinese junk rather than a reconstructed Ming-era vessel belonging to Zheng He's expedition. I called the Cheng Ho cruise agents to book a ride on 30 November 2014 but was informed that the company had stopped operations three months prior to my phone call. The cause of the shutdown was unknown.

Besides private donations and commercial ventures, commemorative events are also held in Singapore. For example, Singapore celebrated the 600th anniversary of Zheng He's maiden voyage in 2005 by installing the Dragon's Teeth Gate replica display near Labrador Park. For my fieldwork, I visited the park on 12 October 2014. There is a meaningful and important reason for the commemoration event.

"Singapore's port is very well known but there is nothing to showcase our maritime achievements, both to the locals as well as tourists," said STB's assistant director for culture and heritage, Ms Goh Kershing. "Cheng Ho's anniversary gave us an opportunity to highlight this heritage."

This was an interesting use of narratives about Zheng He for a multitude of purposes. Interestingly, Longyamen (Dragon's Teeth Gate) itself is not primarily associated with Zheng He but with a trader. Here is how the National Heritage Board of Singapore narrated the presence of Longyamen in Chinese historical consciousness:

> During the 14th century, the ancient mariner and trader Wang Da Yuan is said to have sailed through this passageway. In this travel tales, he recorded that the Fujian mariners knew these two rock outcrops as "Lung ya men" or "Dragon's Teeth Gate" because they reminded the mariners' of the two pegs at the bow of their ships, between which passed the ropes of the ships' anchor. These two pegs were known to the mariner's as "Dragon's Teeth". (Copied from site inscription by the author during his fieldwork trip to the former Dragon's Teeth Gate on 12 October 2014)

This example indicated that commemoration was independent of the historical narrative that indirectly linked Zheng with the rock. The Singapore National Library Board (NLB)'s collection has several books related to Wang Da Yuan's study of Singapore. Its own write-up considers Wheatley's work to be an influential English-language source.

> Wang's account of Singapore has been translated several times; the most commonly available translation is by Wheatley [6]. Wang mentions three place names in conjunction with Singapore. The first is Temasek, which refers to the general area of Singapore and the nearby islands. The second is Longyamen, which means "Dragon's Tooth Strait" in Chinese. The third is Banzu, which is named after the Malay word pancur ("spring of water").[52]

[52]National Library Board (NLB), Wang Dayuan 1349, dated 2014 in the NLB eresources website [downloaded on 8 December 2014], available at http://eresources.nlb.gov.sg/history/events/61d49d33-d5cd-48fc-b91b-652ca64e87c4. This article also quoted: Wheatley, P. *The Golden Khersonese: Studies in the Historical Geography of the Malay Peninsula before A.D. 1500.* Kuala Lumpur: University of Malaya Press, 1961, 301.

While Longyamen was not directly discovered by Zheng He, its naming by Wang in the late Yuan dynasty was linked to the 600th anniversary of Zheng He's voyages through Chinese navigational traditions and histories. Longyamen was in fact known as Batu Berlayer ("Sailing Rock") to the local Malays. At the same time, however, the link between Admiral Zheng He and the rock, according to a *Straits Times* narrative, was Zheng's possible use of the rock for navigational purpose.[53] Other than heritage and tourism establishments, there is a group of Zheng He enthusiasts in Singapore.

> The admiral's records of his epic travels show that Singapore has always been one of the greatest ports in the world, said the secretary of the Friends of Admiral Zheng He Society, Mr Chung Chee Kit.[54]

According to the same report, the Society, founded in 2003 by fans of Zheng, had around 40 members in 2005.[55]

Singapore's initiative to commemorate the 600th anniversary of Longyamen was also reported by the Xinhua News agency that quoted the tourism chief of Singapore in the following passage:

> "In the Zheng He celebrations, we celebrate a mariner who was larger than life. He transcended boundaries in his voyages," Lim [Neo Chian, Chief Executive of Singapore Tourism Board] added. "These celebrations demonstrate the strong influences that Zheng He left in the region".[56]

This example indicated the convergence of tourism initiatives, historical narratives and media interests. In Singapore, besides institutional narratives, public intellectuals and local history fans also engaged in Zheng He-related

---

[53] Sim, Glenys, 'Dragon's tooth' Replica to Mark Anniversary of Chinese Explorer dated 23 March 2005 in *The Straits Times* [downloaded on 30 November 2014], available at http://www.wildsingapore.com/news/20050304/050323-2.htm.

[54] *Ibid.*

[55] *Ibid.*

[56] Xinhua News Agency, Singapore Recreates Longyamen to Commemorate Zheng He's Epic Voyages, dated 7 September 2005 in *Zhongguowang* website [downloaded on 8 December 2014], available at http://www.china.org.cn/english/culture/141058.htm.

Figure 17: Left photo of the signboard pointing towards Longyamen taken by the author during fieldwork on 12 October 2014. Right photo shows the view towards the Singapore Straits at the Longyamen site, taken during author's fieldwork on 12 October 2014

conversations. My survey of online materials also indicated the presence of some narratives linking Zheng He to Mazu worship. I decided to see if it is possible to find out any such links in some of Singapore's oldest Taoist temples. I visited four of Singapore's oldest Taoist temples for clues on 7 December 2014 Sunday morning. Some of these temples were also associated with the Hokkien Huay Kuan which runs the Thian Hock Keng temple where a Mazu idol is located. I started fieldwork, not with an archaeologist perspective but a historian of narratives, it did not matter if there were no documentation or artefacts showing a link between Zheng He and Mazu relics, but rather, I was interested to find out if there were consciousness amongst devotees or temple guardians of such a link either through hearsay or legends. I started the research with Jinlan Miao at the Tiong Bahru area, then proceeded to the Taiyang Gong and Chia Leng Kong. At Jinlan Miao, I was advised to go to Thian Hock Keng if I wanted to see a Mazu idol. It was at Taiyang Gong that I was told they had a Sam Poh Buddha but was given the explanation that this was a Buddhist god and had little to do with Sam Poh Kong which was the deified personification of Zheng He. I was unable to detect further links related to Zheng He or Mazu when speaking to devotees and temple guardians in casual, random and unstructured oral conversations. I also spoke to shopkeepers who sold traditional Chinese offerings if they had heard of anyone buying offerings for praying to Cheng Ho and the reply was

Figure 18: In the modern period, a light house beacon used to stand near Longyamen to guide ships towards Singapore through the straits channel, indicating the possible importance of the Longyamen landmark as a navigational tool (picture taken by author during fieldwork on 12 October 2014)

in the negative. The brief fieldwork finding was different from an online source related to the Thian Hock Keng temple where a user indicated such a link. The context in which the connection between Zheng He and Mazu was raised is detailed in the following text. In 2007, the Taoism Singapore Forum engaged in online debates, amongst which included the question of whether the Thian Hock Keng Temple intended to revive Taoist cultural practices through practicing rites associated with this religion.[57] Some selected texts of

[57]Taoism Singapore Forum User Javewu, Title Thian Hock Keng Temple, dated 12 June 2006 in the *Taoism Singapore Forum* website [downloaded on 7 December 2014], available at http://z14.invisionfree.com/taoism_singapore/ar/t513.htm.

Figure 19: A reconstruction of Longyamen (Dragon's Tooth Gate) in Labrador Park with Keppel Harbor and Sentosa Island in the background (photo taken by Chia Lin Sien). [Both photo and caption are reproduced here with Dr Chia Lin Sien's permission.] Photo and text were also previously published here: International Zheng He Society, "605th Anniversary Conference — Zheng He and the Afro-Asian World: An Update" dated 1 July 2009 in the International Zheng He Society Newsletter [downloaded on 12 December 2014], available at http://www.chengho.org/newsletter/2009-Jul-01.php

the online discussion from a user by the nickname of "javewu" are highlighted as follows:

> ... The temple building resonated with the rhythm of the drums, gongs, cymbals and na (Chinese version of the oboe, or something like that), giving us the atmosphere of the temple events that must have witnessed such gathering in the past hundreds of years. Through this ancient music, we were linked to our ancestors, bound together in appreciating the wonders of Mazu as she guided so many Chinese coming to Nanyang. The famous Cheng-Ho (Zheng He) is said to have Mazu in his wooden ships and whenever they encountered fierce storms, they would pray to her for guidance, and it was said that the sea would then calm down again.[58]

---

[58] *Ibid.*

Figure 20: The author ascended the Henderson Waves Bridge which is located at over 70 meters above sea-level at its highest point and glanced down upon the stretch of sea which Zheng He may have traversed near the Longyamen that is located behind the cluster of skyscrapers (fieldwork done on 6 December 2014)

While I could not find links between Mazu and Zheng He in my search, I was able to locate a golden Mazu idol in my fieldwork in my last stop which was the Kai San Temple. There is, however, no association with Zheng He, from my understanding after speaking with devotees and temple guardians.

On 12 December 2014, I tried to follow leads of possible Cheng Ho-related temples in Singapore after I got to know of an online source that revealed the old name of the current Hong Sun Tan Temple [Address: 17 Woodlands Ind Pk E4 S(757750)], which was formerly known as the Sam Poh Keong Temple.[59] I investigated further to see if the "Sam Poh Keong" designation had any relationship with Cheng Ho but to no avail. The Hong Sun Tan Temple is a Taoist facility that worships the Cult of Guangze

[59]Timothy, Chinese Temples in Singapore, dated 13 April 2009 [downloaded on 12 December 2014] in the *Timothy* website [downloaded on 12 December 2014], available at https://oattao.netfirms.com/slowloris9/taoism/temples.htm.

Figure 21: The Golden Mazu idol at Kai San Temple from author's photos taken on 7 December 2014

Junwang and researchers interested in this topic should read Jack Chia Meng Tat's detailed thesis.[60] Even this detailed thesis did not explain the significance of the online source of the original name of Hong Sun Tan Temple. I therefore concluded that this lead did not constitute any significance for the subject matter in this writing.

Therefore, it appears any reference to Zheng He in Singapore is probably based on historical texts, commercial marketing efforts or state-linked commemorative initiatives (e.g. the Longyamen narratives) rather than hearsay, legend or religious narratives.

[60] Chia, Meng Tat Jack, Sacred Ties Across the Seas: The Cult of Guangze Zunwang and its Religious Network in the Chinese Diaspora, 19th Century 2009. A Thesis Submitted for the Degree of Master of Arts. Singapore: Department of History National University of Singapore, 2009.

Malaysia. In Malaysia, fans of the deity and historical figure, Zheng He, organized themselves into an International Zheng He Society. They raised funds, restored shophouses, preserved Ming relics and established a museum. The following passage is extracted from the Society's website:

> Today, the eight shophouses have been completed rebuilt and modeled after historical accounts of what the guanchang looked like. The Cheng Ho Cultural Museum now occupies the premises and a soft opening took place on 28 Sept 2005. Dr Tan's inspiration has become reality in the shape of a first-rate museum (details can be viewed in the pdf files in this website). The Museum has sections that traces the life of Zheng He, the historical background from which he emerged as a high ranking official in the Ming Court; the ships in his mighty fleet; navigational and communications tools and techniques; the cargo carried including ceramics, urns for storing food, traded products and items carried as gifts and tributes; a collection of highly-valuable ceramic pieces; voyages of well-known western pioneering maritime explorers including Vasco Da Gama, Christopher Columbus, Capt James Cook, and other exhibits.[61]

From this passage, it appears Zheng He-related history buffs are more institutionalized in Malaysia compared with Indonesia where the subject of the Admiral is more closely related to religious and community identities and compared with Singapore where narratives are generated mostly by heritage/tourism-related personnel and commercial outfits.

Besides institutional entities, geographical features related to Zheng He can also be located. According to Cheu Hock Tong's thesis, there is a cave in the periphery of Ipoh (Perak) known as Sanbao Dong named after Zheng He with similarly named caves located in Semarang (Java) off Acheh (Sumatra) and Bangkok.[62] Similarly, in cyberspace, I was able to locate Malaysian accounts of local legends in other rural areas of Malaysia. Narratives about

---

[61] International Zheng He Society, About Our Society, undated in the International Zheng He Society [downloaded on 7 December 2014], available at http://www.chengho.org/aboutus.php.

[62] Cheu, Hock Tong, Malay Keramat, Chinese Worshippers: The Sinicization of Malay Keramats in Malaysia Academic Session 1996/97 [downloaded on 8 December 2014] in the *Faculty of Arts National University of Singapore* website. Singapore: Department of Malay Studies National University of Singapore, 1997, 17.

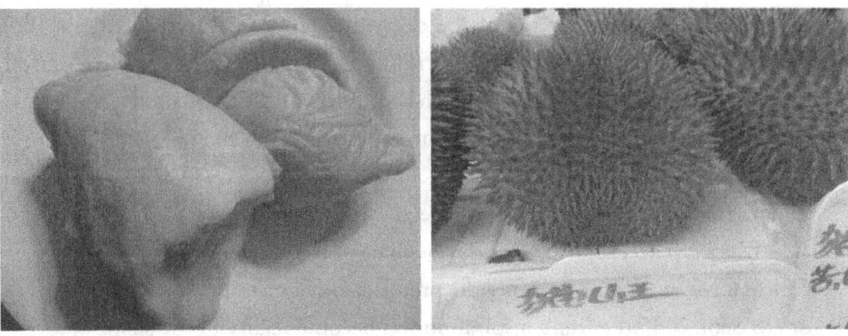

Figure 22: These are the Malaysian Musang King (Civet Cat King in English; Mao Shan Wang in Hanyu Pinyin) one of the priciest durians in the open market

Zheng He can also be found in commercial websites, including the one written by an individual named Kelvin Liew Peng Chuan from Tanjong Tokong, Penang, Malaysia who described how local fishermen in Batu Maung were able to recall Sam Poh Kong's life in detail without realizing this was the deified name of Zheng He.[63] Liew wrote about farfetched local old wives' tales related to Zheng He, including one about the origins of a popular Southeast Asian fruit, the durian:

> … being a newcomer to the island, he wanted so much to explore ... They went on foot, as the local narration goes, and half way through, he had to answer nature's call. A refined man as he, he defecated on a cloth and hung it high above a tree so that it will not soil any passing man or animal ... That tree later bore fruits ... The fruits turned out to be durians ... Due to that too, until today, Penang Chinese would use any fruits but durians for prayer offerings.[64]

Local legends like these add color to Zheng He narratives that are otherwise limited to mostly historical and heritage accounts. The following picture shows the shape and form of a Malaysian durian fruit.

---

[63] Liew, Peng Chuan Kelvin, Admiral Cheng Ho: Man in the Past, Divinity in the Present dated 2009 in the *Penang Heritage City* website [downloaded on 9 December 2014], available at http://www.penangheritagecity.com/admiral-cheng-ho-man-in-the-pastdivinity-in-the-present.html.

[64] *Ibid.*

The International Zheng He Society newsletter dated 1 October 2009 also talks about Zheng He's heritage representation in a temple in Batu Maung on the southeastern end of Penang Island near the Fishing Port, including a painting of Zheng He and his treasure ships on a cliff, an imprint representing his footprint on the ground with coins strewn onto it.[65] Some photographs of the Batu Maung site are as follows:

Interestingly, a *New York Times* article appeared on 18 December 2014 which appears to imply that some Malaysian intellectuals and private sector businessmen in Malaysia and Singapore are claiming ownership over Zheng He's existence and associating him with the Straits of Malacca as much as he is linked symbolically with China.[66] These initiatives by Southeast Asians also attracted the attention of the Chinese leadership. In 2013, an elite Chinese Communist Party (CCP) political figure Jia Qinglin visited the Cheng Ho Cultural Museum in Malacca which is run by an eminent Singaporean scholar and public figure in Zheng He-related history.[67] The fact that Chinese leadership officials have shown interest in Zheng He and Malacca is not surprising, given repeated statements by Beijing that China intends to become a maritime nation, an ambition that is greeted with fear, caution and welcome by different quarters in East Asia. The article contained interesting narratives by stakeholders in Malaccan history. It featured narratives by Zheng Yijun (historian at the Institute of Oceanology Chinese Academy of Sciences) who said that Zheng He started to influence local lifestyles like introducing Chinese clothes and backed the Malacca kingdom against a much stronger Thai kingdom and also David Khor (museum guide) who provided his own perspective that Zheng He's patronage of Malacca and his presence helped to put Malacca on the navigational map of the known world of trading nations at that point of time.

These two individuals represented different kinds of interest in the narrative of Zheng He. One is located in a circle related to tourism, heritage and

---

[65] International Zheng He Society, Zheng He Temple in Batu Maung, Penang Island, dated 1 October 2009 in the International Zheng He Society Newsletter [downloaded on 10 December 2014], available at http://www.chengho.org/newsletter/2009 Oct 01.php.

[66] Wong, Edward, Celebrating the Legacy of a Chinese Explorer, dated 18 December 2014 in *The New York Times* [downloaded on 24 December 2014], available at http://www.nytimes.com/2014/12/19/world/asia/celebrating-the-legacy-of-a-chinese-explorer.html?_r=0.

[67] *Ibid.*

Figure 23: Painting of Zheng He on the cliff side with his treasure ship (photo taken by Dr Chia Lin Sien, used with permission). The photos are also published here: International Zheng He Society, Zheng He Temple in Batu Maung, Penang Island dated 1 October 2009 in the International Zheng He Society Newsletter [downloaded on 10 December 2014], available at http://www.chengho.org/newsletter/2009-Oct-01.php

Figure 24: Traditional Chinese arched gateway to the Cheng Ho Sam Poh Kong (Zheng He Temple). (Photo taken by Dr Chia Lin Sien used with permission here.) The photo is also published in: International Zheng He Society, Zheng He Temple in Batu Maung, Penang Island, dated 1 October 2009 in the International Zheng He Society Newsletter [downloaded on 10 December 2014], available at http://www.chengho.org/newsletter/2009-Oct-01.php

Figure 25: Shrine that deifies Cheng Ho, guarded by two Chinese stone lions with red lanterns hung at the top of the entrance. At the side of the shrine, green porcelain bamboo-shaped architectural accessory is visible. The roof of the temple is covered with Shiwan-like porcelain tiles. (Photo taken by Dr Chia Lin Sien used with permission here.) The photo is also published in: International Zheng He Society, "Zheng He Temple in Batu Maung, Penang Island" dated 1 October 2009 in the International Zheng He Society Newsletter [downloaded on 10 December 2014], available at http://www.chengho.org/newsletter/2009-Oct-01.php

historical interest groups and the other is a professional academic from a state research institution. The former represent interests that commensurate with the leisure, tourism and entertainment industries in other Southeast Asian countries featured in the writing, which are appropriating Zheng He's biographical and navigational histories for profit-making, arousing visitor interest and cultural awareness. The latter is interpreting Zheng He through research and documentation that may or may not be eventually weaved into official histories and perspectives of history. Given the Academy is a ministerial-level organ in China, narrated histories may sometimes become possible references or views about a certain topical area. Both represent narratives that contribute to a grand narrative about Zheng He forwarded by international stakeholders in the subject area.

There are a number of important and interesting directions for near-future Zheng He-related research. In the arena of arts and culture, for example, utilizing aesthetics observations studies, interpretive art historical

Figure 26: Cheng Ho deity inside the temple, flanked by two sides of circular windows with green bamboo-shaped porcelain grills. The author could not locate a similar Cheng Ho shrine in Singapore's coastal areas. (Photo taken by Dr Chia Lin Sien used with permission here.) The photo is also published here: International Zheng He Society, Zheng He Temple in Batu Maung, Penang Island, dated 1 October 2009 in the International Zheng He Society Newsletter [downloaded on 10 December 2014], available at http://www.chengho.org/newsletter/2009-Oct-01.php

ideas as well as preliminary scoping work, there are narratives of the impact of Zheng He's journeys on Southeast Asian culture. One candidate (currently a conjecture) named in this area is the Saman dance. However, a check with the official interpretation of this art form with *Wonderful Indonesia* which is the government's official tourism website reveals that the current interpretation of this art form is an indigenously-developed Acehnese traditional dance created by the religious leader Sheikh Saman in the 16th century,[68] therefore more work needs to be done to translate, interpret and research on the cultural and historical backgrounds and influences received by the dance's originator. It is important to state the limitation that traditional and popular

[68] Discover Indonesia, Aceh's Best: The Saman Dance, dated 2013 in Discover Indonesia Ministry of Tourism, Republic of Indonesia [downloaded on 8 January 2015], available at http://indonesia.travel/en/destination/494/banda-aceh/article/42/aceh-s-best-the-saman-dance.

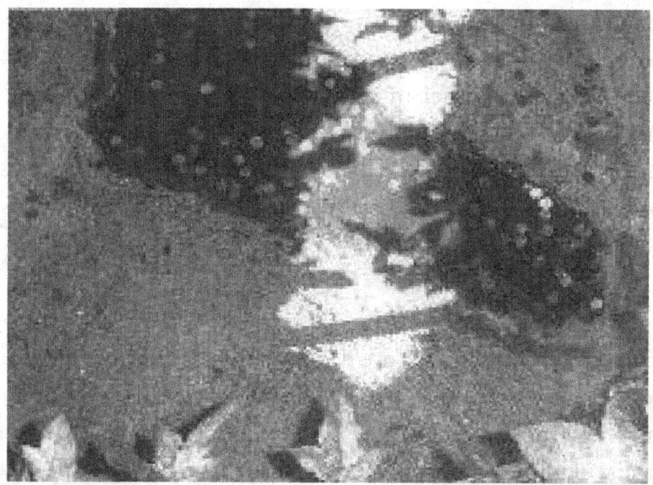

Figure 27: The mythical "footprint" of Cheng Ho with some coins thrown into it for heralding luck and prosperity. (Photo taken by Dr Chia Lin Sien used with permission here.) The photo is also published here: International Zheng He Society, Zheng He Temple in Batu Maung, Penang Island, dated 1 October 2009 in the International Zheng He Society Newsletter [downloaded on 10 December 2014], available at http://www.chengho.org/newsletter/2009-Oct-01.php

cultures are subjected to intense cultural cross-pollination and influences and it is difficult to unambiguously define the precise source of influence for each dance move. But, discussions remain important for contributing to the grand narrative of this important and fascinating art form. For readers interested in this area, a recommended work is the current snippets of information provided by Lilianne Fan, an anthropologist working on Aceh since 1999, and writing a book on history and memory in Aceh, slated for release in 2015.

Another area is to collect YouTube video links of popular narratives of historical interpretations of Zheng He (Cheng Ho). One example is the Indonesia Tourism Youtube Video, *Cheng Ho Great Mosque — Surabaya* dated 10 July 2012[69] that feature a mosque with Chinese-looking decorative designs (based on this video, mostly Qing dynastic architectural features

[69] Indonesia Tourism Video, Cheng Ho Great Mosque — Surabaya, dated 10 July 2012 in Youtube.com [viewed on 8 January 2015], available at https://www.youtube.com/watch?v=VoEDyp-4Xvg.

inside the mosque) and the façade model of an imagined Zheng He treasure ship in the place of worship. The advantage of collecting such videos is that they provide a moving visual image of the tangible and material artefacts under examination but the disadvantage remains the inability to download these videos from the host for archival purposes for research and also insufficiency of background information of the producers of these videos.

Concluding section

Academic and historical studies are more circumspect with their comments about Zheng He's voyages, indicating Zheng's voyages as mainly an important trade catalyst for the region. Lynn Pan associated Zheng He's voyages with regional trade stimulus. Her edited volume featured renowned Southeast Asian scholar Anthony Reid who highlighted the following passage:

> The Zheng He expeditions marked the starting point of Southeast Asia's 'age of commerce'. His fleets stimulated the production of pepper, clove, nutmeg and sappanwood, and the distribution networks that brought these items to the major entrepots and took cloth, rice and manufactured goods in exchange to the production centres. Demand for Southeast Asian products in China leapt, with pepper and sappanwood becoming for the first time items of mass consumption in the 15th century.[70]

There are points of commonalities between these narratives on trade related to Zheng He's voyages. First, they offer center-periphery perspectives. In Tan and Pan's narratives, the periphery of Southeast Asia (in the Sinocentric world view) or overseas Chinese benefited from Zheng's role in opening up maritime routes and facilitating trade with China. Second, this exchange of goods is an incentive for Chinese traders to settle in Southeast Asia and become intermediaries between the Ming regime and the local rulers of kingdoms in the region. These Chinese traders became the seeds of settler communities throughout the region, including the Peranakans. Third,

[70] Reid, Anthony, "Chinese and Southeast Asian interactions" in *The Encyclopedia of the Chinese Overseas* edited by Lynn Pan. Singapore: Chinese Heritage Center/Archipelago Press/Landmark Books, 1998, 50.

it supports the idea of a vassal system, whereby local rulers can maintain these vigorous trade links by partaking in a tributary system where China is acknowledged (at least in the symbolic manner) as the center of the Sino-centric world order.

On the other hand, it is possible not to exceptionalize Zheng He's voyages. Wang's seminal work on the Nanhai trade reminds us that regional trade had been alive well before Zheng He's voyages, starting from coastal trade and eventually expanding to regional and then inter-regional trade. Seen in this context, with the participation of the Arab, Malay, Southeast Asian and Persian traders before the onset of Yuan or Ming dynasties, the seas around Southeast Asia had already become a regional trading lake. The regional order therefore is predicated over reciprocal trade between willing kingdoms rather than conceptualizing it as a hegemonic center with a distant reactive periphery. As merchants from large trading units reach out for trade, they need to find willing partners in the recipient smaller kingdoms for reciprocity, regardless of motivations (religious, profit-making or diplomatic reasons).

The "Maritime Silk Road (MSR)" narratives of Zheng He may become part of the updated discourse on Chinese plans to revive the Maritime Silk Road which covers the span of trading cities from Fuzhou to Italy (the "one road" component of the "one belt one road" concept (known as Belt and Roads initiative in official Chinese terminology). Other interpretations see the Maritime Silk Road ending in Antwerp, Belgium, at the European end of the Maritime Silk Road.

Bibliography

Bloomberg, Chinese Premier's Silk Road Trip Marks Advance on Russia's Patch, dated 16 December 2014 in *Todayonline* website [downloaded on 18 December 2014], available at http://www.todayonline.com/chinaindia/china/chinese-premiers-silk-road-trip-marks-advance-russias-patch.

Cheong, Weng Eang, *The Hong Merchants of Canton Chinese Merchants in Sino-Western Trade*. Richmond Surrey Great Britain: Nordic Institute of Asian Studies, 1997.

Cheu, Hock Tong, Malay Keramat, Chinese Worshippers: The Sinicization of Malay Keramats in Malaysia Academic Session 1996/97 [downloaded on 8 December 2014] in the *Faculty of Arts National University of Singapore* website. Singapore: Department of Malay Studies National University of Singapore, 1997.

Chia, Meng Tat Jack, Sacred Ties Across the Seas: The Cult of Guangze Zunwang and its Religious Network in the Chinese Diaspora, 19th Century 2009. A Thesis Submitted for the Degree of Master of Arts. Singapore: Department of History National University of Singapore, 2009.

China Daily/Asia News Network, Discover Historic Gems Galore in Fujian's Cities, dated 23 December 2014 in *The Straits Times Classified*. Singapore: SPH, 2014, C1.

ComeSingapore.com, Cheng Ho Cruise, dated 2010–2011 in the ComeSingapore.com website [downloaded on 30 November 2014], available at http://comesingapore.com/tourist-directory/review/278/cheng-ho-cruise.

deAlwis, Akshan, The New Silk Road: A True Win–Win or a Perilous Future?, dated 31 December 2014 in the Huffingtonpost.com *The World Post* website [downloaded on 2 January 2015], available at http://www.huffingtonpost.com/akshan-dealwis/the-new-silk-road-a-true-_b_6400992.html.

Discover Indonesia, Aceh's Best: The Saman Dance, dated 2013 in Discover Indonesia Ministry of Tourism, Republic of Indonesia [downloaded on 8 January 2015], available at http://indonesia.travel/en/destination/494/banda-aceh/article/42/aceh-s-best-the-saman-dance.

Escobar, Pepe, China Is Building a New Silk Road to Europe, And It's Leaving America Behind, dated 16 December 2014 in *Mother Jones* website [downloaded on 18 December 2014], available at http://www.motherjones.com/politics/2014/12/chinas-new-silk-road-europe-will-leave-america-behind.

Escobar, Pepe, Go West, Young Han: How China and the New Silk Road Threaten American Imperialism, dated 1 January 2015 in Salon.com website [downloaded on 1 January 2015], available at http://www.salon.com/2014/12/31/go_west_young_han_how_chinas_new_silk_road_threatens_american_imperialism_partner/.

Goh, Brenda, China Pays Big to Expand its Clout Along the New Silk Road, dated 10 November 2014 in the *Reuters* website [downloaded on 18 December 2014], available at http://www.reuters.com/article/2014/11/10/us-china-silkroad-idUSKCN0IU27R20141110.

Gosset, David, China's Grand Strategy: The New Silk Road, dated 8 January 2015 in *The Huffington Post* [downloaded on 12 Jan 2015], available at http://www.huffingtonpost.com/david-gosset/chinas-grand-strategy-the_b_6433434.html.

Hefner, Robert W, Introduction: Multiculturalism and citizenship in Malaysia, Singapore, and Indonesia in *The Politics of Multiculturalism* edited by Robert W. Hefner. Honolulu: University of Hawaii Press, 2001, 1–58.

Indonesia Tourism Video, Cheng Ho Great Mosque — Surabaya, dated 10 July 2012 in Youtube.com [viewed on 8 Jan 2015], available at https://www.youtube.com/watch?v=VoEDyp-4Xvg.

International Zheng He Society, 605th Anniversary Conference — Zheng He and the Afro-Asian World: An Update, dated 1 July 2009 in the International Zheng He Society Newsletter [downloaded on 12 December 2014], available at http://www.chengho.org/newsletter/2009-Jul-01.php.

International Zheng He Society, Zheng He Temple in Batu Maung, Penang Island, dated 1 October 2009 in the International Zheng He Society Newsletter [downloaded on 10 December 2014], available at http://www.chengho.org/newsletter/2009-Oct-01.php.

Jiang, Xueqing, Pledge Made to Support 'One Belt One Road', dated 31 December 2014 in *China Daily* USA website [downloaded on 1 January 2015], available at http://usa.chinadaily.com.cn/epaper/2014-12/31/content_19210598.htm.

Lalwani, Bharti, Cross-Cultural Influences Shape the Island of Sumatra, dated 2 November 2010 in *Focus*, Magazine Culture360.org website [downloaded on 26 November 2014], available at http://culture360.asef.org/magazine/cross-cultural-influences-shape-the-island-of-sumatra/#sthash.JbQiXkIY.dpuf.

Lee, Khoon Choy, *Golden Dragon and Purple Phoenix*. Singapore: World Scientific, 2013.

Liew, Peng Chuan Kelvin, Admiral Cheng Ho: Man in the Past, Divinity in the Present, dated 2009 in the *Penang Heritage City* website [downloaded on 9 December 2014], available at http://www.penangheritagecity.com/admiral-cheng-ho-man-in-the-pastdivinity-in-the-present.html.

Lo, Jung-pang, *China as a Sea Power 1127–1368*. Singapore: National University of Singapore and Hong Kong University Press, 2012.

Lye, Liang Fook and Loh Yi Chin, Xi Jinping's "Silk Road" Strategy, dated October 2014 in EAI Bulletin, 16(2). Singapore: East Asian Institute, 2014, 5.

Mackie, J.A.C., "Business relations with non-Chinese" in *The Encyclopedia of the Chinese Overseas* edited by Lynn Pan. Singapore: Chinese Heritage Center/Archipelago Press/Landmark Books, 1998, 126–127.

National Library Board (NLB), Wang Dayuan 1349, dated 2014 in the *NLB eresources* website [downloaded on 8 December 2014], available at http://eresources.nlb.gov.sg/history/events/61d49d33-d5cd-48fc-b91b-652ca64e87c4.

Pan, Lynn (ed.), *The Encyclopedia of the Chinese Overseas*. Singapore: Chinese Heritage Center/Archipelago Press/Landmark Books, 1998.

Pavlicevic, Dragan, China's New Silk Road Takes Shape in Central and Eastern Europe, dated 9 January 2015 in Jamestown Foundation China Brief Volume: 15 Issue: 1 [downloaded on 15 January 2015], available at http://www.jamestown.

org/single/?tx_ttnews%5Btt_news%5D=43374&tx_ttnews%5BbackPid%5D=7&cHash=dcf45d3bf99b47d32fcb982a34e81371.

Reid, Anthony, "Chinese and Southeast Asian Interactionsn" in *The Encyclopedia of the Chinese Overseas* edited by Lynn Pan. Singapore: Chinese Heritage Center/Archipelago Press/Landmark Books, 1998, 50–52.

Seagrave, Sterling, *Lords of the Rim*. Great Britain: Bantam Press, 1995.

Seagrave, Sterling, *Lords of the Rim*. US: Putnam's Sons, 1995.

Sender, Henny, China's lenders are best placed to fix the region's infrastructure, dated 24 December 2014 in the *Financial Times*, 2014, 12.

Sim, Glenys, 'Dragon's tooth' Replica to Mark Anniversary of Chinese Explorer, dated 23 March 2005 in *The Straits Times* [downloaded on 30 November 2014], available at http://www.wildsingapore.com/news/20050304/050323-2.htm.

Singapore Tours, Admiral Cheng Ho Cruise, dated 2010 in the Tours in Singapore.com website [downloaded on 30 November 2014], available at http://www.toursinsingapore.com/singapore-sightseeing/admiral-cheng-ho-cruise.html.

Skeldon, Ronald, "The Case of Hong Kong" in *The Encyclopedia of the Chinese Overseas* edited by Lynn Pan. Singapore: Chinese Heritage Center/Archipelago Press/Landmark Books, 1998, 67–70.

Smith, Rachel, Stanford Historian Sees New Perspectives on Chinese Border Disputes in Declassified Qing Dynasty Maps, dated 29 May 2014 in *Stanford Report* [downloaded on 27 November 2014], available at http://news.stanford.edu/news/2014/may/declassified-chinese-maps-052914.html.

Tan, Ta Sen, *Cheng Ho and Islam in Southeast Asia*. Singapore: Institute of Southeast Asian Studies, 2009.

Tan, Ta Sen, Cheng Ho Spirit and China's Soft Power in the *International Zheng He Society* website [downloaded on 7 December 2014], available at http://www.chengho.org/downloads/CH_spirit_China_soft_power_1.pdf.

Taoism Singapore Forum User Javewu, Title Thian Hock Keng Temple, dated 12 June 2006 in the *Taoism Singapore Forum* website [downloaded on 7 December 2014], available at http://z14.invisionfree.com/taoism_singapore/ar/t513.htm.

The Jakarta Post, Semarang's Temple, A Tribute to Adm. Zheng He, dated 17 November 2000 in *The Jakarta Post* [downloaded on 26 November 2014], available at http://www.thejakartapost.com/news/2000/11/17/semarang039s-temple-a-tribute-adm-zheng-he.html.

Tiezzi, Shannon, China's $1 Trillion Investment Plan: Stimulus or Not?, dated 8 January 2015 in *The Diplomat* website [downloaded on 13 January 2015], available at http://thediplomat.com/2015/01/chinas-1-trillion-investment-plan-stimulus-or-not/.

Tourism of Indonesia i Norsk, Tourism of Indonesia i Norsk, dated 29 December 2011 in the *Tourism of Indonesia i Norsk* website [downloaded on 23 December 2014], available at http://tourism-n.jazz.or.id/category/sumatra/page/3/.

Vogue Mum, Restoran CHENG HO (AMY SEARCH) Will it be My Last Trip?, dated 14 March 2009 in *Voguemom Blog* [downloaded on 23 December 2014], available at http://voguemom.blogspot.sg/2009/03/restoran-cheng-ho-amy-search-will-it-be.html.

Wade, Geoff, The Zheng He Voyages: A Reassessment, dated October 2004 in the Asia Research Institute Working Paper Series No. 31. Singapore: National University of Singapore Asia Research Institute, 2004, 1–27.

Wang, Gungwu, *China and the Chinese Overseas*. Singapore: Times Academic/ Eastern Universities Press/Marshall Cavendish, 2007.

Wang, Gungwu, *The Nanhai Trade*. Singapore: Times Academic Press, 1998.

Wheatley, P, *The Golden Khersonese: Studies in the Historical Geography of the Malay Peninsula Before A.D. 1500*. Kuala Lumpur: University of Malaya Press, 1961, 301.

Wonderful Indonesia Indonesia's Official Tourism Website, The Chinese "Peranakan" Cultural Festival in Batam, dated 4 November 2012 in the *Wonderful Indonesia* website [downloaded on 26 November 2014], available at http://www.indonesia.travel/en/event/detail/566/the-chinese-peranakan-cultural-festival-in-batam.

Wong, John, Reviving the Ancient Silk Road: China's New Economic Diplomacy, dated 9 July 2014 in *the Straits Times* [downloaded on 26 November 2014], available at http://www.straitstimes.com/news/opinion/invitation/story/reviving-the-ancient-silk-road-chinas-new-economic-diplomacy-20140709.

Xinhuanet, Malaysia Ready for Greater Cooperation with China in Maritime Silk Road: Former Ambassador, dated 13 December 2014 in the *Xinhuanet* website [downloaded on 13 December 2014], available at http://news.xinhuanet.com/english/china/2014-12/13/c_133852521.htm.

Xinhuanet, Silk Roads Initiatives Enters New Phase: Think Tank, dated 15 December 2014 in Xinhuanet.com website [downloaded on 18 December 2014], available at http://news.xinhuanet.com/english/china/2014-12/15/c_133856803.htm.

Xinhuanet, Xi Suggests China, C. Asia Build Silk Road Economic Belt, dated 7 September 2013 in the *Xinhuanet* website [downloaded on 18 December 2014], available at http://news.xinhuanet.com/english/china/2013-09/07/c_132700695.htm.

Yahuda, Michael, *Hong Kong China's Challenge*. London and NY: Routledge, 1996.

Chapter 8

China's One Belt One Road Initiative: A Literature Review

LIM Wen Xin

The massive and ambitious One Belt One Road (OBOR) initiative spanning over 60 countries was unveiled by President Xi Jinping in 2013. This strategy, to be pursued in the next decade, not only serves as the main instrumental economic, political and foreign policies of the Xi's government, but also a significant hallmark of China's rise as a global economic power. Since the announcement, the discourse of the OBOR has dynamically evolved and eclectically incorporated the non-hegemony promise, vision of a multipolar world, peaceful rise of China and the idea of doing what is necessary for China's national interest without infringing upon others. Many media, consultancy, think tank and academic literatures have studied the plan in detail, analyzing and discussing the economic implications and impacts on development brought about by the strategic initiative. Nevertheless, some international critics and skeptics tend to associate the Chinese scheme with a political agenda, refuting the Chinese claim that it is merely an economic initiative.

Apparently, the OBOR initiative for many states is an individual assessment of national interests and how they can benefit from it or encounter detriments. An important part of the strategy is strengthening Beijing's economic influence and dominance in the South China Sea and Central Asia, the latter used to be part of the Soviet Union's traditional sphere of influence. With the presence of other geopolitical powers and when domestic politics in each affected states come into play, China is likely to face multiple hurdles and challenges which might complicate the implementation of its grand strategy. It is thus not difficult to anticipate major efforts in persuading these countries of the benefits of massive investments in railway infrastructure and industrial modernization.

The ultimate adjudicating factor is in the details of the OBOR and the newly established institutions such as the Asian Infrastructure Investment Bank (AIIB) and the Silk Road Fund. It also depends on how China is able to overcome the deficit of trust and suspicions among countries, convincing each individual country that the OBOR is genuinely a sincere plan for joint economic development and a win–win approach for all sovereign states.

To address a spectrum of opinions in this aspect, this writing gathers, consolidates and reviews the current level of information, presenting the readers with different interpretations of the OBOR, the economic and political implications of the plan, and possible challenges that it would encounter including the internal challenges and external factors.

The OBOR initiative from different angles

The newly-mooted OBOR proposal can be regarded as President Xi Jinping's move to redefine China's foreign policy to commensurate with China's rise. Chinese officials reiterate that the OBOR initiative is based on open multilateral cooperation, a useful complement to the existing international order and a catalyst to rejuvenate the global economy. Given the scope and significance of the OBOR initiative, Chinese Foreign Minister Wang Yi stated during the 2015 National People's Congress that in 2015, "making all-round progress in the Belt and Road initiative" constitutes the "key focus" for Chinese diplomacy.[1] Apart from that, official sources highlight the idea that OBOR will uphold the Five Principles of Peaceful Coexistence: mutual respect for each other's sovereignty and territorial integrity, mutual non-aggression, mutual non-interference in each other's internal affairs, equality and mutual benefit, and peaceful coexistence.[2] It is said that the plan will

[1] Foreign Minister Wang Yi Meets the Press. Ministry of Foreign Affairs of the People's Republic of China, dated 8 March 2015 [downloaded on 13 November 2015], available at http://www.fmprc.gov.cn/mfa_eng/zxxx_662805/t1243662.shtml; Sheng Zhong, Much Expected of 'One Focus and Two Main Themes'. *People's Daily*, 10 March 2015.

[2] Vision and Actions on Jointly Building Silk Road Economic Belt and 21st-Century Maritime Silk Road. National Development and Reform Commission of the People's Republic of China,

espouse economic globalization, open market economy and cultural diversity in the spirit of open regional cooperation.

The Chinese Ministry of Foreign Affairs (MFA) identifies three major geoeconomics and geopolitical purposes of the OBOR. First, internally, it will accelerate the development and growth of the western interior and turn it into the "frontier in opening up to the world". Second, by enhancing connection and the productivity of the developing Asian countries, it elevates the status of Asia in the world industrial chain. Third, it intends to form a community of destiny for China's relations with the region.[3] The OBOR initiative is sometimes referred to as a new kind of "strategy" designed to support the larger effort enunciated by Xi Jinping, to strengthen Beijing's periphery diplomacy and create a "new type of major country relations", both of which are based on intensive cooperation and a win–win approach to international politics and economics.[4] Jin Yongming claimed that the OBOR could be seen as "an important step to ensure safe navigation, improving relations with relevant countries and maintaining security".[5] Zhong Sheng describes the OBOR initiative as "a masterstroke of deepening China's reform and opening up and furthering peripheral diplomacy".[6]

---

dated 28 March 2015 [downloaded on 10 November 2015], available at http://en.ndrc.gov.cn/newsrelease/201503/t20150330_669367.html.

[3] Comments of Li Ziguo, deputy director of One Belt and One Road Studies Center of Ministry of Foreign Affairs Institute for International Studies, in Huangfu Pingli and Wang Jianjun, "How to Play Well the One Belt and One Road Symphony."

[4] Xue Li and Xu Yanzhuo stress the importance in developing the One Belt One Road strategy of relations with four major powers within the Eurasian area: Kazakhstan ("undoubtedly the strongest country in Central Asia"), Indonesia ("the world's largest Muslim country"), Japan ("as a global economic heavyweight"), and India ("with unrivaled cultural confidence and high political ambitions"). They argue that Beijing should consider working with these powers to found a "'G5-Asia' to strengthen economic ties among this group, thereby promoting overall Asian economic cooperation." See Xue and Xu, "China Needs Great Power Diplomacy in Asia." Also see "Make Concerted Efforts to Promote the Strategy of 'One Belt, One Road'."

[5] Coltrane, Mason, China's Former Glory to be Found in the "One Belt, One Road" Initiatives, *Yibada*, dated 30 January 2015 [download on 2 November 2015], available at http://en.yibada.com/articles/11258/20150130/china-s-former-glory-to-be-found-in-the-one-belt-one-road-initiatives.htm.

[6] Zhong Sheng, Epoch-Making Significance of "Silk Road Economic Belt and 21st century Maritime Silk Road" Proposal. *People's Daily*, 25 February 2014.

Not mentioned in the authoritative Chinese sources is that the 21st Century Maritime Silk Road constitutes "the crucial strategic direction of China's rise ... indicating a belief that developing the route will be critical to the country's entire development program."[7] National Defense University professor and strategist Liang Fang claimed that "the security of the sea lanes involved in the One Belt, One Road undertaking will ultimately require very significant capabilities, including carrier battle groups on station".[8] In other words, "the One Belt, One Road concept is linked, in the views of some Chinese military and naval analysts, with robust blue water naval capability dedicated to sea lines of communication (SLOC) defense."[9] William Yale wrote in *The Diplomat* that "the Maritime Silk Road, and especially Chinese infrastructure investment, is implicitly intended to facilitate more frequent People's Liberation Army Navy (PLAN) deployments in the Indian Ocean and beyond to secure the reliable logistics chains across SLOCs throughout Southeast and South Asia."[10] This could also be regarded as a strategic move for China to equip itself with stronger logistical maritime links in view of the preponderance of the United States navy force and influence in the region.

According to the non-Chinese commentators, Nadege Rolland (2015) suggests that "the proposed new Silk Road is a tool for promoting national economic development by boosting exports, enhancing access to natural resources, and providing support to important domestic industries". He suggests the new Silk Road can be identified as China's "infrastructure diplomacy" and "strategic motivation" to reinforce "relations along the country's continental periphery and a way to reduce dependency on the Southeast

---

7 Clemens, Morgan, The Maritime Silk Road and the PLA: Part One; and Clemens Morgan, The Maritime Silk Road and the PLA: Part Two. *China Brief* 15, No. 7, dated 8 April 2015 [downloaded 16 November 2015], available at http://bit.ly/1G5NVzn.

8 Liang, Fang, How Risky is the Maritime Silk Road? National Defense Reference, dated 11 February 2015 [downloaded on 20 November 2015], available at http://www.81.cn/jwgd/2015-02/11/content_6351319.htm.

9 Swaine, Michael D, Chinese Views and Commentary on the "One Belt, One Road" Initiative. Hoovers [downloaded 25 November 2015], available at http://www.hoover.org/sites/default/files/research/docs/clm47ms.pdf.

10 Yale, William, China's Maritime Silk Road Gamble. *The Diplomat*, dated 22 April 2015 [downloaded on 10 November 2015], available at http://thediplomat.com/2015/04/chinas-maritime-silk-road-gamble/.

Asian Straits of Malacca through which 80% of China's energy supplies from the Middle East and West Africa due to a fear of maritime blockade imposed by the United States in the event of a conflict in east Asia" (Nadege, 2015).[11]

Li Mingjiang, an Associate Professor at S. Rajaratnam School of International Studies (RSIS), Singapore Nanyang Technological University regards this grand strategy as China's "new round of opening up" as it dovetails with China's aspirations in various aspects. First, it helps to accelerate China's economic restructuring; second, it provides lucrative opportunities for Chinese companies in overseas market; third, China can export its overproduced steel and construction materials through OBOR's infrastructure projects; lastly, it helps to develop China's western region as Xinjiang is the core of the Silk Road Economic Belt.[12] On the other hand, David Dollar suggested that against the backdrop of China's economic slowdown, "domestic reform is a much more promising road to deal with China's surplus problem and to rebalance its economy away from such a heavy reliance on investment". He provided four areas of rebalancing including the household registration system (*hukou*), the inter-governmental fiscal reform, financial reform and the opening up of service sectors for more market competition (David Dollar, 2015).[13]

Most scholars insist that the OBOR initiative does not target the United States. As early as October 2012, Professor Wang Jisi (2015) from the Peking University talked about the need for China to carry out a geopolitical rebalance but refused to consider this concept as to target the United Sates rebalancing strategy.[14] Li Ziguo also said in a roundtable organized by Liaowang, "the OBOR is not a response to America's rebalancing in Asia-Pacific or to

---

[11] Nadege, Rolland, China's New Silk Road [downloaded on 22 April 2016], Available at http://nbr.org/research/activity.aspx?id=531.

[12] Li Ming Jiang, China's "One Belt, One Road" Initiative: New Round of Opening Up? S. Rajaratnam School of International Studies, dated 15 April 2015 [downloaded on 9 November 2015], available at http://www.rsis.edu.sg/wp-content/uploads/2015/04/CMS_Bulletin0015.pdf.

[13] Dollar, David, China's rise as a regional and global power: The AIIB and the 'one belt, one road', Brookings, dated 2015 [downloaded on 22 April 2016], available at http://www.brookings.edu/research/papers/2015/07/china-regional-global-power-dollar.

[14] Wang Jisi, 'March West'. The Rebalancing of China's Geopolitics. *Global Times*, dated 17 October 2012 [downloaded on 14 November 2015], available at http://opinion.huanqiu.com/opinion_world/2012-10/3193760.html.

the Russia's Eurasian Union (EEU), but a new model of economic cooperation".[15] Sun Hao argues that the OBOR is not a response to US pressure and suggests that the plan should be utilized "as a tool in the rapprochement between Asian and European economies".[16] Most Chinese sources, characteristically, reject the comparison of the OBOR with the Marshall Plan, which the Chinese media tend to characterize as an American political tool to gain geopolitical preeminence in the Western Europe nations and to contain the Soviet Union. Zheng Xie from the *Global Times* wrote "China's OBOR is not an alliance and comes with no political strings attached" to rebut the claims of Western outlets, which have described the program as China's Marshall Plan".[17] Sheng Dingli from Fudan University clarified that the Chinese OBOR is vastly different from the Marshall Plan which was a short-term strategy to help rejuvenate only the European economy. He argues that the "OBOR is a very ambitious program entailing a vast amount of resources through multilateral collaboration with no single country dominating the process".[18] The Sino-centric perspective clearly rejects the idea of OBOR as an instrumental tool for extending China's economic influence.

Zheng Wang[19] looks into the problem of regionalism and put forward a positive outlook of China's greater leadership and its role in institutional building and regional integration. While Asian countries are immensely disparate in size, culture and wealth, Wang asserted that China initiatives such as the OBOR and AIIB would be imperative "to reduce tensions, restore confidence and provide integration and connection for regional

[15]Godement, Francois, One Belt, One Road: China's Great Leap Outward. European Council on Foreign Relations [downloaded on 25 November 2015], available at http://www.ecfr.eu/page/-/China_analysis_belt_road.pdf.

[16]New Type of Major Power Relations as the Global Foundation. *Shenzhen Shangbao*, dated 8 June 2015 [downloaded on 14 November 2015], available at http://szsb.sznews.com/html/2015-04/08/content_3189311.htm.

[17]Zheng Xie, "One Belt, One Road" is not Chinese Marshall Plan. *Huanqiu*, dated 16 November 2014 [downloaded on 14 November 2015], available at http://opinion.huanqiu.com/opinion_world/2014-11/5204124.html.

[18]Shen Dingli, China's "One Belt, One Road" Strategy Is Not Another Marshall Plan. China–US Focus, dated 16 March 2015 [downloaded on 16 November 2015], available at http://www.chinausfocus.com/finance-economy/china-advances-its-one-belt-one-road-strategy/.

[19]Wang Zheng, China's Institution Building, Leading the way to Asian Integration. Georgetown Journal of Asian Affairs [downloaded on 25 November 2015], available at https://asianstudies.georgetown.edu/sites/asianstudies/files/GJAA%202.1%20Wang,%20Zheng_0.pdf.

development" He also proposed "the United States to work with China in shaping this process, and to push regional institution-building and integration in a positive direction" as this is also in interest of the United States.

OBOR's vast scale has created a new economic paradigm for China and the world, but funding and financial support remains a crucial factor to realize this long-term strategy. With the proposed plan, how fundamentally important are the financial institutions that provide funding and loan — the AIIB, Silk Road Fund and the New Development Bank BRICS (NDB BRICS). More importantly, AIIB successfully attracted 57 founding members, including America's closest allies — the United Kingdom (UK), Australia and South Korea. Leading economic news journal *Caijing*'s journalists wrote that "by creating the AIIB, China is putting pressure on the West to further the reform of the existing institutions as well as offering developing countries an alternative: a multilateral cooperative banking organization led by emerging powers".[20] She Jianguang and Shui Shangnan called the AIIB "a multilateral development bank for a new age".[21] Shui Shangnan says that "the AIIB is the subject of global interest" because it is a "new type of institution which unlike the World Bank, is eager to promote liberal Western values".[22]

Economic and political implications

With the Silk Road Economic Belt focusing on enhancing economic engagement and the Maritime Silk Road eyeing to bring together China's coastal hubs and Europe, scholars suggest that economic implications generated could be conspicuous. Tom Orlik and Fielding Chen (2015) put forward the idea that the OBOR "has the potential to make a long-lasting economic impact as the potential demand is enormous" (Tom & Chen, 2015).[23]

[20] Godement, Francois, One Belt, One Road: China's Great Leap Outward. European Council on Foreign Relations [downloaded on 25 November 2015], available at http://www.ecfr.eu/page/-/China_analysis_belt_road.pdf.

[21] *Ibid.*

[22] Shui Shangnan, If the OBOR only Focuses on Mutual Benefit, it Won't Succeed, *Gongshiwang*, dated 13 April 2015 [downloaded on 12 November 2015], available at http://www.21ccom.net/articles/economics/dongjian/20150413123546_all.html.

[23] One Belt, One Road Assessing the Economic Impact of China's New Silk Road, Bloomberg Briefs, dated 2 July, 2015, [downloaded on 12 November 2015], Available at http://www.bloombergbriefs.com/content/uploads/sites/2/2015/07/SC_062615-OBOR.pdf

Scott Kennedy opined in an interview that the OBOR has become an integral part of China's economic policy to cushion the effect of the domestic economic doldrums and "to help make use of China's enormous industrial overcapacity and ease the entry of Chinese goods into regional markets".[24] Yi Zhu (2015)[25] notes that "the large-scale investments needed to build the One Belt, One Road plan will boost demand for steel" and helps to redirect the steel surpluses at home to countries along the new trade link. John Mathai (2015) wrote that the OBOR could "boost shipping and cargo demand as planned infrastructure investments improve ports that dot the silk route" which previously have difficulties in handling increasing ship size and freight traffic due to "depth restrictions and lack equipment capacity" (Mathai, 2015). According to Scott Kennedy, the OBOR is not a regional free trade area agreement and it "reflects China's preference to avoid formal treaties with measurable compliance requirements in favor of less formal arrangements that give it flexibility and allow it to maximize its economic and political skills".[26]

Apart from the economic perspectives, the multifaceted OBOR initiative will inevitably create a political impact within and beyond the region. Interestingly, Willy Lam (2015) argues that domestically, the OBOR initiative will enhance Xi Jinping's control over the economy, empowering his leadership in the Chinese bureaucratic system. It is said that "the infrastructure, based scheme fits hand-in-glove with President Xi's insistence on the "top-level design" of economic development, leads to the revival of central planning as well as boosting the pivotal role of state-owned enterprise (SOE) conglomerates, and enables Beijing to enforce more effective control over its domestic regions". As a result, President Xi Jinping's mammoth OBOR strategy has gained him more power, "as well as his cronies and advisors in the Party-state apparatus". Finally, he remarked that "Premier Li Keqiang and his

[24] Kennedy, Scott, Building China's "One Belt, One Road". Center for Strategic and International Studies, dated 3 April 2015 [downloaded on 12 November 2015], available at http://csis.org/publication/building-chinas-one-belt-one-road.

[25] One Belt, One Road Assessing the Economic Impact of China's New Silk Road, Bloomberg Briefs, dated 2 July 2015 [downloaded on 12 November 2015], available at http://www.bloombergbriefs.com/content/uploads/sites/2/2015/07/SC_062615-OBOR.pdf

[26] Kennedy, Scott, Building China's "One Belt, One Road". Center for Strategic and International Studies, dated 3 April 2015 [downloaded on 1 November 2015], available at http://csis.org/publication/building-chinas-one-belt-one-road.

relatively liberal ministers in the State Council, or central government, have been increasingly sidelined".[27]

The OBOR has also recently become a buzzword among politicians and diplomats, dominating the agenda of various conferences, summits and meetings. While China's immediate neighbors are likely to benefit from the substantial infrastructure investment and industrial modernization generated by the OBOR, regional politicians have positively articulated their will to work with China, hoping that the lofty plan of OBOR could help deepen the political and economic ties with China. Specifically, the OBOR echoed ASEAN's master plan on connectivity to spur regional economic development. Magdalene Teo, Brunei Ambassador to China stated that the plan "augurs very well with ASEAN's masterplan on connectivity" and both sides are working towards enhancing greater connectivity between China and ASEAN.[28] Ivan Frank Olea, Minister and consul from the Philippines embassy said that the OBOR could help share China's prosperity around the region.[29] Malaysia's Transport Minister Datuk Seri Liow Tiong Lai said at the opening ceremony of the One Belt and One Road, China–Malaysia Business Dialogue that "Malaysia can play the role of a coordinator for China to expand into the markets of other ASEAN and neighboring countries". He observes that the improved transport network will allow Malaysian businessmen to explore the "vast opportunities in tourism, trade, ports, education and industrial development brought about by this belt-road cooperation".[30]

Singapore which enjoys a deep and broad relationship with China due to the camaraderie forged by the past leaderships of both countries — Deng

---

[27] Lam, Willy, One Belt, One Road Enhances Xi Jinping's Control Over the Economy. The Jamestown Foundation, dated 15 May 2015 [downloaded on 12 November 2015], available at http://www.jamestown.org/programs/chinabrief/single/?tx_ttnews%5Btt_news%5D=43914&cHash=859e508bc4e133a688b4ca5bd57bf1c2#.VkmfgdIrLcs.

[28] Koh, Jeremy, ASEAN Diplomats Welcome China's One Belt, One Road Initiative. *Channel News Asia*, dated 16 November 2015 [downloaded on 12 November 2015], available at http://www.channelnewsasia.com/news/asiapacific/asean-diplomats-welcome/2265422.html.

[29] *Ibid.*

[30] Ho Wah Foon, Belt-Road to Benefit Businesses in Malaysia. *Asiaone Business*, dated 2 August 2015 [downloaded on 9 November 2015], available at http://business.asiaone.com/news/belt-road-benefit-businesses-malaysia.

Xiaoping and Lee Kuan Yew — has been following the development of the Belt and Road initiative with an open mindset. Senior Minister of State for Transport Josephine Teo at a forum on the 21st Century Maritime Silk Road said that "countries in the region, including Singapore, would benefit from participating in the cocreation of this initiative and given Singapore's roots as a regional trading hub, it should adopt a more active role in key areas of connectivity, namely transport, finance and trade." She also subtlelty pointed out that China should share ownership of the OBOR with countries along the route so that "participating countries could see themselves as being able to influence the outcome and retain a sense of ownership over the pace and texture of collaboration".[31]

Marching into Central, South and West Asia

It is expected that the Silk Road Economic Belt will reduce the traveling time from China to Europe via Central and Western Asia through the construction of high-speed railway to promote greater trade, financial, economic and cultural activities. Leung Kin Pong listed a slew of economic benefits which the European Union could obtain from the grand proposal. The alternative land route improves the logistical matter to maximize cost-efficiency as "railways linking China and Europe have already diminished the number of days of shipment to around average 15 days, compared with 30–40 days required by sea". Also, as Chinese SOEs and companies are encouraged to explore and "invest in the overseas markets and ideally along the cities of the Silk Road, Chinese investment in European companies has been increasing tremendously since 2009 to reach US$18 billion in 2014".[32] He stated in his report that according to the European Commission President Jean Claude Junker,

---

[31] Patrick, John Lim, China's One Belt, One Road Initiative Could Usher in New Growth: Josephine Teo. *Channel News Asia*, dated 27 July 2015 [downloaded on 11 November 2015], available at http://www.channelnewsasia.com/news/business/singapore/china-s-one-belt-one-road/2010212.html.

[32] 'One Belt One Road' — Implications for the European Union. European Union Academic Programme Hong Kong, dated 2 June 2015 [downloaded on 11 November 2015], available at http://euap.hkbu.edu.hk/main/wp-content/uploads/2015/06/EU-Business-News-Insights_Issue-15_One-Belt-One-Road-implications-for-the-EU.pdf.

the Chinese OBOR also complements with the EU Investment Plan[33] by bringing in additional funding.[34]

As the Silk Road Economic Belt spans across Central Asia to reach Europe, Chinese economic involvement in Central Asia is likely to increase. China and Central Asia trade has skyrocketed from US$1 billion in 2000 to US$50 billion in 2013. China is currently the largest trading partner of all the countries in the region, except for Uzbekistan. Michelle Leung (2015) opined that China's cement companies alone will reap long-term benefits from the mammoth cement demand that is set to be generated by the OBOR initiative. She claims that "average cement output per capita in Central Asian nations is 300 kilograms which is less than the global average of 600 kilograms and China's 1,800 kilograms, implying large potential demand" (Leung, 2015).[35] Tao Wang and Rachel Yampolsky note that China has poured in US$30.5 billion investment in the region between 2005 and the first half of 2014. [36] Most of the ongoing projects are related to the resources and power sector which include "extensive network of oil and gas pipelines, oil and gas exploration, power plant financing, and even electric grid construction in Tajikistan".[37] The emblem of China National Petroleum Corporation (CNPC) is also visible everywhere at the gas and oil stations in Kazakhstan. Adopting the angle of resource trade, Qishloq Ovozi highlighted that Beijing's major interest in Central Asia is natural resources. "China imports oil from Kazakhstan; natural gas from Turkmenistan, Kazakhstan, and Uzbekistan; uranium from Kazakhstan; operates gold mines in Kyrgyzstan and Tajikistan; and is searching for rare earths in

---

[33] The EU scheme will unlock public and private investment of at least €315 billion from 2015 to 2017. The initial investment provided by the EU and the European Investment Bank will be €21 billion and it will require additional funding from other investors to reach a multiplier effect of 1:15 in real investment in the economy.

[34] *opcit.*

[35] One Belt, One Road Assessing the Economic Impact of China's New Silk Road, Bloomberg Briefs, dated 2 July 2015 [downloaded on 12 November 2015], available at http://www.bloombergbriefs.com/content/uploads/sites/2/2015/07/SC_062615 OBOR.pdf

[36] Tao Wang and Rachel Yampolsky, Will China and Russia's Partnership in Central Asia Last? *The Diplomat*, dated 21 September, 2015 [downloaded on 13 November 2015], available at http://thediplomat.com/2015/09/will-china-and-russias-partnership-in-central-asia-last/.

[37] *Ibid.*

Tajikistan".[38] With China's growing economic and political prowess, Alexander Cooley (2015) suggests that "China's role in the region is shifting from external commercial partner to a more comprehensive regional provider of collective goods including economic mediation and governance, development financing and even emergency lending".[39]

Singular economic focus is however insufficient for China to pave its way in Central Asia. Zhang Hongzhou suggests that China may face multiple hurdles while building its Silk Road Economic Belt in Central Asia. Deeply rooted and complicated internal conflicts as well as the presence of other major powers in Central Asia can lead to political skirmishes in the region. He thus proposed China to drive "a gradual and incremental process, to adopt a bilateral approach, to explore on agricultural cooperation and to integrate Central Asia into the Pan Asia Production Network to build a regional supply chain and minimize direct competition".[40]

Another major argument in Chinese OBOR initiative is that China is vying for geopolitical power and influence in Central Asia. The OBOR proposal is deemed to deplete Russia's influence in the Central Asia region as it was once under Russia's traditional sphere influence. Russia's mounting suspicion and uncertainty is in tandem with China's frequent interference and encroachment in the Central Asia region. Specifically, when the China Silk Road Economic Belt was announced, the Russian officials regarded it as likely to compete with Vladimir Putin's pet project, the EEU.[41] Alexander Gabuev (2015) suggests that "the only way Russia can preserve its influence, then, is to recalibrate its role in the region to accommodate its own ambitions

---

[38] Pannier, Bruce, How Far Will China Go In Central Asia? Radio Free Europe Radio Liberty, dated 8 June 2015 [downloaded on 13 November 2015], available at http://www.rferl.org/content/qishloq-ovozi-chinese-influence-growing-roundtable/27060377.html.

[39] Cooley, Alexander, China's Changing Role in Central Asia and Implications for US Policy: From Trading Partner to Collective Goods Provider. Prepared Remarks for "Looking West: China and Central Asia" US–China Economic and Security Review Commission, dated 18 March 2015 [downloaded on 5 November 2015], available at http://www.uscc.gov/sites/default/files/Cooley%20Testimony_3.18.15.pdf.

[40] Zhang Hongzhou, Building the Silk Road Economic Belt: Problems and Priorities in Central Asia. May 2015, S. Rajatratnam School of International Studies Policy Report.

[41] Michel, Casey, Putin's Eurasian Union Doomed to Irrelevance by China's Silk Road, dated 5 October 2015 [downloaded on 30 November 2015], available at http://www.worldpoliticsreview.com/articles/16858/putin-s-eurasian-union-doomed-to-irrelevance-by-china-s-silk-road.

and Beijing's quest for raw materials" (Gabuev, 2015).[42] Tao Wang and Rachel Yampolsky on the other hand argue that Beijing and Moscow might not share a similar vision for Central Asia. While "Russian sees Central Asia as its own backyard, to be defended against Western expansion in favor of keeping the existing order, China, by contrast, sees Central Asia as a strategic corridor of its OBOR initiative linking the Europe, sharing prosperity and conveying inclusiveness in a changing international order." This would then impede a valuable and productive partnership and cooperation between the two giants in the Central Asia region.[43]

Some arguments are made that Central Asian countries could possibly embrace a strategic move by hedging against China while befriending Russia or the United States to survive the tussle between big powers. Among all Central Asian countries, Kazakhstan play an imperative role as three of the planned Silk Road routes are passing through the country. Kishore Mahbubani (2015)[44] claimed that "China's decision to launch the OBOR initiative could not be more timely for Kazakhstan, but it would also be wise for Kazakhstan to hedge its bets and work with Russia, India, Japan and the European Union to enhance connectivity in the region" (Mahbubani, 2015).

Finally, unlike the mainstream argument, Garret Mitchell (2014) put forward the idea that China's continuing economic forays into Central Asia are not at the expense of Russia's privileged position in the region. He argues that Russia's longstanding status and substantial role in Central Asia, through "a combination of energy, culture, and military bonds that run much too deep" will not be easily exhausted by China's economic engagement in the short to medium term.[45]

---

[42] Gabuev, Alexander, Post-Soviet States Jostle For Role in One Belt One Road Initiative [downloaded on 22 March 2016], available at http://economists-pick-research.hktdc.com/business-news/article/International-Market-News/Post-Soviet-States-Jostle-For-Role-in-One-Belt-One-Road-Initiative/imn/en/1/1X000000/1X0A3A8Y.htm.

[43] Tao Wang and Rachel Yampolsky, Will China and Russia's Partnership in Central Asia Last? *The Diplomat*, dated 21 September 2015 [downloaded on 19 November 2015], available at http://thediplomat.com/2015/09/will-china-and-russias-partnership-in-central-asia-last/.

[44] Mahbubani, Kishore, How Kazakhstan can make geopolitical waves, World Economic Forum, dated 7 August 2015 [downloaded on 7 January 2016], Available at https://www.weforum.org/agenda/2.

[45] Mitchell Garret, China in Central Asia: The Beginning of the End for Russia? *SLOVO* 26, 2014, 18–31.

From the Southeast Asian perspective, Beijing is leveraging on its neighboring countries' common need for development and China's capacity in fulfilling its regional role in Asia as the basis to construct the Chinese architecture and order. Cheng Chwee Kuik notes that the AIIB is likely to boost ASEAN's internal integration and prompt "other powers to compete with China to reduce Beijing's growing political clout". He also cautioned that "if Beijing preferred institutional goals contradict those of ASEAN", it might undermine ASEAN centrality and cohesion.[46]

Other commentators and scholars are focusing their attention closer to South Asia. Interestingly, Laurence Vandewalle perceived China's OBOR initiative as "China pivots to Central, South and West Asia", which is similar to the US pivoted towards East Asia. Specifically, he highlighted that China and Pakistan are "all-weather friends" which their relation is on firm footing. The China–Pakistan Economic Corridor (CPEC) is the first project that taps on the Silk Road Fund and is a project "for a network of railways, roads and pipelines connecting Pakistan's port city of Gwadar in the province of Balochistan with the Chinese city of Kashgar in the landlocked Xinjiang province". In particular, the strategic location of the Gwadar port rendered China with maritime safety and military advantage as it "offers a direct access route to the Indian Ocean and the possibility to bypass the Malacca Straits ... even a foothold for the Chinese People's Liberation Army".[47]

Apart from the Central, South and West Asia, OBOR also add momentum to Africa which China has active engagement with. Africa which is blessed with abundant of natural resources has maintained a vibrant economic cooperation with China. Yun Sun (2015) mentioned two important implications of OBOR on Africa which are the development of infrastructure facilities and the "transfer of labor-intensive industries". However, he cautioned the sporadic political risks and volatile investment environment in Africa, nudging China to formulate "more systematic, well-coordinated and

---

[46] Cheng-Chwee, Kuik, An Emerging 3rd Pillar in Asian Architecture? AIIB and Other China-led Initiatives. Asia Pacific Bulletin, dated 26 March 2015 [downloaded on 19 November 2015], available at http://www.eastwestcenter.org/system/tdf/private/apb305.pdf?file=1&type=node&id=35025.

[47] Vandewalle, Laurence, Pakistan and China: Iron Brothers Forever? Directorate-General For External Policies Policy Department, June 2015 [downloaded on 19 November 2015], available at http://www.europarl.europa.eu/RegData/etudes/IDAN/2015/549052/EXPO_IDA(2015)549052_EN.pdf.

industry-specific plans to convince Africa and the world" that it will bring real benefits and job opportunities to the region.[48] Mark Bohlund and Tom Orlik (2015) also opined that while the inclusion of Africa in the OBOR strategy helps to bridge facilities gaps in Africa, "the misuse of increased fiscal space by some African states means China's investment adds to debt risks".[49]

Challenges and risks

Some opine that the OBOR initiative is a speculative bubble as it involves three continents and 65 nations with diverging interests, motives, priorities and agendas. If China is going to be the sole proposer, builder and maintainer of this grand strategy, it could encounter a hard time with many challenges and impediments ahead.

Relatively few authoritative Chinese sources genuinely examine what would be required to complete such an endeavor in a profitable beneficial manner.[50] Skeptics and critics however suggested different ideas that are worth consideration. Francois Godement called the OBOR a "grandiose" plan with little concrete details.[51] Jia Qingguo opined that, great as the project's potential may be, China should not be over enthusiastic and succumb to "wishful thinking" by neglecting the management of multilateral ties with countries along the route.[52]

---

48 Yun Sun, Inserting Africa into China's One Belt, One Road strategy: A New Opportunity for Jobs and Infrastructure? Brookings, dated 2 March 2015 [downloaded on 12 November 2015], available at http://www.brookings.edu/blogs/africa-in-focus/posts/2015/03/02-africa-china-jobs-infrastructure-sun.

49 One Belt, One Road Assessing the Economic Impact of China's New Silk Road. *Bloomberg Briefs*, dated 2 July 2015 [downloaded on 12 November 2015], available at http://www.bloombergbriefs.com/content/uploads/sites/2/2015/07/SC_062615-OBOR.pdf.

50 Swaine, Michael D, Chinese Views and Commentary on the One Belt, One Road" Initiative,Hoovers,[Downloaded 25 November 2015], Available at http://www.hoover.org/sites/default/files/research/docs/clm47ms.pdf

51 Godement, Francois, One Belt, One Road: China's Great Leap Outward. European Council on Foreign Relations [downloaded on 25 November 2015], available at http://www.ecfr.eu/page/-/China_analysis_belt_road.pdf.

52 Jia, Qingguo, One Belt, One Road: Urgent Clarifications and Discussions of a Few Major Questions. *Renmin Luntan*, dated 19 March 2015 [downloaded on 25 November 2015], available at http://theory.rmlt.com.cn/2015/0319/377863.shtml.

While the grand proposal promises more connectivity and exchanges that China covets, report from *The Economist* published a risk assessment report, outlining some possible prospects and challenges in the OBOR. Specifically, it underlined the risks across ten different categories including security, legal and regulatory, government effectiveness, political instability and infrastructure. Through rigorous risk assessments in different countries, the report highlights some possible scenarios in countries like Kazakhstan, Vietnam and Malaysia. It concluded that "the strong policy support behind OBOR may prove a weakness if Chinese actors, be they government planners, SOEs or private companies, fall into a false sense of security that government support will guarantee their success". Thus, careful planning is needed to avoid heavy price paid in the process of realizing this grand strategy.

While the OBOR involves the Middle East and Arabian states, it is very likely that China will need to deal with the devastated political turmoil, social unrest and transnational terrorism in the region, as well as ethnic tension within China. Hu Zhiyong said terrorism is the "destabilizing force" and could have a "knock-on effect" in the South and Central Asia.[53] Siqi Gao (2015) argued that "one of the biggest roadblocks on China's Silk Road Economic Belt is the Islamic Caliphate (ISIS), which has occupied large areas in the Middle East and threatened to include China's Xinjiang as part of its territory". With Xinjiang being envisioned as "a major component and beneficiary of the Silk Road Economic Belt", the increased railway transportation will connect Xinjiang to Central Asia, facilitating the movement of terrorists from the other parts of the Muslim world. Xinjiang could be a recruiting station or breeding ground for terrorism with improved connectivity in the region. Internally, the sensitive issue of identity, cultural differences and religion could be resuscitated and evoke tension and violence.[54] It will then depend on how Chinese government is determined to deal with external challenges, to resolve ethnic complexity in domestic China, to expand its influence in the Arab World, and to take more responsibility globally.

---

[53] Hu Zhiyong, How to Understand the Political Risks of 'One Belt One Road'. *Aisixiang*, dated 2 March 2015 [downloaded on 13 November 2015], available at http://www.aisixiang.com/data/84494.html.

[54] Gao Siqi, China's Soft Power in the Arab World through Higher Educational Exchange. Honors Thesis Collection, Paper 290, 2015 [downloaded on 13 November 2015], available at http://repository.wellesley.edu/cgi/viewcontent.cgi?article=1334&context=thesiscollection.

As China's soft power follows its hard power to permeate the territory of the beneficiaries, challenges loom bigger. Huang Yiping and Chu Yin discuss "the limits of China's capabilities, warning that the project could be derailed by ham-fisted great power diplomacy, insensitive to political risk, or excessive central planning.[55] Zhang Yunling highlights the presence of a few challenges in the process of constructing OBOR. These include suspicions between China and the involving countries along the route, China's existing disputes with its neighbors, investment and financial risks in the developing countries and China to expect quick results from OBOR.[56] In particular, the heated South China Sea disputes and many territorial issues could sour relations between China and the respective countries, leading to unintended consequences and stagnation.

There is also a deficit of trust between China and the regional and peripheral powers. At the current moment, it remains unsure whether individual states will conform and respond to China's seemingly great vision of building connectivity for the common interest and better future of all. Linda Jakobson and Rory Medcalf (2015) suggested a "sharp divergences in perceptions regarding China's maritime strategy strategic objectives". While China perceived its own move in the India Ocean an effort to "safeguarding energy and economic lifelines to the Middle East and Africa", India could comprehend such action as China "thwarting India's regional pre-eminence … including through military power projection and influence over third parties such as Sri Lanka and Pakistan".[57] As China purports to uphold the concept of "community of common destiny", lack of trust and the perception gap could be the main impediment to baffle China's regional ambition.

---

[55] Huang Yiping, Don't Let 'One Belt, One Road' Fall into the Trap of Japan's Overseas Investments. *Zhongguo Gaige Wang*, dated 10 February 2015 [downloaded on 10 November 2015], available at http://opinion.caixin.com/2015-02-09/100782544.html.

[56] Zhang Yunling, Analysis says One Belt One Road Faces Five Challenges. *Xiaotang Caizhi*, dated 23 March 2015 [downloaded on 20 November 2015], available at http://finance.sina.com.cn/china/20150323/152821784549.shtml.

[57] Jakobson, Linda and Rory Medcalf, The Perception Gap: Reading China's Maritime Strategic Objectives in IndoPacific Asia. The Lowy Institute for International Policy, June 2015 [downloaded on 1 November 2015], available at http://www.lowyinstitute.org/files/the-perception-gap-reading-chinas-maritime-strategic-objectives-in-indo-pacific-asia.pdf.

Professor Tommy Koh, Ambassador-at-Large at the Singapore Ministry of Foreign Affairs opined that China should adopt an open and inclusive policy to evolve the Chinese OBOR project to being a regional project so that it can gain the trust of its neighbors.[58] Ben Simpfendorfer (2015) advised the Chinese SOEs to collaborate and work closely with foreign companies to gain local knowledge in order to maneuver smoothly in the overseas market. He commented that "history shows that the old Silk Road only flourished during periods of stability along the route", and so the success of Chinese OBOR will highly depend on political will and regional security.[59]

Concluding remarks

The past glory and prosperity of the Chinese empire revolve around the Silk Road which promotes immense merchandizing, trading and cultural exchanges. Today, the Chinese action plan to revive the historical Silk Road due to its growing economic and political clout, to a certain extent, reflects its magnificence and effluence in the past. The OBOR is an outcome of domestic need and external pressure.

Given the broad scope of the OBOR plan, there is no unilateral interpretation on the OBOR initiative. Most of the writings associate the OBOR with the economic, political and military outreach of China against the backdrop of globalization and regional integration and connection. Chinese sources routinely deny and reject the criticisms about China's clandestine agenda to influence, confine, dominate, intimidate, or generally leverage or manipulate other states involved in the undertaking. Chinese nearly altruistic goals in the OBOR are likely to be questioned by various parties and face multifarious challenges including regional instability, investment and credit risks, geopolitical influence of major powers and suspicion and mistrust from other states. Countries will assess their national interests according to conditions for using

---

[58] Chong Koh Ping, The S'pore Connect In 'One Belt, One Road' Initiative. *Straits Time*, dated 28 July 2015 [downloaded on 13 November 2015], available at http://www.straitstimes.com/business/the-spore-connect-in-one-belt-one-road-initiative.

[59] One Belt, One Road Assessing the Economic Impact of China's New Silk Road, *Bloomberg Briefs*, dated 2 July 2015 [downloaded on 7 November 2015], available at http://www.bloombergbriefs.com/content/uploads/sites/2/2015/07/SC_062615-OBOR.pdf.

the OBOR funding facilities, geopolitical priorities, domestic political situations, external factors and national resources and how the Belt and Road Initiative + AIIB + BRICS Bank *vis-à-vis* current existing established institutions like Asian Development Bank (ADB) best serve their needs.

The success or failure of the One Belt One Road concept will depend on the resources that Beijing is willing and able to devote to it, the adroitness of China's leaders and entrepreneurs in maneuvering in the international market and system, and the ability of China in shaping the regional preference.

Chapter 9

The South China Sea and the Maritime Silk Road Proposal: Conflicts can be Transformed

Katherine TSENG Hui-Yi

Development of the South China Sea dispute: A conflicting trend?

The trend of territorialization: The Dash-Line claim as a maritime boundary

Ever since the submission of the dash-line map as an integral part to China (PRC)'s claim on the South China Sea to the Commission on the Limits of the Continental Shelf (CLCS) in 2009,[1] there is a developing trend that China (PRC) has intended to evolve this dash-line claim into a marker that serves as a maritime boundary. Several incidents help reify this observation.

For one thing, China (PRC) has reiterated on several occasions two critical elements in its claim. China (PRC) contends that it has had sovereignty over all land features lying within the dash line. Subsequently, its claim of "sovereign rights in the waters and sea bed" within the dash-line boundary limits is justified and asserted rigorously in the regional arena. Accordingly, patrols and law-enforcement actions conducted by the Chinese Marine

[1] Commission on the Limits of the Continental Shelf (CLCS) Outer limits of the continental shelf beyond 200 nautical miles from the baselines: Submissions to the Commission: Joint submission by Malaysia and the Socialist Republic of Viet Nam. United Nations, Divisions for Ocean Affairs and The Law of The Sea, submitted on 06 May 2009 (updated on 03 May 2011) [downloaded on 20 November 2015], available at http://www.un.org/Depts/los/clcs_new/submissions_files/submission_mysvnm_33_2009.htm.

Police are justified as an exercise of its rights and interests in the said area. These contentions have implied the Chinese have aspirations to the dash-line claim, however implicit, that this dash line serves as a boundary line including all land features lying inside it, and also functions as a maritime boundary by which all waters inside it belong to the sovereign right of China (PRC).

Moreover, the ongoing arbitration initiated by the Republic of the Philippines against the PRC in January 2013, on certain issues in the South China Sea,[2] further places these issues in contention, to which the Chinese approach shows a clear intention to use the dash line as maritime delimitation.

In this ongoing arbitration, the complex distinction between "maritime delimitation" and "maritime limits" leads to two totally different interpretations by the respective disputants. For China (PRC), the essence of the subject-matter of the arbitration is territorial sovereignty over several maritime features in the South China Sea.[3] China (PRC) opines, accordingly, that the tribunal does not have jurisdiction, since an issue of territorial sovereignty over maritime features falls beyond the scope of interpretation or application of the Convention.[4] For the Philippines, it seeks from the tribunal explanations of what a submerged feature, low-tide elevation entails in terms of maritime interests, and clarifications of China (PRC) dash-line claim's effect on maritime interest and limits.[5] In a word, China has regarded this dash-line claim as a form of maritime delimitation, while for the Philippines, clarification of maritime zoning standard is already clearly prescribed in the Law of Sea Convention.

In this context, the dash line serves dual functions, as it denotes a way to confirm a maritime boundary, so that Chinese sovereignty covered any structural feature, and arguably, water situated within them and therefore

---

[2]The arbitration is registered with the Permanent Court of Arbitration. More information can be found in the website of Permanent Court of Arbitration, "The Republic of the Philippines vs. The People's Republic of China" [downloaded on 20 November 2015], available at http://www.pca-cpa.org/showpage.asp?pag_id=1529.

[3]See the Chinese position paper, The Position Paper of the Government of the People's Republic of China on the Matter of Jurisdiction in the South China Sea Arbitration Initiated by the Republic of the Philippines, para. 3.

[4]*Ibid.*

[5]The Republic of the Philippines, Notification and Statement of Claim, 22 January 2013. See also, International Tribunal for the Law of the Sea, Press Release, 25 April 2013.

sovereignty over them should not be questioned. This dash line also can be regarded, along with its function in delimiting a maritime boundary in the South China Sea, as a Chinese methodology of generating "maritime limits".

This dash-line claim serving dual functions has provoked criticism among claimants and stakeholder countries. For one thing, this dash-line claim may blur the distinction between the concept of "maritime delimitation" and "maritime limits". Further, this dual function would increase/deepen the suspicions of other claimants that China (PRC) does not intend, with any possibility, to resolve the dispute under the aegis of the Convention and general international law. This possibility, however perceived, would further fester deep-seated hostility among other claimants against China (PRC), which may easily spoil inter- and intra-state relations in this region. In this regard, it is a challenging, while not totally impossible, mission for China (PRC) to unilaterally declare a modern attestation of the dash-line claim, in defiance of the established law of the sea regime and general international law.

Implications

Contesting legal developments combined with tensed geopolitical events in the South China Sea since 1973 have increased to certain levels such that territorial quarrels among China and Association of Southeast Asian Nations (ASEAN) claimants are in fact interrupting, or at least, hindering the amicability necessary for inter-state cooperation in many aspects. The lack of effective cooperation mechanisms in a variety of issues, such as fishing regulation and maritime environmental administration, is unfortunately one direct outcome of these territorial disagreements. All claimant parties need to start tackling the ongoing urgent issues of depletion of fishing resources, increasing costs of maritime traffic and loss of lives on the sea.

Beyond territorial claims

Briefly put, the real issue in South China Sea is about agenda-setting and shaping the regional maritime order in coming decades, in both political and legal terms. The wrestling match is between the regional great power, China and the only hegemonic power since the end of World War II, the US.

Leaving aside strategic maneuvering and power politics, the real menace is the immediate realization and application of the dash-line claim. To some extent, the essence of the South China Sea issue is actually related to the agenda-setting and rule-making power contestation between regional power of China and global hegemony, of the US. Accordingly, a corollary issue is how should ASEAN claimants' South China Sea positions be interpreted by observers?

Several ASEAN claimants have been involved in a race for maritime resource development and occupation of land areas in the South China Sea.[6] Their willful occupation over islands and rocks, and predation of maritime resources, can hardly be justified under the name of "efforts of asserting sovereign rights and territorial claims". Any exercise of one's right at the cost of others' expenses, beyond reasonable limit, can be deemed as an abusive and harmful development, which should be condemnable and punishable. Yet, the Law of the Sea has not addressed this issue of "the reasonableness of sovereignty claim contestation".[7] This would require relevant international legal principles to fill in this vacuum.

---

6 This is the "push envelope" approach, relied on by ASEAN claimants to test the bottom line of China regarding unregulated and uncoordinated maritime resource development activities. ASEAN claimants hold the view that they have to grab the chance to develop and exploit maritime resources as much as possible, before China gets stronger and powerful enough to prevent their activities.

7 UNCLOS in several provisions stipulate that before final maritime delimitation agreements are reached, states make every effort to enter into provision arrangements, while being restrained from activities that may jeopardize and impair the reaching of an ultimate delimitation. These obligations may be inherently conflicting. One dilemma is that, when states' sovereignty claims overlap, a duplication of such entitlement which enables states' exercises of exclusive right in the said areas may lead to unilateral acts by the states involved. This dilemma seems to be more contentious in the Exclusive Economic Zones (EEZ) zoning instead of zoning of territorial waters which takes place only after the decision of sovereignty attribution of land features. To some extent, the EEZ zoning is thornier, as it contains not only a decision on the calibration of the "zoning", but also a decision by the adjudicator between rival claims which are duly proved, more justified and more "reasonable". Two provisions in the Convention touched on this issue, Articles 74(3) and 83(3), in which states are obliged to spare no efforts in not engaging in activities that would prejudice the final settlement of the dispute. Yet, this latter requirement imposes realistic difficulties in an area where territorial and EEZ claims have overlapped, and may have conflicted against each other. See, Note 10, Law of Sea Convention, Articles 74(3) and 83(3).

Further, in South China Sea, tensions fluctuate and have become one flashpoint that easily topples over efforts for regional developments in various aspects. While sentiments remain boiling in certain claimant countries, it is a totally different picture in the other. This cleavage demonstrates that, with disputed subjects remote in the sea, where no civilian could easily reach and land, the very "emptiness" of these islands (as in people's cognition and memory) makes them the ultimate patriotic symbols, or "logos of nationhood in a global media age".[8] Southeast Asian politicians have much freedom to define what these territorial conflicts mean to their respective populations. In recent round of tensions, Vietnam has served a good example, exemplifying how the government could lead and shape public opinions in an event that easily sparkles up national sentiments.[9]

It is in this sense that even when holding high the banner of international law, overtures and behaviors of ASEAN claimants are still controversial. By relying heavily on legal discourses, flexibility and rooms for maneuvering, at times in extra- and non-legal scenarios, are quickly shrinking. Further, to resort to judicial means for dispute resolution at international level, is time consuming and financially costly.

It is under this context that the recently proposed initiatives of building a Silk Road Economic Belt and a 21st century Maritime Silk Road (MSR) by China should be brought into discussions. The pragmatic mindset and substantial benefits entailed in these initiatives should not be easily shrugged off.

---

[8] Kaplan, Robert D., *ASIA'S CAULDRON — The South China Sea and the End of a Stable Pacific* (London: Random House, 2014); Pollmann, Mina, Government Narratives in Maritime Disputes. *The Diplomat*, 10 July 2014.

[9] As a common tactic for the government to shape public and lead opinions, Vietnam's approaches serve one example. The Vietnamese government is believed to have resorted to diverting domestic attention from its domestic mal-governance by winning sympathy from international public opinion and recognition. Hanoi has apparently shifted the emphasis of its propaganda machine to promoting Vietnam's image as a victim of China's growing national prowess and malicious intents on the South China Sea. For example, on January 2014, Vietnamese state-run media was marking for the first time the anniversary of a 1974 naval battle with China in which 74 soldiers from US-backed South Vietnam were killed. The move appeared to be aimed at boosting the legitimacy of the government in regard to its tricky dealings with China, which was the subject of popular, nationalist anger. *Source*: Pham, Nga Shift as Vietnam Marks South China Sea Battle, *BBC*, 15 January 2014.

Situating the South China Sea issue in the MSR initiative

The MSR in the One-Belt-One-Road initiative

The "One Belt, One Road" initiative (OBOR) starts with the idea that nearby countries in Central Asia — spread along the traditional Silk Road — could benefit from more transport infrastructure, some of which China could finance bilaterally.[10] Further, the idea of a maritime road — that is, the expansion of infrastructure along the seagoing routes from the Chinese coast through Southeast Asia to the Indian Ocean and all the way to Europe further embellishes this ambitious proposal.

Yet, as grand as the slogan may sound, in English the name is misleading, although confusions could be most effectively be dismissed through actual implementation efforts. In other words, this initially vague initiative has been fleshed out in detail after March, 2015.[11]

Succinctly put, looking in more depth at these details, two points that highlight the intended purpose and the pattern of implementation merit reiterations. For one thing, it is not targeting only a single trading route, be it on the northwest part of the Chinese mainland or the southeast maritime area of the Indo-China Peninsula. Rather, it is about building networks of connectivity. The geographical linkages envisaged by the "belt" (in the northwest) and the maritime "road" (in the southeast) cover multiple locations. Second, physical infrastructure to promote connectivity points is a critical, but not the entire main content of OBOR. Rather, connectivity can be elaborated in multiple connections in trade, investment, finance, and flows of tourists and students.[12]

---

[10] China's Initiatives on Building Silk Road Economic Belt and 21st century Maritime Silk Road. *Xinhua News* [download on 20 November 2015], available at http://www.xinhuanet.com/english/special/silkroad/index.htm, Summers, Tim, What Exactly is 'One Belt, One Road'? September 2015, 71(5); Hornby, Lucy, China's 'One Belt One Road' plan greeted with caution. *Financial Times*, 20 November, 2015.

[11] China Unveils Action Plan on Belt and Road Initiative. *Xinhua News*, 28 March 2015.

[12] Infrastructure Connectivity a Priority in Belt and Road Initiative. *Xinhua News*, 28 March, 2015; Xi on "Belt and Road": Not China's solo but inspiring chorus. *Xinhua News*, 28 March 2015.

A 21st century MSR: The déjà vu wears well

In OBOR, a 21st century MSR is believed to be inspired by historical maritime trading routes from southeast coastal China through the South China Sea and beyond, by extending these routes to continents and countries where trade volumes are currently small, but hold future growth potential, such as East African and the Mediterranean areas. Besides this historical legacy, China's rapidly deteriorating neighborly relations with other states in the South China Sea also hint at how this modern maritime trade route unfolds.

Briefly put, the South China Sea issue is now enmeshed in a malicious cyclical pattern, of involving not only claimant states, but also other extra-regional stakeholder countries. Proliferation of actors have, to a considerable degree, rendered the dispute even more intractable, as any single compromise between two parties may have spillover effects to a third country. The Sino-Filipino arbitration initiated in January 2013 and still ongoing at this point of writing, continues to highlight such uncertainties in the South China Sea scenario. *Inter alia*, a trend of territorialization in China's interpretation and contestation of the South China Sea claim is triggering alarm bells.

In short, with a territorializing dash-line claim, would the OBOR initiative be overshadowed, and be deprived of required momentum for its further implementation? To answer this inquiry, a retrospective approach is necessary and justified, traceable back to the time before the arrival of European colonialism and the regional order that facilitated the growth of the MSR.

Before European dominance in East and Southeast Asian maritime order

The world system before the rise of European hegemony was, not in a strict sense, segmented, or sectoral, in terms of the unit used to gauge involving participants. In this pre-European era, it was not the nation state, or companies established as its proxies that endeavored to advance national policies in newly-colonized overseas territories, but local principalities and polities in Southeast Asia already had their own versions and interpretations of state, territory, governance and world order. While it was by no means sharing a developed system of transcontinental communication links and networks like present day, a system of world trade which facilitated not only trans-continental trades, but even cultural exchanges, was integrating a large number of advanced societies stretching between the extremes of north-western Europe and China.

That said, two characteristics underpin the understanding of this pre-European world system. For one thing, it was observed that transition of this world system to a new one might result in changes in different regions and states, some of which might not be prepared for such changes, or lack the capabilities to address challenges brought about by the changes.

Another characteristic is that the periodic modifications to the world system that makes economies obsolete and bring about state failures, sometimes development and progress are accomplished at the price of economic decline or economic underdevelopment of large world regions. Flourishing societies and their visible and intangible cultural influences mutually counterbalance each other's extent of influence in a complex world system. In fact, transitions in the world system like the rise of western predominance in the 16th century vividly demonstrate the internalized equilibrium in the world system.

Control over the South China Sea was operated quite differently in the era before the arrival of European colonialism and imperialism.

First, the South China Sea was situated en route trade links connecting politically and culturally diverse subsystems in the Near and Far East. Scholar contended that these trading routes could be grouped into three larger circuits, in which the South China Sea constituted one critical sea lane of communication in the Far Eastern circuit extended from Constantinople to China.[13] However, the Straits of Malacca and of Sunda, between Southern Sumatra and Java appeared to be more crucial than the great swaths of waters in the South China Sea. The latter was deemed as a dangerous waterway that can cause great mortalities and loss of wealth.[14]

---

[13] Abu-Lughod, Janet L., *Before European Hegemony: The World System A.D. 1250–1350.* New York: Oxford University Press, 1989; Abu-Lughod, Janet, The Shape of the World System in the Thirteenth Century. *Studies in Comparative International Development*, 22(4) 1987, 3–25; Tansen, Sen, The Phases and The Wider Implications of the Re-configuration of The India–China Trade, *Buddhism, Diplomacy, and Trade: The Realignment of India–China Relations, 600–1400.* Rowman & Littlefield, 2015, 212–247.

[14] Tønnesson, Stein, The South China Sea in the Age of European Decline. *Modern Asian Studies*, 40(1), 2006, 1–57; Womack, Brantly, The Spratlys: From Dangerous Ground to Apple of

Second, maritime order in the South China Sea at that time was relatively calm. It was observed that through China, the overland subsystem that had connected it westward to the Black Sea and the eastern sea subsystem that connected it to the Straits region and beyond were joined together in an all-important loop.[15] The entire world system functioned smoothly when the connection through China operated well. Actually, this was the original apparatus upon which the 21st century OBOR initiative was sketched out.

At that time, Chinese and the Southeast Asian polities conducted tributary and merchant trade. By far the leading technological and naval power until the 14th century, China actually had no need to invoke its naval power. With the Chinese having no ambitions on overseas expansion of territories and resource predation, maritime order in South China Sea remained calm and, for most of the time, a good breeding ground for inter-regional trades. Local principalities in maritime Southeast Asia viewed the ocean as free and open, and a resource for wealth and opportunities.[16] This also echoed the observation that in this region, trade created countries, or state entities, albeit in many different manifestations.[17]

In this sense, lessons from this pre-European world system in the South China Sea are cogent, that a confrontational approach in maritime space

Discord. *Contemporary Southeast Asia*, 33(3), December 2011, 370–387; Tønnesson, Stein, The Paracels: The "Other" South China Sea Dispute. *Asian Perspective*, 26(4), 2002, 145–169; Schofield, Clive H. (ed.) *A Geographical Description of the Spratly Islands and an Account of Hydrographic Surveys Amongst Those Islands.* Durham, U.K.: IBRU, 1995. Also, see the IBRU-Centre for Border Research website, https://www.dur.ac.uk/ibru/.

[15] See, Note 13.

[16] A consensus was reached among scholars that in pre-colonial Southeast Asia, the inter-principalities system could be termed as the *mandala* system. Several characteristics featured its operation, such as overlapping sovereignty, patrimonial authority and vaguely definable and continuously shifting territorial boundaries. See further, Acharya, Amitav, "Imaging Southeast Asia", in *The Making of Southeast Asia: International Relations of a Region.* Ithaca: Cornell University Press, 2013, 51–104; Dieter-Evers, Hans, Understanding The South China Sea: An Explorative Cultural Analysis. *International Journal of Asia Pacific Studies*, 10(1), 2014, 77–93.

[17] See, Note 16. Generally speaking, trades made states in Southeast Asia. Nevertheless, there were different types of states, for instance, city-state ports (Malacca and later, Singapore), ancient kingdoms in main continent (Angkor, Siam and Bagan), and principalities with a more diverse pattern of sovereign projection and confrontational connection with neighboring polities (Srivijaya and Majapahit).

partitioning and resources utilization may not help dispute resolution and conflict management. Further, this historical retrospect also sheds light on how a 21st century MSR plan unfolds, and its implementation carried through.

Crisscrossing the South China Sea in the 21st century MSR

Situating the South China Sea dispute in the MSR initiative

Recent tensions in the South China Sea have drawn considerable attentions within and outside the region.

Situations in the South China Sea are infused with a rising consciousness of self-interest and realist strategic expediency. Protecting self-interest is demonstrated in significant developments in improving maritime capabilities among certain ASEAN claimants in these past months (second half of 2015 at the point of writing). Realism and strategic expediency are largely seen through the engagement of some extra-regional, non-claimant countries in the South China Sea, such as the US. Their stakes in the South China Sea vary, so do their involvements and prospects.

In recent rounds of tensions, several ASEAN claimant countries are engaged in defensive diplomacy, and a race in military capability building.[18] However, amid this region-wide military capability racing, China directs its efforts in island-reclamation and enlargement in the South China Sea, which

[18]The Philippines announced in December 2014 that a sum of US$885 million will be used for force modernization program. Several countries, including France and Korea, have submitted bids for procurement deals. This is opined by Rear Admiral Caesar Taccad, head of the Philippine Navy's weapon systems, on 17 December 2014. Malaysia has adopted similar measures, when Prime Minister Najib Razak announced that Malaysia's defense budget would increase in 2015, with a hike of another 10% as compared to the 2014 expenditures. This increase includes defense procurement and research budget, which will rise up by 6%. Huan, Eric, Tight Budgets Hamper Malaysia's Naval Ambitions. Marine Link, 19 March 2015; By Parameswaran, Prashanth, Malaysia as ASEAN Chair in 2015: What to Expect? *The Diplomat*, 22 November 2014. Vietnam was also involved in an intense round of defense diplomacy in end 2014 and early 2015, involving naval port visits, dialogues in a miscellaneous defense-related issues and exchanges of high-level delegations. *Inter alia*, a trend to upgrade defense dialogues, and to broaden the scope of cooperation merits attentions.

raise keen concerns among ASEAN countries. These worries mainly question if these artificial island constructions would be dedicated for military usage.[19]

On 9 April 2015, the spokesperson of China's Foreign Affairs Ministry explained in length and detail about the rationale of China's land reclamation efforts.[20] The spokesperson raised many dimensions, including providing public goods of maritime search and rescue, disaster prevention and mitigation, environmental protection and safeguarding China's sovereignty over land features in the South China Sea.

This episode vividly reflects a most disturbing concern of ASEAN claimants to China's South China Sea policies, namely, island reclamation and construction work. Have these island reclamation works portended China's next step, that of making the dash-line claim as a maritime boundary in which territorial rights are to be exercised in an exclusive manner?

It is with these worries that ASEAN claimants had started the race-up of maritime resource development, regardless of the pending territorial disputes and possible encroachment upon the right and interest of other parties. With the initiative of establishing a 21st century MSR, a window of opportunity is open to ASEAN to address these fears, and for China, to re-adjust its overture in more sustainable and mutually-beneficial engagement in international affairs.

The key will be, how the Road plan, with the essence of cooperation and coprosperity, helps transform and refine China's South China Sea claim, not treating the sea as an obstacle, but an aid to the realization of the Road plan. If China fails to reconcile between its South China Sea claim and the Road plan and ensure that the Road plan was able to attract ASEAN claimants' participation despite the South China Sea dispute,

---

[19]The increasing Chinese military presence is likely to unsettle the region with a growing sense of unease and rivalry.

[20]Quoting the spokesperson's words, According to Hua, China's "maintenance and construction work" on garrisons located in the Spratlys has the following purposes: *[O]ptimizing their functions, improving the living and working conditions of personnel stationed there, better safeguarding territorial sovereignty and maritime rights and interests, as well as better performing China's international responsibility and obligation in maritime search and rescue, disaster prevention and mitigation, marine science and research, meteorological observation, environmental protection, navigation safety, fishery production service and other areas.*

implications can be problematic. China may lose the credentials needed in its transition of its role as a regional great power, with great development potential and an outlook of promoting coprosperity among neighboring countries via the Road plan. With this fact turning into a reality, would China's further development at both regional and international level be overshadowed and compromised?

It is these issues, all bundled-up, that lead to the observation of faltering peaceful resolutions of the South China Sea issue, the Road plan would be, highly likely, attenuated to mere policy propaganda or diplomatic discourses. Under such a context, not only the Road plan is likely to be aborted, but also China's greater ambitions of establishing a new type of great-power relations with the US and other international subjects may be shattered.

Some proposals

The connection between the South China Sea and the Road plan has been established. Yet, these inquiries should not be counted as a total rejection of the Road plan and OBOR initiative. Rather, they are to shed light on how China's South China Sea claims can be adjusted to render constructive assistance to the implementation of the Road plan.

Of primary importance is that the dash-line claim as a maritime boundary is maintained in an open manner. In other words, sovereign rights and the management of maritime spaces defined by this dash-line maritime boundary should be conducted in a flexible, yet effective manner.

In order for the dash-line claim — deemed as a maritime boundary — not to be a political burden and a legal hazard, it should be operated with an open manner. The underlying logic is that operation of the dash-line maritime boundary should be related to the concept of "border control", and not "border security".[21] Border control is a broader concept, and border security, a narrower one.

---

21 Robert, J. R. John, Victor Prescott, Gillian Gillian and Doreen Triggs, *International Frontiers and Boundaries: Law, Politics and Geography*. Leiden: Martinus Nijhoff Publishers, 2008, 23–90; Prescott, J.R.V., *The Geography of Frontiers and Boundaries*. London: Routledge, 2015, 33–55; Kristof, Ladis K.D., The Nature of Frontiers and Boundaries. *Annals of the Association of*

In practice, border control covers an array of measures, ranging from border security maintenance to negotiations and conversations in local communities and national capitals. In short, border controls concerns both effectiveness and efficiency in terms of management measures to alleviate disputes and transform rivalries into coprosperity. Unlike border security measures, border controls frame a symbiotic relationship with all involving parties, and transform confrontations into mutual prosperity. Two arguments can be elaborated here to support this idea.

For one thing, China (PRC) has, for generations, been a dominating power in South China Sea, which was then a peripheral border land that marks the farthest reach of its cultural, commercial and political impacts. Even with intrinsic limitations that comes with a maritime domain, the Han Chinese civilization, as compared to the Nusantara/Malay culture, by and large, appeared more likely to have a concept of bounded territorial domain, which had been laid upon the great swathes of waters in the South China Sea. Yet, its concept and management of this territory-like maritime space was not exclusive in nature. Instead, Chinese governance appeared to be fluctuating, contextual and dependent upon the wax and wane of its own national prowess.

Second, implementation of the dash-line claim to create an open-end territorial water could only be successful in a multilateral forum when its promulgation and implementation had generated common interests beneficial to all regional countries. In other words, a multilateral approach, with the goal of the provision of public goods, is the most preferred option. Public goods can be of a wide range.

In this aspect, to keep this regional cooperation mechanism in full function requires fulfillment in the following areas: technology, finance, will to cooperate and conflict management in a non-forceful way.

American Geographers, 49(3), 1959, 269–282. Regarding the evolution of boundary in Southeast Asia, see Solomon, Robert L., Boundary Concepts and Practices in Southeast Asia. *World Politics*, 23(1), 1970, 1–23; Leng, Lee Yong, *Southeast Asia: Essays in Political Geography.* Singapore: National University Press, 1982, 9–16; Leng, Lee Yong, The Colonial Legacy in Southeast Asia: Maritime Boundary Problems. *Contemporary Southeast Asia*, 8(2), 1986, 119–130; Acharya, Amitav, "Imaging Southeast Asia", in *The Making of Southeast Asia: International Relations of a Region*. Ithaca: Cornell University Press, 2013, 51–104; Lamb, Alastair, *Asian Frontiers*. New York: Frederick A. Praeger Inc., 1968, 39.

Yet, the South China Sea dispute clearly has shown a picture of diversified interests with sometimes conflicting considerations. Also, how the public perceives this issue depends heavily on the parochial interests of the agents that have the power to mediate access to these sites. Yet, the immediate underlying interests are economic, geopolitical and strategic. The Road plan, which emphasizes common interests of coprospect and coexistence, helps provide an alternative resolution. It advocates that disputes in South China Sea should not be escalated frenetically and should be dealt in a more pragmatic and beneficial manner.

Conclusion

In March 2015, an action plan was published to flesh out implementation of the 21st MSR (the Road plan hereafter) plan.[22] Fujian province and the southeast coast of China are the core area from which the Road is extended. South China Sea is sitting at the throat of the Road, as the route proceeds southward to Southeast Asia and moves westward via the Malacca Straits into the Indian Ocean. Several countries, including ASEAN claimants, along the Road have expressed keen interests of their participation in the plan.[23] Recursively, a fair observation is that the South China Sea issue serves one key event to determine how the Road plan is perceived at regional and international societies.

The OBOR is a Chinese initiative promoted by President Xi Jinping and sometimes known as China's answer to the Marshall Plan (although Beijing rejects that analogy). It is certainly designed to serve a variety of national goals. *Inter alia*, connections between the MSR and South China Sea dispute

---

[22] China Unveils Action Plan on Belt and Road Initiative. *Xinhua News*, 28 March 2015.

[23] ASEAN countries are generally interested in this Road initiative, because of their dire needs for financial aids and technological assistance of infrastructure construction. Vietnam, the Philippines, Cambodia, Indonesia and Thailand all hold esteems regarding this Road initiative. For more detailed of the development of the "One Belt One Road" initiative, see China's Initiatives on Building Silk Road Economic Belt and 21st century Maritime Silk Road. *Xinhua News* [downloaded on 20 November 2015], available at http://www.xinhuanet.com/english/special/silkroad/index.htm.

are, while implicit on the surface, having great potentials for conflict management and alleviation of mutual rivalry. Yet, it depends on first, how China's South China Sea claim, in particular the dash line, is to be developed, and second, if these efforts could be termed in a way sensible to both the need of China and ASEAN claimants.

Section D

The Overland Silk Road

Chapter 10

The One Belt One Road Narratives

LIM Tai Wei

Origins of the One Belt One Road (OBOR) plan

According to international media sources, the OBOR became operational in 2011 when the first direct train from Chongqing to Duisburg Germany started its journey and shipping within the OBOR maritime route began from Chinese port locations on a journey to Antwerp, Belgium.[1] Others date the genesis of this reinterpreted Silk Road on 18 November 2014 when a train carrying 82 freight containers of 1,000 tons of export-made items departed from a large warehousing facility in Yiwu (Zhejiang 300 km south of Shanghai) to Madrid where it arrived on 9 December 2014.[2] The far end of this railway system may eventually be Rotterdam, Duisburg and Berlin[3] in the near future. *The Economist* is even more explicit in its economic analysis (as opposed to media observers keen on discussing geopolitical implications) of the Chinese Belt and Road Initiative:

[1] Goh, Brenda, China Pays Big to Expand its Clout Along the New Silk Road, dated 10 November 2014 in the *Reuters* website [downloaded on 18 December 2014], available at http://www.reuters.com/article/2014/11/10/us-china-silkroad-idUSKCN0IU27R20141110.

[2] Escobar, Pepe, China Is Building a New Silk Road to Europe, And It's Leaving America Behind, dated 16 December 2014 in *Mother Jones* website [downloaded on 18 December 2014], available at http://www.motherjones.com/politics/2014/12/chinas-new-silk-road-europe-will-leave-america-behind.

[3] *Ibid.*

> As Chinese manufacturers move inland, getting their products to European markets has become more complicated. The journey back to the coast and halfway around the world by sea takes up to 60 days — an eternity for the latest iPads and other "fast fashion" products. Kazakhstan offers a backdoor route. Trains from Chongqing in south-west China to Duisburg in Germany, 10,800 kilometres (6,700 miles) via Kazakhstan, Russia, Belarus and Poland, supposedly take just 14 days.[4]

This narrative may be amongst the first in the international media to highlight the connection between the Silk Road and China's Go-West policy, relocating manufacturers from expensive first-tier Eastern coastal cities inland to the West where labor costs are cheaper. It also highlights the narrative that European markets (and, along the way, Middle Eastern, Central Asian and South Asian markets) will become increasingly important for Chinese exports. Thus, the rationale for the Belt and Road Initiative, conforming to Escobar and Goh's diachronic analyses. At the start of 2015, more articles started appearing, analyzing the impact of the OBOR initiative on Central and Eastern Europe (CEE). Geographically-oriented, Dragan Pavlicevic's article in the Jamestown Foundation published on 9 January 2015 was a relatively detailed article on the initial phase of the OBOR initiative in CEE. He noted the possibility of Central and Eastern European benefiting from the overland route between China and Europe and specified the two points of connections between the two regions: the Greek Port of Piraeus and railway between Belgrade and Budapest as well as a southern China–Europe land–sea express line.[5]

As Escobar's sensational article became circulated through the international syndicated media on the first day of 2015, another Silk Road-related article written by a Sri Lankan student leader Akshan deAlwis was circulated by *Huffington Post*, an influential left-leaning liberal online media outlet.

[4] *The Economist*, The New Silk Road Hardly an Oasis, dated 15 November 2014 in *The Economist* [downloaded on 18 December 2014], available at http://www.economist.com/news/asia/21632595-kazakhstan-turns-geography-advantage-china-builds-new-silk-road-hardly-oasis.

[5] Pavlicevic, Dragan, China's New Silk Road Takes Shape in Central and Eastern Europe, dated 9 January 2015 in Jamestown Foundation China Brief Volume: 15 Issue: 1 [downloaded on 15 January 2015], available at http://www.jamestown.org/single/?tx_ttnews%5Btt_news%5D=43374&tx_ttnews%5BbackPid%5D=7&cHash=dcf45d3bf99b47d32fcb982a34e81371.

The tone of this article was alarmist and its author also stated openly his hope that Sri Lankans would democratically vote against Chinese influence in the military infrastructure of his country.[6] The article offers some insights into local reactions and responses in South Asia towards the OBOR perspective from an individual public intellectual and activist, who represent one sliver of many different perspectives held by the vast spectrum of political views related to the Chinese initiative.

There are at least four differences between this narrative and Escobar or Goh's views: (1) part of the article highlights Thailand as the main recipient and beneficiary of Chinese outreach, therefore putting the focus of his narrative closer to the Chinese periphery (unlike Escobar who mentioned a possible German–Russian–Chinese triumvirate at one point in his article); (2) it argues that the Maritime Silk Road (MSR) is larger in scale than the Overland Silk Road where more than US$1.4 billion were spent in the author's home country of Sri Lanka to service Chinese maritime vessels (as opposed to Escobar who argued that the overland route was designed to take away trade from the MSR) [*Note*: It is quite likely that some of these facilities were built before OBOR was announced, and was conceptualized as part of the military strategy of "String of Pearls" reported in the international media and may not officially be construed as part of the current Chinese initiative, at this point, the linkage is unclear]; (3) the author used the word "patron" to describe the Chinese Silk Road initiative but did not clearly define or elaborate on what he meant. Popular rendition of this phrase tend to associate it with the ideas of Zheng He's vassal state diplomacy or it could refer to a more a-historical usage of the term to mean a patron–client relationship, both of which connote the meaning of Chinese dominance (a stronger word would be "protection" as was the case in Zheng He forces' role in Malacca that was facing a stronger Thai kingdom), non-territorial aggrandizement and indirect forms of Chinese economic hegemony; (4) deAlwis also mentioned an interesting statement without further details on how the Chinese initiative can be an economic catch-up opportunity for the rest of Asia to reach the standards of the four tiger economies of

---

[6] deAlwis, Akshan, The New Silk Road: A True "Win–Win" or a Perilous Future?, dated 31 December 2014 in the Huffingtonpost.com *The World Post* website [downloaded on 2 January 2015], available at http://www.huffingtonpost.com/akshan-dealwis/the-new-silk-road-a-true-_b_6400992.html.

Hong Kong, Singapore, South Korea, Taiwan, suggesting readings of uneven economic development in Asia and also the possibility of an alternative model that had made the four dynamic economies successful [the four tiger economies are often associated with Japan's fast growth model that was once lauded by the World Bank as a "miracle" and reinforced by Western notions of capitalism, political and corporate governance as well as democratization pulses].[7]

deAlwis' narrative presented the scenario of the OBOR as an additional (although it was not clear whether he also meant "alternative") developmental system for Asian countries that are not the four tiger economies or Japan (which is presented as an "alternative" modernization but deAlwis was ambiguous if he also meant "rival" to OBOR). He centered his attention on the more immediate periphery of China, especially South Asia where he comes from and Southeast Asia (particularly Thailand). And he wanted to convey the possibility of a possible patron–client relationship although the shape and form is not elaborated upon. Taking his narrative and combining it with Escobar's, a global picture emerges that is complex, ambitious and deeply nuanced. The world system tapestry presented by deAlwis and Escobar are more contentious and ambiguous rather than settled and clearly defined when it comes to Chinese intentions for gaining geopolitical economic advantage. It indicates that observers, activists and analysts are not quite decided on whether the MSR or the Overland Silk Road (dubbed High-Speed Railway or HSR diplomacy) takes precedence in Chinese plans. The Chinese leadership themselves may be testing the waters on this pragmatically without dogmatically following a policy paradigm with options to modify the plans as they go along. The Zhongnanhai or Beijing leadership may also be exercising strategic ambiguity, not deciding or formulating a definite concept on this which may also be an object of internal political tussle. Whatever the reason that accounts for this ambiguity, Escobar and deAlwis' narratives of the MSR *vis-à-vis* HSR may occupy chatter and speculations about the OBOR initiative for some time to come.

On 8 November 2014, the Chinese promised to dispense funds amounting to a US$40 billion Silk Road fund with the broad objective of improving transport and trade links, in addition to the US$50 billion already allocated

---

[7] *Ibid.*

to the Beijing-initiated Asian Infrastructure Investment Bank (AIIB) and the BRICS Bank. The BRICS Development Bank funds energy, telecommunications and transportation infrastructure with a starting capital of US$50 billion and China/India as its major shareholder.[8] A major question arose as to how China will disperse its funds. The key word that is mentioned in the international media, top leaders and policy makers' statements as well as the scholarly conference and seminars that I attended was "connectivity" — how to link up the entire belt of countries along both Overland and MSR so that trade can be stimulated. Up till December 2014, details were not forthcoming from Chinese sources on how their Silk Road-related budget will be utilized. Along with observers and the international media, this began to cause some countries located along both the overland as well as the MSR to seek more details about the initiative.

In seeking this reaction from the Chinese government, the immediate response can be divided into three ways: (1) to use official and track II channels to ask for more details so that states in the designated regions of the Silk Road initiative can react accordingly to maximize their economic benefits from the scheme; (2) to pre-empt any issues incompatible with national interests by first opposing the institutions associated (or perceived to be associated) with the scheme such as opposition to the AIIB; (3) regardless of the shape and form of the Silk Road initiative which is expected to be organic and dynamic both in implementation and development, to persuade Beijing to be more transparent and conform to international norms by integrating with the international community, e.g. the early persuasion to Beijing to locate the headquarters of the AIIB in Seoul, Singapore, Jakarta and perhaps even the semi-autonomous Hong Kong rather than Shanghai or Beijing. These questions are pondered internally within China as well, between an internationalist faction keen to see the Silk Road initiatives as part of China's opening up with greater transparency and harmonization with international norms vs. those keen to construct an international trade and commerce system with firmer Beijing control.

---

[8] Escobar, Pepe, China is Building a New Silk Road to Europe, And it's Leaving America Behind, dated 16 December 2014 in *Mother Jones* website [downloaded on 18 December 2014], available at http://www.motherjones.com/politics/2014/12/chinas-new-silk-road-europe-will-leave-america-behind.

The Chinese Track II and academic institutions held major conferences in Istanbul and Hong Kong to discuss plans about the Beijing-led Belt and Road Initiatives in mid-December 2014. These conferences reveal several nuggets of information. First, there is some emphasis on lifting the living standards of countries (including those with per capita gross national income that is 46.4% of the international average standards) in the Eurasian Zone-Road sections of the Silk Road.[9] *Xinhuanet* featured support from government ministers for the scheme from Balkan states like Montenegro and Serbia.[10] Maritime countries like Malaysia have also stated more concrete intentions to construct infrastructure for tapping into the MSR. "We are in the process of developing port cities collaboration between Qinzhou Port (of China) and the Kuantan Port (of Malaysia)," former Malaysian ambassador to China Abdul Majid Ahmad Khan said at a forum on ASEAN development on 13 December 2014, reported by China's Xinhua news agency.[11] These revelations indicated that the MSR fund could possibly target underperforming economies, help them construct infrastructure, and also enhance connectivity with middle-income economies like Malaysia through cooperation in port facilities.

The manner or operating philosophy in which these funds would be managed and dispensed were also revealed by Chinese President Xi Jinping on 7 September 2013 at the Nazarbayev University in Astana, Kazakhstan. He mentioned that China and other countries like those in Central Asia can first compare their plans on economic development while infrastructure links can be enhanced with the guiding philosophy that China "respects the development paths and policies chosen by the peoples of regional countries, and will never interfere in the domestic affairs of Central Asian nations".[12]

---

[9] *Xinhuanet*, Silk Roads Initiatives Enters New Phase: Think Tank, dated 15 December 2014 in *Xinhuanet* website [downloaded on 18 December 2014], available at http://news.xinhuanet.com/english/china/2014-12/15/c_133856803.htm.

[10] *Ibid.*

[11] *Xinhuanet*, Malaysia Ready for Greater Cooperation with China in Maritime Silk Road: Former Ambassador, dated 13 December 2014 in the *Xinhuanet* website [downloaded on 13 December 2014], available at http://news.xinhuanet.com/english/china/2014-12/13/c_133852521.htm.

[12] *Xinhuanet*, Xi suggests China, C. Asia Build Silk Road Economic Belt, dated 7 September 2013 in the *Xinhuanet* website [downloaded on 18 December 2014], available at http://news.xinhuanet.com/english/china/2013-09/07/c_132700695.htm.

This pronouncement resembled Chinese past practices in which they dispensed aid without strict pre-conditions that both led to praise amongst African leaders for the Chinese role in uplifting the continent economically and also criticisms from human rights groups for dispensing aid to brutal regimes or economies unprepared for economic take-off without proper accounting oversight and procedures. In other words, there are mixed reactions to the Chinese model of infrastructure investment strategies. Further details were provided on 31 December 2014 by the US version of *China Daily*. According to Cheng Jun, general manager of Bank of China's (BoC) global trade services department, the criteria for dispensing the fund is based on the following factors: (1) "economic and trade relations with China"; (2) "their [recipient countries'] goods for export and import"; (3) "related Chinese import and export companies … to find how we [China] can help our companies further open the overseas market".[13]

"China will never seek a dominant role in regional affairs, nor try to nurture a sphere of influence", he added.[14] This is again a familiar format that has dynamically evolved and eclectically incorporated the non-hegemony promise, vision of a multipolar world, peaceful rise of China and the in-vogue idea of doing what is necessary for China's national interest without infringing upon others. There are those who support and oppose this worldview. Those who support this worldview see the consensus as one that opens up an alternative developmental path for those who choose to place growth above political liberalization and competitive politics or system that have been time-tested by developed economies. With regard to the BRICS Bank, both India and China declared broad and ambiguous terms of "justice, equity and transparency" as conditions for their loan dispensing.[15] For most

---

[13]Jiang, Xueqing, Pledge Made to Support 'One Belt One Road', dated 31 December 2014 in *China Daily* USA website [downloaded on 1 January 2015], available at http://usa.chinadaily.com.cn/epaper/2014-12/31/content_19210598.htm.

[14]*Xinhuanet*, Xi suggests China, C. Asia Build Silk Road Economic Belt, dated 7 September 2013 in the *Xinhuanet* website [downloaded on 18 December 2014], available at http://news.xinhuanet.com/english/china/2013-09/07/c_132700695.htm

[15]Escobar, Pepe, China is Building a New Silk Road to Europe, And It's Leaving America Behind, dated 16 December 2014 in *Mother Jones* website [downloaded on 18 December 2014], available at http://www.motherjones.com/politics/2014/12/chinas-new-silk-road-europe-will-leave-america-behind.

countries, the Chinese vision and more established developmental paths of the developed economies are not mutually exclusive, there are overlaps between these two choices. It provides more diversity of choices for funding and infrastructure development. For the critics, the problems they see with this institutional structure range from challenging the status quo of the prevailing world order of trade and politics to the charge of neo-Colonialism in resource extraction.

In terms of implementation priorities, some argue that China's main target is Central Asia and projects covered in the OBOR will eventually proliferate to other regions and will not only include train infrastructure but also ports and eventually energy pipelines.[16] The evidence for this, according to this school of thought, is the direction of Chinese capital flow. China's capital flow to Central Asia: US$30 billion in contracts with Kazakhstan; US$15 billion with Uzbekistan; US$8 billion for Turkmenistan and US$1 billion to Tajikistan.[17] The Chinese authorities' close relations with Putin's Russia is another evidence: the trans-Siberian high-speed rail reduces transit time between Beijing and Moscow from 61/2 days to only 33 hours.[18] These evidences further point to the narrative that the landed routes will eventually pare down the volumes transported on the maritime routes.

The contestations and processes of achieving equilibrium and constant negotiations between the different views of constructing and setting up an economic world or regional geopolitical orders are natural for ambitious schemes as similar ambivalent attitudes were present in grand schemes formulated in the past. Witness the debates over Fortress Europe when a pan-European economy was establishing, the production networks set up by Japan in East Asia, Soviet bloc of collectivized economies, the Organization of the Petroleum Exporting Countries (OPEC) unity in the face of geopolitical crises. All of them were seen as challengers to prevailing world orders at one point of time and were eventually harmonized or integrated into the world order. There are no indications thus far that the Chinese have intentions to overturn or replace the current international economic system. Also there are signs of outreach from perceived or imagined rival institutions.

[16] *Ibid.*

[17] *Ibid.*

[18] *Ibid.*

The Asian Development Bank (ADB) President may not agree with the AIIB idea, for example, but have belatedly welcomed cooperation between the two. Thus far, the OBOR also does not seem to have any hostile features incompatible with Asia-Pacific Economic Cooperation (APEC), World Trade Organization (WTO), Trans-Pacific Partnership (TPP), Free Trade Area of the Asia Pacific (FTAAP), Regional Comprehensive Economic Partnership (RCEP) organizations. In fact, the Chinese appear to harmonize or complement some of these institutions.

A more detailed micro-mechanism of managing the funds slated for the OBOR initiative was expected around mid- or late-December 2014 but details were not forthcoming by that time. Instead, on the very last day of 2014, small slivers of information with regard to the financial and funding mechanism for the OBOR were released in the English language edition of *China Daily* circulated in the US. Up till that point of time, it represented the most detailed announcement of the OBOR funding mechanism, stating that the BoC Ltd. has scheduled a planned US$20 billion credit infusion into the initiative's projects in 2015 and will dispense over US$100 billion from 2015–2018, therefore, *de facto* and *de jure* making it the main financial bankrolling institution for the initiative in the immediate future.[19] US$100 billion is not a small sum for the bank because up till 30 September 2014, the BoC had supported 1,332 overseas projects operated by Chinese firms with loan offers of US$115.2 billion,[20] which means the money allocated for 2015–2018 is equivalent to all of the global loan offers made by BoC prior to the OBOR initiative pledge. It represents a major source of support for a state initiative formulated at the highest levels of Chinese elite leadership in Zhongnanhai.

It is necessary to mention some concerns about the Silk Road by other stakeholders before discussing some of the positive features and concrete measures of the initiative at this early stage. Only a few are briefly discussed here and the intention is not to be reductionist but to mention some formidable obstacles. Some of these narratives may be perceptions but perceptions are sometimes as important as concrete developments in issues

---

[19] Jiang, Xueqing, Pledge Made to Support 'One Belt One Road', dated 31 December 2014 in *China Daily* USA website [downloaded on 1 January 2015], available at http://usa.chinadaily.com.cn/epaper/2014-12/31/content_19210598.htm.

[20] *Ibid.*

related to international relations, geopolitics and economic competition. According to some journalistic writings, Beijing intends to pare down the 90% of world trade that still travels by maritime routes by increasing freight transportation overland through HSRs.[21] *The Economist* lend possible indirect support for this argument:

> Most containers still travel by sea, which is considerably cheaper — about $4,000 each rather than $9,000. But the gap is narrowing as European manufacturers start filling the empty carriages going back to China with high-priced products such as luxury cars.[22]

The equilibrium or balance between overland and maritime trade routes in Chinese initiatives has already been highlighted in the international media. Such a prospect if not properly explained or managed may put maritime trading nations on their toes. Some observers see the AIIB institution as a challenge to the ADB. ADB is a US and Japan institution with a combined 31% contribution of the bank's capital and 25% of its voting power.[23] Veteran contemporary China sinologist and economist John Wong highlighted the smart features of the Belt and Road Initiative and provided a balanced analysis with some concerns as well:

> China is essentially leveraging its geo-economic power in order to achieve larger geo-political objectives … In the case of the Overland Silk Road, China's efforts run the risk of creating suspicion and conflict with Russia. Many Central Asian states fall into Russia's traditional sphere of influence.

---

[21] Escobar, Pepe, China is Building a New Silk Road to Europe, And It's Leaving America Behind, dated 16 December 2014 in *Mother Jones* website [downloaded on 18 December 2014], available at http://www.motherjones.com/politics/2014/12/chinas-new-silk-road-europe-will-leave-america-behind.

[22] *The Economist*, The New Silk Road Hardly an Oasis, dated 15 November 2014 in *The Economist* [downloaded on 18 December 2014], available at http://www.economist.com/news/asia/21632595-kazakhstan-turns-geography-advantage-china-builds-new-silk-road-hardly-oasis.

[23] Escobar, Pepe, China Is Building a New Silk Road to Europe, And It's Leaving America Behind, dated 16 December 2014 in *Mother Jones* website [downloaded on 18 December 2014], available at http://www.motherjones.com/politics/2014/12/chinas-new-silk-road-europe-will-leave-america-behind.

> As for the Maritime Silk Road, China's immediate diplomatic challenge is obviously how to untangle its deep-rooted territorial disputes with neighbours such as Japan, Vietnam and the Philippines.[24]

This is a very succinct, timely, well couched, balanced and important reminder of China's vulnerabilities and weak points when it comes to the geopolitical feature of the Belt and Road Initiative. *Bloomberg*'s report on the Belt and Road Initiative also expressed similar concerns by some experts from Russia:

> "So far, China has understood Russia's sensitivities and has not challenged Moscow on political and security issues ... China, for the first time in 200 years or so, has become a more powerful and dynamic country than Russia ... I expect the Chinese to be smart and clever when dealing with Russia, without provoking it unnecessarily ... Should they, however, suddenly become abrasive and aggressive instead, a rupture in relations will follow," said Mr Dmitri Trenin, director of the Moscow Centre at Carnegie Endowment for International Peace, he said.[25]

Essentially, it is quite well understood that Beijing is yielding the dividends from Russia's fallout with Washington and European majors, particularly after the Crimea issue. Beijing will have to deepen the bilateral relationship further to prevent any flip-flops or frictions in the future which are bound to occur between neighbors and also institute measures that will bring the bilateral relations into the post-Putin era. Beijing's collective leadership will have to cope with political elite power structures in the Kremlin. Beijing also understands that the Kremlin was a pioneer and forerunner in Eurasian regionalism. As *The Economist* pointed out, in 2011, Kazakhstan,

---

[24] Wong, John, Reviving the Ancient Silk Road: China's New Economic Diplomacy, dated 9 July 2014 in the *Straits Times* [downloaded on 18 December 2014], available at http://www.straitstimes.com/news/opinion/invitation/story/reviving-the-ancient-silk-road-chinas-new-economic-diplomacy-20140709.

[25] *Bloomberg*, Chinese Premier's Silk Road Trip Marks Advance on Russia's Patch, dated 16 December 2014 in *Todayonline* website [downloaded on 18 December 2014], available at http://www.todayonline.com/chinaindia/china/chinese-premiers-silk-road-trip-marks-advance-russias-patch.

along with Russia and Belarus, formed a customs union, and the Treaty on the Eurasian Economic Union became effective on 1 January 2015.[26]

Besides Russian presence, *The Economist* also pointed out other challenges in the Eurasian region. They include Russian swaggering (Ukraine, recent mobilization of troops near its border with Kazakhstan), European reluctance to trade with Russia, Russian obstacles to goods traveling to Europe at times of bad relations, domestic problems like corruption in Central Asia, elitist dominance of wealth creation, susceptibility to commodity fluctuations, criminal groups, etc.[27] While Central Asia remains Russia's traditional sphere of influence, stronger Sino-Serbian and China–CEE ties run into a traditional sphere of influence for the EU as the latter worry whether Sino-CEE cooperation may be used as a vehicle by Beijing to split the EU.[28] To this, China answered that it would make sure infrastructure projects observe EU legal benchmarks as Brussels has political influence in the CEE region and will make its voice known on Sino-CEE collaborations.[29]

Besides Central Asia and Russian influence as well as the presence of the EU in Central and Eastern European, deAlwis's article in *Huffington Post* covered a few more challenges summarized here, including: (1) local nationalism, including the author deAlwis' home country of Sri Lanka, which has traditionally railed against Western imperialism and dominance but remain friendly to China's funding opportunities, according to deAlwis; (2) the case of Thailand which has accepted Chinese railway projects in two areas but simultaneously asking Japan to modernize its entire railway system (same case for South Asians, playing one Asian power against another, in their case, a hedge against India); (3) poor existing infrastructure, including Thailand's

---

[26] *The Economist*, The New Silk Road Hardly an Oasis, dated 15 November 2014 in *The Economist* [downloaded on 18 December 2014], available at http://www.economist.com/news/asia/21632595-kazakhstan-turns-geography-advantage-china-builds-new-silk-road-hardly-oasis.

[27] *Ibid.*

[28] Pavlicevic, Dragan, China's New Silk Road Takes Shape in Central and Eastern Europe, dated 9 January 2015 in Jamestown Foundation China Brief, Volume: 15 Issue: 1 [downloaded on 15 January 2015], available at http://www.jamestown.org/single/?tx_ttnews%5Btt_news%5D=43374&tx_ttnews%5BbackPid%5D=7&cHash=dcf45d3bf99b47d32fcb982a34e81371.

[29] *Ibid.*

own railway system and, while the Chinese have mastered the technology of HSR, according to deAlwis, it is still "nascent" [deAlwis' benchmarks are unknown but he may be comparing Chinese railway experience with the French, German or the Japanese]; (4) fear of Chinese export potential, perhaps referring to being overwhelmed by more affordable Chinese products and skilled Chinese laborers, something mentioned before in other writings on Chinese presence in Africa, for example, and in Southeast Asia in earlier media reports.[30]

Escobar's (correspondent for *Asia Times*) attention-grabbing article cited before appeared in several sites/versions. In the 2015 New Year Day version, Escobar stated that there are a large number of challenges facing the OBOR Chinese initiative. China which is emerging as a major (not the only one but the main player) funder of the Silk Road initiative is facing tremendous economic challenges as it mitigates having 43% of its overall investments in infrastructure construction,[31] in other words an overreliance of economic activity on construction work. From the points mentioned earlier, there are several external and internal factors that may impede development of the OBOR initiative, including external geopolitical issues of mutual accommodation of China's rising strength and Russia's traditional stronghold in Central Asia and internal factors like China's ability to have sustainable economic development in order to bankroll these ambitious initiatives.

Not all correspondents from the West are alarmist about the OBOR initiative. Some like Henny Sender argue that China is "best placed to fix the region's infrastructure" through a "new generation of financial institutions" like the AIIB, the BRICS New Development Bank, and the Silk Road

---

[30] deAlwis, Akshan, The New Silk Road: A True "Win–Win" or a Perilous Future?, dated 31 December 2014 in the Huffingtonpost.com *The World Post* website [downloaded on 2 January 2015], available at http://www.huffingtonpost.com/akshan-dealwis/the-new-silk-road-a-true-_b_6400992.html.

[31] Escobar, Pepe, Go West, Young Han: How China and the New Silk Road Threaten American Imperialism, dated 1 January 2015 in Salon.com website [downloaded on 1 January 2015], available at http://www.salon.com/2014/12/31/go_west_young_han_how_chinas_new_silk_road_threatens_american_imperialism_partner/.

Plan with a combined US$100 billion funding.[32] Sender believes that the main motivation for China lending is to encourage the growth of new markets for Chinese export products, benefiting its construction firms such as China State Construction and Engineering as well as meeting Asian infrastructure requirements that come up to US$8 trillion before the year 2020.[33] Along the same lines, other narratives claim that the OBOR is part of a massive stimulus package to inject funds into an investment-dependent economy like China. According to Shannon Tiezzi's article in *The Diplomat*, unnamed reports mentioned that China would allocate US$16.3 billion for infrastructure development in central and western China (Xinjiang, for example, is the planned gateway to the West) so that they can be better prepared as part of the OBOR initiative while outward bound investments are also planned for other countries in the region covered by the OBOR initiative (Beijing is in railway talks with 28 different countries in a bid to sell their railway technologies).[34]

Another article in the Western media related to OBOR written with optimism is David Gossett's post in *The Huffington Post*. Interestingly, when David Gosset (Director of Academia Sinica Europaea at China Europe International Business School) wrote a media commentary on China's OBOR initiative, he preferred to compare it with the Tang dynasty's overland version instead of the Ming dynasty route traveled by Zheng He.[35] This hinted that the bulk of his analysis was focused mainly on the overland "belt" rather than the maritime "road". Many points are mentioned in this piece but three interesting but highly controversial arguments were forwarded that hitherto were not recorded yet in other narratives: (1) it proposed the option of Japan choosing to "reconnect with the depth of its Eurasianness and become a constructive force in the making of a cooperative Eurasia" but

---

[32] Sender, Henny, China's Lenders are Best Placed to Fix the Region's Infrastructure, dated 24 December 2014 in the *Financial Times*, 2014, 12.

[33] *Ibid.*, 12.

[34] Tiezzi, Shannon, China's $1 Trillion Investment Plan: Stimulus or Not?, dated 8 Jan 2015 in *The Diplomat* website [downloaded on 13 January 2015], available at http://thediplomat.com/2015/01/chinas-1-trillion-investment-plan-stimulus-or-not/.

[35] Gosset, David, China's Grand Strategy: The New Silk Road, dated 8 January 2015 in *The Huffington Post* [downloaded on 12 Jan 2015], available at http://www.huffingtonpost.com/david-gosset/chinas-grand-strategy-the_b_6433434.html.

further details were not elaborated; (2) Gossett proposes that the OBOR is "offering Taipei an opportunity to benefit from his [Xi Jinping] grand strategy and a space, besides APEC, for more international visibility"; (3) the article claims that "Fully embraced by the European Union and other Eurasian actors, the New Silk Road will take 65 percent of the world population toward an unprecedented level of cohesiveness and prosperity".[36]

Point 1 is a particularly sensitive topic given that 2015 is the 70th anniversary of the end of WWII and preparations are underway for Russia and China to organize conspicuous commemoration ceremonies at a time when Sino-Japanese ties are only beginning to thaw slightly. Point 2 is just as controversial because, at the time of Gossett's writing, Taiwanese voters had just voted for the opposition party overwhelmingly in an indication to the Nationalist Party (Kuomintang) in Taiwan as well as Beijing that they do not view incumbent President Ma's reconciliatory policies towards China positively. At the point of this writing, it remains to be seen what the opposition party Democratic Progressive Party (DPP)'s intentions are (given that the party has followers belonging to a spectrum of political colors from light to dark green, i.e. mild to strong independence advocates). Point 3 is equally controversial since the EU and Central Asian actors have to thread between Beijing, Russian and also US interests carefully. Therefore, the support or responses are not entirely unqualified and without caveats. Given the three points above, I would argue that Gossett's narrative is probably the most interesting and controversial as well as politically contentious that I have come across thus far.

Besides media narratives, I also referred to think tank reports and bulletins for information on the OBOR policy. One of the comparatively balanced reports that I came across was authored by Lye Liang Fook (Assistant Director of the East Asian Institute) and his intern coauthor Loh Yi Chin. They argued that China's "Silk Road" Strategy (the OBOR initiative) has benefits and opportunities but also face hurdles when implementing it.[37] Summarizing this narrative, the hurdles mentioned in the article can be divided into several points: (1) the initiative involves the "long-term

---

[36] *Ibid.*

[37] Lye, Liang Fook and Loh Yi Chin, Xi Jinping's "Silk Road" Strategy, dated October 2014 in EAI Bulletin, 16(2). Singapore: East Asian Institute, 2014, 5.

commitment and political will" of the agencies and states involved; (2) the importance of managing expectations as the process will be slow, dependent on collaboration and require sustained momentum; (3) the third point mentioned by many observers is Russia's traditional influence in the Central Asian region; (4) neighboring states' perceptions of Beijing's robust and "assertive" foreign policy and the anxieties about overdependence on China; (5) the potentialities of the OBOR initiative being an indirect challenge to the US trying to rebalance to Asia.[38] To cope with these challenges, the authors see the need for Beijing to demonstrate the ability to work out joint projects, convince others of its goodwill, display the qualities of patience, political determination and diplomatic skills.[39]

Ultimately, the Belt and Road initiative offers a choice of developmental funding based on each individual country's assessment of their national interests at this moment. The ultimate adjudicating factor is in the details, each individual economy or state will assess the national interests according to conditionalities, geopolitical priorities, domestic political situations, external factors and national resources and how the Belt and Road Initiative + AIIB + BRICS Bank *vis-à-vis* current existing established institutions like ADB best serve their needs. Kazakhstan's position is reflective of such sentiments. *Bloomberg* reported on 16 December 2014 that Kazakhstan says it wants "to be on good terms with all the major powers like China, the United States and the European Union, as well as Russia, a nation with which it has long-standing historical, economic and political ties".[40] The same message appeared to emanate from Sri Lanka on 9 January 2015 as pro-Beijing Mahinda Rajapaksa conceded electoral defeat to Maithripala Sirisena, who announced he was keen on a more balanced relationship between Pakistan, India, Japan and China. This electoral event affected Beijing's MSR plans as Sri Lanka is a major node in the MSR's Indian Ocean component. Under the Rajapaksa administration, the Chinese navy had previously sent two submarines to berth in Sri Lanka and

---

38 *Ibid.*, 5.

39 *Ibid.*, 5.

40 *Bloomberg*, Chinese Premier's Silk Road Trip Marks Advance on Russia's patch, dated 16 December 2014 in *Todayonline* website [downloaded on 18 December 2014], available at http://www.todayonline.com/chinaindia/china/chinese-premiers-silk-road-trip-marks-advance-russias-patch.

construction firms to build a Monaco-sized city on land reclaimed near Colombo whose fate is unclear under the incoming Sirisena administration. Like Kazakhstan, Sri Lanka does not want to be caught in the position of having to choose sides in big power rivalry in the region. The Kazak and Sri Lankan reactions serve as natural limitations to China's OBOR policy and are instructive in predicting responses to the policy by major states in the Asian region.

Chapter 11

The One Belt One Road Initiative — Who's Going to Pay For It?

Henry CHAN Hing Lee

"One Belt One Road" or OBOR has evolved as the latest buzzword in China studies of late. A lurking issue on people's mind is how China is ever going to pay for such an ambitious undertaking and ensure its ultimate collection of the loans associated with OBOR initiative. Will the endeavor, resembling the traditional 10-year-project associated with each leader turnover, be forgotten after next leader comes in at 2022?

This Chapter will look briefly at the birth of the ambitious OBOR, then analyze the economic rationale behind OBOR, the funding institutions of the OBOR initiative, including existing mechanisms that China has developed in its overseas investment and loan programs, which can easily be adopted and scaled up for OBOR-related activities, and will end with the outlook for OBOR.

The birth of an ambitious plan

In contrast to public perception, the idea of the "Silk Road Economic Belt" concept was not first raised by President Xi Jinping, in September 2013, in an address to Kazakhstan's Nazarbayev University. Simeon Djankov, an acknowledged early thinker on the Silk Road initiative and currently a visiting senior fellow at the Peterson Institute for International Economics, revealed that he first heard the idea, in October 2011, in Warsaw at an impromptu summit of 22 heads of government from Central and Eastern Europe (CEE), which included some of the former Commonwealth of

Independent States (CIS) republics, such as Georgia and Armenia, with then visiting Chinese Prime Minister Wen Jiabao. Simeon Djankov was the Finance Minister and Deputy Prime Minister of Bulgaria from 2009 to 2013 and was representing Prime Minister Boyko Borisov in that summit. The impromptu meeting was called with just a few days notice by Polish Prime Minister Donald Tusk upon the request of Prime Minister Wen.

In the Warsaw meeting, Premier Wen revealed that the Chinese government had worked with academics since 2010 on the idea of bringing different countries along the old Silk Road economically closer through the proposed new initiative of "New Silk Road". The impromptu meeting was to solicit the attending countries' perspective on this unilateral initiative. In the subsequent one-on-one private meetings, Premier Wen further revealed that China wanted to know more about the Silk Road countries in order to explore investment and infrastructure business exchange with these countries. He acknowledged that Chinese companies have not been successful in the many European Union-funded (EU) infrastructure projects in new EU countries, like Bulgaria, Romania and Poland, in the past despite Chinese companies submitting the lowest bid. Somehow objectively or subjectively, Chinese companies proposals were consistently rejected for quality reasons. He admitted that China had no experience as contractors and investors in the CEE countries and it must learn more about these countries to break into the market. The Chinese hopes that the "New Silk Road" initiative will help the Chinese companies overcome the latecomer disadvantage and break into the CEE market.[1]

The impromptu summit in October 2011 subsequently laid the groundwork of annual China–CEE summit, which started in 2012 at Warsaw, followed by subsequent summits at Bucharest, Belgrade and Suzhou. Chinese government has set up the "Secretariat for Cooperation between China and CEE Countries" to deal with communication, coordination and implementation of cooperation work between China and CEE countries. The secretariat is headed by a foreign vice minister with members from 18 Chinese government ministries and 16 national coordinators from 16 CEE countries. A China–CEE Investment Cooperation Fund of USD$500 million was set up with China's Export–Import Bank (Exim Bank) holding 94% shares and

[1] Djankov, Simeon, Multilateral Development Banks & Asian Investment: Room for More? Lecture. Washington, September 30, 2015.

Hungarian Exim Bank holding the rest 6%. The fund has a standby credit line facility of USD$10 billion from Chinese commercial banks.

The account of Simeon Djankov puts 2010 as the genesis of the idea "Silk Road Economic Belt" and the basic economic rationale of the Chinese initiative is clear. President Xi's proposal of the new "21st Century Maritime Silk Road" in his address to the Indonesian parliament at Jakarta in October 2013 is just a simple extension of the same idea to a different geographical area.

"Silk Road Economic Belt" and "21st Century Maritime Silk Road" ideas were subsequently combined into the "One Belt, One Road" (OBOR) initiative. The plan is to enhance China's trade and financial linkage with countries along OBOR through the creation of an unbroken transport and infrastructure network made up of "Silk Road Economic Belt" countries across Western and Central Asia to Europe and the "21st Century Maritime Silk Road" extending from China to Southeast Asia and passing Middle East to Europe. OBOR countries cover 2/3 of the global population and more than 1/3 of the global GDP; it is the most ambitious infrastructure program to be ever placed on the table of world economic history.

The fact that the OBOR initiative was launched in 2013, almost 3 years after its 2010 academic genesis and 2 years after its first unofficial debut in Warsaw means that China would have gained some operational experience on OBOR projects by now. In fact, China had scrapped the sticky sovereign guarantee provision in many of the infrastructure projects at CEE in the past 2½ years and replaced the funding method from sovereign guarantee loan to project finance. The change has facilitated many infrastructure projects in many CEE countries.[2] China has developed some operational expertise in handling overseas infrastructure loans or investment and is enjoying some good initial success. The challenge now is to replicate the earlier success when it scales up the program and try to minimize the natural pitfalls associated with long-term investment.

Economic rationale behind OBOR

The narrative of Simeon Djankov places the economic rationales at the center of OBOR initiative, the rising importance of China in the global

---

[2] *Ibid.*

economy rightfully places it in a position to look for ways to seek a higher profile and secure its new gains on global economy. We will look at the economic rationales of China to initiate OBOR.

Becoming more influential

It is generally agreed that a closer economic relationship through trade and investment is one of the best ways to forge alliances with strategically important countries. Since the 1997 Asian financial crisis until present date, China has adopted infrastructure investments as an economic counter-cyclical measure. As a result, China has built up cost-effective expertise in many areas of basic infrastructure such as power, port, highway, railway and telecom from the extensive infrastructure development. Multilateral development banks (MDBs) such as International Monetary Fund (IMF), World Bank (WB) and Asian Development Bank (ADB) have noted the success of infrastructure investment to underpin economic growth and they are recommending their member states to significantly increase infrastructure investment. ADB estimates that, between 2010 and 2020, Asia requires US$8 trillion on infrastructure investment and a significant portion of which can be met provided sound financing methods are used.[3] McKinsey cited that US$57 trillion is needed to be spent on building and maintaining infrastructure worldwide between 2013 and 2030 just to keep up with global growth.[4] The ability of many developing countries to embark on necessary infrastructure investments is hampered by their poor domestic savings and available expertise, as well as poor current account status that hurts their ability to import the required technology. We have noted that most of the countries under OBOR initiative are either unrated or rated below investment grade.[5]

China's ability to offer cost-effective infrastructure solution and provision of necessary financing fits well to the needs for many of these countries.

---

[3]Rathbone, Mark and Oliver Redrup, Developing Infrastructure in Asia Pacific: Outlook, Challenges and Solutions. PricewaterhouseCoopers Service LLP, 2014.

[4]Palter, Robert and Herbert Pohl, Money Isn't Everything (but We Need $57 Trillion for Infrastructure). *Infrastructure Journal & Project Finance Magazine*, 1 March, 2013.

[5]Van Praagh, Anna, Multilateral Development Banks & Asian Investment: Room for More? Lecture. Washington, 30 September 2015.

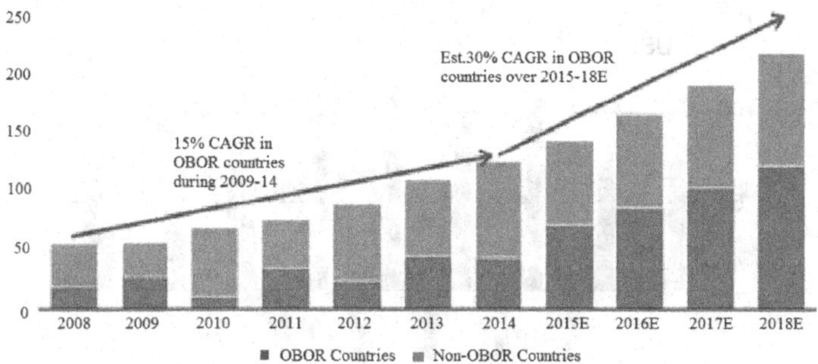

Figure 1: China annual outward investment inside and outside OBOR regions (US$ billion)

Source: Ministry of Commerce, China Global Investment Tracker complied by the American Enterprise institute and The Heritage Foundation, USB estimates

Figure 1 shows the increasing share of OBOR countries in the overseas direct investment (ODI) of China.

Increasing Chinese goods and services export

Some sectors facing overcapacity problems in the domestic market are in demand overseas, e.g. railway equipment, construction, building materials and capital. We should note that exporting capital, importing foreign demand and addressing overcapacity issues are just different aspects of the same issue — China's excessive savings need an outlet. Chinese government used to be a happy passive investor in low-yielding US Treasury bonds before, now the government evidently wants to shift part of the savings to higher risk but real commercially-related direct lending and/or investment to OBOR countries. Such a transition, if executed properly, will benefit the real economy of China much more than the passive US Treasury holdings. In 2014, Chinese companies' ODI had surpassed foreign direct investment (FDI) to China and the trend is likely to continue.[6] Figure 2 highlights the change of China's role from an investment destination to an investment source.

[6] David, Cui, Tian Tracy and Tai Katherine, One Belt & One Road, Great Expectation. Lecture. China, 16 March 2015.

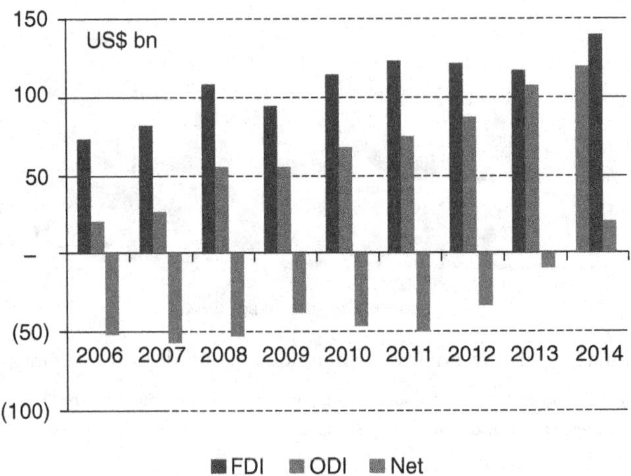

Figure 2: China FDI vs. ODI in value

Source: CEIC, BofA Merrill Lynch Global Research

A greater say in global financial architecture

China's economic size is not in tune with its representation in the existing global financial architecture essentially formed around 1944 Bretton Woods agreement, especially IMF, WB and the ADB. China's nominal GDP share in 2014 was almost 14% of the world, but its outstanding voting share assignment in the three institutions were only 4%, 4.42% and 5.5%, respectively. The implicit voting bloc arrangement among European countries, the US and Japan also meant that management of these institutions is always skewed towards the vested interest of the Europeans in IMF, the Americans in WB and the Japanese in ADB. Different approaches in dealing with the Asian financial crisis in 1998 and Euro crisis post-2008 have raised the issue of discrimination among members in IMF. Budget constraints of developed members of WB and ADB had forced them to shift focus from asset-heavy model of development loan granting to asset-light model of soft technical advisory assistance and cofinancing arrangements, leaving a huge funding gap in developing countries' infrastructure requirements.

Reform efforts at these institutions to reflect China's rising economic status as the biggest trading country and holder of largest foreign exchange reserves with over 30% of total global official reserves are not always successful.

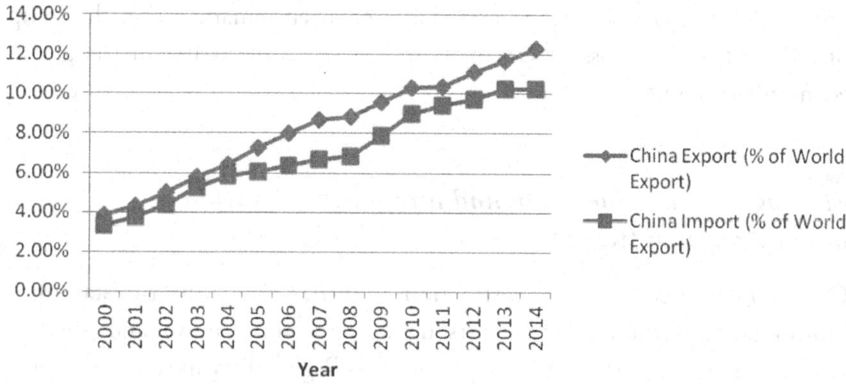

Figure 3: Chain trade (% of world trade)

US Congress withheld the 14th general quota increase plan of IMF that was approved in 2010 and that would have increased China's share in IMF from 4% to 6.4%. What US Congress will do to the 15th general quota increase slate to be approved by IMF in the immediate future is even more questionable, the new round will further increase China's share to 10.5% and cut US share to 14.9%. It will be the first time that US share will fall below 15% in IMF history and deprive US of the effective veto power. IMF charter stipulates that certain major decisions require 85% approval. Figure 3 highlights the spectacular rise of Chinese share of global trade in recent years.

China's launch of Asian Infrastructure Investment Bank (AIIB) holds the potential to significantly affect the global landscape of MDB financing. Though the bank will only start its operation from 2016 and the first loan release is targeted at 2Q 2016. The designated AIIB President, Jin Liqun's promise of a clean, lean and green bank that will uphold the highest social and environmental standard, minimize undue loan conditionality and work on faster loan processing speed than its rival highlighted the existing MDBs' deficiency in meeting its member's need.[7] AIIB had generated incredible public attention of any new multilateral financial institution.

[7] Donnan, Shawn, and Demetri Sevastopulo, AIIB Head Vows to Be Clean, Lean & Green-and Fast. Dated 25 October 2015 in *FT.com*. [downloaded 28 October 2015], available at http://www.ft.com/intl/cms/s/0/b6f95846-7b0d-11e5-a1fe-567b37f80b64.html?ftcamp=crm/email/20151025/nbe/AsiaMorningHeadlines/product#axzz3przV48Pp.

Former US treasury secretary Larry Summers even remarked that the setup of AIIB reflects the loss of US in its role as the underwriter of the global economic system.[8]

Moving up the value chain and internationalization of the Renminbi (RMB)

OBOR may open doors in destination countries for China to establish a foothold in important service sectors, including banking, power and telecom. A wider usage of RMB that comes with OBOR globally will serve as important impetus to expand the influence of China's financial sector overseas. There is market speculation that IMF approved the RMB inclusion in the Special Drawing Right (SDR) on November 2015 after taking into account the potential of a wider and more free use of RMB under OBOR. With better connectivity, in the long term, China may be able to relocate some of the low-end manufacturing capacities to these countries and thus, focus on the more value-added parts of the value chain.

Development of inland provinces

The main force behind regional rebalancing in China today focuses on relocation of manufacturing facilities from affluent coastal region to inland provinces in order to take advantage of cheap land, labor and more lenient environment regulation. The inland migration has been successful in mitigating the outward migration loss of many low-value manufacturing to other countries and also helps to uplift the economies of many inland provinces. However, inland provinces suffer from exports via seaborne route, OBOR will not only open the Central Asia market to the inland provinces manufacturing goods, it will also lower logistic costs significantly for inland provinces in the export market once initial logistic bottleneck is worked out.

---

[8] Summers, Larry, Time US Leadership Woke up to New Economic Era, dated 5 April 2014 in *Larry Summers'* blog [downloaded on 11 December 2015], available at http://larrysummers.com/2015/04/05/time-us-leadership-woke-up-to-new-economic-era/.

Enhancing economic security

When President Obama launched Trans Pacific Partnership (TPP) negotiation that excluded China in 2009, his declared intention of US retaking global leadership in trade negotiation from China caused much chagrin among the Chinese leaders. Many observers attributed the 2010 genesis of OBOR as a pushback against the TPP which was perceived as an attempt to hurt the economic security of China.

European Union is the single biggest trading bloc of China and developing multiple transit routes to Europe through OBOR will enhance the economic security of China. Central Asian countries along OBOR routes also provide some diversification of China's energy import requirement and enhance the Chinese energy security.

Funding institutions involved with OBOR

The following table provides the list of funding institutions of potential OBOR projects. One should note that many of these institutions have been working on Chinese infrastructure export funding for some time and their involvement in OBOR is not a new business area for them. There are misunderstandings in many quarters that OBOR is a new political initiative camouflaged under economic connectivity and decides on political basis rather than economic merit, hence the project risk involved is significant. In actual fact, essentially all of the OBOR projects being signed, worked on and in the few cases finalized under the OBOR initiative in Europe are projects in which the project preparation and evaluation was started with a different entity — either development agency or commercial bank. Many of these projects were basically shelved for one reason or another and did not get to the end. In most cases, the reasons to these projects being blocked are not economic but problems in other areas. The Chinese investors/partners would often return and work out some solutions to the blocking issues and proceed to fund the projects under OBOR. The famous 770 km US$15 billion Moscow–Kazan high-speed rail project is a typical example of such project. The economic merit of the OBOR projects thus far is better than commonly perceived and risk is more manageable as well.[9]

[9] Djankov, Simeon, Multilateral Development Banks & Asian Investment: Room for More? Lecture. Washington, 30 September 2015.

Name	Year	Resources Size (US$ — Billion)	Partners
AIIB	2015	100	57 member state
BRICS Development Bank	2015	100	Brazil, Russia, India, South Africa
Silk Road Fund	2015	40	
China Policy Banks — China Development Bank and China Exim Bank	1993		
Major Chinese Banks — Bank of China, Industrial and Commercial Bank of Chinas (ICBC), China Construction Bank (CCB) … etc.			

AIIB — An Origin against all odds

No MDB, in memory, had generated that much controversy on its formation as compared to the AIIB. AIIB is regarded by some as a rival to the dominance of Bretton Woods institutions like IMF, WB and the Bretton Woods system associated ADB. These institutions are perceived by many developing countries as proxies of developed countries like the United States and are not performing a good job in serving its developing country members. Many Americans also see AIIB as a significant challenger to America's decades-old leadership in Asia.[10] The United Nations took a more positive stance toward AIIB and describe it as "scaling up financing for sustainable development for the concern of Global Economic Governance".[11]

When the UK became the first major Western country to apply to join AIIB in early March 2015, US National Security Council released a statement to *The Guardian* in London: "Our position on the AIIB remains clear and consistent. The United States and many major global economies all

[10] Support for China-led Development Bank Grows despite US Opposition, dated 13 March 2015 in *The Guardian* [downloaded on 15 December 2015], available at http://www.theguardian.com/world/2015/mar/13/support-china-led-development-bank-grows-despite-us-opposition-australia-uk-new-zealand-asia.

[11] World Economic Situation and Prospects 2015-Chapter III International Finance for. UN, 2015 [downloaded on 12 December 2015], available at http://www.un.org/en/development/desa/policy/wesp/wesp_archive/2015wesp-ch3-en.pdf.

agree there is a pressing need to enhance infrastructure investment around the world. We believe any new multilateral institution should incorporate the high standards of WB & other regional MDB... Based on many discussions, we have concerns about whether the AIIB will meet these high standards, particularly related to governance, and environmental and social safeguards... The international community has a stake in seeing the AIIB complement the existing architecture, and to work effectively alongside the WB and ADB."

In addition, UK's decision to join AIIB was criticized by the US government. A US government official told *Financial Times*, "We are wary about a trend toward constant accommodation of China, which is not the best way to engage a rising power."[12] Though the opposition to AIIB has significantly subsided after its founding members' ratification of Article of Agreement in late June 2015, US, Japan and Canada remain out of AIIB. US and Japan have not indicated any interest to join the bank anytime soon, however, many observers expect Canada to join as a non-founding member in 2016. Working relationship between AIIB and IMF, WB and ADB have been smooth and the existing MDBs are in active working meetings with the secretarial of AIIB organizing committee to work out joint infrastructure cofinancing program once AIIB is officially set up in 2016.

AIIB will complete its Article of Agreement stipulating legal formalities by the end of 2015 and will officially be set up in 2016 with 57 founding members composed of 37 regional members and 20 non-regional members.[13] The initial authorized capital is US$100 billion will be headquartered in Beijing. Former Vice Minister of Finance of China, ADB and WB veteran, Jin Liqun will be the inaugural president. President Jin revealed that there are more than 30 countries indicating interest to join AIIB after its official setup.[14] If all of the applicants are accepted by AIIB, its membership will

---

[12]Washington Rebukes Britain's Decision to Join China-backed Asian Infrastructure Bank, dated 13 March 2015 in *The Standard* [downloaded on 12 December 2015], available at http://www.thestandard.com.hk/breaking_news_detail.asp?id=58463&icid=2&d_str=20150313.

[13]List of AIIB founding members and their respective capital shares and voting rights are provided in Appendix 1.

[14]Over 20 Countries on 'waiting List' to Join AIIB: China, dated 19 September 2015 in *Channel News Asia* [downloaded on 12 December 2015], available at http://www.channelnewsasia.com/news/business/over-20-countries-on/2137808.html.

swell to more than 87 and it will have more members than ADB, which at the moment has 67 members made up of 48 regional members and 19 non-regional members.

AIIB — Operational principles

President Jin has stated some operating principles of the bank to address the market concern on issues of governance and transparency of AIIB as well as the unusual large share holding of China in AIIB. It is noted that the US is the largest shareholder of IMF and WB and it holds 16.5% and 16.3% of the voting rights, respectively, of these two organizations at the moment. In the case of ADB, Japan as the largest shareholder holds 13% of voting share. For AIIB, China holds 26.06% and the supermajority provision of major AIIB decision making is approved by 75% voting share. China thus holds an effective veto power on major decisions of AIIB and there are worries that AIIB will become a policy tool of China in its push for OBOR financing. One should note that US also yields effective veto power in IMF and WB as their supermajority provision stipulation is higher at 85%, so a lower shareholding still yields some sense of privileged position for the US at IMF and WB. However, holding effective veto power on major decisions does not mean that the country gets the control of the multilateral agencies. Historically, formal votes are rarely taken at these entities and the executive board strives for consensus on decision making. All these institutions' professional management team yields effective operational control on the business of the bank.[15]

Apparently with the blessing of the Chinese authority, President designate Jin Liqun has put forward the following operational philosophy for AIIB:[16]

First, AIIB is not a policy tool of Chinese government in its OBOR initiative. AIIB is an MDB that must serve the interests of all of its members. In case

---

[15] Posner, Eric and Alan Posner, Voting Rules in International Organizations, Public Law and Legal Theory Working Papers, 2014 [downloaded on 12 December 2015], available at http://chicagounbound.uchicago.edu/cgi/viewcontent.cgi?article=1448&context=public_law_and_legal_theory

[16] President-designate Talks about Plans for the Bank, dated 11 December 2015 in CCTV.com website [downloaded on 12 December 2015], available at http://english.cntv.cn/2015/12/11/VIDE1449826919588145.shtml.

of meritorious OBOR projects that AIIB will offer support, the bank will invest based on policies and loan conditions set by the Board of Governors of the Bank. The bank will pay equal attention to other non-OBOR Asian nations' projects as well.

Second, AIIB is not a challenger to global financial order, it is to complement the existing MDB and will concentrate on infrastructure investment. It will invest in five major areas during its initial stages — energy, transportation, rural development, urban development and logistics. WB and ADB supports AIIB and they are working for areas of cooperation.

Third, AIIB will uphold the highest social and environmental standard among MDBs. It will codify employee conduct, social and environmental standard after public consultation.[17] The bank will strive to be a clean, lean and green bank with faster loan processing speed to meet the needs of its members. It will minimize undue loan conditionality that hampers project implementation.[18]

Fourth, AIIB's management will be professional as well as international. English will be the operational language and USD is the operational currency. Staff are recruited on international basis by merits and compensation is similar to existing MDB standard.[19]

AIIB — The game changer in development banking

AIIB can provide a very helpful role in the success of OBOR infrastructure financing. Infrastructure financing is mostly long term and credit risks run high on people's mind when China embarks on such a large scale project. Though China is successful so far in cherry-picking good projects that failed

---

[17] Consultations on Draft Environmental and Social Framework, dated 1 August 2015 in *AIIB* website [downloaded on 12 December 2015], available at http://www.aiib.org/html/theme/Consultations_Draft/.

[18] Donnan, Shawn and Demetri Sevastopulo. AIIB Head Vows to Be Clean, Lean & Green-and Fast, dated 25 October 2015 in FT.com [downloaded on 28 October 2015], available at http://www.ft.com/intl/cms/s/0/b6f95846-7b0d-11e5-a1fe-567b37f80b64.html?ftcamp=crm/email/20151025/nbe/AsiaMorningHeadlines/product#axzz3przV48Pp.

[19] For the five vice president post openings, AIIB have received more than 140 international applicants and the position will be based on merit rather than nationality.

to get off the ground before and thus, minimizing the associated credit risk, such projects will run out soon and new projects with increasingly complicated backgrounds requiring more extensive expert evaluations will be the business norm going forward. A good MDB definitely possesses some advantage in this regard.

A rising power often gets embroiled in geopolitical disputes with neighbors. Neutral MDB like AIIB provides a forum for sound economic projects to continue amid troubled relations between China and the project recipient country.

An often overlooked issue on MDB credit extension to member countries is that there is never a default in MDB debt to its member. Also the capital increase around the time of global financial crisis indicates strong government shareholder support to MDB. On average, MDB debts are more highly rated than its member's individual sovereign debt. This can significantly lower the funding cost of MDB infrastructure loan. The number of MDB that have become active in capital markets has grown significantly in the past decade and the market is increasingly willing to participate in sound MDB initiated infrastructure loans.[20] This is probably the most important benefit to China from a successful AIIB. AIIB can source funds cheaper than China and mobilize a larger pool of fund on OBOR or other projects if it is successfully ran. Figure 4 highlights the advantage enjoyed by MDB.

AIIB has already introduced a competitive dynamic to the global financial system that was not there before. Both the WB and ADB are reviewing its ratio of operating cost in relation to loan. It is interesting to note that WB gets around 10,000 staff costing US$2.4 billion annually to run a new approved loan volume of US$40 billion, while ADB has around 3,000 staff to run an annual new loan of around US$15 billion. The idea of President Jin Liqun to run the bank with a staff level of 500–600 and an annual new loan approval volume of up to US$15 billion highlights the potential cost-saving measures the existing MDB can implement. The idea of a non-resident board, smaller staff, flatter organization, speedier loan approval procedures are now the topics of the day in many MDBs.[21]

---

[20] Hess, Steven, Multilateral Banks Playing Growing Role in Funding Global Development. Lecture, 30 September 2015.

[21] Industry observer often use 7–9 years as the time frame of a typical WB/ADB medium-size infrastructure from initiation to completion. AIIB had stated they will try to cut the time frame to less than 5 years.

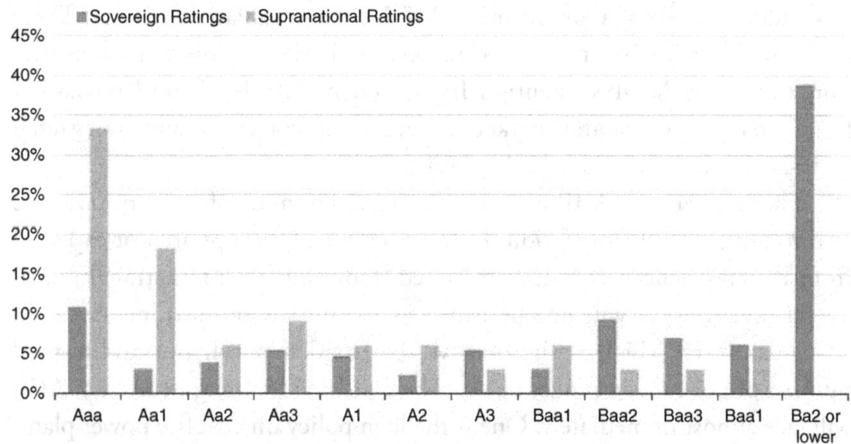

Figure 4: Aaa and Aa rating dominate
Source: Moody's

AIIB has prompted other actors to accelerate their own steps in filling the infrastructure gap. The G20 launched a global infrastructure initiative with a hub in Australia. WB increased its funding and plans to increase more in the future. It also launched a global infrastructure facility that will hopefully serve as a platform to bringing various actors to fund infrastructure development. There are also various new regional programs being set up or under planning by regional MDBs.

AIIB could also contribute or change the existing pattern of infrastructure financing by adopting certain kinds of new financing methods that China had used successfully in recent years in the international infrastructure market. A resource financed infrastructure approach which has been actively practiced by China in recent years is now a serious subject of study by WB staff to verify how the new model can be adopted.

An interesting area to watch is how China's emphasis on infrastructure loans that suit local development needs and de-emphasizing the need of the recipient country to adopt traditional free-market principles of privatization and deregulation might be watched by the existing MDBs.[22] A lot of social issues such as poverty alleviation, democracy, freedom, human rights, religion, women's advancement, climate change, health issues, education

[22] Wang, Hongying, Multilateral Development Banks & Asian Investment: Room for More? Lecture. Washington, 30 September 2015.

were added in recent years in many MDB's loan evaluation criteria. These issues are laudable but they often unnecessarily delay project implementation and divert MDB's attention from their main role of fund mediation from international capital market to developing countries, and overstretch its financial, human and logistic resources.

The secretariat of AIIB has recruited a good number of veteran ADB and WB to jumpstart the operation. Initial operational hiccups are not expected from the experienced core staff recruited. However, an international multilateral organization will not be expected to run smoothly from day 1, in particular, AIIB which is the first MDB that China will run and a good number of policy issues must be set. There are two looming issues that AIIB will face almost immediately. One is the loan policy on coal fire power plant. WB and ADB had refrained from coal fire power plant financing in the past few years and yet coal fire power plant is the cheapest baseload electricity source for developing countries. Should AIIB finance coal fire power plant and if so, what kind of pollutant emission standard and carbon emission standard should it mandate without unduly raising too much electricity cost will be an acid test on the operational skill of the management. Second is the credit rating of AIIB. China is apparently looking at AAA rating in Moody's rating scale and a lower scale will hurt its international funding effort down the road. Will AIIB seek an early credit rating after its setup or will it rely on Chinese financial market funding in the early stage of operation is interesting to watch. President Jin had indicated that in case AIIB does not get a top rating, it will turn to Chinese market to fund its initial operation.[23]

AIIB will surely face a steep learning curve ahead; how long will the management take to overcome hurdles and become a leading MDB will serve as an acid test of China's soft power. In a certain sense, the success or failure of AIIB will also determine the fate of OBOR.

BRICS Development Bank (New Development Bank — NDB)

The bank was set up in 2015 by the five BRICS member countries — Brazil, Russia, India, China and South Africa. Each participant country holds an equal number of shares and equal voting rights, as such, none of the coun-

[23] *Ibid.*

tries will have veto power. The bank's headquarters will be in Shanghai with major officials such as president, chairman of the board and chairman of the board of governors serving on a rotating basis. Indian banker K.V. Kamath was appointed as the inaugural president, the inaugural chairman of the Board of Directors is from Brazil and the inaugural chairman of the Board of Governors will be a Russian. The authorized capital is US$100 billion and the goal of the bank is to "mobilize resources for infrastructure and sustainable development projects in BRICS and other emerging economies and developing countries".

NDB has an authorized capital of US$100 billion and it has set an ambitious lending target of up to US$34 billion annually. The bank can be perceived as a sort of pushback against recent MDB's philosophy of social priorities such as education, healthcare, women's right over physical infrastructure.[24] In terms of founding philosophy, NDB share a lot of similarity with AIIB.

NDB's fortune rise and fall with that of its founding stockholders. The taper scare in 2013 summer expose the economic weakness of three of the five founding members: Brazil, India and South Africa. These three countries are among the fragile five mentioned in the business press. The commodity collapse of 2015 also places another member country, Russia, to economic tailspin. The only economically strong member country, China, is going through its internal economic restructuring and it has launched a similar MDB, AIIB. It is becoming increasingly apparent that China is concentrating its resources on AIIB and NDB is suffering from the absence of an anchor investor.

NDB has made few public statements in relation to its forthcoming debut in 2016. In contrast to the active management style of AIIB's Jin, K.V. Kamath gave few interviews and the public only knew recently that NDB is trying to release its first loan by the second quarter of 2016 and will work with AIIB and other MDB on projects cooperation.

An immediate challenge to NDB is the credit rating it can get from international rating agencies. Based on the current credit rating of Moody's, China's sovereign rating is AA3 while India is BAA3 (the lowest investment

---

[24] Khanna, Parag. New BRICS Bank a Building Block of Alternative World Order, dated 18 June 2014 in *Huffington Post* [downloaded on 12 December 2015], available at http://www.huffingtonpost.com/parag-khanna/new-brics-bank_b_5600027.html.

grade assignment). Brazil's current rating is also BAA3 but are facing reviews and there is a very high likelihood of a downgrade in the immediate future, any downgrade will move Brazil to speculative grade assignment. South Africa's current rating is BAA2 and Russia's current rating is BA1, which are both speculative grade. Even MDB usually enjoys a higher credit rating than individual member states, and NDB's equal stockholding structure means the absence of an anchor player. Initial rating on NDB might not be high and it cannot afford the luxury of AIIB to forego international bond market and turn to domestic market for funding.

The prospect of NDB as a major conduit of OBOR projects is not expected to be significant in the initial stage. Most of its activities will probably be concentrated within its five members.

Silk Road Fund

The US$40 billion fund was set up in 2015 with an impressive shareholder slate. China foreign exchange reserve (SAFE) holds 65% share, China Exim bank 15%, China sovereign country fund China Investment Corporation (CIC) 15%, China Development Bank (CDB) 5%. The combined assets of these four stockholders run an impressive US$7 trillion. The fund will run on a long-term view private equity fund model similar to International Finance Corporation (IFC) of WB. It will also provide investment and financing support for infrastructure, resources, industrial, financial cooperation and other projects involved in the Belt and Road initiative. First president is Madame Jin Qi, who had served as deputy director of People's Bank of China's foreign financial institution department and assistant governor.

The fund's first investment is the US$1.65 billion 720 MW (4 × 183 MW Francis turbine unit) Karot hydroelectric project. The project will generate an annual power output of 3.2 billion Kwh. This Silk Road fund joins China Three Gorges South Asia Investment Ltd. (CTGC) to put up 20% of the equity in the Karot project.

IFC is one of the more successful WB subsidiaries and its leading strategic investor role in Public–Private Partnership (PPP) is well known. Silk Road Fund will probably take on a leading public investor role with China's State-Owned Enterprises (SOEs) taking on the private role in future OBOR-related projects.

China policy banks — CDB & EXIM Bank

China is the biggest overseas contractor today. Chinese Ministry of Commerce data has shown that Chinese contractors' estimated 2015 overseas revenue and new contract win will hit US$160 billion and US$190 billion, respectively. That is a significant increase from US$30 billion and US$70 billion in 2006. CDB and Exim Bank play an indispensable role in China's successful overseas construction market.[25]

CDB was set up in 1994 with an assigned mandate of assisting national government's development policies. One of the mission statements of CDB is "facilitating China's cross-border investment & global business cooperation". CDB raises funds through domestic bond issuance and its bonds are assigned risk-free assets status by the Chinese banking authority. The bank is the second biggest bond issuer of the country, just behind the Ministry of Finance. In 2014, CDB raised RMB 1,175 billion in domestic bond market.

CDB is the biggest development bank in the world. At the end of 2014, its asset is RMB 10.32 trillion, with a loan portfolio of RMB 7.942 trillion, equity standing at RMB 681 billion, profits for 2014 are 97.7 billion and non-performing loan at 0.65%. CDB did not break down its overseas loan portfolio, however, its foreign loan stands at RMB 1.56 trillion at the end of 2014, and this amount most likely reflects a significant portion of its overseas loan support to Chinese contractors. It should be noted that CDB is the biggest foreign currency loan provider in China.[26] CDB extended more than RMB 2 trillion new loan in 2014, a much higher figure than WB's fiscal commitment of US$60 billion (RMB 380 billion) in loans, grants, equity investment and guarantees to partner country and private business.

China Exim Bank is another policy bank set up in 1994 to promote foreign trade and investment as well as development assistance in concessional funding. At the end of 2014, bank assets were at RMB 2.37 trillion, with outstanding loans at RMB 1.74 trillion and profit for the year was RMB 4 billion. It has committed various financial facilities of RMB 995 billion and disbursed RMB 921 billion in 2014. The bank provides fund support to expedite RMB 292.5 billion exports and RMB 140 billion imports. Though

[25] *Ibid.*

[26] "Annual Report 2014. China Development Bank, 2015 [download on 12 December 2015], available at http://www.cdb.com.cn/english/Column.asp?ColumnId=91.

the bank is smaller in scale than CDB, its imprint in overseas markets are just as important as CDB. Most of the CDB resources are devoted to the domestic market and its overseas exposure is not much larger than Exim Bank. The fact that Exim Bank is the only policy bank allowed to provide concessionary loans make it a preferred lender in many cases.

CDB and Exim Bank recently received a capital infusion from the government of US$48 billion and US$45 billion, respectively on July 2015. The move will significantly strengthen their lending capacity in the forthcoming OBOR infrastructure financing. These two institutions are expected to retain their role as dominant player of Chinese infrastructure export in the near to medium term. They have developed certain expertise in handling foreign development funding and overseas concessionary loan granting.

Major Chinese state commercial banks — ICBC, CCB, Agricultural Bank of China (ABC), BOC

A high domestic savings rate that approaches half of GDP and the concentration of financial asset system in the banking sector allows China to build a huge banking system. Figure 5 shows the relative size of China's banking system as

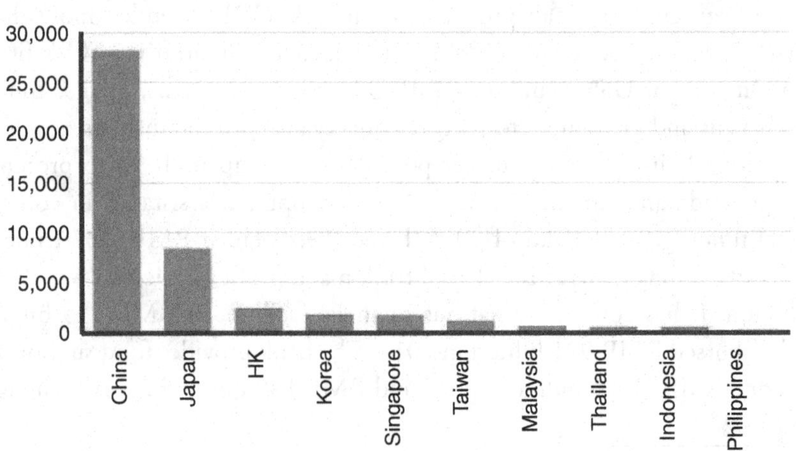

Figure 5: Relative size of different Asian banking markers, US$ billion at YE14E

Source: Central Banks, CEIC, UBS Banks team

compared to its Asian neighbors. We have just highlighted Asian countries as their financial system are much more bank-centric than other regions.

Chinese commercial banks overseas businesses used to concentrate on trade financing. However, OBOR initiative and RMB internationalization have opened many new business areas for these institutions. The burgeoning expansion of banking assets, risk diversification and seeking higher returns all provide justifiable incentives for the commercial banks to venture overseas.

BOC is the biggest Chinese bank overseas, and it recently announced that the bank had lent out US$10 billion to OBOR-related loans in the first half of 2015 and was on the way to reach US$20 billion OBOR-related new lending in 2015. OBOR-related loan will be 16% of its new lending in 2015. For 2016–2018, the bank has committed US$100 billion or 22% of its forecasted new loans to OBOR-related loans. Even at such elevated level of new loan commitment, OBOR-related loans will just be 6% of its loan portfolio by the end of 2018, BOC's assets were at US$2.458 trillion at the end of 2014 and it is the fifth largest bank according to Forbes.

The biggest bank of the world, ICBC revealed that it has pledged US$10.9 billion to 73 overseas project along OBOR countries at the end of 2014.

CCB emerged later than BOC and ICBC, it is increasing its overseas branch network to 30 by the end of 2015 to look for opportunities arising from OBOR-related business.

ABC is a newcomer in overseas banking among the four major Chinese commercial bank and is not expected to be a major player in OBOR-related funding activities in the near future.

Chinese banking system assets are heavily concentrated in the domestic market as the following Figure 6 shows. The current overseas loans make up less than 3% of Chinese banking system total loans, a very low level in the global banking scene for a major trading country and a major economy. BOC is the most experienced in overseas banking business and its plan of US$100 billion in the next 3 years will constitute the bulk of major commercial bank loan commitment to OBOR initiative.

Other players — SOE & SCO Bank

Jakarta–Bandung high-speed rail project is a private commercial partnership with China SOE and Indonesia SOE. This novel approach avoid the sticky

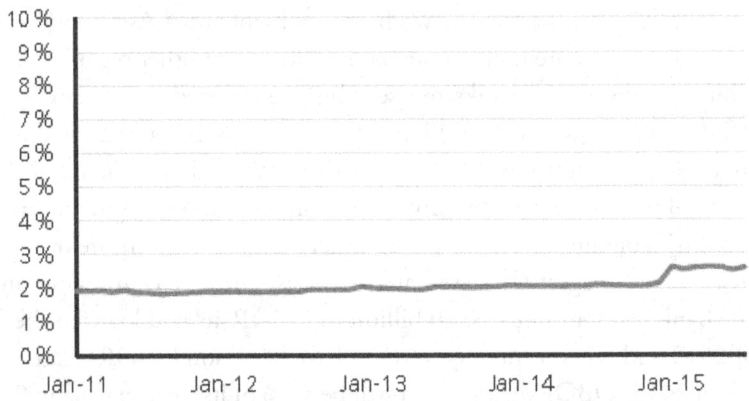

Figure 6: Overseas loans currently make up a fraction of China banking system total loans
Source: PBOC, UBS Banks team

issue of sovereign guarantee for the US$5.5 billion project. We should note the role played by SOE in the initiation, planning, negotiation and execution of the OBOR projects. Their ability to screen out economically sound projects will ultimately decide the success of OBOR initiatives.

Shanghai Cooperation Organization (SCO) is proposing to set up an SCO Bank to expedite OBOR-related project financing. Currently, the market is not looking at the idea too seriously. Out of the eight members of SCO: China, Kazakhstan, Kyrgyzstan, Russia, Tajikistan, Uzbekistan, India and Pakistan, Russia and India already has BRICS Bank to serve its need, Pakistan already received the US$46 billion OBOR funding commitment in April 2015 and Kazakhstan is an important energy partner in Central Asia to China. There seems to be no pressing need for such a new MDB. Institutional build up of a MDB takes time and the proposed SCO Bank is not expected to make material difference to OBOR projects in the immediate future.

Outlook for OBOR

Analysis on the funding source for OBOR indicates that China does possess sufficient financial resources, at the moment, to support its OBOR initiative. China already gained certain level of expertise in the infrastructure export through the SOEs such as China Communication Construction Corporation (CCC), China Railway Group (CRG), China Railway Rolling Stock

Corporation (CRRC), etc. They have obtained good overseas contract opportunities and the policy bank support have brought many of these opportunities to actual project implementation.

China is running an annual current account surplus of around US$300 billion, and committing such amounts of funding to OBOR financing is not going to hurt China's credit standing and financial system stability. Of course, we should note that OBOR is probably the most ambitious cross-border infrastructure initiative ever launched, scaling up earlier bilateral working model between China and the recipient country might not be a simple extension of modeling. The issue of country affordability, loan credit worthiness, long-term political stability and many more risk factors will be coming into the picture.

The Chinese government had set a deadline of 30 October 2015 in its solicitation of provincial inputs on the finalization of OBOR plan, how the plan is laid out will allow a more detailed analysis and lookout for its future prospect. Even in the absence of an integrated plan, Chinese overseas contract wins and execution is already at a high note, whether there is a need to overhaul the system or keep the existing system with a small twist are topics that observers are keenly looking into.

McKinsey estimated that the world needs an annual investment of US$2 trillion on infrastructure spending to keep the current pace of GDP growth. If China can indeed free up its annual current account surplus of US$300 billion for infrastructure investment around the world, particularly OBOR-related developing countries, the impact on global growth and poverty alleviation will be meaningful.

Appendix 1

Initial subscriptions to the authorized capital stock for countries which may become members in accordance with Article 58

Part A — Regional Members	% of Share	% of Vote
Australia	3.76	3.46
Azerbaijan	0.26	0.48
Bangladesh	0.67	0.83
Brunei Darussalam	0.05	0.31
Cambodia	0.06	0.32
China	30.34	26.06
Georgia	0.05	0.31
India	8.52	7.51
Indonesia	3.42	3.17
Iran	1.61	1.63
Israel	0.76	0.91
Jordan	0.12	0.37
Kazakhstan	0.74	0.89
Korea, South	3.81	3.50
Kuwait	0.55	0.73
Kyrgyz Republic	0.03	0.29
Lao People's Democratic Republic	0.04	0.30
Malaysia	0.11	0.36
Maldives	0.01	0.27
Mongolia	0.04	0.30
Myanmar	0.27	0.49
Nepal	0.08	0.33
New Zealand	0.47	0.66
Oman	0.26	0.49
Pakistan	1.05	1.16
Philippines	1.00	1.11
Qatar	0.62	0.79

(*Continued*)

Russia	6.66	5.93
Saudi Arabia	2.59	2.47
Singapore	0.25	0.48
Sri Lanka	0.27	0.50
Tajikistan	0.03	0.29
Thailand	1.45	1.50
Turkey	2.66	2.52
United Arab Emirates	1.21	1.29
Uzbekistan	0.22	0.45
Vietnam	0.68	0.84

Part B — Non-Regional Members	**% of Share**	**% of Vote**
Austria	0.51	0.70
Brazil	3.24	3.02
Denmark	0.38	0.58
Egypt	0.66	0.83
Finland	0.32	0.53
France	3.44	3.19
Germany	4.57	4.15
Iceland	0.02	0.28
Italy	2.62	2.49
Luxembourg	0.07	0.32
Malta	0.01	0.27
Netherlands	1.05	1.16
Norway	0.56	0.74
Poland	0.85	0.98
Portugal	0.07	0.32
South Africa	0.60	0.77
Spain	1.79	1.79
Sweden	0.27	0.50
Switzerland	0.72	0.87
United Kingdom	3.11	2.91
UNALLOCATED	**REST of 100%**	**REST of 100%**

Appendix 2

MDBs rated by Moody's as of September 2015 MDB

	Founding Year	Moody's Initial Rating	Current Rating
Africa Finance Corporation (AFC)	2007	2014	A3/Stable
African Development Bank (AfDB)	1963	1984	Aaa/Stable
African Export-Import Bank (AFREXIM)	1993	2010	Baa2/Stable
Arab Petroleum Investments Corp (APICORP)	1974	2010	Aa3/Stable
Asian Development Bank	1966	1975	Aaa/Stable
Black Sea Trade & Development Bank (BSTDB)	1997	2004	A2/Negative
Caribbean Development Bank (CDB)	1969	1992	Aa1/Stable
Central American Bank for Economic Integration (CABEI)	1960	2002	A1/Stable
Corporacion Andina de Fomento (CAF)	1968	1993	Aa3/Stable
Council of Europe Development Bank (CEB)	1956	1988	Aa1/Stable
East African Development Bank (EADB)	1967	2013	Baa3/Stable
European Financial Stability Facility (EFSF)	2010	2010	Aa1/Stable
Eurasian Development Bank (EDB)	2006	2007	Baa1/Stable
Eurofina	1956	1984	Aa1/Stable
European Bank for Reconstruction & Development (EBRD)	1991	1991	Aaa/Stable
European Investment Bank (EIB)	1958	1976	Aaa/Stable
European Investment Fund (EIF)	1994	2003	Aaa/Stable
European Stability Mechanism (ESM)	2012	2012	Aa1/Stable
European Union (EU)	1993	1997	Aaa/Stable
Fondo Latinoamericano de Reservas (FLAR)	1978	2002	Aa2/Stable
GuarantCo	2006	2014	A1/Stable
Gulf Investment Corporation G.S.C. (GIC)	1983	2002	A2/Stable
International Bank of Reconstruction & Development (IBRD)	1944	1962	Aaa/Stable

(*Continued*)

Appendix 2 (*Continued*)

	Founding Year	Moody's Initial Rating	Current Rating
Inter-American Development Bank (IADB)	1959	1975	Aaa/Stable
Inter-American Investment Corporation (IIC)	1985	2001	Aa2/Stable
International Finance Corporation (IFC)	1956	1989	Aaa/Stablc
International Investment Bank (IIB)	1970	2014	Baal/Stable
Islamic Corporation for the Development of the Private Sector (ICD)	1999	2015	Aa3/Stable
Islamic Development Bank (IsDB)	1975	2006	Aaa/Stable
Nordic Investment Bank (NIB)	1976	1980	Aaa/Stable
North America Development Bank (NADB)	1994	2010	Aal/Stable
PTA Bank	1985	2010	Bal/Stable
Shelter Afrique	1982	2011	Bal/Stable
The West African Development Bank (BOAD)	1973	2015	Baal/Stable

Source: Moody's , Issuers Article of Agreement

Chapter 12

Prospect of Chinese Rail Export Under "One Belt, One Road"

Henry CHAN Hing Lee

Background concept on "One Belt, One Road" (OBOR) and economic corridors

The "Silk Road Economic Belt" concept was first raised by President Xi Jinping, in September 2013, in an address to Kazakhstan's Nazarbayev University. A month later, he proposed the new "21st Century Maritime Silk Road" in his address to the Indonesian parliament at Jakarta. These two initiatives were subsequently combined into the OBOR initiatives. The announced objectives of OBOR are to enhance mutual trust, promote connectivity and share economic prosperity with the aim of reaching a "community of common destiny" for countries in OBOR.

OBOR aims to connect Asia, Europe and Africa along five routes. The first three routes are under "Silk Road Economic Belt": (1) link China to Europe through Central Asia and Russia; (2) link China with the Persian Gulf through Central Asia; (3) link China with Southeast Asia, South Asia and the Indian Ocean. The last two routes fall under "The 21st Century Maritime Silk Road", they are: (4) link China coastal ports to Europe through the South China Sea and Indian Ocean; and (5) link China coastal ports with the South Pacific Ocean through the South China Sea. Appendix 1 shows the conceptual map of OBOR.

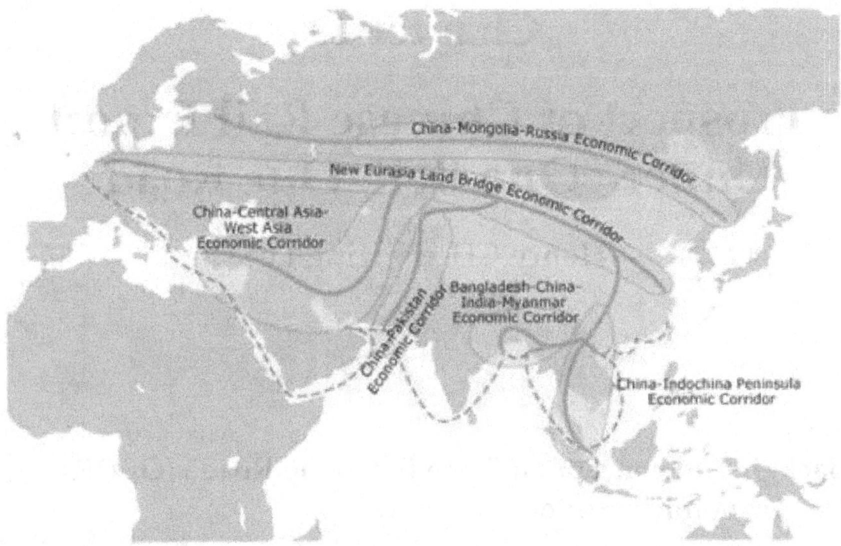

Figure 1: The Belt and Road initiative: Six economic corridors spanning Asia, Europe and Africa

Based on the five routes under OBOR,[1] China has identified six international economic cooperation corridors as shown in Figure 1: (1) China–Mongolia–Russia; (2) New Eurasia Land Bridge; (3) China–Central Asia–West Asia; (4) China–Pakistan; (5) Bangladesh–China–India–Myanmar; (6) China–Indochina Peninsula.

(1) China–Mongolia–Russia economic corridor — There is extensive border trade between the three countries at the moment. In September 2014, the three countries' heads agreed to forge tripartite cooperation on the basis of China–Russia, China–Mongolia and Russia–Mongolia bilateral ties. The three countries agreed to bring together the building of China's Silk Road Economic Belt, the renovation of Russia's Eurasia Land Bridge and the proposed development of Mongolia's Prairie Road. This

[1]The Belt and Road Initiative. HKTDC (Research), dated 19 August, 2015 [downloaded on 17 October 2015], available at http://china-trade-research.hktdc.com/business-news/article/One-Belt-One-Road/The-Belt-and-Road-Initiative/obor/en/1/1X000000/1X0A36B7.htm.

commitment will strengthen rail and highway connectivity and construction, advance customs clearance and transport facilitation, promote cross-national cooperation in transportation, and help establish the China–Russia–Mongolia Economic Corridor. In July 2015, the three leaders held a second meeting in the Russian city of Ufa and agreed to adopt the Mid-term Roadmap for Development of Trilateral Cooperation between China, Russia and Mongolia. The countries will formulate an outline of China–Russia–Mongolia Economic Corridor Cooperation that will align the Silk Road Economic Belt with the establishment of the Eurasia Economic Union and the Steppe Road Initiative. At the same time, the three countries will coordinate their respective economic and trade departments to promote trilateral trade that include the expansion of local currency in reciprocal trading, coordinate customs procedures to facilitate trade and explore the possibility of establishing a joint company for China–Russia–Mongolia rail transport and logistics, as well as investing in infrastructure construction projects. The US$50 billion projects under discussions include a network of 997 km new expressway linking China and Russia, 1,100 km electrified railway, expansion of the pan-Mongolia railway system, new oil and gas pipelines linking Russia and China. Some proposed projects under the China–Russia–Mongolia corridor are shown in Figure 2.

(2) New Eurasian continental economic corridor — The New Eurasia Land Bridge, also known as the Second Eurasia Land Bridge, is a group of railway routes originating from various parts of China running through Xinjiang to various parts of Europe. So far, China has opened eight international freight rail route offering cargo service under "one declaration, one inspection, one cargo release" in the eight routes. Please refer to Appendix 2 for the eight routes.

(3) China–Central Asia–Western Asia economic corridor — This corridor runs from Xinjiang in China and exits the country via Alashankou to join the railway networks of Central Asia and West Asia before reaching the Persian Gulf, the Mediterranean coast and the Arabian Peninsula. The corridor mainly covers five countries in Central Asia (Kazakhstan, Kyrgyzstan, Tajikistan, Uzbekistan and Turkmenistan) as well as Iran and Turkey in West Asia. The third China–Central Asia Cooperation Forum in June 2015 committed to jointly build the Silk Road

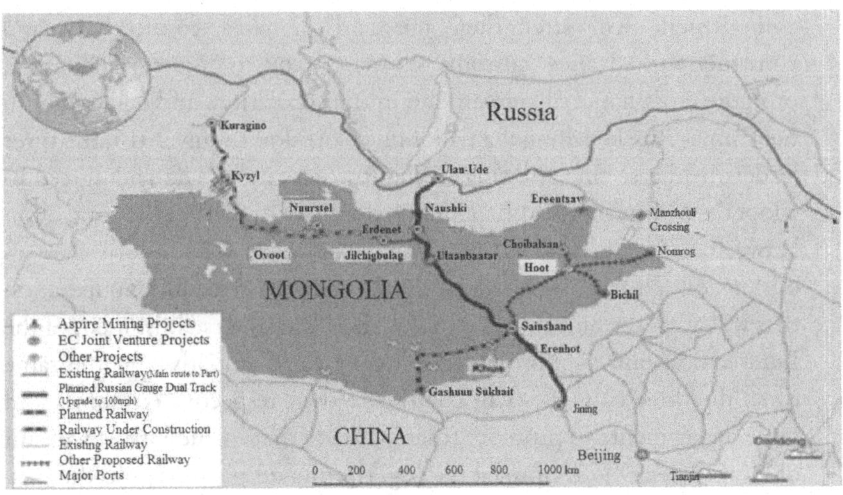

Figure 2: Proposed projects for China–Russia–Mongolia economic route

Economic Belt. Prior to that, China has signed bilateral agreements on the building of the Silk Road Economic Belt with Tajikistan, Kazakhstan, Uzbekistan and Kyrgyzstan. The national development strategies of the five Central Asian countries — including Kazakhstan's "Road to Brightness", Tajikistan's "Energy, Transport and Food", and Turkmenistan's "Strong and Happy Era" — all share common ground with the establishment of the Silk Road Economic Belt and the countries concerned will coordinate their national plans to the regional OBOR plans.

(4) China–Pakistan Economic Corridor — The idea is to build a 3,000 km economic corridor running from Kashgar, Xinjiang, in the north, to Pakistan's Gwadar Port in the south. In April 2015, China made a commitment to invest in projects and lend a total of US$46 billion to jump-start the program. So far, this is the biggest overseas investment project announced by China. The two governments have mapped out a provisional long-term plan for building highways, railways, oil and natural gas pipelines and optical fiber networks stretching from Kashgar to Gwadar Port. The whole program will take 10–12 years to complete. As of September 2015, more than 20 projects have been approved and the corridor is expected to be operational within 3 years.

(5) Bangladesh–China–India–Myanmar Economic Corridor — In December 2013, the official representatives from the four countries formed the Bangladesh–China–India–Myanmar Economic Corridor Joint Working Group and discussed the development prospects, high priority areas for cooperation and cooperation mechanisms for the economic corridor. Eventually, they reached consensus on cooperation in areas such as transportation infrastructure, investment and commercial circulation and people-to-people connectivity. They have also established the Bangladesh–China–India–Myanmar Economic Corridor joint study program.

(6) China–Indochina Peninsula Economic Corridor — Chinese Premier Li Keqiang put forward three suggestions to enhance economic cooperation of the six countries (Cambodia, China, Laos, Myanmar, Thailand and Vietnam) in the fifth Leaders Meeting on Greater Mekong Sub-regional Economic Cooperation in December 2014 at Bangkok: (1) to jointly plan and build an extensive transportation network, as well as industrial cooperation projects; (2) creating a new mode of cooperation for fundraising; and (3) promoting sustainable and coordinated socio-economic development. Currently, the countries along the Greater Mekong River are engaged in building nine cross-national highways, connecting east and west and linking north to south. A number of these construction projects have been completed. Guangxi, for example, has already finished work on an expressway leading to the Friendship Gate and the port of Dongxing at the China–Vietnam border. The province has also opened an international rail line, running from Nanning to Hanoi, as well as introducing air routes to several major Southeast Asian cities.

Initial action plan on OBOR

In March 2015, the Chinese government released an action plan regarding the principles, framework, cooperation priorities and mechanisms in the Belt and Road Initiative. The plan states that "Countries along the Belt and Road should improve the connectivity of their infrastructure construction plans and technical standard systems, jointly push forward the construction of international trunk passageways, and form an infrastructure network connecting all sub-regions in Asia, and between Asia, Europe and Africa step by step".

China has put up US$40 billion Silk Road Fund and initiated the establishment of US$100 billion Asian Infrastructure Investment Bank (AIIB) to complement its existing export funding agency China Development Bank (CDB) and China Export-Import Bank (Ex-Im Bank) to provide funding for physical infrastructure in developing countries along the OBOR route. The list of 64 countries identified by China in the OBOR program is in Appendix 2. We should note that the concept of OBOR reflects the Chinese desire to promote mutual beneficial developmental economics with friendly neighbors. The OBOR boundaries are fluid and dynamic. China's role as the architect, financier and builder of the OBOR community requires the active cooperation of the partner countries and China is still in the process of soliciting the participation of many of the identified countries at the moment. Countries will be added to OBOR as well as taken away from the list depending on the availability of sound projects and interest of the countries concerned. OBOR is a new concept and is only 2 years old, and most of the economic corridor projects are stuck at discussion stage sans the China–Pakistan economic corridor projects.

Infrastructure connectivity is a priority in the implementation of the OBOR initiative. Observers are focused on the rail connectivity in the OBOR Initiative. The unprecedented speed and scale that China has set up its passenger High-Speed Rail (HSR) system, from virtually zero to 19,000 km in less than a decade's time, at a significantly lower cost that even a lower middle-income country with per capita of US$3,000 can afford has turned many neighboring countries to take a second look at using rail as a viable land transport backbone for passengers *in lieu* of the post WWII transport network norm of highways and airports.

During the six nationwide railway "Speed Up" campaigns which China embarked on, the experience the Chinese gained in upgrading conventional track to run trains at sub-high speed of up to 180 km/h at a fraction of the cost of building a new line has also captured the attention of many developing countries interested at using rail system. Until the first Chinese standard Jakarta–Bandung HSR contract was awarded on 16 October 2015, the conventional rolling stock up to 180 km/h combo passenger–cargo rail system is the main export product and technology of China.

This chapter will look at the recent history of Chinese railway developments, in particular the HSR technology. Analyzing its strength and weakness as the means of connectivity in the OBOR on the economic corridor framework, in particular, we will highlight the economic and geopolitical challenges that these projects are likely to face and lay down conditions that will determine the outcome of these projects.

Chinese development of HSR

In early 1990s, Chinese commercial train service ran at an average speed of only 48 km/h under a congested railway network and it was steadily losing its market share to air transportation and the expanding highway network. Ministry of Railway (MOR) proposed to build a high-speed railway between Beijing and Shanghai in early 1990. This proposal was accepted by the central government, however, raging debates ensued inside China on whether the country should adopt conventional high-speed wheel technology or maglev technology at that time. This has caused significant delays in the project and construction did not start until the 2000s. In 2004, the State Council in its *Mid-to-Long Term Railway Development Plan*, adopted conventional track HSR technology over maglev for the Beijing–Shanghai HSR and three other north–south HSR lines. This decision ended the debate and cleared the way for rapid construction of standard gauge (1,435 mm), passenger dedicated HSR lines in China. While the discussion on HSR was going on, MOR embarked on a series of nationwide "Speed Up" campaign to increase the service speed and capacity on existing lines. Measures employed include double-tracking, electrification, improvements in grade (through tunnels and bridges), reductions in turn curvature, installation of continuous welded rail, development of new locomotives and modernizing of signaling systems. Appendix 3 provides the summary of the six nationwide rail speed upgrades. What is more astonishing is that the new technologies employed during the "Speed Up" projects were almost all developed indigenously. This experience not only made China the world technology leader in the upgrading of conventional track to either sub-high speed passenger lines (top speed below 200 km/h in the route) or combo cargo–passenger line, it has also laid the foundation for the subsequent speedy absorption of HSR technologies from foreign joint venture partners after 2004. Upgrading existing tracks to run sub-high speed train is a technological area often neglected by major developed countries' rolling stock companies but this know-how offers significant economic benefits to developing countries where old rail network can be rehabilitated to provide cheaper alternatives.

HSR Technology import through joint venture

China is a latecomer to the HSR industry. Japan ran the world's first HSR Shinkansen in 1964, France TGV in 1981 and that of Germany ICE in 1991, whereas China only started building the Beijing–Shanghai HSR in 2004. China's early high-speed trains were imported or built under technology transfer agreements with foreign train-makers including Alstom, Siemens, Bombardier and Kawasaki Heavy Industries.[2] In 2004, Railway Ministry tasked its two rolling stock manufacturing arms, China South Rail (CSR) and China North Rail (CNR) to work with foreign technical partner to produce rolling stock for HSR project under technical transfer agreement,[3] the electric multiple unit (train sets) produced were given the designations CRH-1 through CRH-5:

(1) CRH-1 series are produced by Bombardier's joint venture CSR Sifang (Qingdao) Transportation (BST);
    - CRH-1A: an eight-car version; maximum operating speed of 250 km/h, derived from Bombadier Regina design.
    - CRH-1B: a modified 16-car version; maximum operating speed of 250 km/h, derived from Bombadier Regina design.
    - CRH-1E: a 16-car high-speed sleeper version; maximum operating speed of 250 km/h, derived from Bombadier Zefiro 250 design.

(2) CRH-2 series are produced by CSR Sifang under license from Kawasaki with designs derived from Shinkansen E2-1000 series.

[2] Railway Ministry practically owned all railways in China before March 2013 and it likewise manufactured all rolling stocks and rail related equipment. China Railway Corporation (CRC) took over all assets of Railway Ministry in March 2013.

[3] CSR and CNR were merged at mid-2015 to form China Railway Rolling Corporation (CRRC).

- CRH-2A: an 8-car version; maximum operating speed 250 km/h.
- CRH-2B: a modified 16-car version of CRH-2; maximum operating speed of 250 km/h.
- CRH-2C (Stage one): an 8-car version; maximum operating speed of 300 km/h.
- CRH-2C (Stage two): an 8-car model; maximum operating speed of 350 km/h.
- CRH-2E: a 16-car version of CRH-2 with sleeping cars, maximum speed of 250km/h.

(3) CRH-3 is produced by CNR under license from Siemens ICE-3 (class 403)

- CRH-3: an 8-car model, maximum operating speed of 350 km/h.

(4) CRH-5A is produced by CNR under license from Alstom, derived from Alstom Pendolino ETR 600.

- CRH-5A: an 8-car model, maximum operating speed of 250 km/h.

The Chinese Railway Ministry had set the target of achieving indigenous HSR technology at the top priority when they licensed the imported technology in mid-2000s. Chinese train-makers, after receiving transferred foreign technology, have been able to achieve a considerable degree of self-sufficiency in making the next generation of high-speed trains by developing indigenous capability to produce key parts and improvising upon foreign designs. China currently holds many new patents related to the internal components of these train sets since they have re-designed major components so the trains can run at a much higher speed than the original foreign train designs. China has developed indigenous technology in the 380 km/h category and the models CRH 380-A, CRH 380-AL, CRH 380-B, CRH 380-BL, CRH 380-CL were all locally designed and built. The only foreign participation in the rolling stock industry is the Bombadier Sifang Transportation (BST) with its production of CRH 380-D (known as Zefiro 380 internationally) and CRH 380-DL models for the Chinese market. The most popular model today in the Chinese 380 km/h market is the CRH 380-A.

China has established its unique Chinese HSR technical specification. The rolling stock industry claimed a local content ratio of more than 80% and many observers put it as the most successful absorption of foreign technology in Chinese economy.

State of Chinese railway industry

Since HSR service was introduced on 18 April 2007, China has built the world's most extensive HSR network with operating length more than 55% of the world's total. Average daily ridership has grown from 237,000 in 2007 to 2.49 million in 2014, making the Chinese HSR network the most heavily used in the world. Cumulative ridership has reached 3.25 billion by end of 2014. China's nationwide HSR network covers 28 of the country's 33 regions.[4] HSR in China can be broken down into four sub-groups: The first is the newly built passenger designated lines (PDLs) that just run HSR passenger service; the second is newly built conventional rail lines, mostly in western China, that can carry high-speed passenger and freight trains; the third is certain regional "intercity" HSR lines that are also dedicated to passenger service alone; the fourth is the conventional track railways that were upgraded to run mixed passenger and freight lines. Most of the rail lines now under construction belong to one of the first three categories. Nearly all HSR lines and rolling stock in China are owned and operated by the CRC.

Spillover effect in the Chinese HSR development

The spectacular growth of the HSR in China significantly improved the land transport efficiency of China. The system runs more than 58% of passenger train routes and carry close to 40% of train passenger number in December 2014.[5] Aside from the convenience of shorter travel times, the key to the successful migration of ordinary train passenger to HSR lies in affordability.[6] From the perspective of absolute fare to relative fare, Chinese HSR is very affordable to the riding public as the following Figure 3 and Table 1 show.

The spillover effects of HSR to the efficiency of the economy are very positive. Railway has overall cost advantages vs. other means of transportation.

---

[4] All 33 regions in the country is expected to be covered by HSR by 2018.

[5] December 2014 New Train Schedule (2014年12月新列車運行圖), dated 11 November 2014 [downloaded on 28 December 2014], available at www.huoche.net/show_312560.

[6] During 2008–2013, total rail passenger volume continued to grow at 7.6% annually, but with a change in traffic composition. While conventional rail traffic grew 1.5% annually, HSR traffic has increased 39% per annum since 2008. The introduction of CRH services has not caused a reduction in ridership on the conventional network, but has instead fueled accelerated growth, which the previous network, close to its full capacity, was unable to serve.

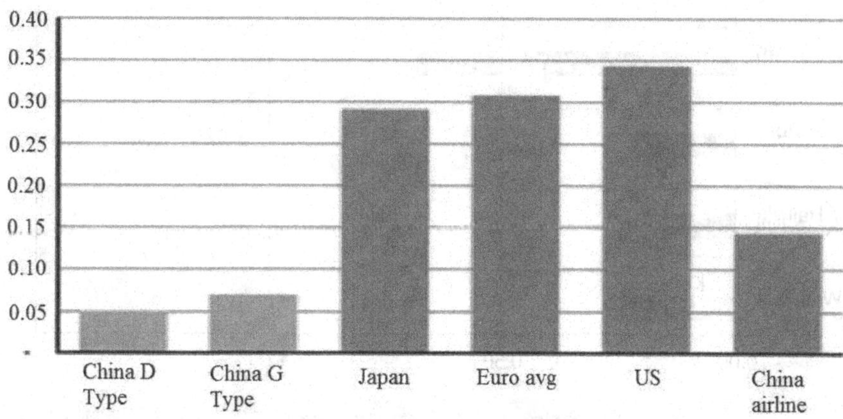

Figure 3: China HSR train passenger ticket prices compared with global prices and China airline tickets (US$/km)
Source: UBS

Table 1: HSR fare as percentage of monthly income per 100 km

	Nominal HSR Fare-euro/km	Average Monthly Salary (Euro/Month)	Percentage (%) of Monthly Income per 100 km HSR
China	0.04	500	0.80
Spain	0.19	1800	1.05
France	0.22	2210	0.81
Germany	0.27	2080	1.29
Italy	0.25	1870	1.33
Japan	0.22	1930	1.14

Author's calculation based on 2013/1/15 Takungpao

Just measuring in terms of energy efficiency, it compares well with other modes as well. Figure 4 and Table 2 highlight these two points.[7]

Traditional economic evaluations of major transport infrastructure investment focus on the direct costs and benefits arising from travel, including user time savings, operator cost savings and reduction of externalities

[7]Table on energy consumption use Standard Coal Equivalent (SCE) as energy measurement unit, 1 SCE = 8.14 kWh.

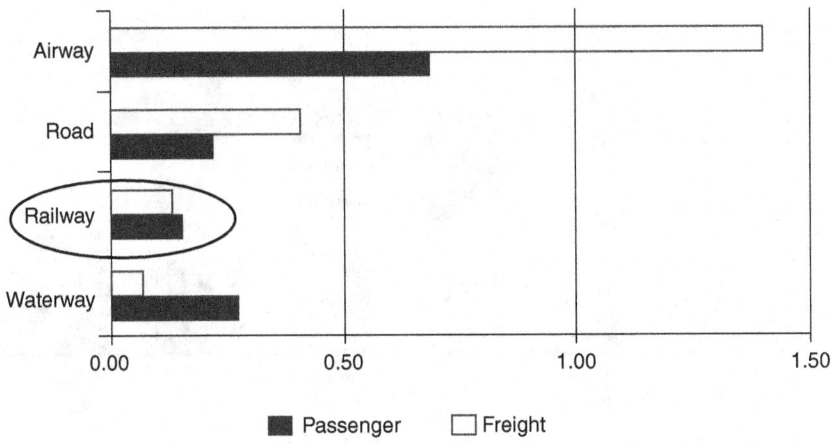

Figure 4: Railway has cost advantage vs. other transportation means

Source: MOR, MOC, Xinhua Net

Table 2: Energy consumption comparison of the different modes of transportation

	Cargo kg SCE/kt.km	**Passenger kg SCE/person.km**
Ordinary Railway (diesel)	3.6	0.018
Ordinary Railway (electrified)	1.4	0.007
High-speed Railway (electrified)	na	0.01
Large vehicle	18.2	0.015
Cars	na	0.043
Shipping	3.1	na
Civil Aviation	91	0.068

Note: 1 standard coal unit = 8.141 kWh

Source: Logistic companies, shipping campanies, airline campanies, B of A Merrill Lynch Global Research estimates

that include air pollution, noise and accidents. The wider economic impacts are too tenuous to be reliably quantified and therefore often neglected. However, China has surprisingly shown strong economic agglomeration benefits in just a few years after adoption of HSR.[8] This significant economic

[8] In economies, agglomeration are the benefits that firms obtain by locating near each other. This concept relates to the idea of economies of scale and network effects. As more firms in related

growth effect from agglomeration in favor of city cluster encourages the formation of three mega growth areas in China: Beijing–Tianjin–Hebei; Yangtze River Delta; and Pearl River Delta. China's drive to build intercity HSR in the last 2 years is quite unique in the world HSR construction history. This reflects the trend that the economic agglomeration effects are becoming more and more apparent.

A World Bank (WB) study noted the unusually strong contribution of HSR to China's regional economic development, urbanization and industrial upgrading.[9] Although benefits from these three areas are too early to be quantifiable, Chinese experience does show a dynamic interaction of properly executed transportation infrastructure and economic growth in both short and long terms. Chinese successes in HSR have drawn the attention of many developing countries and the term "Rail Diplomacy" was a buzzword in 2013 and 2014 until its replacement by OBOR.

An interesting technology spillover area from China's development in HSR is in the area of urban rail transport. Urban rail transport includes subway and light rail, with tram and maglev being an insignificant player. China has intensified urban rail transport infrastructure investments to improve the city traffic conditions. Cost estimates based on approved lines show that China in general spent around RMB 500–700 million/km (US$80–110 million/km) on city subway construction. This figure is very low by international standards and most observers believe that the Chinese civil work and rolling stock contractors achieved such efficiency through the learning curve from the HSR construction. By the end of 2015, 23 Chinese cities were running their urban subway rail networks and China will expand its urban rail networks significantly in the next few years.[10] Figures 5 and 6 show the Unit investment of urban rail transit and operating length of urban rail transit system in China.

---

fields of business cluster together, their costs of production may decline significantly (firms have competing multiple suppliers, greater specialization and division of labor result). Even when there are competing firms in the same sector cluster, there may be advantages because the cluster attracts more suppliers and customers than a single firm could achieve alone.

[9] Salzberg, Andrew, Richard Bullock, Ying Jin and Wanli Fang, High-Speed Rail, Regional Economics and Urban Development in China. World Bank Office (Beijing), *China Transport Topics*, No. 08, January 2013.

[10] Twenty-three cities running subway are Beijing, Changsha, Chongqing, Chengdu, Dalian, Guangzhou/Foshan, Hangzhou, Harbin, Hong Kong, Kunming, Nanjing, Nanchang, Ningbo, Qingdao, Shanghai, Shenyang, Shenzhen, Suzhou, Tianjin, Wuhan, Wuxi, Xian and Zhengzhou.

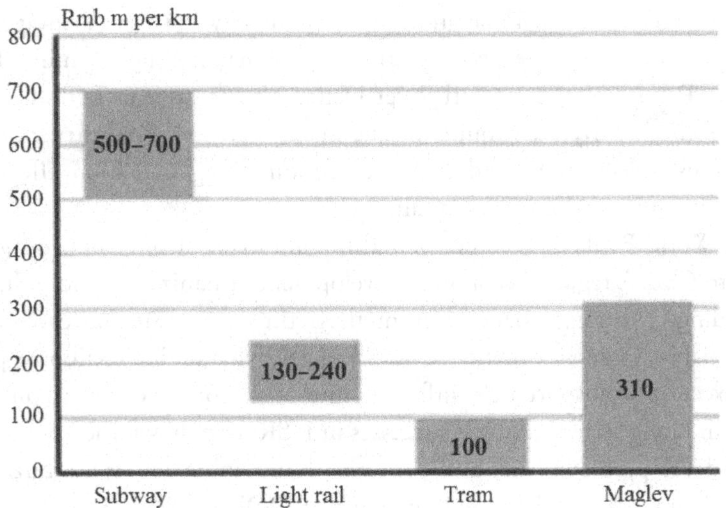

Figure 5: Unit investment in RMB/km for Urban Rail Transit
Note: Magiev includes vehicle equipment purchase
Source: UBS estimates

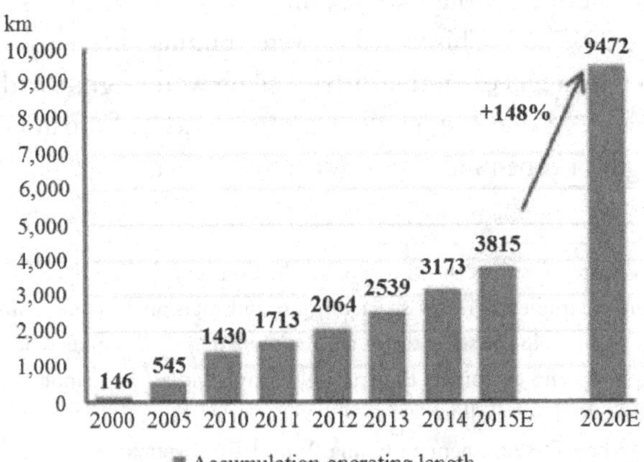

Figure 6: Operating length of the urban rail transit system in China
Sources: China Associate of Metros, UBS estimates

China is investing heavily in HSR as well as conventional rail system to improve its land transportation network. The proportion of HSR will increase in the composition of the rail network as shown in Figures 7 and 8. Appendix 4 shows the China rail track length and Appendix 5 shows annual HSR annual ridership.

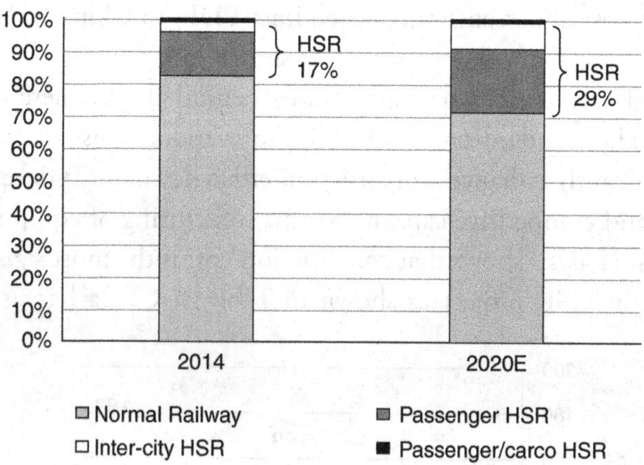

Figure 7: Breakdown of different lines in operating rail length in China

Sources: China Railway Corporation, Ministry of Railways, UBS estimates

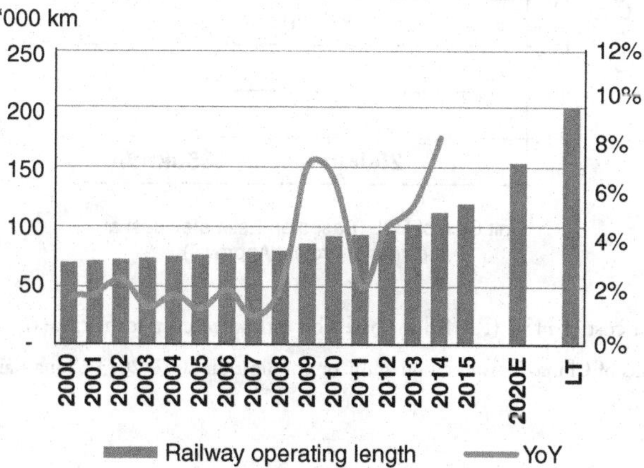

Figure 8: Railway operating length in China

Sources: China Railway Corporation, Ministry of Railways, UBS estimates

Comparative advantage of Chinese rail system in global export market

The strongest comparative advantage of Chinese rail system is its cost efficiency. WB provided the earlier financing to some of the HSR projects and it probably has the best cost factor data aside from Chinese government. WB pointed out that China has a commanding cost advantage in turnkey HSR system, unit cost of passenger dedicated line (PDL) in Chinese HSR is about 1/3 to 2/3 to those of other countries as shown in Figure 9.[11]

WB had identified two main reasons behind the Chinese cost advantage[12]: (1) The standardization of design of various construction elements which significantly enhances construction efficiency and (2) development of innovative and competitive capacity for manufacturing of equipment.

WB cost analysis shows that construction cost is the most significant cost component in HSR project as shown in Table 3. China has used its scale

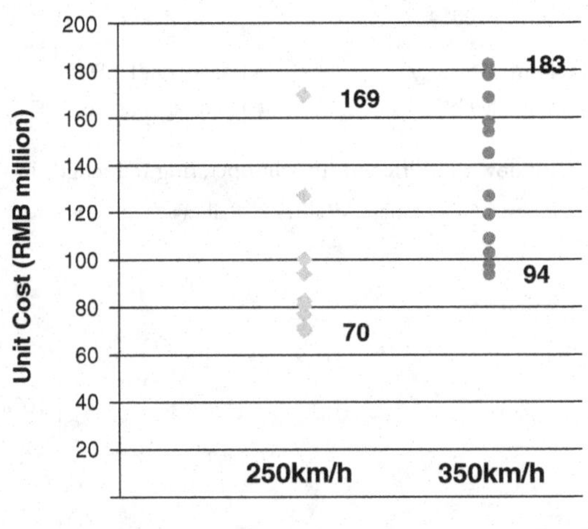

Figure 9: Unit cost of HSR (RMB/km) based on estimated cost at the time of project approval

Source: Year books of China Transportation and Communication 2007–2013/China Railway Yearbooks

---

[11] Olivier, Gerald, Jitendra Sondhi and Nanyan Zhou, High-Speed Railways in China: A Look at Construction Costs. World Bank office (Beijing), *China Transport Topics*, No. 09, July 2014.

[12] *Ibid.*

Table 3: Percentage of total project cost based on WB-financed HSR lines

Element	350 km/h	250 km/h	200 km/h
Land acquistion and resettlement	4	4–8	6–9
Civil works	48	50–54	44–51
Embariment	6	7–12	13–15
Bridges/viaducts[12]	41*	13–25	25–27
Tunnels	0*	16–29	2–13
Track	9	9–11	6–7
Signaling and communications	4	3	4
Electrification	5	4–5	4–5
Rolling stock	15	3–4	5–7
Buildings including stations	2	2–4	3–5
Other costs	Balance	Balance	Balance

*An exception is Shizheng Railway that has 69% of track on viaduct accounting for 41% of cost and no tunnels

Beam Launching Equipment

Figure 10: Specialized beam carrier and launching equipment used in HRS viaduct construction

advantage and developed a standardized design for various construction elements that significantly lowers costs. Figure 10 is an example of such standardization of two specialized equipment developed on viaduct construction. Table 4 shows the typical track civil work cost and the relatively small premium of viaduct over embankment cost as well as the low price of track.

China HSR with a maximum speed of 350 km/h has a typical infrastructure cost of about US$17–21 million/km, with a high ratio of viaducts and

Table 4: Range of average unit construction costs of HSR lines financed by WB (RMB in million per km of double track)

Element	**350 km/h**	**250 km/h**	**200 km/h**
Land acquisition and resettlement	4	5–9	5–8
Civil Works	57	56–62	42–43
Embankment	24	31–42	23–28
Bridges/viaducts	71	57–73	59–62
Tunnels	—	60–95	51–68
Track			
*Track (ballast-less)**	10	10–13	
Track (*ballasted*)*			5–7
signaling and Communications	5	3	3–4
Electrification	6	4–5	4

*Ballast-less slab track is used for 350 and 250 km/h PDLs while ballasted track is employed for 200 km/h railways
Source: PSR/PAD for projects

tunnels. Similar construction in Europe, having design speed of 300 km/h is in the order of US$25–39 million/km and the figure is estimated to be as high as US$52 million/km for California. Chinese contractors have delivered projects within budget and construction time frames under most difficult terrain conditions as shown in Table 5.[13] Budget overruns and delays are extremely rare.[14] For instance, the WB-financed 857 km Guiyang–Guangzhou line, which traverses 270 tunnels and 510 valleys across the geographically challenging landscapes in Guizhou, took only 6 years to complete with the final budget amended to RMB 94.6 billion on completion from the initial projected budget of RMB 85.8 billion estimated 7 years earlier. Its completion is considered an outstanding engineering achievement.

[13]The Guiyang–Guangzhou line is 1,856 km long with 83% of the tracks in tunnels and bridges, its maximum design speed is 250 km/h. The project completed in 5 years with the cost capped at RMB 147 m/km.

[14]There is a delay of several months on project completion post July 2011 Wenzhou train accident, the government ordered a review of all projects under construction. However, all lines are finished on budget.

Table 5: Railway Projects Supported by the WB in China

Project	Max. Speed kph/Type	Length km	Total Estimated Cost RMB b	Unit Cost RMB m/ km	Bridges + viaduct + Tunnels (% of route km)	Period of Construction
Shijiazhuang–Zhengzhou	360 PDL	366	43.9	123	69	2008–2012
Guiyang–Guangzhou	250 PDL	867	94.6	110	80	2008–2014
Jilin–Hunchun	250 PDL	360	39.6	110	66	2010–2014
Zhangjiakou–Hohhot	250 PDL	286	34.6	121	67	2013–2017
Nanning–Guangzhou	200 Mixed	463	41.0	89	53	2008–2014
Harbin–Jiamusi	200 Mixed	343	33.9	99	48	2014–2017

Notes: 1. Total project cost includes the cost of project preparation, land acquisition, construction of the railway and regular stations contingencies rolling stock and interest during construction. The cost of railway excluding cost of project preparation, rolling stock and interest during construction is estimated at about 82% of the total cost

2. Cost Reference: GG-Revised FSR December. 2010, NG-PAD May 2009, Shi-Zheng PAD May 2008, Jilin-PAD 2011, Zhang-Hu-FSR, Halla-Revised Feasibility study October. 2010/PAD

The extensive HSR construction in China provides valuable construction knowledge for the Chinese railway builder: the 904-km Harbin–Dalian HSR line and 3607-km Lanzhou–Xinjiang HSR are all considered engineering wonders.[15,16] Many observers put the civil work expertise of China in railway construction, particularly in HSR construction, as the most significant comparative advantage it enjoys in global railway construction market. It is interesting to note that in the aborted 210 km Mexico–Queretaro HSR project, China was the sole bidder as the construction period of 2.5–3 years will not be met by all other international competitors. Interest accumulated during construction is a major cost component for major infrastructure projects and

[15] Harbin–Dalian is the world's first alpine high-speed railway operating at high latitude and low temperature. The train has to operate in the same trip under a minimum of –40°C to maximum 40°C temperature conditions at a maximum speed of 350 km/h.

[16] The line is the first desert running HSR that goes through desert wind zone. It passes through 3,607 altitude tunnel along the way and it is the highest operating HSR.

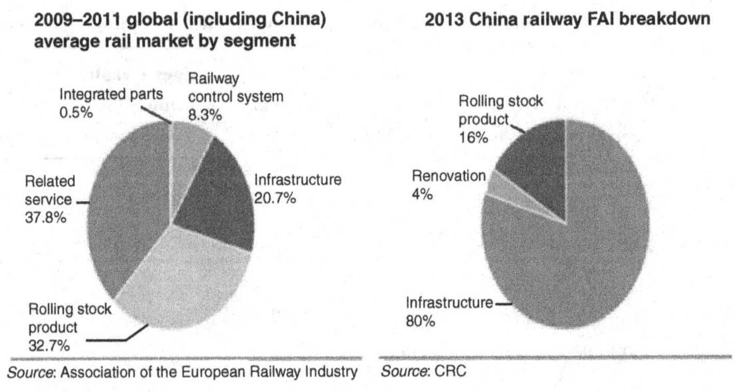

Figure 11: Breakdown of cost segments in HSR construction

the Chinese ability to materially shorten construction periods are a major source of competitive advantage.

The second important cost advantage of China lies on its development of innovative and competitive capacity manufacturing of equipment.[17] Chinese rolling stock generally cost around one-half to two-third to that of international competitors.[18] Comparisons based on Figure 11 on global system cost between 2009 and that of China in 2011. China's design fee and rolling stock cost is much lower than the comparative global standard. Apparently, the scale effect plus the innovation skills of the designers and equipment manufacturers are the main reasons behind the cost savings. China has managed to develop innovative and competitive capacity for manufacture of equipment.[19]

China has just released a complete set of China Technical Standards on HSR in 1Q 2015. Technical standard setting puts China's HSR on equal footing with ICE of Germany, TGV of France and Shinkansen of Japan as the fourth international HSR standard. It is worthwhile to note that Chinese standard has a high degree of compatibility with TGV and ICE in the area

[17] 张瑜, "高铁出海激浪环球大潮　国产化推进激发 6 股巨大空间", 中国证券报, 19 December 2014, www.yicai.com/news/2014/12/4054254.html.

[18] Li, Jacqueline LT Outlook Positive; Buy CSR, New Neutral CNR. *Rail Equipment — China*, Bank of America Merrill Lynch, 21 October 2014.

[19] 张瑜, "高铁出海激浪环球大潮 国产化推进激发 6 股巨大空间", 中国证券报, 19 December 2014.

of electrical system, in contrast to the Shinkansen system. It is generally acknowledged that TGV and ICE system is superior in the electrical system area and adopting their standard significantly improved the Chinese HSR system reliability.

Cost competitiveness in construction and rolling stock means that even China is a latecomer in the HSR industry and its technology will not be acknowledged as the leading one.[20,21] However, it can still compete on a commercial basis in global HSR projects. Since the with regard to Wenzhou accident in 2011, statistics prove that Chinese has shaken off doubts on the two critical areas of reliability and safety.[22] In fact, Chinese HSR had carried more than three billion passengers without any issue since then. Average daily passenger volume of three million attest to the reliability and safety of the system. Chinese HSR construction consortium is probably the only entity that can offer turnkey HSR Engineering, Procurement and Construction (EPC) rail project in any country under short construction time frame.

Aside from the above-mentioned advantages in the HSR area cited by WB, China enjoyed some significant comparative advantage in the ordinary rail area: (1) the experience that China gained in the six "Speed Up" exercises makes it the only country in the world with extensive operating experience on rail speed-up using conventional track upgrade, most of the complete turnkey rail project that China won in recent years is in this area.[23] (2) China

---

[20] With 55% of the world's running line and the longest line under construction, China will end up running 60% of the world's HSR for some time. This huge installed base could mean future improvement on line technology and will most likely come from China.

[21] CRRC, the merged entity of CSR and CNR and *de facto* single manufacturer of rolling stock in China, is estimated to get an annual sales of RMB 230 billion in 2015 and a research budget of RMB 9 billion. Its research budget is bigger than its four former technical partners combined.

[22] July 2011 Wenzhou accident in which a stationary train was hit at the track by another 100 km/h running train in stormy weather, resulting derailment of a few cars falling off the viaduct had caused 40 mortalities and over a 100 injured. HSR accident does happen as Germany had an accident in 1998 with 101 fatalities. Spain had an accident in 2013 with 71 fatalities. Japan is the only country that never had any fatalities in its 50 years of HSR operation.

[23] Kenya is building the world's first Chinese standard modern railway in Nairobi–Mombasa line (485 km long, design speed maximum of 120 km/h, costs at US$3.804 billion to be completed in 2017). Thailand agreed to use Chinese standard to build Nongkai–Mapta Phut (734 km long, design speed maximum of 180 km/h and upgradable to 250 km/h, line completion in 2022) and Kaeng Khoi–Bangkok (133 km long, design speed maximum of 180 km/h and

often sets up training institutes in the recipient country to share latest management and technical innovations that the huge network of China has generated. This is quite a unique offering among rail equipment exporting companies and certainly very attractive to the recipient country.[24]

Prospects of Chinese rail export under OBOR

(1) China–Mongolia–Russia Economic Corridor

The Mid-term Roadmap for Development of Trilateral Cooperation among China, Russia and Mongolia is in the preliminary planning phase and plans are not expected to take shape for some time. Trilateral rail linkage cooperation under discussion is not expected in the immediate future.

Bilateral rail cooperation between Russia and China is proceeding in a meaningful way, the most notable recent development is the contract win of a Chinese-led consortium with Russian companies on the RUB 20.8 billion contract to design the 770 km Moscow–Kazan HSR that is expected to cost RUB 1.06 trillion. Chinese companies are expected to win the contract of the design if it can offer an acceptable financing term to Russia. Moscow–Kazan HSR will be part of the 7,000 km RMB 1.5 trillion Beijing–Moscow HSR passing through Kazakhstan line if the project were to go ahead.

China has proposed to build the 7,000 km Beijing–Moscow HSR and extend the HSR line from border town Hunchun in Jilin to Vladivostok, 138 km away, on May 2015. Both offers did not solicit enthusiastic responses from Russia. We should note that Russia's rail gauge is 1,520 mm and the Chinese standard gauge is 1,435 mm, improving rail connectivity between China and Russia will face this important constraints of break of gauge. While Siberian Russia has a land area of 13.1 million sq. km and accounts for 77% of Russian territory, it only has 40 million or 27% of national population. The area is historically not on the top of economic development

---

upgradable to 250 km/h, line completion in 2022). Hungary–Serbia railway will use Chinese technology to build the Budapest–Belgrade line (400 km at US$4 and will probably follow European standard).

[24] CRC is developing rail base express service on small volume less than rail container goods. Chinese experience in this area is keenly watched by many overseas train operator as China is a major player in e-commerce.

agenda of Russia. Rail connection on Russia's Far East which calls for huge resources commitment is not likely to happen in the immediate future. We should also note that Russia has a historical concern on its sparse population base in Siberia and always looks at a foreign offer of Siberian investment with hesitation. A case in point is the project to build the Russian section of the bridge across the Amur River in Heilongjiang. The bridge will connect Tongjiang in Heilongjiang Province with Nizhneleninskoye, a village in Russia's Jewish Autonomous Oblast and will facilitate the development of a new rail link between China and Russia. An intergovernmental agreement on building the new bridge was signed back in 2008. China undertook the bulk of the work (1.9 out of the total 2.2 km) and plans to complete its section by the end of 2016. Whereas the relevant Russian agencies did not start building their section of the bridge until President Putin interceded personally on September 2015.

Bilateral rail cooperation between China and Mongolia face similar problems as the China–Russia cooperation. Mongolian railway gauge is the same the Russian railway gauge at 1,520 mm whereas the Chinese railway gauge is 1,435 mm. The break of gauge prevents smooth cross border train travel. Mongolian territory has 1.57 million sq. km but its sparse population base of three million make new long distance passenger rail service economically hard to justify.

On the cargo rail side, Mongolia has shown flexibility on the issue. In October 2014, Mongolian parliament has given special authority to allow a 260 km Ukhaa Khudag (part of the Tavan Tolgoi coal field) and Oyu Tolgoi (copper/gold mine) to connect to Chinese border town of Gashuun Sukhait using 1,435 mm standard gauge for a seamless connection with China's railway network, rather than on the 1,520 mm Russian gauge used elsewhere in Mongolia. Another special authority was given to construct a standard gauge cargo line to run from central Mongolia to Bichigt in Sükhbaatar Province and cross into China at Zhuengadabuqi of East Ujimqin Banner, under Inner Mongolia's Xilingol League. Railway cooperation between China and Mongolia in the future will probably concentrate more on cargo line and border passenger linkage. The most important cargo between China and Mongolia is the coal export from Mongolia to China, in which China is curtailing coal consumption and switching to cleaner energy such as natural gas. Immediate prospects for new cargo line construction in Mongolia are not bright.

Long-term prospects of new cargo rail project between China and Mongolia depend on the cargo movement between China and Europe. Out of three land routes between China and Europe: (1) China–Kazakhstan–Europe; (2) China–Russia–Europe; (3) China–Mongolia–Russia–Europe, the Mongolian route offers significantly shorter distance.

(2) New Eurasia Land Bridge Economic Corridor–Asian Europe Cargo Link — What Really Impedes It?

China started Chongqing–Duisburg cargo service in 2011. By September 2014, there were eight major cargo routes connecting China to Europe as shown in Table 6.

In 2014, the trains made 308[25] trips along the route, carrying 26,070 containers and 700,000 tons of goods. The number of trips are a significant increase from just 80 trips in 2013. However, these railway connections still face many hurdles and long-term commercial problems, which must be worked out: (1) Generally, the west-bound cargo volumes are not a problem, however, Europe–China east-bound goods are often minimal. Hence, cargo schedules for China to Europe are well scheduled but schedules from Europe back to China are often irregular; (2) Figure 12 highlights the most important complicating technical factor toward train linkage in OBOR — the differences of rail gauge at national border. As mentioned, the break of gauge

Table 6: The eight cargo lines running from China to Europe

Date	Route	Time Taken	Distance
2011	Chongqing–Duisberg	15 Days	11,179 km
2012	Wuhan–Prague	15 Days	11,000 km
2013/4	Chengdu–Lodz	14 Days	9,826 km
2013/7	Zhengzhou–Hamburg	15 Days	10,214 km
2013/9	Suzhou–Warsaw	15 Days	11,200 km
2014/12	Yiwu–Madrid	18 Days	13,053 km
2015	Changsha–Duisberg	13 Days	11,808 km
2015	Hefei–Poland	18 Days	9,820 km

25 中国制造挺进欧洲：8条中欧货运班列领跑"一带一路. 凤凰财经. 19 April 2015. [downloaded on 16 October 2015], available at http://finance.ifeng.com/a/20150419/13645326_0.shtml?wratingModule=1_15_103.

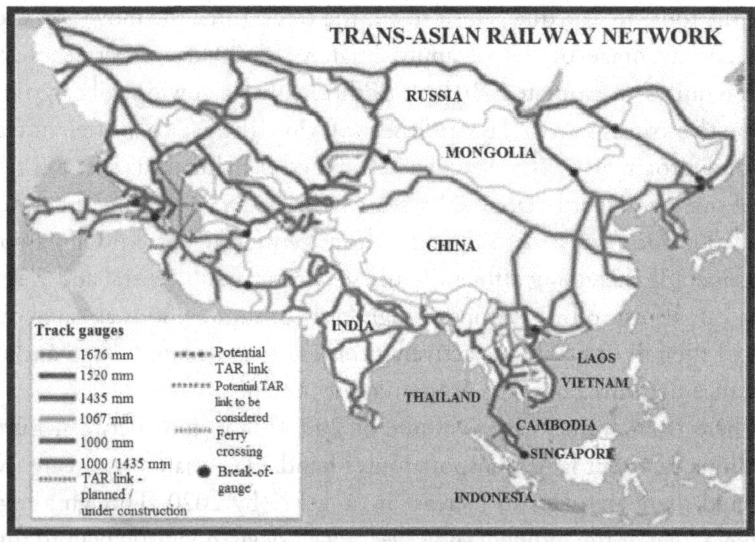

Figure 12: Different gauge in Trans-Asian railway network

problem requires mechanized facilities to move shipping containers from train to train. Former Commonwealth of Independent States (CIS) countries all use a 1,520 mm wide rail, while China and European countries use the standard 1,435 mm rail gauge. A China–Europe cargo train must move its containers from standard gauge to 1,520 gauge in one border crossing, continue the journey and change back to standard gauge in the next border crossing. For a 64 standard container train, the process takes 1.5–2 hour and significantly adds cost; (3) Train transit and operating fees in Europe are much higher as compared to China, it is estimated that while China charges around US$0.39/km-container, corresponding charges in European section is around US$0.80–0.97/km-container. It is estimated that Chinese local government sponsors the cargo linkage by providing US$1,000–$2,000 per container subsidies despite the fact that rail line is charging a 20–30% freight premium over ocean voyage.

In spite of all these problems, China is working on various solutions to improve the operation of the Europe–Asia cargo link: (1) CRC is developing more feeder routes to feed higher valuable cargo to the eight main routes, the plan is to add 45 feeder routes in 2015. Higher value cargo can justify increasing higher cargo freight rate; (2) China is working with countries along the route to expedite transit to cut the travel time, the move will widen the time advantage of rail of approximately 15–20 days over sea voyage which requires an estimated 40 days. Additionally, narrowing rail cargo transit time to a consistent 15 days or lesser will close the gap to air freight travel time of approximately 2–3 days. The estimated benchmark is that rail travel cost of one container is US$6,000, sea voyage is US$4,000 and air travel is US$16,000 for a container originated from central or western China going to Europe; (3) Increasing affluent Chinese consumers in central and western China can afford to buy European high-end consumer goods as east-bound cargo of the rail line. CRC is actively promoting east-bound cargo and that could meaningfully boost the economics of the line.

There is an annual cargo volume of 200 million tons between Europe and China. Current land transport routes handle less than 1% of cargo volume, and there are plans to increase it to 5–7% by 2020. Though a highly unlikely target at the moment, however, a well-devised logistic plan to divert a few million tons to the land rail line is highly probable in the next few years. These lines too can easily turn profitable under such a plan in a few years. Building new lines in the near future is probably not economically justifiable.

(3) China–Central Asia–West Asia Economic Corridor

The most significant rail project with Chinese contractors in West Asia is the US$1.2 billion, 530-km section of the Ankara–Istanbul HSR line between Eskişehir and İnönü in western Turkey. However, the line is built with European Union (EU) standard with significant European content.

Uzbekistan is building a 129-km Pap–Angren railway line and using Chinese contractors on a 19 km tunnel through the Kamchik Pass that connects the Fergana Valley with the rest of Uzbekistan. The countries in Central Asia: Kyrgyzstan, Kazakhstan, Tajikistan, Uzbekistan use 1,520 mm Russian rail gauge which creates a break of gauge issue with rail connectivity to China. The unfavorable terrain and sparse population density of these countries also make rail economics doubtful. No major rail projects are currently on the table.

(4) China–Pakistan Economic Corridor

Pakistan is the first major beneficiary in the OBOR initiative of China. The US$46 billion Chinese investment and loan package agreement reached in April 2015 placed the implementation of railway projects almost to a certainty.

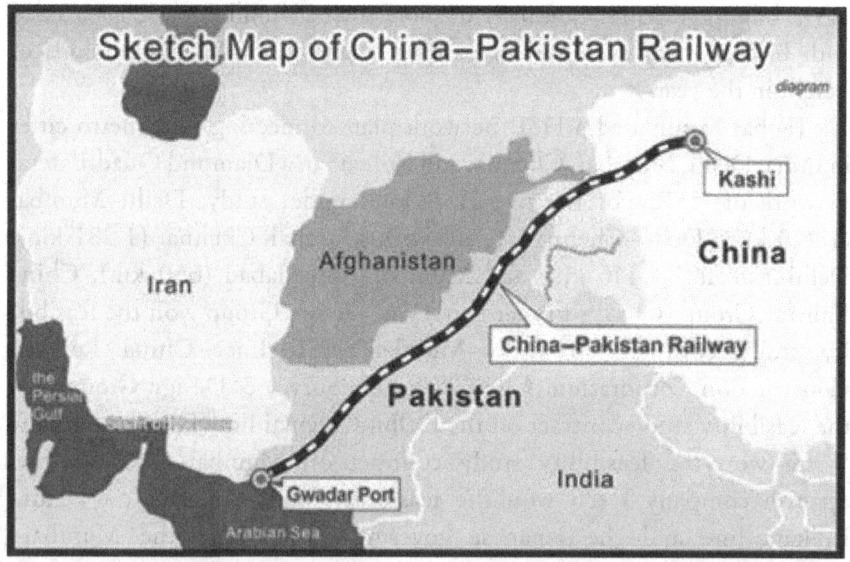

Figure 13: Sketch of the China–Pakistan Railway

The Havelian–Khunjerab railway construction is starting soon. This line runs 750 km in Pakistan and links Havelian through the 4,730 m high Khunjerab Pass to connect to Kashgar through 350 km of Xinjiang. The line will use standard 1,435 mm gauge, a departure from the legacy railway gauge of 1,676 mm in most of Pakistan today. Two other railway projects currently under evaluation are the Karachi–Peshawar mainline and Khunjerab railway. Once the two projects are implemented, China will be able to connect directly to Arab Sea through the Gwadar port and the railroad linking Xinjiang and Gwadar as shown in Figure 13.

A successful implementation of the Havelian–Khunjerab railway linkage will not only demonstrate the engineering skills of the Chinese contractors, but will also shows their social skills in convincing the local Muslim tribal groups of the merit of transport development. This potentially holds significance in view of recent radicalization of Islam in the Middle East.

(5) Bangladesh–China–India–Myanmar Economic Corridor on India Rail Project

India Rail (IR) runs one of the world's largest railway networks comprising 115,000 km of track over a route of 65,808 km. In 2014–2015, IR carried

8.397 billion passengers annually or more than 23 million passengers a day with half of them as suburban passengers and 1,058.81 million tons of freight in the year.

IR has formulated a HSR network plan connecting four metro cities in India: Delhi, Mumbai, Chennai and Kolkata in a Diamond Quadrilateral network of HSR. For the five HSR lines under study: Delhi–Mumbai (1,200 km), Delhi–Chennai (1,745 km), Mumbai–Chennai (1,281 km), Delhi–Kolkata (1,446 km) and Mumbai–Ahmedabad (650 km). China Railway Group (CRG)'s Eryuan Survey & Design Group won the feasibility study contract on Delhi–Mumbai HSR line. China Railway Construction Corporation (CRCC)'s Siyuan Survey & Design Group won the feasibility study contract on the Delhi–Chennai line. French company Systra won the feasibility study contract on Mumbai–Chennai line. Spanish company Iveco won the feasibility study contract on Delhi–Kolkata line and the Japanese government provided the Mumbai–Ahmedabad feasibility study.

China is expected to dominate in the Indian HSR market: (1) India is proposing HSR to be a Public–Private Partnership (PPP) initiative. It has been historically seen that PPP railway projects in India depend on China for manufactured train sets. Private sector Metro projects in Mumbai and Gurgaon which are built in PPP are depending on train sets manufactured in China, as cost is the main factor. This is in contrast to government funded Metro projects in India that also look at other criteria such as manufacturing within India, technology transfer, etc.; (2) China has already built a personal relationship with many of the senior employees of the Indian Railways with sponsored visits to China and training programs conducted in China under "Sino-Indian Memorandum of Understanding & Implementation Plan on Cooperation in Railways". India Railway is interested in using the Chinese heavy haul technology to improve the cargo line as well as learning Chinese experience to increase the speed of passenger train to 160–200 km/h on dedicated conventional line — an area of technology that China possess as a result of its six "Speed Up" exercise. IR has awarded the speed raising project study on the Chennai–Bangalore–Mysore conventional line to CRG; (3) Government indicated budget for the line is around US$20 million per km for a 350 km/h top speed track, a figure that favors the low cost producers. In the Japan-funded study on 505 km Mumbai–Ahmedabad HSR line, the indicated budget is US$15.44 billion and the unit cost is over US$30 million/km and it will take 6 years to finish; (4) Indian train passenger volume averages 12 million daily ridership (excluding city metro) and yet the fare is among the lowest in the world, the cheapest fare on a 100 km trip is less the US$1.00 and even air-conditioned 100 km first-class sitting trip is less than US$7.00. Huge passenger volumes and low fares will make cost efficiency one of the primary concerns to IR, and this favors China.

Cross border rail connection between China and India is not viable as the Himalayas serve as a natural barrier and territorial disputes also make direct China–India train link not possible. China has announced that by 2020, Qinghai–Tibet railway line will extend 253 km from Shigatse to Gyirong on the border of Nepal and China. There is a talk for extending the Shigatse–Gyirong to Kathmandu by 2022, however, scant information is available and Indian opposition is expected. The press has also reported that the less than 200 km rail link between Shigatse and Yadong, a Chinese border town with Bhutan and India, will be completed before 2020.

In March 2011, Indian and Chinese rail authorities expressed interest to build a HSR link that would link New Delhi with Kunming, China via Myanmar. The rail link would use the railway under construction from Manipur, India to Myanmar and the Yunnan–Myanmar railway being discussed then, however, the discussion stopped after Myanmar stopped its railway program with China.

The main impediment between China–India collaboration lies in geopolitical concerns which are beyond the realm of economics.

(6) China–Indochina Peninsula

There are currently three rail connection proposals to connect Kunming, the capital of Yunnan Province in southwest China with Singapore. The eastern route via Vietnam, central route via Laos and the western route via Myanmar would eventually converge in Bangkok, Thailand which forms a single line, would be extended to Singapore via Malaysia.

The eastern route construction was stopped by Vietnam in 2010 after the chilling of relations between China and Vietnam. China continues to build the 466 km connecting Kunming to the border town of Hekou using standard gauge, the line runs along the historical Yunnan–Vietnam line built by the French and it is completed in 2014. There are intense market speculations that Vietnam will proceed with the construction of the 389 km Hekou–Haiphong line, the Vietnam section of Yunnan–Vietnam rail, using 1,435 mm standard gauge. Bilateral trade between China and Vietnam will reach US$65 billion in 2015 with China as the biggest trading partner of Vietnam and Vietnam as the second biggest trading partner of China in ASEAN. Economic incentives are strong enough to build the rail connection between the two countries.

As for the central route through Laos, China commenced construction of its section to the Laos border of Xishuangbanna on August 2015 and there is speculation that construction on the 530 km Laos section to Vientiane, the capital of Laos, will commence shortly after repeated delays since 2010. The Laos section will cost US$6.8 billion and the project is not economical on a stand-alone basis. Laos is a country of 6.8 million population with nominal GDP less than US$12 billion in 2014, and a Chinese construction company had pulled out of Laos rail project in 2013 on account of the poor economics.

Laos rail project is not feasible on a stand-alone basis, however, if the line is connected to Bangkok as part of the Pan Asian network then it could be economically justifiable. Construction on US$8.4 billion, 867 km Nong Khai–Bangkok–Rayong line running at 180 km/h started in November 2015 after an agreement was reached in August 2015, the project will be completed in just 3 years. Nong Khai is the border town of Thailand around 25 km from Vientiane.

Economic linkage between China and Thailand is increasing very fast with the export of Thai fruit to China as shown in Figure 14. Passenger potential between China and Thailand is also encouraging, annual Chinese tourist to Thailand is expected to exceed 7 million in 2015. Laos' inclusion in the China–Thai railway connection can ameliorate the poor economics of Laos railway construction in a stand-alone basis.

As for the western route, construction is underway on the 690 km Yunnan Dali–Yunnan Ruili route, and it extends the Chinese railway network to the Yunnan–Myanmar border. The work on the Myanmar section was interrupted in 2011 and no news on the resumption is reported.

The Pan-Asian rail connection section running from Kunming to Vientiane to Bangkok will be completed before 2020 if all plans proceed as announced. Malaysia–Singapore HSR connection had reached the design phase and the tentative running schedule is 2023. The Pan-Asian rail connection is seen in Figure 15.

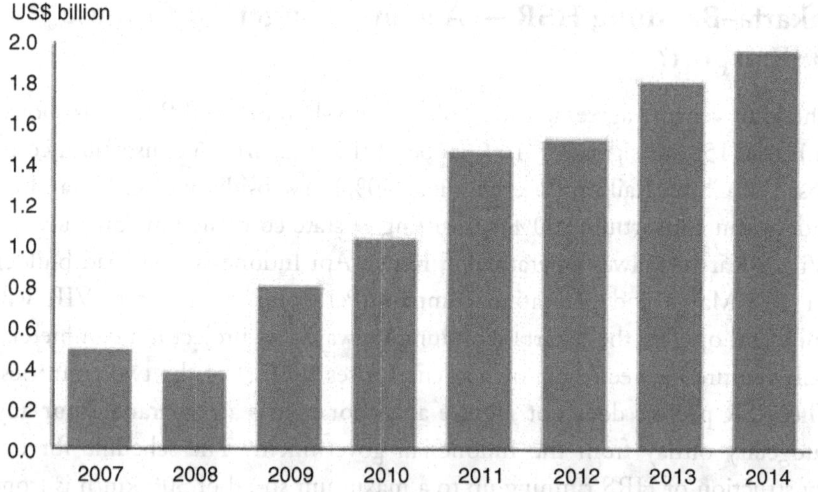

Figure 14: Exports of fresh fruits to China from Thailand have boomed post-2008

Sources: UBS, UN Comtrade

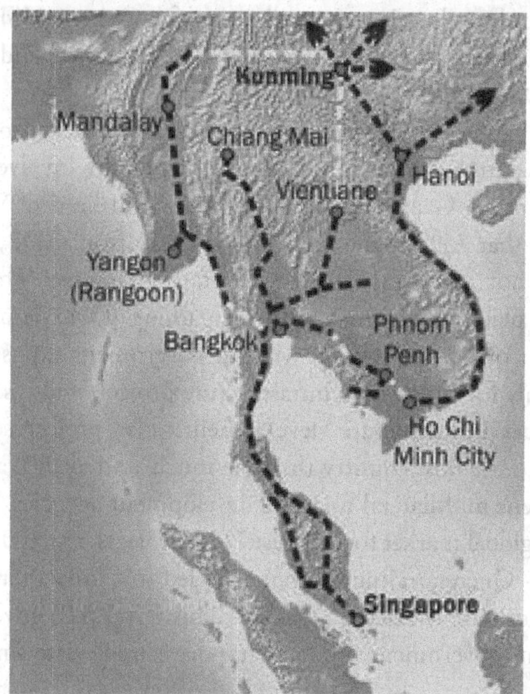

Figure 15: Map of the proposed routes for the Kunming–Singapore Railway

Jakarta–Bandung HSR — A game changer for Chinese HSR export?

The joint venture agreement to build Jakarta–Bandung HSR line, as shown in Figure 15, was signed on 16 October 2015 at Jakarta. A consortium composed of China Railway International (40%), a subsidiary of CRC, and an Indonesian consortium (60%) consisting of state construction company PT Wijaya Karya, railway operator PT Kereta Api Indonesia, toll road builder PT Jasa Marga and plantation company Perkebunan Nusantara VIII will build and operate the Jakarta–Bandung railway. The project is a commercial B2B venture between state-owned enterprises (SOEs) of the two countries. The HSR project does not require an Indonesian state guarantee nor any budgetary outlay from the Indonesian government. The schedule for the construction of HRS running up to a maximum speed of 300 km/h is from 2015 to 2018. The line will cut travel time between the two cities from more than 3 hours at the moment to 40 minutes. Commercial operation will commence in 1H 2019.

Jakarta–Bandung line is a groundbreaker for Chinese HSR export, it is the first complete HSR export using Chinese standards and it holds the potential to be a game changer as well.

First, the line probably does not require any outlay from either the Indonesian government or Indonesian state companies involved in the project. Sahala Lumban Gaol, Chairman of the JV and head of Wijaya Karya, told the media that 75% of the funding will come from CDB, and the project loan will not carry any Indonesian state guarantee. The Indonesian consortium is planning to finance the remaining 25% via a global bond issue. A project of US$5.5 billion without government exposure is a game changer not only for Indonesian infrastructure project, it also serves as a new model of global infrastructure development. The project setup is more advantageous to the host country than the much-touted PPP approach promoted by current multilateral financial development agencies. The first tender win in the global market for Chinese HSR projects, the 210-km US$3.75 billion Mexico–Queretaro line was not awarded to China after the tender as a result of last minute Mexico budget cut. This novel B2B government SOE partnership sans government funding support can alleviate similar problem down the road.

Second, most developing countries either face budgetary hard constraints in their development of infrastructure projects or high funding risk premium issues that significantly raise project cost and render many projects financially infeasible. The novel way of structuring the deal essentially means shifting a portion of Chinese foreign exchange in US treasury to a developing country through direct investments and debts. This can significantly reduce the funding requirements and costs and turn the project to become a commercially viable one. Jakarta–Bandung project demonstrates that a commercially viable project can proceed with minimal state funding, provided that it can secure a reliable, cost-efficient technology partner and cheap financing option. These two critical gaps are the strength of Chinese EPC provider who double as project investors. Indonesia has an ambitious five year infrastructure development of US$400 billion for the next five years. Government budgetary support can fill only US$80 billion and the gap of US$320 billion must be filled through multiple channels. The B2B model used in Jakarta–Bandung line can free valuable resources for Indonesia to complete its infrastructure plans. The favorable condition provided by China also allows it to cherry pick the most commercially stand-alone infrastructure project on the table and minimize its project macro risk.

Third, all project feasibility studies points to average daily passenger volume of at least 45,000 in the coming Jakarta–Bandung line, with a potential of higher daily passenger volumes. At the announced fare of Rp 200,000 (US$15.00) and minimum annual revenue of US$250 million, the project can turn a profit in the fifth to sixth year, an outstanding achievement for HSR lines.[26] Conventional wisdom prior to Chinese investments on HSR is that a country must be a high income country with per capita annual income of over US$12,000 for HSR to be commercially feasible. Even China started planning its HSR at a per capita level of US$1,000 plus in the 1990s and it demonstrated that a high middle income country with per capita of US$6,000 can profitably run a well–planned line. There are

[26]The 275-km Xiamen–Fuzhou and 1318-km Beijing–Shanghai turned a profit in the third & fourth year of operation, these two lines are probably the record holder for HSR profitability in HSR history.

lingering doubts on whether the experiences will hold true in other countries. A successful Jakarta–Bandung HSR will entice many developing countries with twin major cities population distribution pattern and a distance of 100–200 km upward between the cities to seriously look at the feasibility of HSR as their transportation backbone. A good number of cities will fall into this category.

Fourth, the elevation profile of the Jakarta–Bandung route indicates a steep elevation of 600 m over a 20 km stretch between 80 and 100 km of the line. Construction of such a line in 3 years is an engineering feat to many countries, while China had built the 1,318 km Beijing–Shanghai line in a record 31 months and operated the line in 38 months. There are persistent questions on whether such a civil engineering performance can be achieved outside China. An on-schedule performance of the Jakarta–Bandung line can demonstrate China's leading civil engineering technology in HSR. China's HSR has demonstrated that railways are enhancing productivity, GDP-boosting, and wealth-creating. Jakarta–Bandung can well show that effect and entice many developing countries to follow the HSR bandwagon. China is the only country with full set of products that can cater to different operational environment, from the tropical heat of Hainan to frigid cold of Heilongjiang to arid Xinjiang, from earthquake prone Szechuan to muddy coastal Guangdong to the 1,900 m elevation of Kunming. Figure 16 shows the challenging elevation profile of the Jakarta–Bandung HSR.

Fifth, Jakarta–Bandung will build on Chinese technical standards as Indonesia is a well-known earthquake zone. Its successful operation will lay all concerns on Chinese technical ability, safety and intellectual property issues to rest, a similar prejudice faced by Japanese manufacturers in the 1960s and the Korean manufacturers in 1990s. HSR is a highly visible symbol of technological capability and reliability of a country, a successful HSR line can well be the coming-out party for Chinese high technology exports.

Sixth, the Indonesian–Chinese joint venture has stated that it will work on HSR project elsewhere in ASEAN and Indonesia is the anchor member of ASEAN. The Jakarta–Bandung line is part of 750-km Jakarta–Bandung–Cirebon–Surabaya, the JV enjoys the firstcomer advantage for the rest of

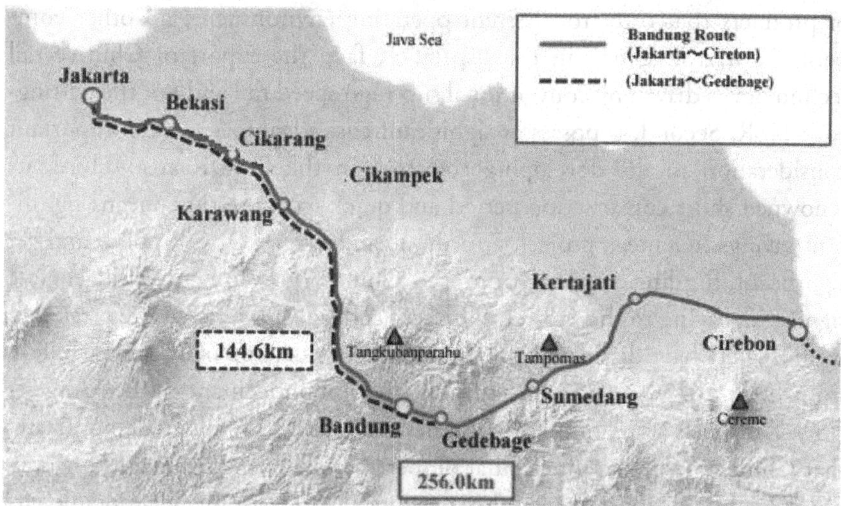

Figure 16: Jakarta–Bandung HSR route extend to Gedebage, Cirebon (part of Jakarta-Surabaya HSR line)

Jakarta–Surabaya line as well as other rail projects in ASEAN. The ability of Chinese EPC contractor to offer a favorable 60% local content in the project is very favorable to the host country.

Seventh, China's ability to complete the project in 3 years reflect its unique construction expertise in HSR, the competing offer from Japan takes 1–2 more years to finish the project. In the aborted 210-km Mexico–Queretaro HSR contract, Chinese contractor came out as the sole bidder, many observers pointed out that the short construction period of 2.5–3 years is the main reason behind other international companies' withdrawal from the project. The shortened construction period means significant savings on interest under construction.

Conclusions

China possesses significant comparative advantages in the export of both rail construction know-how or rolling stock in either conventional cargo or passenger sub-high speed segment and HSR segment. First, it can offer a full set of products that cater to different operating environment, no other competitor can rival China in this aspect. In fact, the export of Chinese rail technology is driven by conventional sub-high speed rail and not the cutting-edge HSR. Second, it possesses significant cost advantage, a very important consideration to the developing countries in the OBOR area. Third, its renowned short construction period and quick response time means significant savings in a mega project. Fourth, it can leverage OBOR policy and get significant funding support from the Chinese government and generate significant saving to the project. Fifth, concerns over Chinese system reliability and safety have dissipated after accident-free ridership of over three billion from 2011 to 3Q 2015. In addition, the announcement of Los Angeles (LA)–Las Vegas HSR line using Chinese standard technology demonstrates that Chinese owns the intellectual property it is offering overseas. However, OBOR railway export potential hype comes mainly from the academic circles and the Chinese local governments. Economic justifications and geopolitical realities are often neglected. As the business sector gets more and more involved in the implementation phase of OBOR in both China and other OBOR countries, reality on the ground will creep in. In any case, Chinese connectivity to the OBOR world will definitely improve with the rail export and the convenience of speedy travel will definitely benefit more and more people.

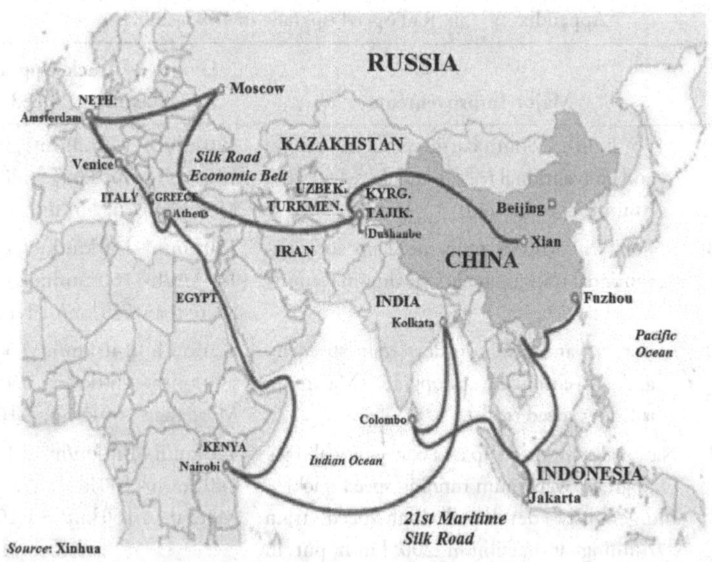

Appendix 1: Conceptual map of Silk Road Economic Belt and 21st Century Maritime Silk Road

Appendix 2: 64 Counties along the "One Belt, One Road"

		China, Mongolia, Russia;
Southeast Asian countries	(11):	Brunei, Cambodia, East Timor, Indonesia, Laos, Malaysia, Myanmar, Singapore, Philippines, Thailand, Vietnam.
Asian countries	(8):	Afghanistan, Bhutan, Bangladesh, India, Maldives, Nepal, Pakistan, Sri Lanka.
Middle East & North Africa countries	(16):	Bahrain, Egypt, Iran, Iraq, Israel, Lebanon, Jordan, Kuwait, Oman, Palestine, Qatar, Saudi Arabia, Syria, Turkey, UAE, Yemen.
Central and Eastern European countries	(16):	Albania, Bosnia and Herzegovina, Bulgaria, Croatia, Czech Republic, Estonia, Hungary, Latvia, Lithuania, Macedonia, Montenegro, Poland, Romania, Serbia, Slovakia, Slovenia.
Central Asian countries	(5):	Kazakhstan, Kyrgyzstan, Tajikistan, Turkmenistan, Uzbekistan.
The other six CIS countries	(6):	Armenia, Azerbaijan, Belarus, Crewe Georgia, Moldova, Ukraine.

Appendix 3: Six Rail Speed upgrade in 1997–2007

Date	Major Improvements	Length of Track Upgraded (Maximum Speed)
1997/4	Major North – South corridors train speed up and conventional track upgrade (Maximum running speed track).	120 km/h – 140 km/h: 1,398 km 140 km/h – 160 km/h: 588 km More than 160 km/h: 752 km
1998/10	Major NS corridors train speed up and conventional track upgrade (Maximum running speed track).	120 km/h – 140 km/h: 6,449 km 140 km/h – 160 km/h: 3,522 km More than 160 km/h: 1,104 km
2000/10	Major NS and EW corridors train speed up and conventional track upgrade (Maximum running speed track).	120 km/h – 140 km/h: 9,581 km 140 km/h – 160 km/h: 6,458 km More than 160 km/h: 1,104 km
2001/11	National train speed up and conventional track upgrade (Maximum running speed track). Indigenously developed high-speed train running at maximum 200 km/h put in service. National ticket sales online in one single network.	120 km/h – 140 km/h: 13,166 km 140 km/h – 160 km/h: 9,779 km More than 160 km/h: 1,104 km
2004/4	National train speed up and major corridor conventional track all upgraded to >160 km/h. Some major corridor lines run at maximum speed of 200 km/h	
2007/4	National train speed up and all major corridor lines run at maximum speed of 200 km/h. Indigenously developed 250 km/h trains put into service.	

Source: [downloaded on 31 December 2014], available at http://news.sina.com.cn/z/chinarailwayts/

Appendix 4: China rail track length

Year	Km	± % p.a.
1949	21,800	—
1955	25,600	+ 2.71
1960	33,900	+ 5.78
1965	36,400	+ 1.43
1970	41,000	+ 2.41
1975	46,000	+ 2.33

(*Continued*)

Appendix 4: (*Continued*)

Year	Km	± % p.a.
1980	53,300	+ 2.99
1985	55,000	+ 0.63
1990	57,800	+ 1.00
1995	62,400	+ 1.54
2000	68,700	+ 1.94
2005	75,400	+1.88
2010	90,504	+ 3.65
2014	112,000	+ 5.33

Appendix 5: China HSR annual ridership

HSR	Million Ridership	± % p.a.
2007	61.21	—
2008	127.73	+ 108.68
2009	179.58	+ 40.59
2010	290.54	+ 61.79
2011	440.00	+ 51.44
2012	486.00	+ 10.45
2013	672.00	+ 38.27
2014	893.20	+ 32.92

Chapter 13

Rethinking the Outputs of Chinese High-Speed Railways

ZHANG Huang and LI Jie

Introduction

On 30 January 2015, affected by the decline of international oil prices, the government of Mexico announced an indefinite postponement of the high-speed railway project that runs from Mexico City to Queretaro. This is the second time that China encountered setbacks in exporting its high-speed railway projects in this country. On 4 November 2014, a high-speed railway contract between China and Mexico was abruptly canceled. Equipped with cutting-edge technology, the export of Chinese high-speed railway plays an important role in politics, economy and culture in China itself and abroad as part of railway diplomacy. However, as a new initiative, this process also faces inevitable challenges and obstacles, which requires the Chinese government's rational and in-depth analysis. Chinese high-speed railway transportation technology serves the functions of economic and social development. The profound benefits of exporting Chinese rail technologies overseas are applicable to national politics, economy and culture. However, as a new development in terms of technological exports, challenges and setbacks are inevitable in the process of marketing the new product and product implementation in overseas market. How does one treat and cope with the challenges on high-speed railway overseas output? It is an important issue worthy of attention by the Chinese government.

From the Chinese perspective, the Chinese system's selling points include mature technology, high performance price ratio and abundant operation experience. However, these advantages may not be enough to offset the importance of unimpeded access to the sale of high-speed railways to overseas customers. Two setbacks Chinese companies encountered in the Mexico market reflect the strategic nature of Chinese high-speed railways from the perspective of its destination countries' national interests. In November 2014, the Mexican government canceled a US$3.7 billion contract to build the bullet train that was awarded earlier to a Chinese-led consortium, in spite of the legal validity of the entire bidding process. The news garnered international attention, as it had been touted in the media as the "No. 1 Overseas Order" for China's high-speed railway for a significant period of time. The stated reason for this abrupt withdrawal is because there was only one bidder in the bidding process, which drew the skepticism from the public about the transparency of the competitive tender system. As indicated in the government announcement, Mexico expected a fair bidding result without any skepticism from both society and its Congress.

The Chinese model

The deeper reason lies in a prevailing systemic defect in China's overseas project model. For a long time, Chinese enterprises have been relying too much on networking with the host countries' government when trying to expand their business abroad, as they believe, above all, that a close relationship with local authorities and elite class is essential to the success of their overseas projects. Another fundamental reason is a chronic disease in Chinese overseas engineering industrial practices for a long time. When expanding overseas markets, Chinese enterprises always implement the so-called 'the upper-level line', which was highly dependent on the receptivity of the local host government. In this concept, the development of large-scale infrastructure project is based on cultivating close contact with the local government and local elites. This strategy has yielded great successes in Africa and some South American countries for Chinese economic diplomacy in the past. Its advantage lies in the provision of official support and protection by the state for effective high administrative access and material resources, however, the drawback is the lack of communication and contact with the local public and the mass media (and other stakeholders in the project).

Indeed, by following this pattern, Chinese enterprises achieved great success in the overseas projects in Africa and some South American countries.

This model efficiently takes advantage of local administrative access to decision making at the highest levels of government, therefore Chinese enterprises acquire decisive advantage over overseas businesses. However, on the other hand, the downside to this model is that a communication channel linking to the opinions of local people and media is missing, which is considered to be an inherent defect in this economic diplomacy model. It is exactly because of this flaw in the economic diplomacy model that China encountered unprecedented resistance from Mexico, given constantly-fluctuating political conditions in this country. Especially against the background of "Iguana mass kidnapping" incident, the absence of both bidding competitors and transparency easily resulted in critical voices from the media, thus instigating skeptical sentiment amongst the population at large. With the presence of a highly developed mass media industry and a formidable political opposition in Mexico, "the upper-level line" has encountered unprecedented resistance, especially against the background of the "Iguala incident". The twin absence of both bidding competitors and the public's right to information about the bidding process resulted in public opinion backlash and provoked probing questions from the public.

The second setback that happened in 2015 exposed the lack of knowledge about the international investment environment for China. Chinese enterprises are unfamiliar with latent risks in making international investments, such as international political and financial risks, operational and technological innovation challenges and so forth. Intertwined with each other, these factors often result in a large gap between expectations and actual investment returns. This second setback in Mexico exposed Chinese deficiencies in knowledge and experience when it comes to Chinese enterprises navigating through the international investment environment. Compared to the domestic investment environment, the international investment environment is more unfamiliar territory for Chinese companies. The risks from international geopolitics and domestic politics, finance, operational and technological innovation interact with each other in a complex manner, leading to a large difference between the actual income obtainable and the expected returns from the investment project. As early as 2013, the unrest and economic recession in Thailand resulted in the interruption of "interchanging high-speed railway with rice" plan which was preliminarily reached between China and Thailand. From the perspective of overseas expansion of national interests, a slight error in judgment for the international investment environment may also cause the serious reduction of investment benefits, because China currently lacks enough power and specialized agencies to protect overseas investment. It is one of the errors contributing to the cancellation of the Chinese high-speed railway project in Mexico.

Mexican perceptions

In addition to the impact of investment pattern and investment environment, there is also a factor that cannot be ignored, that is, the Mexican government decision-making body has a cautious and skeptical attitude with regard to the economic output of Chinese high-speed railway. The former Mexican ambassador to China, Guajardo said on Twitter: "before the visit to China, the president canceled the contract to send out a strong signal: we are not turning to China for grace." (切格瓦斯,墨西哥前驻华大使谈高铁毁约: 不向中国求恩惠 http://news.hexun.com/2014-11-08/170190240.html.

The former Mexican ambassador to China talked about high-speed railway project, by indicating that Mexico is not turning to China for "grace" (the same word implies "favor" or "kindness".) (*Source*: 切格瓦斯, 墨西哥前驻华大使谈高铁毁约: 不向中国求恩惠 http://news.hexun.com/2014-11-08/170190240.html.) This speech is thought provoking. From a historical perspective, it often conveyed a strong colonial flavor when one country built railways in the territory of other countries. For example, at the beginning of the 20th century, western powers carved China up like a pie. As a Chinese history article points out: "where there were railways built by big powers, there were their orbit." (胡滨 十九世纪末帝国主义瓜分中国铁路利权的阴谋活动(一八九八—一八九九)《历史研究》***1956*** 年第 ***5*** 期| 89–104 页; [in English] Bin, Hu, The Conspiracy Which Imperialism Divided up the Rights of Chinese Railway Rights by the End of Nineteenth Century (1898–1899), history research, 1956 (5), 89–104.)

After World War II, technical assistance from developed countries to developing countries often attached harsh political conditions or economic conditions. Because the Chinese companies obtained construction rights to large projects at a low bid price, it may lead to a new wave of "China threat theory" from opponents of deals made with China. The opponent may ask some questions like: Whether building high-speed railway will result in

Chinese economic penetration? Once dependence on Chinese economic reaches a "dangerous" level, it prompts some observers to ask whether Mexico will play a passive economic role in its economic relationship with China. This may be the important factors influencing the decision-making process of the Mexican government in procuring high-speed railways.

Understanding local markets

The contrast between advantages of Chinese high-speed railway and predicament of high risks in overseas output testify to the fact that there are factors which influence technology transfer that are not solely related to the level of sophistication of technology and market demand. According to the theory of technological sociology, the growth of technology is a process and outcome of social construction. There are many other factors that also affect the development of technology, such as national culture, social psychology, political parties, aspirations of the general public and other subjective factors. Thus, the output of Chinese high-speed railway not only need to meet market demands, but also the connection between culture and psychology of the masses and all other stakeholders. The Chinese government or state-owned enterprises (SOEs) should acknowledge the diversity of social cultures, understand historical traditions, regime features, media influence, consumption propensities, the diversity of customs and habits of consumers in countries, which want to import Chinese high-speed railways. For example, in societies where the "auto culture" is highly developed, such as Western Europe and the US, high-speed railway can carry the implication of weakening the freedom to travel. Therefore, Chinese companies should achieve a seamless link between high-speed railways and other public vehicles, and provide one-stop public service to meet transportation needs instead of a stand-alone project. This may be a crucial factor when it comes to selling Chinese high-speed railway systems to Western Europe and the US.

Policy recommendation

For neighboring countries, in order to build networks of high-speed railway starting from China, Chinese companies and the state should not only avoid the traditional "tributary system" and civilization mentality, but also avoid cross-cultural barriers faced in exporting high-speed railway systems by maintaining an inclusive and open attitude, and carry out cooperation in high-speed railway construction under equal terms and conditions with an understanding of the cultural identity of destination markets. Marketing Chinese High-Speed Rail to the world may also trigger a new round of the "China threat theory". In line with deliberate interpretations by some foreign media, Chinese internationalization attempt in the field of building railway traffic through constructing a high-speed railway network, which radiates outwards to surrounding countries, and building traffic arteries across the South American continent, is directly related to its intentions and national interests in politics, economy, strategy and so on. For countries that are suspicious about the Chinese high-speed railway, especially neighboring countries around China, China should be more proactive and patiently explain its peaceful development intention. In essence, the sale and exportation of Chinese high-speed railway systems is a normative economic activity regulated by the market mechanism against the backdrop of globalization, just like other products and commodities made in China. China should express its cooperative, win–win intentions clearly, at the same time, attract a wide range of local technical elites, administrative elites and labor force in carrying out high-speed railway design projects, operation and maintenance. China and others countries can work together to share the bigger economic cake of exporting high-speed railway, while the presence of high-speed railway benefits local communities and people.

Section E

Region Specific Section — Country Case Studies

Chapter 14

One Belt One Road, China and Europe: Economic Strategy and Pragmatic Economies

Winglok HUNG

Introduction

This chapter aims to explain "One Belt One Road" (OBOR) with the use of Professor Yan Xuetong's analytical framework of international system. The central question of this chapter is "Why is Europe more important than other regions in China's OBOR economic strategy?" In this first part I explain my conception and understanding of OBOR. OBOR is a new economic strategy. In the remaining parts, I continue to examine China's economic strategies and relations with Europe under the framework of OBOR. As OBOR is fundamentally different from an American-led private investment and trade liberalization since the Second World War, China's OBOR attempts to construct a new international system after the global financial crisis in 2008. In the conclusion, I return to the same puzzle of why Europe is important in China's OBOR strategy to establish a new international order.

On 7 September 2013, China's President Xi Jinping first proposed the idea to build a Silk Road Economic Belt between China and Central Asia at the Nazarbayev University in Astana, Kazakhstan.[1] A month later, the idea of the 21st century Maritime Silk Road was advocated during China's President Xi Jinping's visit to Indonesia. In the Third Plenary Session of the 18th

[1] Chinese President Delivers Speech at Nazarbayev University. *China Daily*, 8 September 2013 http://news.xinhuanet.com/english/photo/2013-09/08/c_132701546.htm.

Central Committee of the Communist Party of China, the strategies of the Silk Road Economic Belt and the 21st century Maritime Silk Road were confirmed.[2] In December 2013, the Chinese Foreign Minister, Wang Yi, mentioned that the Silk Road Economic Belt and the 21st century Maritime Silk Road aimed to develop long-term strategic objectives, directions and framework with China's periphery neighbors in the next 5–10 years in an interview with the Chinese official newspaper *People's Daily*.[3]

"One Belt One Road" is still an ongoing project. It is possible that this strategy will evolve because of changing international political and economic circumstances. Meanwhile, it seems that different people perceive this strategy very differently. For example, some academicians may perceive OBOR as China's new economic paradigm that focuses on connectivity and cooperation among different countries in the world. Some foreign government officials may perceive OBOR as China's strategy to start a discriminatory trade and investment system exclusively with emerging countries.[4] It was even found that Chinese media reports contradicted each other. For instance, *China Review News* (中国评论) articulated that China should first enlarge its influence in the Southeast Asia region under OBOR while *Xinhua News* (新华社) suggested that China should focus more on One Belt rather than One Road as it is expected to face opposition from Association of southeast Asian Nations (ASEAN) countries.[5] However, I do not agree with the view that China's OBOR attempts to exclude developed countries, such as countries in Europe. This chapter aims to argue that

---

[2] Sun Jiuwen, Gao Zhigang zhu bian, 孙久文, 高志刚主编, *Si chou zhi lu jing ji dai yu qu yu jing ji fa zhan yan jiu* 丝绸之路经济带与区域经济发展研究 [*Research on Silk Road Economic Belt and Regional Economic Development*]. Beijing: Jing ji guan li chu ban she. (北京: 经济管理出版社, 2015). All the Chinese reference sources were translated by the author.

[3] 'Zhong guo te se da guo wai jiao de cheng gong shi jian (2013 niandu tebie baodao) — Wai jiao bu zhang Wan Yi tan er ling yi san nian zhong guo wai jiao' '中国特色大国外交的成功实践(2013年度特别报导)—外交部长王毅谈二〇一三年中国外交' [Successful implementations of great power diplomacy with Chinese characteristics (Special reports of 2013) — Minister of Foreign Affairs Wang Yi highlighted China's diplomacy in 2013], *Ren Min Ri Bao* 人民日报 [*People's Daily*], 19 December 2013, 3.

[4] Personal experience. One Belt One Road International Forum. Hong Kong Convention and Exhibition Centre, 24 July 2015, Hong Kong.

[5] Chinese Media on the "One Belt, One Road" Strategy. *Chinascope* (73), 2015, 38.

Europe is vital in China's OBOR strategic plan. More details will be discussed in the following section.

Literature review of OBOR

Since the "One Belt One Road" was confirmed in late 2013, there has been a dearth of academic reports, especially in the English language on the topic of "One Belt One Road". When the term "One Belt One Road" was searched in the document title box with the term "China" via ProQuest search engine, only two scholarly works were found.[6] However, when the term "New Silk Road" was used for searching, 1,857 results of scholarly publications were found. Apparently, English literature preferred the name "New Silk Road" rather than "One Belt One Road" for discussion. For example, Chris Devonshire-Ellis recently published a book titled *China's New Economic Silk Road: The Great Eurasian Game & The String of Pearls*. In addition, there are other journal articles with the title of "New Silk Road".[7]

---

[6] Chinese Media on the "One Belt, One Road" Strategy. *Chinascope* (73), 2015, 38.; Yan, Mengzhao and Shumin Li., Chinese Firms' International Market Entry to Main Participating Countries of "One Belt One Road." *The Institute of Electrical and Electronics Engineers, Inc.(IEEE) Conference Proceedings,* June 2015, 1–6. ProQuest search result [downloaded on 12 November 2015] available at http://search.proquest.com/results/13533FEBCC654250PQ/1/$7b$22limiters$22:$5b$5d,$22mqlversion$22:$221.1$22,$22v$22:$221$22,$22sort$22:$22relevance$22,$22param$22:$7b$22NAVIGATORS$22:$22navsummarynav,sourcetypenav, decadenav$28filter$3d110$2f0$2f*,sort$3dname$2fascending$29,yearnav$28filter$3d1100$2f0$2f*,sort$3dname$2fascending$29,yearmonthnav$28filter$3d120$2f0$2f*,sort$3dname$2fascending$29,monthnav$28sort$3dname$2fascending$29,daynav$28sort$3dname$2fascending$29,pubtitlenav,objecttypenav,languagenav$28filter$3d200$2f0$2f*$29$22,$22RS$22: $22OP$22,$22chunkSize$22:$2250$22,$22instance$22: $22prod.academic$22,$22ftblock$22:$22740842+1+149000+149001+149113+113+670831+740848+670829+660845+660843+660840$22, $22removeDuplicates$22:$22true$22$7d, $22serializer$22:$22std1.5$22, $22searchterms$22:$5b$7b$22name$22:$22$22,$22qry$22:$22ti$28$27One+belt+one+road$27$29+AND+$28china$29$22, $22fld$22:$22citationBody$22,$22top$22: $22AND$22$7d$5d, $22navs$22:$5b$5d,$22meta$22:$7b$22UsageSearchMode$22: $22Advanced$22, $22dbselections$22:$22allAvailable$22, $22SEARCH_ID_TIMESTAMP$22:$221447328537306$22,$22siteLimiters$22:$22SourceType, +DocumentType,+ Language$22$7d,$22querytype$22:$22advanced:OS$22$7d?accountid=14426.

[7] Devonshire-Ellis, Chris, *China' New Economic Silk Road. The Great Eurasian Game and the String of Pearls* (Hong Kong: Asia Briefing Ltd., 2015).

There is a further challenge in conducting this literature review. "One Belt One Road" actually refers to two concepts "The Silk Road Economic Belt" (One Belt) and "The 21st Century Maritime Silk Road" (One Road). Theoretically, it is possible for China to perform well in One Belt but fail in One Road. Therefore, the general description on the topic of "China's New Silk Road" used in the literature might not always be discussing the two concepts separately.[8] Without detailed clarification, it will be difficult for us to review and explain arguments from the English literature. By contrast, China's scholarly work has relatively clearer classification of two separate subjects. There are books and journal articles on "The Silk Road Economic Belt",[9] "The 21st century Maritime Silk Road"[10] and the whole OBOR project.[11] To facilitate discussion, I will review the literature regarding

---

[8] This point will be discussed in the next part.

[9] For example, Liu Huaqin, 刘华芹, *Si chou zhi lu jing ji dai: Ou ya da lu xin qi ju* 丝绸之路经济带: 欧亚大陆新棋局 [*Silk Road Economic Belt: The New Eurasia Opportunity*], (Beijing: Zhongguo shangwu chu ban she (北京: 中国商务出版社, 2015); Sun Jiuwen, Gao Zhigang zhu bian, 孙久文, 高志刚主编, *Si chou zhi lu jing ji dai yu qu yu jing ji fa zhan yan jiu* 丝绸之路经济带与区域经济发展研究 [*Research on Silk Road Economic Belt and Regional Economic Development*]. (Beijing: Jing ji guan li chu ban she, 2015 (北京: 经济管理出版社, 2015).

[10] For example, Zhao jiang lin zhu bian 赵江林主编, *21 Shi ji hai shang si chou zhi lu: Mu biao, shi shi ji chu yu dui ce yan jiu* 21 世纪海上丝绸之路: 目标构想、实施基础与对策研究 [*The 21st Century Maritime Silk Road: Target, Implementation and Policy Suggestions.* Beijing: She hui ke xue wen xian chu ban she, 2015) (北京: 社会科学文献出版社, 2015); Shiyu, Zhang, Zhang Yong bian zhu 张诗雨, 张勇编着, *Hai shang xin si lu: 21 shi ji hai shang si chou zhi lu fa zhan si lu yu gou xiang* 海上新丝路: 21 世纪海上丝绸之路发展思路与构想 [*New Maritime Silk Road: The 21st Century Silk Road: Ideas and Implementation.* Beijing: Zhong guo fa zhang chu ban she, 2014 (北京: 中国发展出版社, 2014).

[11] For example, Zhangjie zhu bian 张洁主编, Zhongguo zhou bian an quan xing shi ping gu: Yi dai yi lu yu wai wei zhan lüe 中国周边安全形势评估: "一带一路"与周边战略 [*China's Regional Security Environment Review 2015: "One Belt One Road" and Its Regional Strategy.* Beijing: She hui ke xue wen xian chu ban she, 2015 (北京: 社会科学文献出版社, 2015); Xiangyang, Li, 李向阳, *Yi dai yi lu: Ding wei, nei han ji xu yao you xian chu li de guan xi* 一带一路: 定位、内涵及需要优先处理的关系 ["*One Belt One Road" Orientations, Contents and Challenges*] (Beijing: She hui ke xue wen xian chu ban she, 2015) (北京: 社会科学文献出版社, 2015).; Wang, Yiwei 王义桅, *Yi dai yi lu: Ji yu yu tiao zhan* 一带一路: 机遇与挑战 ["*One Belt One Road*": *Opportunities and Challenges*]. Beijing: Ren min chu ban she, 2015 (北京: 人民出版社, 2015).

themes and arguments on OBOR rather than focus on the written language of the publication.

First, some papers generally lack a clear definition of "One Belt One Road". These papers might be considered good research articles in their subfields but possibly did not have a substantial connection with China's OBOR. For example, one academic journal had recently published two special issues on the topic "New Silk Road Project" in mid-2015.[12] A few papers were based on the conference presentation held in Macau in June 2013.[13] Serious readers may be uncertain of whether the 'new' OBOR strategy is similar to the "old" China's foreign policy in the different explanations and interpretations of the Silk Road. For example, the "New Silk Road" project is regarded as "massive trade and infrastructure networks which would foster closer economic ties between East Asia and Europe, and promote economic cooperation among most of the countries in the two continents".[14] What is the meaning of "economic cooperation"? Are there any similarities between the existing bilateral trade agreements and OBOR? Also, shall we include Japan, Russia or Mongolia in the discussion of "East Asia"? If so, why did Japan appear to distance itself from OBOR while Russia, South Korea and Mongolia joined Asian Infrastructure Investment Bank (AIIB) as founding members? This tendency to discuss OBOR may cause further confusion to both academic and non-academic scholars.

Furthermore, how OBOR will affect China's current economic relations with other countries is uncertain. This approach critically examined China's foreign relations and its domestic tension. For example, China's bilateral relations with its neighboring countries such as India and Turkey have been comprehensively studied.[15] Scholars analyzed the domestic ethnic tension

---

[12] Shen, Simon, Special Issue: New Silk Road Project. *East Asia: An International Quarterly*, 32(1), 2015, 1–5.; New Silk Road Project (Part 2). *East Asia: An International Quarterly*, 32(2), 2015, 101–205.

[13] For example, Mackerras Colin, Xinjiang in China's Foreign Relations: Part of a New Silk Road or Central Asian Zone of Conflict? *East Asia: An International Quarterly*, 32(1), 2015, 40, acknowledgments.

[14] Bill Chou, Xuejie Ding, A Comparative Analysis of Shenzhen and Kashgarin Development as Special Economic Zones. *East Asia: An International Quarterly*, 32(2), 2015, 118.

[15] For example, Mackerras, Colin, Xinjiang in China's Foreign Relations: Part of a New Silk Road or Central Asian Zone of Conflict?. *East Asia: An International Quarterly*, 32(1), 2015,

and social development in Xinjiang. Research on the social development in Xinjiang Uyghur Autonomous Region, studied from 1999 to 2009, also showed that Uyghurs are not necessary involved in the policy-making process.[16] Nevertheless, the papers did not explicitly present a clear correlation between China's foreign relations and domestic conflicts with the exact plans or practices of OBOR. It seems unclear how China's Xinjiang ethnic riots in 2009 will affect China's economic strategy in 2015 and how China's OBOR will also affect its economic strategy with India, Russia or Turkey.

Second, most researchers focus on China's attempt to enforce a greater political (or geopolitical) relationship with emerging countries in OBOR. This branch of literature often links up with China's political and military power in the world. In the *Blue Book of Asia-Pacific*, published by the Chinese Academy of Social Sciences, it was suggested that China's growing emphasis to build a good relationship with Central Asian and South Asian countries is in order to balance the US's and possibly Russia's influence in Central Asia or Asia.[17] OBOR is regarded to be a part of China's assertive foreign policy under the leadership of President Xi Jinping.[18] Some papers have argued that China should strengthen its relations with Russia and Central Asian countries to counterbalance American hegemony.[19] China

25–42; Colakoglu, Selcuk, "Dynamics of Sino-Turkish Relations: A Turkish Perspective. *East Asia: An International Quarterly*, 32(1), 2015, 7–23; Mukherjee, Kunal, Comparing China and India's Disputed Borderland Regions: Xinjiang, Tibet, Kashmir, and the Indian Northeast. *East Asia: An International Quarterly*, 32(2), 2015, 173–205; Shichor, Y, Pawns in Central Asia's Playground: Uyghurs Between Moscow and Beijing. *East Asia: An International Quarterly*, 32(2), 2015, 101–116.

16 Cappelletti, Alessandra, Developing the Land and the People: Social Development Issues in Xinjiang Uyghur Autonomous Region (1999–2009). *East Asia: An International Quarterly*, 32(2), 2015, 137–171.

17 Li Xiangyang zhu bian, Ya tai lan pi shu: Ya tai di qu fa zhan bao gao 2015 Yi dai yi lu 李向阳主编, 亚太蓝皮书: 亚太地区发展报告(*2015*) 一带一路 [*Blue Book of Asia Pacific: Annual Report on Development of Asia-Pacific (2015) One Belt One Road*]. Beijing: She hui ke xue wen xian chu ban she, 2015. (北京: 社会科学文献出版社, 2015), BI Zong baogao 总报告[General Report], 1–10.

18 Tiezzi, Shannon, Where is China's Silk Road Actually Going? *The Diplomat*, 30 March 2015 [downloaded on 19 November 2015], available at http://thediplomat.com/2015/03/where-is-chinas-silk-road-actually-going/

19 Zhangjie zhu bian 张洁主编, Zhongguo zhou bian an quan xing shi ping gu: "Yi dai yi lu" yu wai wei zhan lüe 中国周边安全形势评估: "一带一路"与周边战略 [*China's Regional*

intends to strengthen its maritime routes to facilitate economic trading. However, China has yet to build political and strategic trust with various countries.[20] In brief, political relationships are important for economic cooperation. This argument can be found in the discussions of One Belt or One Road. If China can dominate the sea route and the South China Sea or the route in Central Asian regions, China will be more likely to rise as a dominant power in the 21st century.

It is worth mentioning that Kazakhstan competed with Beijing in the bid to host the 2022 Winter Olympics in 2014. If China's ultimate aim was to build a friendly political relationship with Kazakhstan, then why did the Beijing authority choose not to give up the bidding so that Kazakhstan would have a higher chance to win the bid and be thankful to the Chinese government? If economic and political aspects are completely separate for discussion, it seems that focusing too much on the possible political dimension of OBOR does not highly correlate with OBOR as an economic strategy.

Third, cultural and geographical factors are critical in OBOR. The ancient Silk Road contributed to the spread of Buddhism and Chinese porcelains. China's Silk Road Economic Belt starts from Yunnan, Tibet, Xinjiang and other western regions rather than China's coastal areas or urbanized cities such as Beijing or Nanjing. The geographical locations, religions, human activities and resources are not similar to those in the eastern part of China. For instance, China has more grassland in its western regions.[21] The percentage of grassland is geographically similar to five Central Asian countries: Kazakhstan, Kyrgyzstan, Uzbekistan, Turkmenistan and Tajikistan. In the

---

Security Environment Review 2015: "*One Belt One Road*" *and Its Regional Strategy*]. Beijing: She hui ke xue wen xian chu ban she, 2015 (北京: 社会科学文献出版社, 2015), 16.

[20] Chaturvedy Rajeev Ranjan, New Maritime Silk Road: Converging Interests and Regional Responses. Institute of South Asian Studies (ISAS) Working Paper, National University of Singapore, No. 197, October 2014, 1–20.

[21] Lin Ma, Liu Dazhi and Teng Fei, 马林 刘大志, 滕飞, Si chou zhi lu jing ji dai yu wo guo cao yuan ke chi xu fa zhan zhan lue yan jiu, 丝绸之路经济带与我国草园可持续发展战略研究 [Silk Road Economic Belt and Study on China's Grassland Sustainable Development Strategy], Zhang Lijun zhu bian 张丽君主编, *Si chou zhi lu jing ji dai: Gou jian yu fa zhan yan jiu*丝绸之路经济带: 构建与发展研究 [*Silk Road Economic Belt: Ideas and Development Study*]. Beijing: Zhong guo jing ji chu ban she (北京: 中国经济出版社, 2015), 251–262.

plan of OBOR, tourism, cultural and religious exchanges are emphasized to promote economic cooperation.[22]

Physical and human geography will reshape methods for economic transaction. For example, people rely on donkeys rather than automobile cars for transporting goods to climb over mountains in China's western regions. Religions, culture and local unique products such as silk, tea, china porcelain wares were highlighted in the ancient history of China's Silk Road.[23] From a geographical perspective, the economic strategy in China's western regions might be different from the urbanized plan which China started and gradually implemented from the 1980s. Cultural stakeholders hope that the unique Chinese art products and Chinese ancient philosophy of arts can be promoted to other regions through One Belt and One Road routes.[24] These cultural products are greatly different from McDonald's hamburger restaurants, Starbucks coffee shops or Coca-Cola soft drink cans that exist in most globalized cities. They offer an alternative.

Forth, this approach focuses on economic and investment activities. Studies have focused more on infrastructure projects, increased investment in both Asia and Europe.[25] There are relatively few papers substantially concerned with the China — European Union (EU) relationship in the discussion of One Belt or One Road. However, Europe is the final destination in China's One Belt strategy[26] with Africa expected to be a strategic point in

---

[22] Zhao Kejin, 赵可金, Yi dai yi lu de Zhong guo fang lue yan jiu 一带一路"的中国方略研究, *Xin jiang shi fan de xue xue bao* 新疆师范大学学报 [*Journal of Xinjiang Normal University (Philosophy and Social Sciences)*], (1), 2016, 22–23.

[23] Sun Jiuwen, Gao Zhigang zhu bian, 孙久文, 高志刚主编, *Si chou zhi lu jing ji dai yu qu yu jing ji fa zhan yan jiu* 丝绸之路经济带与区域经济发展研究 [*Research on Silk Road Economic Belt and Regional Economic Development*]. Beijing: Jing ji guan li chu ban she, 2015 (北京: 经济管理出版社, 2015), Chapter 5.

[24] Pan Tianbo, and Hu Yukang, 潘天波, 胡玉康, Si lu qi yi yu zhong guo mei xue si xiang de chuan bo 丝路漆艺与中国美学思想的传播, *Xin jiang shi fan de xue xue bao* 新疆师范大学学报[*Journal of Xinjiang Normal University (Philosophy and Social Sciences)*], 35 (2), 2014 89–95.

[25] For example, Scott Kennedy, David A. Parker, "Building China's 'One Belt, One Road'", publication. Center for Strategic and International Studies, Washington, DC [downloaded on 22 November 2015], available http://csis.org/publication/building-chinas-one-belt-one-road.

[26] Hu Angang, Ma Wei and Wan Yilong 胡鞍钢, 马伟, 鄢一龙, '"Si chou zhi lu jing ji dai": Zhan lue, ding wei he shi xian lu jing', '"丝绸之路经济带": 战略内涵、定位和实现路径' [Connotation, Definition, and Passage of "Silk Road Economic Belt"], *Xin jiang shi fan de xue*

OBOR.[27] It was suggested that Rotterdam, the Netherlands will be the final stop in the One Belt route from Shenzhen, China via Myanmar, India, Pakistan, Iran, Turkey and Bulgaria.[28] There are advantages for establishing an economic network with Europe. Most European countries recorded a high GDP per capita, have an advance level of economy and technology, scientific technology and cultural activities. As a result, China may focus more on trading, education and cultural exchanges in Europe while focusing on energy resources in the Central Asia region in OBOR.[29]

Overall, it seems that most of the details of OBOR are not completely publicised. Particularly, the exact practices or policies of OBOR are still not very clear. Furthermore, how long their plans will last remains unknown. It is unclear whether OBOR will last for 5 or 10 years or for as long as 20 or 30 years. Nevertheless, it is still possible for China to implement the One Belt and One Road project despite not many people understanding clearly the idea. Similarly, I believe that few scholars and even Chinese government officials thoroughly understood China's open-door policy in former Chinese leader Deng Xiaoping's economic blueprint in late 1970s, even though the market reform has been implementing and evolving in the last few decades in China.

Defining OBOR

One Belt One Road emphasizes its "newness" and it is neither an American-led globalization nor European-type free trade economic zone. In an exclusive report published by the Chinese Academy of Social Sciences, it summarized that the current regional economic cooperation mechanism can be conceptualized

---

xue bao 新疆师范大学学报 [*Journal of Xinjiang Normal University* (*Philosophy and Social Sciences*)], 35(2), 2014, 1–10.

27 Lin Yifu, 林毅夫, "'Yi dai yi lu" xu yao jia shang "yi zhou"', "'一带一路"需要加上"一洲"', *Dang zheng lun tan* (*Gan bu wen zhai*) 党政论坛（干部文摘）, (4), 2015, 32.

28 Dumitresu George Cornel, Central and Eastern European Countries Focus on the Silk Road Economic Belt. *Global Economic Observer,* 3(1), 2015, 144–153.

29 Hu Angang, Ma Wei and Wan Yilong 胡鞍钢, 马伟, 鄢一龙, Si chou zhi lu jing ji dai: Zhan lue, ding wei he shi xian lu jing', 丝绸之路经济带：战略内涵、定位和实现路径' [Connotation, Definition, and Passage of "Silk Road Economic Belt"], *Xin jiang shi fan de xue xue bao* 新疆师范大学学报. *Journal of Xinjiang Normal University* (*Philosophy and Social Sciences*), 35(2), 2014, 2–4.

into five major categories: (1) Economic Free Zone, (2) Tariff Alliance, (3) Common Economic Market, (4) Economic Integration, (5) Political and Economic Integration. Nowadays, only Europe has the above five categories at the same time.[30] OBOR does not aim to reproduce the European model. By contrast, it is defined as a new strategy.

This short chapter defines OBOR mostly based on a special report published by the Chinese Academy of Social Sciences.[31] First, OBOR is an economic strategy that aims to target the world market and not the domestic market. Second, OBOR helps to promote economic integration between China and strategic countries or partners. Third, OROB is an economic strategy with the assistance of diplomatic practices. In the past, Chinese companies, especially small and medium Chinese enterprises, explored their business opportunities abroad by mostly relying on their own networks and resources. Now, China's official diplomacy helps domestic companies to develop overseas business networks under the OBOR strategy. Forth, OBOR attempts to promote economic integration beyond existing mechanisms such as the World Trade Organization (WTO), Free Trade Area of the Asia Pacific (FTAPP), the Trans-Pacific Partnership (TPP) and the Transatlantic Trade and Investment Partnership (TTIP).[32]

The historical background of the ancient Silk Road is worth noting. It was popular from the Han Dynasty (206 BC–AD 220) to the Ming Dynasty (AD 18th century) before the emergence of western imperialism and colonialism started from the 19th century. Before the age of imperialism, China explored the "West" including India, Iraq, Iran rather than the United States or Japan for trading goods or cultural exchanges.[33] The ancient Silk Road passed through Central Asia, the Persian Gulf and the Arab region to

---

30 Li Xiangyang, 李向阳, *Yi dai yi lu: Ding wei, nei han ji xu yao you xian chu li de guan xi* 一带一路: 定位、内涵及需要优先处理的关系 [*"One Belt One Road" Orientations, Contents and Challenges*]. Beijing: She hui ke xue wen xian chu ban she, 2015 (北京: 社会科学文献出版社, 2015), 21.

31 *Ibid.*, 15–19.

32 *Ibid.*, 15–19, with minor addition and explanation by the author.

33 The author acknowledges Professor Chang Chak-yan on this point.

reach Europe and Africa.[34] In roughly 600 BC, the tradition of Persian statecraft was well established. Both the Roman Empire and the Parthian Empire dominated the majority of the Middle East region.[35] The region experienced a sophisticated culture of commerce, which attracted Chinese in Han Dynasty to explore. Fundamentally, OBOR might be inspired by the period of the Ancient Silk Road under the age of globalization.

Assumptions, hypothesis, method and limitations

Great powers are assumed to be rational powers. China and two European countries namely Britain and Germany are considered to be great powers, while France, Italy and Spain are considered to be middle powers. Great powers are assumed to have state capability to adjust and decide international norms, however, states are never certain about the intentions of other states before the implementation of economic or diplomatic practices. Middle powers are less likely to decide or set international norms. Power is defined as a combination of three elements: the number of people who can work and fight; economic productivity and the effectiveness of the political system.[36]

Nations are no longer the only actors in the international system or the international order. This chapter does not share the liberalist assumption that economic cooperation must bring harmony between nations or even world peace. Furthermore, there are now some extreme non-state actors or networks such as Islamic State (ISIS), Al-Qaeda that can greatly disturb the social order. This is not the main purpose of this chapter to discuss whether economic integration must achieve peace or harmony in the international system. The current international configuration is assumed to be unipolar and the United States is the only dominant power after the Cold War period. I assume that

[34]Heng li Ji xin ge 亨利. 基辛格 [Henry Kissenger], Hu li ping deng yi 胡利平等译 [Translated by Hu Liping *et al.*], *Shi jie zhi xu*世界秩序 [*World Order*]. Beijing: Zhong xin chu ban she 北京: 中信出版社, 2015), 116–118.

[35]Zheng chi yan 郑赤琰, Cong san ge jiao du kan 'yi dai yi, 从三个角度看'一带一路, [Examining "One Belt One Road" from three perspective] *Yin ni jian dian* 印尼焦点 [*Indonesia Focus*], (4), 2015.

[36]To facilitate our discussions, 'the international system' and 'the international order' are used interchangeably in this chapter.

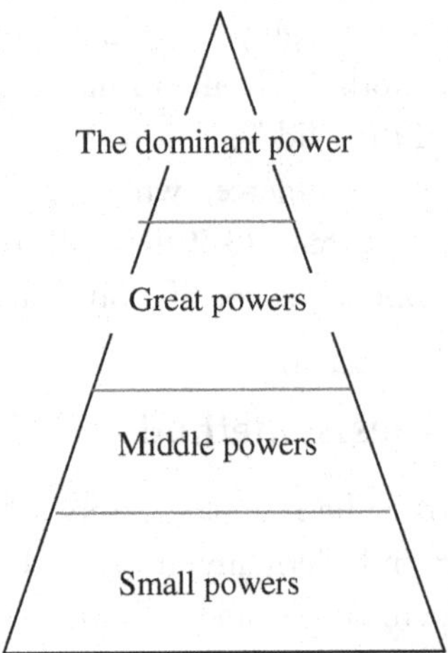

Figure 1: Class power pyramid[37]

there is no second dominant power in the system. In a classic power pyramid, the world consists of one dominant power, great powers, middle powers and small powers as showed in Figure 1:

The following hypotheses can be proposed:

Hypothesis 1: One Belt One Road is a new economic strategy to China and the world. Since it is an economic strategic plan, OBOR stresses economic benefits rather than political benefits to China and/or other countries.

Hypothesis 2: Company but not country is an important actor to generate profits.

Hypothesis 3: Existing economic norms are no longer feasible and new economic norms should be built.

Scholarly work, online materials and Chinese media reports on OBOR and Europe from December 2013 to October 2015 will be analyzed. Some

[37] With reference to Tammen Ronald L, *et al., Power Transitions: Strategies for the 21st Century.* New York: Chatham House Publishers, 2000, 7, Figure 1.1.

arguments will also be based on the author's personal observations, conversations with scholars and public lectures attended on the topic of the OBOR economic strategy. There are limitations in this chapter. The OBOR strategy is examined entirely based on open sources such as media reports, books, journals and public lectures. The author has no connection with any Chinese government officials or entrepreneurs. It is possible that the exact motivation or practices of OBOR may not be the same as what can be found in public and open sources. It is also possible that entrepreneurs and business companies understand and practise the OBOR economic strategy differently from what has been published.

Analytical framework: Yan Xuetong's analysis of international system

As discussed earlier, OBOR is a new economic strategy. This section borrows the framework of international system to illustrate how this new economic strategy will transform the system.[38] In Professor Yan Xuetong's study about transformation of the international system, the international system is generally composed of three elements, namely international actors, international configuration and international norms.[39] In ancient times, Europe consisted of Kingdoms and China consisted of various vassal states such as the states of Qin, Chu, Qi and so on as inter-state actors. The international configuration is present in the form of unipolar, bipolar or multipolar. International norms usually refer to the common standard in international affairs and include the norm of sovereignty, the norm of annexation, the norm of occupation or the norm of non-interference and non-annexation.[40]

The international system will be only transformed when at least two components are changed in the system. Table 1 sums up the components in

[38] Yan Xuetong, 阎学通, *She jie quan li de zhuan yi*: *Zheng zhi ling dao yu zhan lue jing zheng* 世界权力的转移: 政治领导与战略竞争 [*The Shift of World Power. Political Leadership and Strategic Competition*]. Beijing: Beijing da xue chu ban she, 2015 (北京: 北京大学出版社, 2015).

[39] *Ibid.*

[40] *Ibid.*, 76–78.

Table 1: Three components in the international system

	International Actors	International Configuration	International Norms
The Middle Ages System (5th–15th century)	The pope and kingdoms	Multipolar	Norms of annexation
The Westphalian System (AD 1648–1792)	Nations-states	Multipolar	Norms of sovereignty
The Vienna System (AD 1814–1913)	Nations-states	Multipolar	Norms of interference
The Yalta System (AD 1945–1991)	Nations-states	Bipolar	Norms of non-interference and non-annexation
The Yalta System (The Post-Cold Era, AD 1991–2014)	Nations-states, International organizations (e.g. WTO, IMF)	Unipolar	Norms of non-interference non-annexation
One Belt One Road System (AD 2015–)	Nations-states, Business corporations	Multipolar	Pragmatic economy norms

Note: This table is an edited version with reference to Professor Yan Xuetong's "The Shift of the World Centre and its Impact on the Change of the International System".[41] The post-cold war era and OBOR system were added by the author

the international system during different periods. The last row shows that three components are expected to change in the OBOR economic strategy.

Why focus on "Europe"?

It was argued that Europe has always been the center of the world since the 19th century.[42] If China and Africa, the Middle East or Latin America strengthen economic integration and set new economic norms, it is difficult

[41] Yan Xuetong, The Shift of the World Centre and its Impact on the Change of the International System. *East Asia: An International Quarterly*, 30(2), 2013, 227, Table 1.

[42] Yan Xuetong, The Shift of the World Centre and its Impact on the Change of the International System, *East Asia: An International Quarterly*, 32(2), 2015, 221–222.

to argue whether the "international" order is transformed as these regions have not been generally regarded as the center of the world economies in the past few centuries. Africa has been even described as a "shadow" in the present neo-liberal international order.[43] As China is located in Asia, any changes between China and other Asian countries are more likely to be regarded as a transformation of the "regional" system rather than "international" system. However, if any two of the three criteria namely international actors, international configuration and international norms in Europe are changed, it is more likely to argue that the international order may be transformed.

Banks and geopolitics: Establishing the AIIB

There is a Chinese saying from *Sun Tzu's The Art of War*, 'Grain (army provision) comes first before moving three troops' (三军未动，粮草先行). In modern period, people need to ensure that they have enough cash or financial resources before implementing any strategy.[44] As OBOR is a strategy, China should first think of a feasible way to backup this economic strategy. After the financial crisis in 2008, it resulted in the collapse of Lehman Brothers and the merge of the global insurance and financial services organization, American International Group (AIG). Other international giant banks such as Citigroup, HSBC Holdings, Standard Chartered and other financial institutes appeared to have certain problems in managing a large sum of funding and therefore, it is important to establish a new international financial institute for funding OBOR.

Hence, the AIIB was established. AIIB, a Chinese-led initiative was proposed in October 2013.[45] This was announced just after a month when Xi Jinping delivered the idea of One Belt in Kazakhstan, September 2013. After proposing the establishment of AIIB, 21 Asian countries agreed to join

---

[43] Ferguson, James, *Global Shadows: Africa in the Neoliberal World Order*. Durham: Duke University Press, 2006.

[44] McCredie, Karen, *Sun Tzu's The Art of War: A 52 Brilliant Ideas Interpretation*. Oxford: Infinite Ideas, 2008, 17–18.

[45] About us, AIIB's official website [downloaded on 23 November 2015], available at http://www.aiib.org/html/aboutus/AIIB/.

AIIB.[46] In March 2015, the United Kingdom announced that the country intended to join AIIB and other European countries including Austria, Germany, Finland, France, Italy, the Netherlands, Portugal and Spain later joined AIIB as founding members.[47] According to an official document, AIIB will finance projects that promote sustainable development and regional cooperation.[48]

Although China did not explicitly explain the reasons for setting up the AIIB, it is important to compare it with two other similar institutes namely the World Bank and the Asian Development Bank. Media reported that the World Bank is now led by the United States while the Asian Development Bank is dominated by Japan, so China is now setting up a new financial institute.[49] Nevertheless, this media report did not articulate the fact that the US has been recovering from the global financial crisis in 2008 and Japan's economy has been staggering for decades. America and Japan might plan to reserve financial budget to deal with domestic economic crisis and the existing capital and financial resources may not be enough to fund large infrastructure projects overseas. As a result, it is logical for China to establish AIIB to back up the OBOR economic strategy. AIIB becomes a great financial alterative especially with the involvement of European countries.

International actors of the international system will not be changed as AIIB is similar to other international organizations such as the International Monetary Fund (IMF) and the World Bank in the international system. However, the international configuration may be changed. International configuration is determined by two major factors: comparative strengths and strategic relationships of major power.[50] As China, Germany and the United Kingdom are considered to be the great powers, the international

---

46 Zhong guo chou jian ya tou hang 21 guo you yi can jia 中国筹建亚投行 21 国有意参加' [China planned to establish AIIB, 21 nations intended to join], *Xiang gang shang bao* 香港商报 *Hong Kong Commercial Daily*, 22 October 2014, A19.

47 50 guo qian ya tou hang xie ding 50 国签亚投行协定 [50 nations signed AIIB aggrement], *Wen hui bao* 文汇报. *Wen Wei Po*, 30 June 2015, A08.

48 Articles of Agreement, AIIB [downloaded on 23 November 2015], available at [http://www.aiib.org/uploadfile/2015/0814/20150814022158430.pdf.

49 Why China is Creating a New "World Bank" for Asia. *The Economist*, 11 November 2014.

50 Yan Xuetong, A Bipolar World is More Likely Than a Unipolar or Multipolar One. China–US Focus, Carnegie-Tsinghua Center for Global Policy, 20 April 2015.

configuration will be changed from unipolar to multipolar as other great powers have the authority to create and establish an international financial institute. Also, it is expected that the economic power of China, Germany and the United Kingdom will further increase due to these countries sharing the economic profits from OBOR.

Chinese and European firms in OBOR

Firms are expected to be involved in OBOR. Without the involvement of Chinese firms, OBOR would simply be regarded as another China's foreign assistance program.[51] In the plan of OBOR, various Chinese actors such as private companies, state-owned companies, non-government organizations, cultural and educational institutes will explore overseas economic opportunities.[52] Particularly, small and medium business firms and individual business owners who were seldom informed by the Chinese authorities on how to develop their overseas businesses.[53] Although China has achieved an astonishing economic growth since the 1970s, few people in Europe can name a single Chinese company in the 2010s.[54] In 2013, when China's OBOR was confirmed as a national grand strategy, China only had 23 companies listed in the global top 500 compared to the 184 US firms on the same list.[55] Furthermore, most of the top 10 companies are owned by the US such as Apple, ExxonMobil, Berkshire Hathaway, WalMart, Microsoft, IBM, Nestle. PetroChina company (ranked fourth in the world) was the only Chinese company listed in top 10 in 2013.[56]

---

[51] Li Xiangyang, 李向阳, *Yi dai yi lu: Ding wei, nei han ji xu yao you xian chu li de guan xi* 一带一路：定位、内涵及需要优先处理的关系 [*One Belt One Road" Orientations, Contents and Challenges*], Beijing: shi hui ke xue wen xian chu ban she (北京：社会科学文献出版社, 2015), 27.

[52] *Ibid.*, p. 28.

[53] Winglok Hung, *The Travails of Chinese Businesses in Present-day Uganda.* Saarbrücken, Deutschland: LAP Lambert Academic Publishing, 2014.

[54] Nolan, Peter, *Chinese Firms, Global Firms: Industrial Policy in the Age of Globalization.* New York : Routledge, 2014, xvii.

[55] FT 500, 2013 [downloaded on 6 December 2015], available at http://www.ft.com/indepth/ft500.

[56] *Ibid.*

In fact, Chinese leaders highly regard overseas Chinese firms. For example, in November 2012, former Chinese President Hu Jintao encouraged more Chinese companies to expand their overseas businesses in order to enhance cooperation in an international environment and develop a number of world class international companies.[57] I believe that this is one of the main reasons why OBOR has a strong emphasis on Chinese companies. China's OBOR engagement with European countries will have a large impact as there are already well-established international firms in Europe. The cooperation between Chinese and European firms may help to expand their economic influence in other regions under OBOR.

The involvement of Chinese companies will change the actors in the international order system. It would be difficult to imagine Coca-Cola Company's CEO Muhtar Kent traveling with the American president to various countries and signing significant business deals with respective governments. However, a few Chinese companies accompanied China's President Xi Jinping during his official trip to America in September 2015.[58] During President Xi's official visit to the United Kingdom in October 2015, Mr Wang Chuanfu, CEO of BYD automobile company, was on the trip and signed a contract with British companies worth RMB 6.5 billion RMB when Chinese President Xi arrived in London on 21 October 2015.[59] It seems that Chinese company representatives have a role in China's OBOR and companies may become a new actor in the international system.

International norms and pragmatic economies: Monks and bankers

International norms are complicated and normally take more time for changes to take place. In fact, the internationalization of a norm is a process

57 Nolan, Peter, *Chinese Firms, Global Firms: Industrial Policy in the Age of Globalization.* New York: Routledge, 2014, xvii.

58 Zhong xing shou ji sui tuan dao fang xi ya tu 中兴手机随团到访西雅图 [ZTE tech company followed the trip to Seattle], *Na fang du shi bao* 南方都市报. *Southern Metropolitan Post,* 25 September 2015, C07.

59 Bi ya di 65 yi jin jun ying xin neng yuan shi chang: he xin jing zheng li shi tie dian chi 比亚迪 65 亿进军英新能源市场: 核心竞争力是 "铁电池"', *21 shi ji jing ji bao dao 21,* 世纪经济报道 *21st Century Economic Review*, 27 October 2015, 21.

of socialization.[60] Norms are defined as a set of values and collective beliefs shared by a community.[61] For example, we accept the result of "winner takes it all" in classical liberal economics. Traders have no responsibility to respect the values of religious and environmental groups unless those values affect their market profit, or those values are enforced legally. In the field of international relations, "norms are standards of behaviour in terms of rights and obligations".[62]

If we regard that international norms are based upon people's views of national interests for their own benefits,[63] it is possible that people in Europe are looking forward to establishing new international norms to overcome their economic adversities. European countries are desperate for any changes, especially in economic norms to improve domestic economies and to help those who lost their jobs during the prolonged economic recession. But how do norms change exactly? It is important to note that OBOR starts from the western regions of China, passes through Nepal, Iraq, Central Asian and the Middle East regions and finally reaches Europe. In the aforementioned regions, there are village farmers, monks and small-scale business people. In these regions, few are educated with a bachelor degree in economics but they can still manage their lives well.[64] There seems to be no stock markets, investment bankers and financial advisors in these regions.

Nowadays, the western liberal economic approach apparently widens income gaps, creates environmental damage and increases unemployment. By contrast, there are more monks than hedge fund bankers in Tibet. Nature, religion and culture are well preserved, and their economies are "localized"

---

[60] Yan Xuetong, International Leadership and Norm Evolution. *The Chinese Journal of International Politics*, 4(3) 2011, 236.

[61] With reference to Elster Jon, *Explaining Social Behavior: More Nuts and Bolts for the Social Sciences*. Cambridge: Cambridge University Press, 2007, 353.

[62] Krasner, Stephen, 'Structural causes and regime consequences: Regimes as intervening variables', in *International Regimes*, edited by Stephen Krasner. Ithaca and London: Cornell University Press, 1983, 2.

[63] Finnemore, Martha, 'Constructing norms of humanitarian intervention', in *The Culture of National Security: Norms and Identity in World Politics* edited by peter J. Katzenstein New York: Columbia University Press, 1996, 154.

[64] Braham, Laurence J, *Fusion Economics: How Pragmatism is Changing the World*. New York: Basingstoke Palgrave Macmillan, 2014.

rather than "globalized".[65] The people in these regions face adverse conditions of impoverishment and environmental degradation but they often seek solutions with local wisdom. Money or profit may not be the most important norm in their economy. It is equally important to mention that people in Bhutan are often regarded as the happiest people in the world. Norms are fundamentally intrinsically related to people's interests and shape their social and economic behavior.

Furthermore, norms of non-interference may be gradually adjusted as some regions (e.g. Iraq and Syria) may need external peacekeeping forces to maintain order for businesses. From this perspective, norms may change as China further integrates their way of doing business under OBOR. At this moment, I am not really certain how economic norms will be exactly changed. But culture and religion are important factors. The new norms may not be the same liberal norms that originated from Adam Smith's ideas of market.

Conclusion

Why is Europe more important than other regions in China's OBOR economic strategy? This short chapter argues that OBOR is a new economic strategy. The financial crisis in 2008 further exposed existing global economic problems and still requires a new international order to maintain peace. OBOR was established under this international context. There are many papers focusing on China's relations with emerging countries under the framework of OBOR. I admit that China's relations with emerging countries are important but only China's successful interactions with Europe will transform the existing international system. Europe is important as it has always been the center of the world, particularly since 19th century. Furthermore, there are world leading business companies in Europe. As mentioned before, three components of the world international system including international actors, international configuration and international norms are expected to change if OBOR is successfully practised.

After the global financial crisis in 2008, senior scholars, foreign policy advisors and experts such as Henry Kissinger have been searching for a new

---

[65] *Ibid.*, especially Chapters 4 and 5.

global order.[66] I believe that China, Southeast Asian countries, the Middle East regions and the African continent all have a role in OBOR and that Europe is particularly crucial in this transformation.

Acknowledgments

The author would like to acknowledge the input from Professor Jan van der Harst and Professor Chang Chak-yan at different stages of writing this chapter. The author was also inspired by Laurence J Braham's two lectures on the current world's economy at The Kee Club, Hong Kong and at Tsinghua University, Beijing in 2015. Comments on my earlier draft by Patrik Anderson are greatly appreciated. Last, the author would like to thank Serena Chan for her patient and kind editing help. Needless to say, all the faults are the author's sole responsibility.

Bibliography

In Chinese

Academic journals and books

王义桅,《"一带一路": 机遇与挑战》, 北京: 人民出版社, 2015.

刘华芹,《丝绸之路经济带: 欧亚大陆新棋局》, 北京:中国商务出版社, 2015.

孙久文, 高志刚主编,《丝绸之路经济带与区域经济发展研究》, 北京: 经济管理出版社, 2015.

李向阳,《"一带一路": 定位、内涵及需要优先处理的关系》, 北京: 社会科学文献出版社, 2015.

李向阳主编,《亚太蓝皮书: 亚太地区发展报告(2015) 一带一路》, 北京: 社会科学文献出版社, 2015.

赵可金,《"一带一路"的中国方略研究》,《新疆师范大学学报》, 2016 年第 37 卷第1期, 页22–33.

赵江林主编,《21世纪海上丝绸之路: 目标构想、实施基础与对策研究》, 北京: 社会科学文献出版社, 2015.

张洁主编,《中国周边安全形势评估: "一带一路"与周边战略》, 北京: 社会科学文献出版社, 2015.

张诗雨, 张勇编着,《海上新丝路: 21世纪海上丝绸之路发展思路与构想》, 北京: 中国发展出版社, 2014.

66 Kissinger, Henry, *World Order*. New York: Penguin Press, 2014.

林毅夫,《"一带一路"需要加上"一洲"》,《党政论坛（干部文摘）》, 2015 年 4 期, 页 32.
胡鞍钢, 马伟, 鄢一龙,《"丝绸之路经济带": 战略内涵、定位和实现路径》,《新疆师范大学学报》, 2014 年第 35 卷第 2 期, 页 1–10.
阎学通,《世界权力的转移: 政治领导与战略竞争》, 北京: 北京大学出版社, 2015.
潘天波, 胡玉康,《丝路漆艺与中国美学思想的传播》,《新疆师范大学学报》, 2014 年第 35 卷第 2 期, 页 89–95.
[美] 亨利. 基辛格, 胡利平等译,《世界秩序》, 北京: 中信出版社, 2015.

Magazine

郑赤琰,《从三个角度看'一带一路'》,《印尼焦点》, 第 46 期, 2015 年 8 月, 页4–5.

Newspapers

《21世纪经济报道》,《比亚迪 65 亿进军英新能源市场: 核心竞争力是"铁电池"》, 27 October 2015 第 21 版.
《人民日报》,《中国特色大国外交的成功实践 (2013 年度特别报导)—外交部长王毅谈二〇一三年中国外交》, 19 December 2013, 第 03 版.
《文汇报》,《50国签亚投行协定》, 30 June 2015, 第 A08 版.
《南方都市报》,《中兴手机随团到访西雅图》, 25 Sepember 2015, 第C07版.
《香港商报》,《中国筹建亚投行 21国有意参加》, 22 October 2014, 第 A19 版.

In English

Academic journals and books

Anonymous, Chinese Media on the "One Belt, One Road" Strategy. *Chinascope* (73), 2015, 38.
Braham, J. Laurence, *Fusion Economics*: *How Pragmatism Is Changing the World*. New York: Basingstoke Palgrave Macmillan, 2014.
Cappelletti, Alessandra, Developing the Land and the People: Social Development Issues in Xinjiang Uyghur Autonomous Region (1999–2009). *East Asia*: *An International Quarterly*, 32(2) 2015, 137–171.
Chou, Bill and Xuejie Ding, A Comparative Analysis of Shenzhen and Kashgarin Development as Special Economic Zones. *East Asia*: *An International Quarterly*, 32(2) 2015, 117–136.
Colakoglu, Selcuk, Dynamics of Sino-Turkish Relations: A Turkish Perspective. *East Asia*: *An International Quarterly*, 32(1), 2015, 7–23.
Cornel Dumitreseu, George, Central and Eastern European Countries Focus on the Silk Road Economic Belt. *Global Economic Observer*, 3(1), 2015, 144–153.

Devonshire-Ellis, Chris, *China's New Economic Silk Road: The Great Eurasian Game and The String of Pearls*. Hong Kong: Asia Briefing Ltd., 2015.

Kissinger, Henry, *World Order*. New York: Penguin Press, 2014.

Elster, Jon, *Explaining Social Behavior: More Nuts and Bolts for the Social Sciences*. Cambridge: Cambridge University Press, 2007.

Ferguson, James, *Global Shadows: Africa in the Neoliberal World Order*. Durham: Duke University Press, 2006.

Hung, Winglok, *The Travails of Chinese Businesses in Present-day Uganda*. Saarbrücken, Deutschland: LAP Lambert Academic Publishing, 2014.

Mackerras, Colin, "Xinjiang in China's Foreign Relations: Part of a New Silk Road or Central Asian Zone of Conflict? *East Asia: An International Quarterly*, 32(1), 2015, 25–42.

McCredie, Karen, *Sun Tzu's The Art of War: A 52 Brilliant Ideas Interpretation*. Oxford: Infinite Ideas, 2008.

Mukherjee, Kunal, Comparing China and India's Disputed Borderland Regions: Xinjiang, Tibet, Kashmir, and the Indian Northeast. *East Asia: An International Quarterly*, 32(2), 2015, 173–205.

Nolan, Peter, *Chinese Firms, Global Firms: Industrial Policy in the Age of Globalization*. New York: Routledge, 2014.

Shen, Simon, Special Issue: New Silk Road Project. *East Asia: An International Quarterly*, 32(1), 2015, 1–5.

Shichor, Y, Pawns in Central Asia's Playground: Uyghurs Between Moscow and Beijing. *East Asia: An International Quarterly*, 32(2), 2015, 101–116.

Tammen, Ronald L *et al.*, *Power Transitions: Strategies for the 21st Century*. New York: Chatham House Publishers, 2000.

Yan, Xuetong, International Leadership and Norm Evolution, *The Chinese Journal of International Politics*, 4(3), 2011, 233–264.

Yan, Xuetong, The Shift of the World Centre and its Impact on the Change of the International System. *East Asia: An International Quarterly*, 30(2), 2013, 217–235.

Chapters

Finnemore, Martha, "Constructing norms of humanitarian intervention" in *The Culture of National Security: Norms and Identity in World Politics* edited by Peter J. Katzenstein. New York: Columbia University Press, 1996, 153–185.

Krasner, Stephen, "Structural causes and regime consequences: Regimes as intervening variables" in *International Regimes* edited by Stephen Krasner. Ithaca and London: Cornell University Press, 1983, 1–22.

Magazines

The Economist, Why China is Creating a New 'World Bank' for Asia. 11 November 2014.

Tiezzi, Shannon, Where is China's Silk Road Actually Going? *The Diplomat*, 30 March 2015 [downloaded on 19 November 2015], available at http://thediplomat.com/2015/03/where-is-chinas-silk-road-actually-going/.

Newspaper

China Daily, Chinese President Delivers Speech at Nazarbayev University [downloaded on 11 November 2015], available at http://news.xinhuanet.com/english/photo/2013-09/08/c_132701546.htm.

Online sources

About Us, AIIB website [downloaded on 23 November 2015], available at http://www.aiib.org/html/aboutus/AIIB/.

Articles of Agreement, AIIB website [downloaded on 23 November 2015], available at http://www.aiib.org/uploadfile/2015/0814/20150814022158430.pdf.

FT 500, 2013, *Financial Times* website [downloaded on 6 December 2015], available at http://www.ft.com/indepth/ft500.

Working papers

Kennedy, Scott and David A Parker. Building China's "One Belt, One Road". Publication. Center for Strategic and International Studies, Washington, DC [downloaded on 22 November 2015], available at http://csis.org/publication/building-chinas-one-belt-one-road.

Rajeev, Ranjan Chaturvedy, New Maritime Silk Road: Converging Interests and Regional Responses. Institute of South Asian Studies (ISAS) Working Paper, National University of Singapore, No. 197, October 2014, 1–20.

Yan, Mengzhao and Shumin Li, Chinese Firms' International Market Entry to Main Participating Countries of 'One Belt One Road. The Institute of Electrical and Electronics Engineers, Inc. (IEEE) Conference Proceedings, June 2015, 1–6.

Yan, Xuetong, A Bipolar World is More Likely Than a Unipolar or Multipolar One. China–US Focus, Carnegie-Tsinghua Center for Global Policy, 20 April 2015.

Chapter 15
China's Pivot to Central and South Asia

LIM Tai Wei*

Historical background

In its historical narrative, the Silk Road refers to contacts dating back to the Han Dynasty in 200 BC when the Chinese emissary Zhang Qian was dispatched from the Chinese capital of Changan (now known as Xian) to Central Asia to establish trade and commercial ties. He was also sent to search for the famous "blood-sweating" horses in the Kingdom of Ferghana (Tashkent) to bring them back for Chinese horse-riding regiments. His expedition pioneered a caravan route that eventually saw China establishing trade contact with kingdoms in Central Asia. The transportation tool of choice was camels. Persian and Central Asian riders plied the Silk Road especially through the dry and inhabitable Taklamakan desert (also known as the Gobi desert) on their tough Bactrian camels. Images of these camels had been immortalized in tri-color (*sancai*) pottery models fired in Tang China.

Non-Chinese products traded on the Silk Road included the dates, grapes and melons from Kashgar, Arabian glassware, Persian carpets from

---

* This chapter was first published as a limited circulation background brief/working paper: Lim Tai Wei, China's Pivot to Central and South Asia dated 12 August 2015 in East Asian Institute Background Brief 1050. Singapore: National University of Singapore East Asian Institute, 2015. Dr Lim Tai Wei is an adjunct Research Fellow at the East Asian Institute (EAI), National University of Singapore and Senior Lecturer at SIM University (UniSIM). He thanks Prof Zheng Yongnian, Director of EAI and Ms Jessica Loon for their editorial guidance and inputs. He is especially thankful to Prof John Wong for access to his articles published in *The Straits Times* and an unpublished conference paper on Central Asia.

Herat, African slaves, African ivory, Indian and East African spices from Zanzibar, pearls from Arabic locations like modern day Kuwait, gold, cotton from India, gemstones from Indochina and Ceylon, etc. Over time, great cities that used to thrive along this Silk Road had disappeared into the sands of the desert like the trading city of Samarkand and the great Islamic city of Baghdad that was later sacked by the Mongol nomadic raiders. The overland route was eventually supplanted by maritime trade networks.

One Belt One Road (OBOR)

Contemporary China under the Xi Jinping administration has plans to revive this historical route through an initiative known as the OBOR. The Chinese OBOR initiative is not a new concept; in the past, the Ottoman Empire had similarly reached out to Central Asia while Turkey had a new Silk Road project and Russia has its own outreach to ex-Soviet Republics in Central Asia.[1] The OBOR is the latest major policy initiative by the Xi administration to tap into this region. In fact, this initiative is so important to China that President Xi declared that this would be his only major foreign policy initiative for the entire period of his administration.

The OBOR initiative basically has two routes, one overland route reaching outwards from trading hubs like Yiwu to locations as far away as Madrid and Germany. In geographical term, "Central Asia extends from the Caspian Sea in the west to the border of western China in the east. It is bounded on the north by Russia and on the south by Iran, Afghanistan and China. The region comprises five former Soviet republics of Kazakhstan, Uzbekistan, Tajikistan, Kyrgyzstan and Turkmenistan".[2] The other route in the OBOR initiative is a Maritime Silk Road (MSR) that resembles the current trade sea-lanes from the Middle East through the Gulf, the Indian Ocean, down the Straits of Malacca through the South China Sea and eventually to Northeast Asia. The overland route will be the focus here.

To lend economic resources to the OBOR initiative, the Chinese government started funding institutions like the Silk Road Fund, Asian

---

[1] Wong, John, From Silk Road to Economic Bridge, dated 17 June 2015 in *The Straits Times* [downloaded on 1 July 2015], available at www.straitstimes.com.

[2] *Ibid.*

Infrastructure Investment Bank (AIIB) and the BRICS Bank. The financial muscles of state-owned enterprises (SOEs) were deployed behind the OBOR initiative: "The People's Bank of China and the Ministry of Finance have been heavily involved in drawing up its program, and they have also brought in China's two policy banks (China Development Bank China Imports and Exports Bank), the State Administration for Foreign Exchange (SAFE), China Investment Corporation (CIC) and some SOEs like the Three Gorges Corporation".[3]

Central Asia in focus

On 7 September 2013 at the Nazarbayev University in Astana, Kazakhstan, Chinese President Xi Jinping mentioned that China and other countries like those in Central Asia can first compare their plans on economic development while infrastructure links can be enhanced with the guiding philosophy that China "respects the development paths and policies chosen by the peoples of regional countries, and will never interfere in the domestic affairs of Central Asian nations".[4] Some argue that China's main target for the OBOR's overland component is Central Asia, including not only train infrastructure but also ports and eventually energy pipelines.[5] The evidence for this, according to this school of thought, is the direction of Chinese capital flow. China's capital flow to Central Asia amounted to US$30 billion in contracts with Kazakhstan; US$15 billion with Uzbekistan; US$8 billion for Turkmenistan and US$1 billion to Tajikistan.[6] On the surface, the Nazarbayev University speech by President Xi resembled past Chinese practices of conducting "no-strings attached" economic diplomacy; in reality, Chinese OBOR and AIIB initiatives have become

---

[3] *Ibid.*

[4] *Xinhuanet*, Xi Suggests China, C. Asia Build Silk Road Economic belt, dated 7 September 2013 in the *Xinhuanet* website [downloaded on 18 December 2014], available at http://news.xinhuanet.com/english/china/2013-09/07/c_132700695.htm.

[5] Escobar, Pepe, China is Building a New Silk Road to Europe, And it's Leaving America Behind, dated 16 December 2014 in *Mother Jones* website [downloaded on 18 December 2014], available at http://www.motherjones.com/politics/2014/12/chinas-new-silk-road-europe-will-leave-america-behind.

[6] *Ibid.*

more sophisticated with the integration of market-driven practices and some imposition of environmental conditions.

Possible developmental challenges facing Central Asian economies

A big differentiating factor between East Asia and Central Asia is in their population. The former is lightly populated and so it does not face the same pressures as the heavily populated latter region in industrialization to develop the economy.[7] Economically, Central Asian economies faced a number of geographical weaknesses such as not having access to the sea for trade and overdependence on commodities trade (cotton, oil, gas and agricultural produce).[8] Overdependence on natural resources export brings along with it the usual challenges of vulnerability to price volatility. If Central Asia wishes to modernize (assuming there is social consensus to do so), then the region would need to go through a similar process that East Asian development is familiar with. These features would include the growth of mass education, infrastructure investments, industrialization, skills and management training, etc. These are items that China can offer.

Steel and coal

For industrialization and modernization to take place, be they European, American, Japanese, Chinese or most East Asian experiences, two of the most important commodities are steel and coal (oil was a latecomer as a major source of energy). There is almost no exception to this cardinal rule. The industrial revolutions in Europe and America followed the same path for hundreds of years, making steel magnates and coal barons extremely wealthy. Japan, a latecomer to the modernization game and the first East Asian economy to develop, also utilized its own domestic coal resources for the same purpose. The Yahata iron ore plants or the Kyushu coal mines were pioneers in Japan's moderniza-

[7] Wong, John, China's New Silk Road Initiatives and Central Asia Development, dated 28 June 2015–2 July 2015 in The Seminar on the Silk Road and Nazarbayev Theory of Peace. Astana, Kazakhstan: Unpublished, 2015, 15.

[8] *Ibid.*

tion and, in the post-war years, coal was also the main power source for Japan. China's post-1949 modernization followed a Stalinist path to industrialization with the Great Leap Forward that produced steel according to non-market conditions; its post-1979 economic reform initiatives depended on cheap coal and Daqing oil. The post-war European Community (later European Union) was built upon a coal and steel community as well.

The steel and coal industries thus become items of attention in China's OBOR and AIIB initiatives when it comes to modernization and industrialization projects. Any intention for the industrialization of Central Asia occurs at an opportune time because China is simultaneously facing overcapacity. The idle capacity of China's steel industry is twice the size of the United States' steel production; amongst other heavy industries, the Chinese coal industry is also facing decreasing demand and lower profits.[9] The *New York Times* reported that 60% of all train cargo traffic is concentrated on the transportation of coal and this amount fell 11% in December 2014 and 9% in January 2015 compared with the figures a year ago.[10] A slowdown in the steel industry also translated to lower use of coking coal and such slowdown also affected the railway industry which had excess capacity and fell into debt, e.g. China Railway Corporation, an offshoot of the Ministry of Railways with an accumulated debt of 3.5 trillion yuan (US$567 billion), an amount that has increased by 26% since the end of 2012.[11]

With its massive consumption of steel and coal, China can help Central and South Asia create the demand for energy (including coal fuels) in powering the industrialization of these two developing regions.[12] With the coming

---

[9] Zhou, Jiayi, Karl Hallding and Guoyi Han, The "One Belt, One Road" Strategy Risks Exacerbating China's Economic Imbalances, dated 26 June 2015 in *The Diplomat* [downloaded on 1 July 2015], available at http://thediplomat.com/2015/06/the-trouble-with-the-chinese-marshall-plan-strategy/.

[10] Gough, Neil, For Chinese Economy, Strengths Are Now Weaknesses, dated 11 March 2015 in the *New York Times* [downloaded on 1 June 2015], available at http://www.nytimes.com/2015/03/12/business/international/for-chinese-economy-steel-goes-from-strength-to-weakness.html?_r=0.

[11] *Ibid.*

[12] Shah, Saeed (Islamabad) and Jeremy Page (Beijing), China Readies $46 Billion for Pakistan Trade Route, dated 16 April 2015 in *The Wall Street Journal* [downloaded on 28 June 2015], available at http://www.wsj.com/articles/china-to-unveil-billions-of-dollars-in-pakistan-investment-1429214705.

into being of the AIIB, China now has the resources to fund the overland Silk Road. On a longer term basis, the ultimate prize for enhancing China–Central Asia cooperation as well as continued Chinese role in the Shanghai Cooperation Organisation (SCO) is the eventual fruition of a Free Trade Agreement (FTA) between China and Central Asia. This may be one reason for Chinese membership in the SCO despite a dominant Chinese diplomatic principle of not forming alliances (Pakistan is an exception) or joining any regional security pacts (SCO is an exception). OBOR and AIIB are likely to complement this cherished Chinese diplomatic dream of an FTA.

Enter Pakistan

The first country in South Asia that China is concentrating on with regard to economic development is Pakistan, an old and reliable ironclad ally; China has promised to pump US$46 billion into Pakistan's development. Beijing has its own self-interest as well, as with any other bilateral projects between the two states. Beijing wants to develop the neighboring South Asian region so that the threat of terrorism that feeds on underdevelopment can be nipped in the bud and eradicated. Beijing is also initiating meetings with tribal chiefs in Pakistan and Afghanistan to resolve disputes between them. This would have a longer-term effect on insulating Xinjiang from Islamic extremism. This initiative is important because US President Obama's withdrawal of 10,000 US soldiers from Afghanistan would create a power vacuum in that part of the world.

Moreover, if the Pakistani (and Afghanistan) sector can be developed, then China would have access to Iran and the proximate Central Asian markets. There are thus economic benefits to developing the northern regions of South Asia that are contiguous with Central Asia. In the field of energy development which is something essential for industrialization, China is helping to construct US$15.5 billion coal-fired power plants to resolve Pakistan's electricity shortage by increasing another 10,400-megawatt of electricity to the country.[13] Beyond 2018, Beijing will increase Pakistan's electricity supply by an additional 6,600 megawatts at a cost of US$18.3 billion, doubling Pakistan's electricity supply.[14]

---

[13] *Ibid.*

[14] *Ibid.*

Sino-Pakistani exchanges are no ordinary strengthening of a *youhao* relationship; it was an ironclad relationship to Beijing as Pakistan would become what the Chinese foreign minister described as the symphony of the OBOR foreign policy initiative. The overall impact of the Chinese–Pakistani outreach is a potentially win–win situation for all if (1) the projects are transparent; (2) China negotiates successfully through the complex geopolitics and domestic politics of the South and Central Asian regions and (3) the infrastructural connectivity promotes trade and commerce for the region.

India and its coal industry

Pakistan is not the only South Asian country to want to benefit from China's OBOR initiative. Even India, China's rival, is also interested in tapping into Chinese initiatives to develop its coal industry. The unwillingness of the World Bank to fund coal projects due to climate change reasons has prompted India to turn to AIIB for such funding, as revealed by an anonymous Senior Indian bureaucrat: "When you have 1.3 billion people starved of electricity access and the rest of the world has created a carbon space, at this point denying funding is denying access to cheap energy."[15]

India wishes to develop its domestic coal reserves (fifth largest in the world) that currently produces power for 3/5th of the country's electricity, but the country still faces power shortage and is in need of 455 more coal power plants.[16] Approximately 300 million people in India still have no access to electricity.[17] Like Central Asia, India also has industrialization and modernization on its agenda, particularly under current PM Modi's dream of an economically developed India on the world stage with foreign policy leadership. For the short- to medium-term, India still needs to depend on cheaper coal resources even as it gears up to tap into renewable energy sources on a large scale in the near future, like China. India's coal industry is also

---

[15] Kumar, Manoj and Tony Munroe, For India, China-Backed Lender May be Answer to Coal investment, dated 5 November 2014 in *Reuters* website [downloaded on 6 July 2015], available at http://www.reuters.com/article/2014/11/06/us-india-aiib-insight idUSKBN0IP2S020141106.

[16] *Ibid.*

[17] Subramanya, Rupa, Is the Asian Infrastructure Investment Bank Good for India?, dated 15 April 2015 in *Foreign Policy* (FP) [downloaded on 1 July 2015], available at http://foreignpolicy.com/2015/04/15/is-the-asian-infrastructure-investment-bank-good-for-india-coal-china/.

facing a renaissance due to policy issues like accelerated coal mine permits and greater market flexibility in retailing coal and stricter rules for churning out coal fuels.[18] In fact, India and Pakistan in South Asia and Central Asia are not the only regions facing coal shortages; Northeast and Southeast Asia also need cheaper sources of coal energy.

Funding coal-fired power generation

Private sector consultancy sources indicate that the OBOR initiative has the potential to benefit the Chinese coal industry. Liang Dunshi, deputy secretary general of China coal Transport and Distribution Association, opined that China's coal export market is expected to benefit from the country's OBOR initiative by shipping more coal to meet Southeast Asian needs.[19] Vietnam has been importing more coal and exporting less while Thailand and Malaysia are projected to increase coal fuels import in 20 years' time.[20] Vietnam, Indonesia, South Korea, Japan and India as a group will be upping their coal-fired electricity production capacity by as much as 60%, something AIIB can finance in the vacuum of World Bank's refusal,[21] leading to some voices in the West asking for a review of World Bank restrictions.

Even though World Bank rejects coal-fired projects, the AIIB is not the only funding institution; Japan and the United States-dominated Asian Development Bank (ADB) is more flexible than World Bank and funds some coal-fired electricity initiatives if green technologies are used; it permitted US$900 million funds for a 600- megawatt coal power plant in Pakistan,[22]

---

[18] Runde, Daniel, AIIB And US Development Leadership: A Path Forward, dated 30 April 2015 in *Forbes* [downloaded on 1 July 2015], available at http://www.forbes.com/sites/danielrunde/2015/04/30/aiib-us-development-leadership/2/.

[19] Jia, Jessie (ed.), China Coal Export to Benefit From "One Belt and One Road", dated 8 June 2015 in Shanxi Fenwei Energy Consulting Company [downloaded on 1 July 2015], available at http://en.sxcoal.com/121553/NewsShow.html.

[20] *Ibid.*

[21] Runde, Daniel, AIIB And US Development Leadership: A Path Forward, dated 30 April 2015 in *Forbes* [downloaded on 1 July 2015], available at http://www.forbes.com/sites/danielrunde/2015/04/30/aiib-us-development-leadership/2/.

[22] Kumar, Manoj and Tony Munroe, For India, China-Backed Lender May be Answer to Coal Investment, dated 5 November 2014 in *Reuters* website [downloaded on 6 July 2015], available at http://www.reuters.com/article/2014/11/06/us-india-aiib-insight-idUSKBN0IP2S020141106.

the main beneficiary of China-dominated AIIB and OBOR initiatives. From the Chinese perspective, reception towards the OBOR and AIIB had been positively transformative in economic and perhaps political relations. A *China Daily* commentary noted that "[m]ost countries in South Asia actively support China's "Belt and Road" initiatives, and only India shows deep suspicion and concern over the strategy's transparency … The construction of the China–Pakistan economic corridor sets an example for Nepal and Sri Lanka, and will propel India to adjust its attitudes to China's "Belt and Road" initiatives, and the economic corridor connecting Bangladesh, China, India and Myanmar, in which China proposes to promote regional connectivity".[23]

Critical voices

There are however criticisms towards the OBOR and AIIB. A Silk Road-related article written by a Sri Lankan student leader Akshan deAlwis was circulated by *Huffington Post*, an internationally influential liberal online media outlet. The tone of this article was alarmist and its author also stated openly the political stance of hoping that Sri Lankans would democratically vote against Chinese influence in military infrastructure of his country.[24] The election eventually voted against the retention of pro-Beijing PM Rajapaksa. The article offers some insights into some aspects of critical local reactions and responses in South Asia towards the OBOR from an individual public intellectual and activist perspective, which represents one sliver of many different perspectives held by the vast spectrum of political views related to the Chinese initiative.

Akshan deAlwis also mentioned that the Chinese initiative can be an economic catch-up opportunity for the rest of Asia to the standards of the four tiger economies of Hong Kong, Singapore, South Korea and Taiwan, suggesting readings of uneven development in Asia and also the possibility of an alternative model that had made the four dynamic economies successful

---

[23] Li, Yang, "Islamabad a Pivot for China's Involvement in Islamic world, dated 22 April 2015 in the *China Daily* website, chinadaily.com.cn [downloaded on 25 April 2015], available at http://www.chinadaily.com.cn/opinion/2015-04/22/content_20507080.htm.

[24] deAlwis, Akshan, The New Silk Road: A True "Win–Win" or a Perilous Future?, dated 31 December 2014 in the Huffingtonpost.com *The World Post* website [downloaded on 2 January 2015], available at http://www.huffingtonpost.com/akshan-dealwis/the-new-silk-road-a-true-_b_6400992.html.

(the four tiger economies are often associated with Japan's fast growth model that was once lauded by the World Bank as a "miracle" and reinforced by Western notions of capitalism, political and corporate governance as well as democratization pulses).[25] Akshan deAlwis' narrative presented the scenario of the OBOR as an additional (although it was not clear whether he also meant "alternative") developmental system for Asian countries that is not based on the model of the four tiger economies and Japan. He centered his attention on the more immediate periphery of China, especially South Asia where he comes from and Southeast Asia (particularly Thailand). Akshan deAlwis wanted to convey the possibility of a possible patron–client relationship, though the shape and form have not been elaborated upon.

Combining his narrative with positive assessment of the OBOR and AIIB, a global picture emerges that is complex, ambitious and deeply nuanced. The world system tapestry presented by deAlwis are more contentious than settled when it comes to Chinese intentions of gaining geopolitical economic advantage. It indicates that observers, activists and analysts are not quite decided on whether the MSR or the overland Silk Road (dubbed High-Speed Railway or HSR diplomacy) takes precedence in Chinese plans. The Chinese leadership themselves may be testing the waters on this, pragmatically implementing an economic policy for the region with options to modify the plans as they go along. The Zhongnanhai or Beijing leadership may also be exercising strategic ambiguity, not deciding or formulating a definite concept for some aspects of the One Belt One Road initiative. Whatever be the reason that accounts for this ambiguity, narratives and commentaries similar to deAlwis' ideas about the MSR *vis-à-vis* HSR may be a subject of concern for some time to come.

Some operational details

Policy wise, however, things are more concrete in the textual form. In his New Silk Road speech at Nazarbayev University, Chinese President Xi outlined five sectors for future cooperation between China and Central Asia. They include (1) more consultations and communications on economic development; (2) increase connectivity between Pacific and Baltic Sea as well

---

[25] *Ibid.*

as the regions of East, West and South Asia; (3) increase trade and investment; (4) promote trade in local currencies and (5) more exchanges at the non-state level and at the individual level.[26] China's initiatives with railway lines running through the historical Silk Road region provides landlocked Central Asian countries with the connectivity to import and export goods. The Maritime and Overland Silk Roads may even link up in the future, providing Central Asia with indirect access to maritime trade.[27] Eventually, there appears to be in the future a plan to build a mega energy grid involving energy pipelines (probably in oil and natural gas) between China and Central Asia; these pipelines have been planned to link up with the power grids and hydropower facilities in Southeast Asian countries (Association of Southeast Asian Nations (ASEAN) members), as suggested in a CCTV report.[28]

Some challenges and possible Chinese responses

While conformity to market-driven conditions is a demonstration of smart Chinese economic diplomacy, it still needs to overcome geopolitical sensitivities in the Central Asian region. Smart economic diplomacy is not only restricted to the area of economic exchange but also broader geopolitical implications: "China is essentially leveraging its geo-economic power in order to achieve larger geo-political objectives ... In the case of the Overland Silk Road, China's efforts run the risk of creating suspicion and conflict with Russia. Many Central Asian states fall into Russia's traditional sphere of influence". The challenges in the Eurasian region for any multilateral economic initiative include Russian swaggering (e.g. recent mobilization of troops near its border with Kazakhstan), European reluctance to trade with Russia, Russian obstacles to goods traveling to Europe at times of bad relations, domestic problems like

26 Wong, John, China's New Silk Road Initiatives and Central Asia Development, dated 28 June 2015–2 July 2015 in The Seminar on the Silk Road and Nazarbayev Theory of Peace. Astana, Kazakhstan: Unpublished, 2015, 16.

27 Wong, John, China's New Silk Road Initiatives and Central Asia Development dated 28 June 2015–2 July 2015 in The Seminar on the Silk Road and Nazarbayev Theory of Peace. Astana, Kazakhstan: Unpublished, 2015, 2.

28 Zhang, Mengyuan, Energy Cooperation in One Belt One Road Focused, dated 16 June 2015 in CCTV.com [downloaded on 2 July 2015], available at http://english.cntv.cn/2015/06/16/VIDE1434444361462625.shtml.

corruption in Central Asia, elitist dominance of wealth creation, susceptibility to commodity fluctuations, criminal groups, etc.[29]

Therefore, Central Asian actors have to thread between Beijing, Russian and also US interests carefully. The support or responses that they give to Beijing's OBOR initiatives are not entirely unqualified and without caveats. Meanwhile, other than Russia, India also wants a role in the region. P Stobdan, a former Indian ambassador to Central Asia, argued that the Central Asian region is undergoing a process of "de-Europeanization"; trans-national forces like the Islamic State is moving into the region and China has challenged Russian regional monopoly to control trade in the region.[30] From such narratives, it appears India is also interested in projecting its geo-political influence to Central Asia. To avoid being embroiled in geopolitical rivalries with Russia and India, China would do well to stick to the economic agenda that is in common with those of Central Asian states. Kazakhstan and Turkmenistan are relatively more developed than the other Central Asian states but they have commonalities of poverty, unemployment, unindustrial-ized economies and income gaps.[31]

Another way is to use a functionalist approach to utilizing China's geo-graphical advantage in linking India with Central Asia so that Beijing can keep the trade and commercial agendas' momentum on its turf. This is because, ironically, a prescription for Indian re-engagement with Central Asia is to link up with China through the northern corridor of the Ladakh–Xinjiang axis where India can reach Central Asia or the Eurasian landmass; the other way is to become more active in the SCO.[32] Finally, the SCO can also become an important platform for Beijing to have regular consultations

---

[29] *The Economist*, The New Silk Road Hardly an Oasis, dated 15 November 2014 in *The Economist* [downloaded on 18 December 2014], available at http://www.economist.com/news/asia/21632595-kazakhstan-turns-geography-advantage-china-builds-new-silk-road-hardly-oasis.

[30] Stobdan, P, IDSA COMMENT Modi's Visit to Central Asia, dated 6 July 2015 in the Institute for Defence Studies and Analyses (IDSA) [downloaded on 1 July 2015], available at http://www.idsa.in/idsacomments/ModisVisittoCentralAsia_pstobdan_060715.html.

[31] Wong, John, China's New Silk Road Initiatives and Central Asia Development, dated 28 June 2015–2 July 2015 in The Seminar on the Silk Road and Nazarbayev Theory of Peace. Astana, Kazakhstan: Unpublished, 2015, 15.

[32] Stobdan, P, IDSA COMMENT Modi's Visit to Central Asia, dated 6 July 2015 in the Institute for Defence Studies and Analyses (IDSA) [downloaded on 1 July 2015], available at http://www.idsa.in/idsacomments/ModisVisittoCentralAsia_pstobdan_060715.html.

with Russia on Chinese intentions in the Central Asian region to reduce the trust deficit. Moreover, Russian interests, hurt by Western sanctions, have gravitated closer to Beijing's priorities. It is quite likely that Beijing will build upon the convergence of Chinese and Russian common interests in Central Asia.

Chapter 16

Strategic Partnership: The China–Pakistan Relations

LIM Tai Wei*

Background to the alliances in the East Asian context

In the last two weeks of April 2015 and almost contiguous with each other, two sets of relations were strengthened in South Asia and Pacific East Asia. In South Asia, China extended developmental funds of US$46 billion, the single largest sum of funding for China's *youhao* friendship partners, to Pakistan. This was however no ordinary strengthening of a *youhao* relationship; it was an ironclad relationship to Beijing as Pakistan would become the swansong of what the Chinese foreign minister described as the symphony of the One Belt One Road (OBOR) foreign policy initiative.

The Chinese–Pakistani cooperation was based on developmental assistance and economic mutualism as China was building and funding mainly infrastructural projects in Pakistan. The guiding philosophy was also declared to be market-friendly and basically a targeted economic initiative. Building strategic partnerships with different countries is key to China's foreign relations. China avoids building any alliance that is akin to that of US–Japan alliance. Its strategic partnerships aim to promote bilateral relations or solve common problems between or among states. The Chinese

*This writing was first published with limited circulation as a working paper/background brief as: Lim Tai Wei, EAI Background Brief No. 1029 "Strategic Partnership versus Alliance: The China–Pakistan Relations versus the US–Japan Alliance" (by Lim Tai Wei) circulated on 3 June 2015. Singapore: NUS EAI, 2015. Dr Lim Tai Wei thanks Prof Zheng Yongnian, director of EAI and Ms Jessica Loon for their editorial guidance and inputs.

believe that an alliance is often targeted at a third party and a common enemy. Even if an enemy does not exist, the alliance has to create one out of potential rivals. If the Chinese leadership follows suit to forge an alliance along such lines, the world may once again become divided into bipolarities and may invite dangerous proxy conflicts.

The Chinese–Pakistani model was consistent with China's self-declared non-interventionist and economically focused approach to bilateral and multilateral cooperation. This approach has not been static and has dynamically evolved from the doctrine propounded by paramount leader Deng Xiaoping of "lying low" and "biding one's time" to the "Peaceful Rise" idea emphasized in President Hu Jintao's administration and finally to the OBOR initiative by President Xi Jinping. All three doctrines shared some commonalities: (1) they had little or no military-defense elements; (2) they were focused on the idea of peaceful development and (3) economic interests were at the heart of bilateral and multilateral cooperation. Chinese-style strategic partnership focuses on inclusiveness, while the concept of an alliance is exclusive.

As it settles into its role as a big power in the international arena, China may exhibit five main ideas of inclusiveness, development-focused orientation, friend and not enemy-seeking, military-free content in partnership and emphasis on common-goods approach.

The Pakistani partnership: Three schools of interpretation in the initial stage of the US$46 billion Chinese–Pakistani outreach

The China–Pakistan Economic Corridor (CPEC) is a US$46 billion Chinese initiative to fund infrastructure projects in Pakistan as a subsidiary part of the OBOR foreign policy outreach. The international media has begun to focus on the CPEC from mid-April 2015 due to the official visit of President Xi Jinping to Pakistan. For the international media, the amount and magnitude of funding may appear startling, dwarfing Washington's military aid to the same countries. For the more seasoned observers, it conforms to Pakistan's *tiegeermen* (literally "iron-clad brotherly status or comrade" meaning "a strong ally") in Chinese diplomacy.

There were three interpretations of China's latest initiative in Pakistan in the international media, with the economic perspective possibly the most dominant. *The New York Times* editorial on 23 April 2015 is probably the most indicative of such economic analyses of Chinese expanded presence in Pakistan. Three important points were made in the article: (1) infrastructure construction for Pakistan's energy and transportation needs; (2) economic growth in Pakistan to discourage political extremism and (3) de-emphasizing military aid in favor of construction and infrastructure assistance.[1]

The second school of thought is the so-called "big bang" theory. "Big Bang" theory has generally been used to describe dramatic political–economic policy changes that have transformative rather than gradual impacts. Big bang approaches have been ascribed to Boris Yeltsin's attempt to democratize Russia, Hashimoto's initiatives to reform Japan's post-bubble economy and China's attempts to transform Pakistan's economic development and growth. The third school of thought conceptualizes this outreach mostly in political terms. First, political readings of the Chinese–Pakistani economic cooperation conceptualize it as a subsidiary of the OBOR policy.

A *China Daily* commentary noted that "[m]ost countries in South Asia actively support China's "Belt and Road" initiatives, and only India shows deep suspicion and concern over the strategy's transparency ... The construction of the China–Pakistan economic corridor sets an example for Nepal and Sri Lanka, and will propel India to adjust its attitudes to China's "Belt and Road" initiatives, and the economic corridor connecting Bangladesh, China, India and Myanmar, in which China proposes to promote regional connectivity".[2] This reading has three significances. First, it connects the Pakistani outreach with the OBOR; second, it highlights the political purpose of exerting pressure on India to conform to its reading of regional trends; and third, it hints at outstanding work to persuade potential rivals to become stakeholders to cooperate in the OBOR plan.

This international relations implication reading has found official resonance with China's Foreign Minister Wang Yi: "If 'One Belt, One Road' is

[1] The Editorial Board, "China's Big Plunge in Pakistan", dated 23 April 2015 in The Opinion Pages of *The New York Times* [downloaded on 25 April 2015], available at http://www.nytimes.com/2015/04/23/opinion/chinas-big-plunge-in-pakistan.html?_r=0.

[2] Yang, Li, Islamabad a Pivot for China's Involvement in Islamic World, dated 22 April 2015 in the *China Daily* website, chinadaily.com.cn [downloaded on 25 April 2015], available at http://www.chinadaily.com.cn/opinion/2015-04/22/content_20507080.htm.

like a symphony involving and benefiting every country, then construction of the CPEC is the sweet melody of the symphony's first movement".[3] While the international media are critical, suspicious or puzzled by the Chinese–Pakistani outreach in their analyses, most agree on three commonalities. First, giving Pakistan economic aid is overall a positive development to stabilize political uncertainties through economic development. Second, it can help to contain or mitigate religious extremism either originating from or passing through Pakistan. Such efforts are complemented by Western media reports that China is brokering negotiations between Afghan Kabul and the Taliban insurgents/tribal leaders[4] (the Chinese call them *zhanglao* or elders). The international media will watch carefully how China negotiates the path of peace brokering without going down the slippery slope of interventionism.

Third, many media readings agree that China is also concerned about religious extremism entering its Xinjiang border and political movements like East Turkestan independence. Helping Pakistan conforms to its national agenda of maintaining security stability in its Muslim autonomous region. There is thus a number of strong expectations for positive outcomes from the Chinese–Pakistani outreach. Despite realist interpretations, this bilateral cooperation is widely acknowledged as providing functionalist and constructivist benefits at a bilateral level with beneficial multilateral spillovers. Pakistan may be bandwagoning with or hedging against China economically while maintaining a good relationship with the United States at the state level. It may also be balancing against re-energized bilateral relationship between India and the United States. However the overall impact of the Chinese–Pakistani outreach is a potentially win–win situation for all, if the projects are transparent, if China negotiates successfully through the complex geopolitics and domestic politics of the South and Central Asian regions and if infrastructural connectivity promotes trade and commerce for the region.

---

[3] Shah, Saeed (in Islamabad) and Jeremy Page (in Beijing), China Readies $46 Billion for Pakistan Trade Route: Beijing Plans to Pour $46 Billion into Infrastructure Projects, Open New Trade Routes, dated 16 April 2015 in *The Wall Street Journal* [downloaded on 25 April 2015], available at http://www.wsj.com/articles/china-to-unveil-billions-of-dollars-in-pakistan-investment-1429214705.

[4] *Ibid.*

Two different creatures

For China, there is no true alliance as the very term implies a working relationship between a senior and junior partner. With an eye for egalitarianism and non-alignment, China is sensitive to entering any relationship where it becomes a senior partner. It also does not want to be "kidnapped" by the national interests of any potential allies. For much of the Cold War, China became a second force within the socialist camp, isolated by the Soviet Union and embargoed by the West. In the post-Cold War world, it remained a third power that refuses to be embroiled in confrontations between the West and Russia, Arab–Israeli conflicts and the Iranian nuclear issue.

Chapter 17

China's 21st Century Maritime Silk Road: Malaysian Perspectives

KONG Tuan Yuen

Chinese President Xi Jinping held a bilateral meeting with Malaysian Prime Minister Datuk Seri Najib Tun Razak in Manila, Philippines at the Asia-Pacific Economic Cooperation (APEC) meeting on 17 November 2015. Xi said China gave top priority to relations with Malaysia, while Najib believed China–Malaysia relations were at the highest level in history.[1] The ancient China–Malaysia relations is traceable back to 3rd century BC when Malays sailed to coastal regions of China and, much later, Zheng He's naval expeditions during Ming dynasty established protectorate relations with the Sultanate of Malacca. Moreover, Malaysia was the first Association of Southeast Asian Nations (ASEAN) country to recognize China officially and established diplomatic ties in 1974. It laid the groundwork for strong China–Malaysia partnership afterwards.

China has become the largest trading partner of Malaysia for six consecutive years since 2009. The trading amount went from US$12 billion in 2000 to US$108 billion in 2014, mainly in Machinery & Transport Equipment (MT), Mineral Fuels (MF) and Manufactured Goods (MG), and both countries targeted to reach US$160 billion in trading volume by 2017. Nonetheless,

[1] Can China Rebuild its 'Special Relationship' With Malaysia? *The Diplomat* [downloaded on 18 November 2015], available at http://thediplomat.com/2015/11/can-china-rebuild-its-special-relationship-with-malaysia/; and Najib: China–Malaysia Bilateral Ties at its Best Now. *The Star Online* [downloaded on 18 November 2015], available at http://www.thestar.com.my/News/Nation/2015/11/17/Malaysia-China-bilateral-ties-at-its-best/.

the China–Malaysia bilateral investments was not as large as trading volume, despite a number of recent developments such as Memorandum of Understanding (MoU) of Guangdong–Malacca seaport construction and Malaysia–China Kuantan Industrial Park (MCKIP). In addition, Chinese government agreed to give RMB 50 billion (US$7.8 billion) quota to Malaysia under the Renminbi Qualified Foreign Institutional Investor program (RQFII) to boost mutual investment, and to buy more Malaysian government bonds for financial stabilization.

The "One Belt One Road (OBOR)" which combined "the Silk Road Economic Belt" (SREB) and "the 21st Maritime Silk Road" (MSR) was addressed by Chinese President Xi Jinping in late 2013 and has played a prominent role in the Chinese 13th Five-Year Plan. China's OBOR initiatives aimed to strengthen the connectivity with about 60 countries along the routes by measures such as policy coordination, infrastructure facility construction, trade and investment collaboration, financial cooperation, as well as exchanging people contact and communication.

Malaysia is designated as part of the sub-line of SREB which planned to construct Kunming–Singapore railway across mainland Southeast Asia countries. But more importantly, Malaysia plays as a bridge in the MSR because the Strait of Malacca is one of the busiest channels and most of the maritime oil import of China passes through here. That is why China were very active to launch the first joint military drill exercise with Malaysia in Malacca in September 2015.

China is also expected to tighten her relationships with ASEAN countries through working with the chairmanship role of Malaysia in 2015, especially to develop Regional Comprehensive Economic Partnership (RCEP) with ASEAN countries for Free Trade Agreement (FTA), as US had led Trans-Pacific Partnership (TPP) into agreement this year. The *halal* food and Muslim commodities were another maneuver by Chinese government to cope with Malaysia to expand international market through OBOR initiatives. The China–Malaysia *halal* food industrial cooperation such as companies at MCKIP in Malaysia and at Wuzhong Halal Industrial Park in China were established to push through the Halal Food and Muslim Commodities Certification and trade with other Muslim countries. In addition, the issue of industrial overcapacity has become one of the hardest problems to industrial development and economic growth. The Chinese government believed that it can only be solved by shifting production facilities to potential foreign countries. Through China–Malaysia industrial cooperation, it could not only lower the cost of local infrastructure in Malaysia, but also assist Chinese government to reduce stress from internal overcapacity.

In line with the OBOR initiatives, the China–Malaysia collaborative projects were implemented in the form of seaport alliances, coastal cities' cooperation and industrial park establishment. China–Malaysia signed a MoU of seaport alliances on November 2015, which included 6 Malaysia ports and 10 Chinese ports to enhance trade relations and information exchange. Before this MoU, the Port Klang of Malaysia has established the sister ports relationship with most of the 10 China ports in order to boost the logistics, trade and tourism industries.

In terms of exchanges in urban infrastructure construction projects between twinned regions, the province of Guangdong in China and Malacca in Malaysia signed a MoU for establishing a Maritime Industrial Park, Guangdong–Malacca electrical manufacturing industrial estate and Malacca's deep water seaport. Furthermore, Guangdong government was highly interested in building a man-made Malacca island for the development of tourism and maritime industry on that island. Chinese construction companies are also engaged in projects such as land reclamation and bridge construction in Penang of Malaysia.

On the other hand, the MCKIP in Pahang of Malaysia has received RM 13.4 billion for working on investment projects till November 2015, and it is the sister park of China–Malaysia Qinzhou Industrial Park (CMQIP) in Guangxi of China. CMQIP which was established in April 2012, was the third collaboration between China and a foreign country for jointly building an industrial park, behind the China–Singapore Suzhou Industrial Park and Sino-Singapore Eco-city. Under the OBOR initiative, MCKIP and CMQIP both were essential to the Chinese government because they were the flagship projects of China–Malaysia industrial cooperation and are the ideal demonstrative case studies for other ASEAN countries.

Malaysia could benefit from China's OBOR initiatives. Firstly, through the OBOR, China could provide infrastructure investment fund for developing industrial park such as MCKIP and reconstructing seaports like Port Klang and Port Malacca. Secondly, the process of technology transfer will occur from China to Malaysia, especially in the field of infrastructure construction. Thirdly, Malaysia can easily access Chinese market and bring Chinese *halal* food and Muslims commodities to Chinese consumers.

However, Malaysia will also meet challenges including the instability of Malaysia's political and economic situations and a festering ethnic issue in domestic politics. There are also other external factors affecting Malaysia like the impact of the economic slowdown of China, geopolitics in the South China Sea and US perception of Malaysia. These factors may impede or redirect attention away from developing China–Malaysia economic cooperation in terms of OBOR initiatives. Malaysia will keep a two-pronged strategy to maximize its economic interests which are in turn subjected to political impact from domestic affairs to international events. In terms of economic perspectives, Malaysia will fully support China's OBOR initiatives by offering more bilateral collaborative project opportunities and deepening their trade partnership. But in political terms, Malaysia will continue to pay attention to concerns from the domestic ethnic Malays majority and external perceptions of this relationship by other ASEAN countries and the US.

Sino-Malaysia economic relations

Along with APEC held in Manila Philippines on 17 November 2015, Chinese President Xi Jinping met Malaysian Prime Minister Najib Razak and reiterated that China gave top priority to bilateral ties and upgraded comprehensive strategic relations with Malaysia. Najib also stated with high optimism that Sino-Malaysia relations were at their highest level in history. Historically, the provable relations between China and Malaysia goes back to the 3rd century BC when Malays sailed to coastal region of China and expanded their influence from the 14th century AD onwards. During Ming dynasty period, which established protectorate relations with Sultanate of Malacca.

During the famous seven expeditions of Zheng He, his entourage visited Malacca five times. The Chinese merchants traded silk and satins, cloths, ceramic ware from China for rhinoceros horn, ivory, bird nest and spices from Malaysia.[2] Obviously, the trading commodities between both countries

[2] Tong, Guang Rong 2010. Complementary Trade Relations between China and Malaysia, dated 3 March 2014 in Center for Malaysian Chinese Studies [downloaded on 12 November 2015], available at http://www.malaysian-chinese.net/publication/articlesreports/articles/999.html.

were the elementary products, mainly the Chinese medicinal materials from Malaysia and apparel materials from China were traded. The content of trading commodities became richer and richer after the 19th century with Chinese migration to British Malaya (the former name for Malaysia during the colonial era). China also sold the foods, traditional products and sundry manufactures to Malaysia and brought back the woods, bamboo, rattan and rubber.[3] The rubber and textile goods have gradually become the main export goods to China in the period from WWII to the formation of Sino-Malaysian official diplomatic ties, even though some political considerations remained such as the United Nation's embargo on China in the 1950s and anti-dumping legislation enacted against Chinese goods in the 1960s that reduced the export figures coming out of China.

Among the Southeast Asian countries, Malaysia was the first one to officially recognize the People's Republic of China (PRC) when Malaysia's former Prime Minister Tun Abdul Razak visited Beijing and Shanghai in 1974.[4] It was fundamental for Sino-Malaysia's 40 years of diplomatic ties to construct normal trading relations and led to the establishment of the Comprehensive Strategic Partnerships in 2013. China was still not the main trading partner of Malaysia in 2000 and the trading volume from China to Malaysia was only under 4% of Malaysia's total trade volume. However, China has become the largest importer of Malaysian products for six consecutive years since 2009 (Figure 1). The trading amount increased from about US$12 billion in 2000 to about US$108 billion in 2014, a nine-fold increase. In the joint communique of 40th anniversary of diplomatic ties in 2015, both countries promised to make efforts to reach US$160 billion of trading volume in 2017.[5]

The largest export trade category from Malaysia to China was MT, followed by MF and MG in last 15 years (Figure 2). Even though the MT exports decreased from over 60% in 2000 to below 50% in 2015, it was still

---

[3] Wong, John, *The Political Economy of Malaysia's Trade Relations with China*. ISEAS Occasional Paper No. 20, 1974, 3.

[4] Baginda, Abdul Razak, *China–Malaysia Relations and Foreign Policy*. New York: Routledge, Chapter 7.

[5] Zhao, Yinan, China, Malaysia Target $160b Trade Volume. *China Daily* [downloaded on 24 November 2015], available at http://www.chinadaily.com.cn/business/2014-06/01/content_17556223.htm.

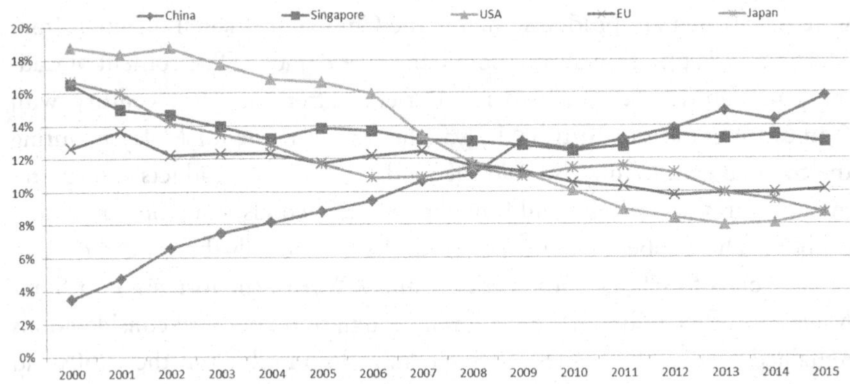

Figure 1: Trade Percentage of Malaysia-Top Five Partners.

Source: CEIC

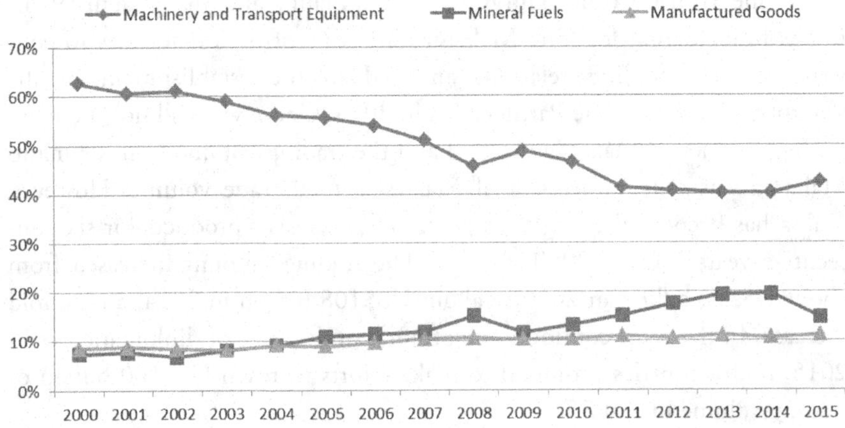

Figure 2: Malaysia top three trade category to China (By SITC)

Source: CEIC

the principal part of Malaysia's trading volume. Actually, China has played an important role in the MT trading with Malaysia. Figure 3 showed that China become the top MT trading partner with Malaysia after 2009 while the trading percentage of US on Malaysia decreased about 10% within these 15 years. The trading dependence of Malaysia on China has been growing stronger, especially after 2009. Malaysia's dependence on China in their bilateral

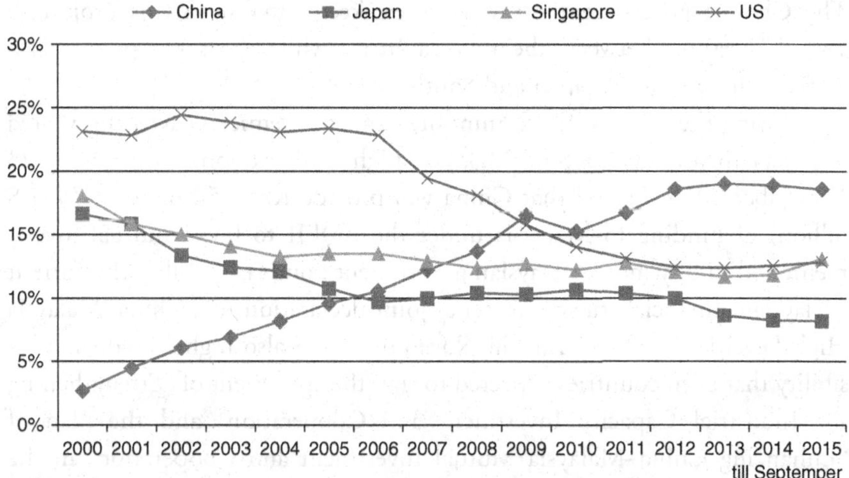

Figure 3: Malaysia: Trade percentage of machinery and transport equipment (by Country)
Source: CEIC

economic relationship is visible because the China economic slowdown has deeply impacted on the Malaysian economy since late last year 2014.[6]

Sino-Malaysian bilateral investments are not as large as their bilateral trading volume, but there are potentially a lot of developments which could trigger rapid growth in the future. For instance, Guangdong signed a MoU with Malacca on 21 September 2015 to enhance mutual cooperation relations, especially to upgrade the deep water seaport of Malacca as a nautical hub.[7] The MCKIP which was officially launched in 2013 has also received a total of RM 13.4 billion worth of investments, mainly from the Guangxi Beibu Gulf International Port Group (China) collaborating with IJM Corporation Bhd (Malaysia), Alliance Steel (M) Sdn Bhd and MCKIP Sdn Bhd. In addition, construction of the Kuala Lumpur–Singapore high-speed rail (HSR) may be the next joint cooperation project for China and Malaysia.

[6] IMF: Malaysia Economy Still Vibrant. *Malaymail Online*, 13 November 2015 [downloaded on 24 November 2015], available at http://www.themalaymailonline.com/malaysia/article/imf-malaysias-economy-still-vibrant.

[7] Melaka Signs MoU with China Province Guangdong. *Bernama*, 21 September 2015 [downloaded on 16 November 2015], available at http://english.astroawani.com/business-news/melaka-signs-mou-china-province-guangdong-74070.

The Chinese government expressed their keen interest in this project in several meetings between the two countries while the same project also attracted interest from Japan and South Korea.

During the 27th ASEAN Summit, Chinese Premier Li Keqiang visited Malaysia to attend the Sino-Malaysia high-level economic forum on 23 November 2015. Li said that China will provide RMB 50 billion (US$7.8 billion) of funding to Malaysia under the RQFII to boost mutual investment, and to buy more Malaysian government bonds to stabilize the current Malaysian financial turmoil.[8] The joint-declaration of China–Malaysia High-Level Economic Forum in November 2015 also highlighted the possibility that both countries expected to sign the agreement of "Strengthening the Industrial Capacity Investment and Cooperation" and the plan of "Enhancing China–Malaysia Mutual Investment and Cooperation" in the future.

China's OBOR initiatives and the role of Malaysia

Chinese President Xi Jinping visited Central Asia and Southeast Asia in late 2013, and advocated to establish "the Silk Road Economic Belt" (SREB) which linked up with the countries located in the original historical Silk Road, and "the 21st Century Maritime Silk Road" (MSR) and included the countries located in the South China Sea, South Pacific Ocean, India Ocean and Europe. The OBOR Prospect and Action Plan" which integrated SREB and MSR was later released by Chinese government in 2015 and featured prominently in the Chinese 13th Five-Year Plan. The China's OBOR initiative is aimed to strengthen the connectivity with about 60 countries along the routes, in terms of policy coordination, infrastructure construction, trade and investment collaboration, financial cooperation, as well as people contact and communication.

The SREB has three main routes which start from inland cities of China. The first route is across Central Asia and Russia to European (Baltic Sea).

[8] Li, Keqiang, Take China–Malaysia Cooperation to A New High. *Keynote Speech at the Malaysia–China High-Level Economic Forum*, dated 23 November 2015 [downloaded on 24 November 2015], available at http://www.fmprc.gov.cn/mfa_eng/zxxx_662805/t1318199.shtml.

The second route is across Central and Western Asia to Persian Gulf and Mediterranean Sea. The third route is across Southeast and South Asia to the Indian Ocean. In contrast, the MSR has two main routes which originate from the coastal port cities of China, including the route across the South China Sea to the Indian Ocean then Europe and another route across the South China Sea to the South Pacific Ocean. Malaysia is locatred in in third route of SREB which planned to construct Kunming–Singapore railway across mainland Southeast Asia countries. More importantly, Malaysia acts as a bridge in the second route of MSR between the various countries surrounding South China Sea and the countries along with the Indian Ocean. In particular, China–Malaysia has prolonged maritime relations since Zheng He's expedition to Malacca in 14th century and the Strait of Malacca itself located in an irreplaceable position.

By geographical location, Malaysia is an important hub for China to connect with Southeast, South and Western Asian countries. The Straits of Malacca is one of the busiest shipping lines in the world, over 79,000 vessels transited in 2014 compared to just 14,000 in Panama Canal in the same year.[9] In terms of transported volume of crude oil and petroleum products, the Strait of Malacca is the second only after the Strait of Hozmuz (Table 1). The oil import of China through this region makes up at least 51% of total oil imported and it comes primarily from the Middle East and 82% of this Middle Eastern oil passes through the Straits of Malacca.[10] This is one of the reasons why the Chinese government was keen to strengthen connectivity with Malaysia through the OBOR initiatives in order to guarantee the accessibility of the Straits of Malacca.

The importance of the Strait of Malacca led China to launch its first joint military drill exercise with Malaysia in Malacca in September 2015, where more than 1,000 Chinese troops participated and it was the largest one

[9] Canal to Bypass Straits of Malacca and Singapore Hard to Justify. *Ship&Bunker*, 22 May 2015 [downloaded on 12 November 2015], available at http://shipandbunker.com/news/apac/387914-canal-to-bypass-straits-of-malacca-and-singapore-hard-to-justify.

[10] Bender, Jeremy, This Pentagon Map Shows How China's Energy Needs Are Driving Beijing's Military and Diplomatic Strategy. *Business Insider*, 14 May 2015 [downloaded on 12 November 2015], available at http://www.businessinsider.sg/this-map-shows-chinas-global-energy-ties-2015-5/?r=US&IR=T#.VlVJfnYrKUk.

Table 1: Volume of crude oil and petroleum products transported

Unit: million barrels per day

Location	2009	2010	2011	2012	2013
Strait of Hormuz	15.7	15.9	17.0	16.9	17.0
Strait of Malacca	13.5	14.5	14.6	15.1	15.2
Suez Canal and SUMED Pipeline	3.0	3.1	3.8	4.5	4.6
Bab el-Mandeb	2.9	2.7	3.4	3.7	3.8
Danish Straits	3.0	3.2	3.3	3.1	3.3
Turkish Straits	2.8	2.8	3.0	2.9	2.9
Panama Canal	0.8	0.7	0.8	0.8	0.8
World Maritime Oil Trade	**53.9**	**55.5**	**55.6**	**56.7**	**56.5**

Source: US Energy Information Administration (EIA), World Oil Transit Chokepoints, dated 11 November 2014, available at http://www.eia.gov/beta/international/analysis_includes/special_topics/World_Oil_Transit_Chokepoints/wotc.pdf. (Accessed on 18 November 2015)

of its kind between Beijing and ASEAN countries.[11] The drill exercise not only included disaster relief, but also search and rescue simulation of hijacked vessel rescue. It implied that the Straits of Malacca was a strategically important channel of China oil imports.

On the other hand, strengthening China–Malaysia relations could tighten up Chinese relations with Southeast Asian countries through Malaysia's current role in the ASEAN. Malaysia was the chair of ASEAN for 2015 and represented ASEAN countries to announce the launch of the ASEAN Community in 27th ASEAN Summit on 21 November 2015.[12] Meanwhile, China was very eager to develop RCEP with ASEAN countries for FTA, particularly since the TPP, another FTA led by US including four ASEAN countries, had reached an agreement in 2015.

[11] China, Malaysia Start Joint Military Exercise. *The Straits Times*, 19 September 2015 [downloaded on 20 November 2015], available at http://www.straitstimes.com/asia/east-asia/china-malaysia-start-joint-military-exercise.

[12] The ASEAN Community means that it became a full-fledged politically cohesive, economically integrated, socially responsible Community, in which all ASEAN members will benefit from the comprehensive integration. To Launch the ASEAN Community, Leaders Gather in Malaysia for the 27th ASEAN Summit. *ASEAN Secretariat News*, 21 November 2015.

Business opportunities in *halal* food and Muslim commodities were another interest by Chinese government to cope with Malaysia through OBOR initiatives. China has 23 million Muslims, just a small portion of 1.6 billion Muslims in the world and they are scattered in many parts of China.[13] Most of the *halal* food and Muslim commodities companies were small-and medium-sized enterprises (SMEs) and only exported their products to local Muslim consumers due to the limited market. Moreover, China's Muslim community was geographically isolated from the other countries' Muslims for a long time. Other Muslim countries still cannot accept the *halal* food and Muslim commodities made in China due to ritual differences. In this circumstance, "the China–Malaysia Halal Food and Muslim Commodities Certification and Industry Cooperation" seminar was held in July 2015 in order to assist China to expand *halal* trade export business with other Muslim countries. Several Halal Food Industrial Parks were also built up to accelerate cooperation by both countries such as the Kuantan Industrial Park in Malaysia and the Wuzhong Halal Industrial Park in China.[14]

Another reason for China's active outreach to Malaysia was to overcome its problem of overcapacity generated through industrial cooperation. The production overcapacity rate of some industries in China, including iron and steel, glass, cement, aluminum, solar panel and power generation equipment, is over 30% that may have led those companies to borrow more to make up for profits.[15] In the short term, the overcapacity causes less fixed investments and directly slows down the economic growth of China. In the long term, there would be more factories going bankrupt if the overcapacity condition continues to deteriorate. The Chinese government was firmly convinced that the industrial overcapacity problems can only be solved by shifting production

---

[13]China's Halal Food Exporters Struggle with Ideological, Trade Barriers. *Global Times*, 26 November 2014 [downloaded on 25 November 2015], available at http://www.globaltimes.cn/content/893789.shtml.

[14]Why China Wants a Bite of the Booming Halal Food Market. *CNBC*, 24 August 2015 [downloaded on 24 November 2015], available at http://www.cnbc.com/2015/08/24/china-wants-a-bite-of-the-booming-halal-food-market.html.

[15]Cheng, Shuahua Wallace, Overcapacity a Time Bomb for China's Economy. *South China Morning Post*, 28 September 2015 [downloaded on 15 November 2015], available at http://www.scmp.com/comment/insight-opinion/article/1862024/overcapacity-time-bomb-chinas-economy.

facilities to potential foreign countries that needed these Chinese products.[16] Thus, Chinese Premier Li Keqiang has highlighted in the Malaysia–China High-Level Economic Forum that China achieved advanced and cost-effective productivity in several areas such as irons and steels, as well as building materials, which can assist in the infrastructure development of Malaysia.[17] Through both countries' bilateral industrial cooperation, it will not only lower the cost of building local infrastructure in Malaysia, but also reduce the Chinese government's stress arising from internal overcapacity.

Collaborative projects: Seaports, cities and industrial parks

In line with the OBOR initiatives, the China–Malaysia collaborative projects are implemented in terms of seaport alliances, coastal cities' cooperation and industrial park establishment such as MCKIP. Malaysia has signed a MoU with China in November 2015 for the establishment of port alliances to enhance trade relations and information exchange. The alliances involved six Malaysian ports located at Bintulu, Johor, Kuantan, Malacca, Penang and Klang and 10 China ports at Beibuwan, Fujian Fuzhou, Guangzhou, Jiangsu Taicang, Ningbo, Dalian, Shenzhen, Haikou, Shanghai and Xiamen.[18] Port Klang is the busiest port in Malaysia and is the second largest container port behind the Singapore amongst ASEAN countries and ranked 13th in the world in 2013.[19] Before the MoU of port alliance, Port Klang had already established the sister ports relationship with most of the 10 Chinese ports

[16] Solution to China's Industrial Overcapacity Setting Up More Factories Overseas, Says Official. *South China Morning Post*, 22 July 2015 [downloaded on 24 November 2015], available at http://www.scmp.com/news/china/economy/article/1842793/solution-chinas-industrial-overapacity-setting-more-factories.

[17] Li, Keqiang, Take China–Malaysia Cooperation to A New High. *Keynote Speech at the Malaysia–China High-Level Economic Forum*, 23 November 2015 [downloaded on 24 November 2015], available at http://www.fmprc.gov.cn/mfa_eng/zxxx_662805/t1318199.shtml.

[18] Msia Signs Eight Govt-to-Govt MoU with China. *New Straits Times*, 26 November 2015 [downloaded on 26 November 2015], available at http://www.nst.com.my/news/2015/11/113395/msia-signs-eight-govt-govt-mou-china.

[19] World Shipping Council, Top 5 World Container Ports http://www.worldshipping.org/about-the-industry/global-trade/top-50-world-container-ports [downloaded on 26 November 2015].

named above in order to boost logistics, trade and tourism exchanges. For instance, Haikou became Port Klang's sister port on 11 November 2015, to cooperate in the fields of sharing shipping lanes, logistics, information exchange and talent training.[20] In addition, Kuantan port has progressively expanded in the Malaysia–China cooperation project, to handle ships over 150,000 deadweight tonnage and became a petrochemical hub in Malaysia and the logistic hub for the East Coastal Economic Special Zone.[21]

Recently, Guangdong of China and Malacca of Malaysia also signed a MoU to establish the Maritime Industrial Park, the Guangdong–Melaka Industrial Estate for electronics manufacturing and investing in the deep seaport of Malacca. Guangdong governor Zhu Xiaodan also expressed his interest in collaborating with Malacca in the construction of man-made Malacca islands for managing the tourist port project and the maritime industry.[22] Seven MoUs were signed from the companies of both sides. The investment projects found in the seven MoUs included Zhuhai International Racing Circuit reconstruction, *halal* food certification cooperation, clinic care, education and research collaboration, intelligent city and infrastructure development at Malacca Gateway, as well as building high technology procurement projects.[23]

In the Penang state of Malaysia, China Communications Construction Company (M) Sdn Bhd (CCCC Malaysia), a wholly-owned Malaysian subsidiary of China Communications Construction Company Ltd. (CCCC), has a land reclamation contract worth RM 2.3 billion for building Seri Tanjung Pinang Phase 2 (STP2).[24] The CCCC group is the largest infrastructure construction and dredging company in China. Before this contract, Beijing-based

---

[20] Haikou Port Sets Up Sister Port Relationship with Malaysia's Port Klang [downloaded on 26 November 2015], available at http://www.whatsonsanya.com/news-32345.html.

[21] Welcome to Kuantan Port Consortium [downloaded on 22 October 2015], available at http://www.ijm.com/infrastructure/port/kuantanport/.

[22] Guangdong Eyes Malacca. *The Star Online*, 22 September 2015 [downloaded on 26 November 2015], available at http://www.thestar.com.my/News/Nation/2015/09/22/Guangdong-eyes-Malacca-Province-sees-potential for-worldclass-port-in-state/.

[23] Seven MOUs Involving Investments Between Malaysia's Melaka, Guangdong Signed Saturday. *Bernama*, 19 September 2015 [downloaded on 12 November 2015], available at http://www.bernama.com/bernama/v8/bu/newsbusiness.php?id=1172767.

[24] China Firm Wins RM 2.3 bil Penang Reclamation Contract. *The Star* 28 October 2015.

China Harbour Engineering Co. Ltd. (CHEC), the main share-holder of CCCC, had undertaken the main construction contract of the Sultan Abdul Halim Muadzam Shah Bridge, also known as the Second Penang Bridge.

The MCKIP in the Pahang state of Malaysia is the sister park of CMQIP in Guangxi China. CMQIP, which was established on 1 April 2012, is the third China–foreign countries Industrial Park, behind the China–Singapore Suzhou Industrial Park and Sino-Singapore Eco-city.[25] Arising from the suggestion of Malaysian Prime Minister Najib, China agreed to establish the MCKIP simultaneously and officially launched the project in February 2013. The MCKIP and CMQIP are critical to Chinese government under the OBOR initiatives because they are the flagship projects of China–Malaysia industrial cooperation and would become the best demonstrative examples of industrial park construction for other ASEAN countries. It will not only attract other countries' participation in the development of both MCKIP and CMQIP, but also encourage them to establish industrial cooperation with China through the "two countries, twin parks" model.

MCKIP targeted making high-end manufacturing industrial items that included stainless steel products, electric and electronics, information communication technology and renewable energy.[26] Until September 2015, MCKIP has totally received RM 13.4 billion investment projects, including RM 4.2 billion of steel production project, RM 3 billion of Kuantan Port expansion project, RM 4 billion of infrastructure project, RM 2 billion of light industry and clay porcelain/ceramic project, and RM 0.2 of renewable energy project (Table 2).

The opportunities and challenges

As Vice Foreign Minister of China said, China will offer US$10 billion (RM 42 billion) as infrastructure loans to Southeast Asian countries through OBOR initiatives.[27] Malaysia would take advantage of China's infrastructure

---

[25] [downloaded on 26 November 2015], available at http://finance.sina.com.cn/roll/20151027/045223585434.shtml.

[26] Malaysia–China Kuantan Industrial Park (MCKIP) Development Achieves Significant Progress. *East Coastal Economic Region News*, 4 April, 2015.

[27] China Offers $10 Billion in Infrastructure Loans for Southeast Asia. *Reuters*, 22 November 2015 [downloaded on 23 November 2015], available at http://www.reuters.com/article/

Table 2: The MCKIP investment projects (total amount RM 13.4 billion, until September 2015)

Year	**Involved Company**	**Project**	**Amounts (RM billion)**
2014	Alliance Steel (M) Sdn Bhd, a subsidiary of Guangxi Beibu Gulf Iron and Steel Co. Ltd. (China)	Modern integrated steel plant, produce high carbon steel and H-shaped steel	4.2
2014	Guangxi Beibu Gulf International Port Group (China) and IJM Corporation Berhad (Malaysia)	Kuantan Port expansion	3
2014	MCKIP Sdn Bhd	Infrastructure	2.5
2015	Malaysia Federal Government Funding	Infrastructure	1.5
2015	Guangxi Zhongli Enterprise Group Co. Ltd. (China)	(1) Light industry (2) Manufacturing of clay porcelain and ceramic	2
2015	Zkenergy (Yiyang) New Resource Science & Technology Co. Ltd. (China)	The development of an engineering and production-based center that will produce renewable energy	0.2

Source: Author integrated info from website of East Coastal Economic Region (ECER) and MCKIP Attracts Two More Investments From China Worth RM2.2 Billion. *Bernama News* 19 September 2015, http://www.bernama.com/bernama/v8/newsindex.php?id=1172780. (Accessed on 20 November 2015)

investment for developing industrial park such as MCKIP and reconstructing seaports like Port Klang and Port Malacca. Apparently, Malaysia needs more funds to comprehensively enhance infrastructure construction within a short time, especially to catch up with the "2020 Vision" to become a developed country.[28] To a certain extent, bilateral cooperation has reinvigorated the

2015/11/22/us-asean-summit-china-aid-idUSKBN0TB0BA20151122#yF2KLPOzaI2Xt bbr.97.

[28]Vision 2020 of Malaysia was addressed by former Prime Minister of Malaysia, Mahathir bin Mohamad, in 1991, during the drafting of the Sixth Malaysia Plan. The vision then was towards making Malaysia in 2020 a fully-developed country in all dimensions, especially in the areas of economic prosperity, social well-being and political stability.

Malaysia Vision 2020 as the current level of Malaysian development still seems far away from reaching the target.

The development of MCKIP will also have positive spillover effects for other industrial parks in the East Coastal Economic Region in Malaysia. One of the MCKIP projects to expand the Kuantan Port will facilitate the growth of other surrounding industrial parks — the Petrochemical Industrial Park, Integrated Biopark, Pekan Automotive Industrial Park and Gambang Halal Park — and provide more logistic capacities and trading possibilities to Kuantan.

Another significant benefit for Malaysia via OBOR initiatives is to receive the technology transfer from China. For instance, University Technology Malaysia signed the MoU with China to transfer the technology of "Moving Bed Bio Reactor" to produce high quality treated water without odor and minimum sludge output this year.[29] The technology has been commonly applied in China on a commercial basis and it could lower the operating costs in Malaysian factories. Chinese companies also invested a production-based center for collaborative efforts to develop renewable energy technology in MCKIP.

From another point of view, China–Malaysia industrial cooperation via OBOR initiatives provides Malaysia not only with an admission ticket to tap into China's potential consumer market, in the agricultural goods such as durian and bird nest to *halal* food and Muslim commodities. This is particularly targeted at the Muslim population in China (23 million) which is more than the Muslim population in Malaysia (19 million), and both can also collaborate to set up an exclusive agency to introduce Chinese *halal* food and Muslim commodities to other Muslims countries.

Broadly speaking, Malaysian government echoes support for the OBOR initiative and deeply believes that it will have positive influence on the economic development of Malaysia. Apart from the Malaysian Prime Minister's supportive statement, Transport Minister Datuk Seri Liow Tiong Lai also pointed out that every ASEAN country, company and individual should not

---

[29] Najib Witnesses Signing of MoU on Transfer of AMBBR Technology from China to UTM. *Eco-Business*, 3 June 2015 [downloaded on 30 November 2015], available at http://www.eco-business.com/news/najib-witnesses-signing-of-mou-on-transfer-of-ambbr-technology-from-china-to-utm/.

miss out from this OBOR-given economic opportunities that amount to US$2.5 trillion of annual trading volume.[30]

Other than the positive returns from capitalizing on these opportunities, Malaysia will inevitably meet with some internal and external challenges that could impede the development of OBOR initiatives. Internally, the instability of Malaysia's political economy and the politically-volatile ethnic issue would adversely impact on the ability of Malaysia to gain from the OBOR initiatives. Externally, the economic slowdown of China, the geopolitics of the South China Sea as well as the strategic perceptions of US would interfere with China–Malaysia cooperation.

The Malaysian economy was hampered by the slump in crude oil prices and political unrests last year. The drop in oil prices negatively impacted on Malaysia's petroleum revenue which accounted for 40% of the total revenues of Malaysia. It also hurt the Malaysian Ringgit, and falling primary commodity export prices such as those of rubber and palm oil, further reduced Malaysia's commodity-dependent revenue. In addition, Prime Minister Najib faced political crisis and mass anti-corruption campaign (Bersih 4.0) after the article from *the Wall Street Journal* uncovered nearly US$700 million of unknown source funds deposited into Najib's personal account.

The shadowy opposition forces in Malaysia with strong views on race and ethnicity often exaggerate the importance of their existence, when political disputes do not conclude quickly. "Seditious" speeches can be easily leveled as a charge against the government's extreme supporters or opposition parties in 2015. The ethnic Chinese will avoidably act in its important role in the China–Malaysia economic cooperation. It will unconsciously trigger the political sensitive of Malays ethnics to doubt whether this development could impact their political position and erode their economic condition.

In the external circumstance, the economic slowdown of China not only directly affect the Malaysian economy due to the largest trading partner relationship between the two of them, but it also raises uncertainties and risks impacting on their collaborative projects with Malaysia. The Chinese economic slowdown may lead to higher debt, including the local government and enterprises. It will lower the projects' achievement rate if Chinese

---

[30] Liow: China's Belt and Road Initiative Offers Vast Opportunities. *The Star*, 3 November 2015.

government needs to reallocate economic resources for local development and the enterprises want to collect funds to repay the loan.

Unlike economic highly positive cooperation with China, Malaysia Deputy Prime Minister Zahid Hamidi had recently criticized the China's sovereignty claims and its artificial island construction in the South China Sea. The criticisms from the Malaysian government was meat not only to soothe the local Malays' sense of nationalism but also assert the integrity of sovereignty, and consider the perceptions of other Southeast Asian countries towards Sino-Malaysian cooperation, especially in the context of ASEAN unity. Besides, Malaysia's alignment with the US also impacts on the development of China–Malaysia economic cooperation, particularly in terms of the TPP which China has not participated yet but will be established soon. Malaysia also needs to consider the balance of power between China and the US, particularly to avoid clashing with the US's "Pivot to Asia" strategy.

In brief, Malaysia will consistently keep a two-handed strategy as the best way to deal with China. In economic hand, Malaysia will make efforts to establish deeper and broader partnership with China through the OBOR initiatives, in order to avoid harming US interests in the Asia-Pacific. In the political arena, Malaysia will echo the ASEAN countries' sovereignty claims in the South China Sea against China's maritime expansion. Malaysia will repeatedly try to maximize its economic interests subjected to comprehensive political considerations and priorities (both domestic and international).

Chapter 18

Japan and its Outreach to Central Asia and Southeast Asia: An Update

LIM Tai Wei

Keeping Central Asia busy: Japanese PM's visit to the region

Central Asia is the traditional backyard for the Soviet Union's geopolitical influence and since the disintegration of the USSR, the region is coming increasingly under Chinese economic influence. This is especially pronounced with the institution of the One Belt One Road economic diplomatic initiative (the overland route was officially announced in Kazakhstan) and the establishment of the Asian Infrastructure Investment Bank (AIIB). As the other major economy in Northeast Asia, Japan is also tapping into the economic potential of the region with Prime Minister Shinzo Abe's one-week official tour of the region in late October 2015 that took him through Mongolia, Turkmenistan, Tajikistan, Uzbekistan, Kyrgyzstan and Kazakhstan (in that order). The last Japanese Prime Minister to visit the region was almost a decade ago and it is also the first time that a Prime Minister from Japan has actually set foot on Turkmenistan, Tajikistan and Kyrgyzstan. And Central Asia is responding to Japanese overtures by hosting him with traditional protocol and hospitality. He also received an honorary doctorate from a university in Turkmenistan. Japan is playing catch-up with Russia and China that have been present in the region for much longer durations. In the post-war years, Russia has been active in the region since the Soviet era. Historically, China has had a long history of engagement since the days of the overland Silk Road from Qin to Ming dynasties.

Compared to Japanese outreach, China has been investing in the region for more than a decade. Economically, China has been successful with offering loans without conditionalities and its socialist system is also compatible with other strongman political systems found in the Central Asian region. In other words, there is compatibility between the two. Central Asia's infrastructure needs is large enough to accommodate all big players coming into the region to work on large construction projects. It already secured affordable low-priced infrastructure construction projects cooperating with China. It has also secured infrastructure equipment for transmitting raw materials from Central Asia to China. Chinese bidding advantages lies in the strength of its state-owned enterprises (SOEs), a model that fits the hybrid socialist political system coexisting with a market economy. Chinese bidding takes the form of one bidding party funded by state banks and guaranteed by the state. Chinese loans and investments are also politically-neutral with a fierce adherence to disinterest in local politics in what used to be called "no-strings attached" loans. Because of these strategies, China is now the region's largest trading partner.

Distinguishing its approach from others, Japan's marketing tack focuses on good quality infrastructure and high value-added industrial processing technologies (e.g. gas, oil, uranium processing plants and chemical fertilizer plants). In other words, Central Asian leaders are keen to process their raw materials in addition to infrastructure and logistical equipment that transport them. In this area, Japan is coming in at the right time because Central Asian economies are reeling from global weakness in commodity prices. Japanese infrastructure, equipment and technologies can help transform their economies based on primary materials to become high value-added industrial processing economies. Japan which is also well-known for high quality agricultural products is providing technologies to Tajikistan to improve its yields in agricultural crop. Japan also hopes to improve lives in Central Asia by providing medical equipment to Uzbekistan. For the purpose of providing high quality equipment, Mr Abe brought 50 leading business sector leaders with him. Along with manpower, Japan is also bringing along a pragmatic mindset. In 1999, Japanese soft loans to Kyrgyzstan was cut because they defaulted on payment, now the loans are resumed again.

Another example of pragmatism is Japan's willingness to help Kazakhstan tap into nuclear power. In the recent past, Japan had shied away from nuclear power cooperation as nuclear energy is still a sensitive topic back home. Japan is the only country in the world to have suffered atomic bombings (Hiroshima and Nagasaki) and also suffered the second most serious nuclear incident in the world in the Great East Japan earthquake with the Fukushima nuclear meltdown. Japan is also sensitive to the fact that some areas within Central Asia used to serve as nuclear weapon testing sites for the former Soviet Union, including Kazakhstan. Politically, Japan has teamed up with Kazakhstan to promote the implementation of the Comprehensive Nuclear Test Ban Treaty (CTBT) as cochairs. The goal is to attain universal adherence and ratification of the CTBT. Partnership between the two is apt because Kazakhstan experienced nuclear tests in its area during the Soviet era while Japan went through the atomic bombings. And now the two countries which had unfortunate nuclear and atomic experiences in the past are collaborating on peaceful and safe civilian nuclear energy uses.

What Japan ultimately offers is experience. Japan's overseas development assistance, loans, aids and investments contributed to the post-war industrialization of Southeast Asia and China and set up production networking in these countries. It has accumulated a wealth of experience in this regard. Japan therefore has the capacity to contribute its experience to developing Central Asia, along with other large economies like China and Russia. Political scientists may call the Japanese entrance into Central Asia "hedging" against Russian and Chinese dominance while economists may consider it as a latecomer catch-up economic decision. Regardless of perspective, the Central Asian developmental pie will be big enough to accommodate all big players, Japan, China and Russia.

Japan's ASEAN diplomacy in end 2015

Besides the overland Silk Road, Japan is also active in the Maritime Silk Road. In fact the term "Maritime Silk Road" was coined by a Japanese researcher on the maritime ceramics trade from Jingdezhen. Given that Japan is an island nation, it is active keeping up relationship-building in Southeast Asia. End 2015, marks a flurry of Association of Southeast Asian Nations (ASEAN) diplomacy for all major powers in the East Asian region and Japan is no exception. At Asia-Pacific Economic Cooperation (APEC) meeting in Manila, the bilateral summit between the Japanese Prime Minister Mr Shinzo Abe and

Filipino President Benigno Aquino III discussed security and defense matters. After the Manila APEC round, the Japanese leader left for Kuala Lumpur (KL) for the ASEAN summit, yet another flurry of diplomatic interactions. In the economic realm, realizing the significance of a combined 600 million-strong consumer market, a young workforce, increasing foreign direct investments, greater net connectivity and tourist arrivals, and the Asia's third largest economy, Japan which has production networks in the region for decades is working with ASEAN partners to strengthen cooperation.

By the end of 2015, the ASEAN Economic Community was set up, an important step that is the start of a long journey to forming a regional economic community. Japanese investments and aid/loans can help the ASEAN Economic Community harmonize its standards for a smoother transition to become a regional organization. The ASEAN Community has three arms: ASEAN Economic Community, Political Security Community and the Socio-Cultural Community. Japan, which is East Asia's oldest democracy with harmonious civil society–state relations, has much to offer in terms of experience for the Socio-Cultural Community. The impetus for hastening the Regional Cooperation for Economic Partnership (RCEP) comes from the successfully-concluded Trans-Pacific Partnership (TPP) talks although challenges remaining for the ambitious regional plan, including harmonizing the standards of a free trade agreement between ASEAN+6 countries, including between economies that do not yet have a bilateral free trade agreement. Japan is a stakeholder in both TPP and RCEP. Currently, the TPP seems to be running faster as President Obama is pushing through a Trade Promotion Bill that allows him to gain powers that can accelerate the process of inking free trade agreements with minimal interference from the US Congress.

On the security front, one month before the ASEAN Summit and APEC Manila on 1 October 2015, Japan led by Cabinet Minister Eriko Yamatani who is the current chairperson of the National Public Safety Commission held the ministerial meeting between Japan and ASEAN on the issues of terrorism and cyber security. Both ASEAN and Japanese Ministers present at the meeting vowed to have greater information exchanges and conversations between them and the cornerstone of this conversation will be the ASEAN–Japan Cybercrime Dialogue founded in 2014. Japan also asked for ASEAN support in resolving the abduction issue whereby North Korean kidnapped Japanese nationals three and four decades ago. KL will host the Japan–ASEAN dialogue on terrorism and cybercrime early 2016. It is here that KL hopes its information and data on extremists and terrorists can be offered in exchange for help in Japanese tracking technologies for human trafficking and cyber-security. KL information may be useful since Japanese citizens had been held hostage and/or executed in the conflict zones in the Middle East.

In the maritime defense sector, Japan worked with the US to raise the issue of South China Sea dispute at the ASEAN Summit meetings (for more on this topic, please refer to Katherine Tseng Hui-Yi's chapter in this edited volume). Both countries are concerned about the freedom of navigation in an area which see US$5 trillion worth of trade that goes through it annually. The US has flown bombers and sent a warship into the disputed area. It is calling for a rule-based maritime-order in the area. A variety of voices emerged in the defense ministers' meeting. Japanese Defense Minister Gen Nakatani called for peaceful cooperation over the South China Sea. The Malaysian Foreign Minister called for a relook at the Code of Conduct over the South China Sea as ASEAN ministers worry over developments in that region. China-friendly ASEAN states like Cambodia preferred to keep the issue out of textual mention for the defense minsters' meeting. Vietnam and the Philippines were keen to have it in the final statement. In all, all parties, regardless of political stance, are keen to see the dispute resolved peacefully and for the waterways to remain free, open and peaceful for navigation.

Section F
Conclusion

Chapter 19
Conclusion

LIM Tai Wei

Positive reviews, cautionary suggestions and narratives of complementarity

Historical narratives of the Maritime Silk Road were discussed in-depth by **Tan Ta Sen** in Section B. He pointed out one early example of globalization in maritime trading history. From 1602 to 1682, China exported through the Dutch East India Company a total of 16 million pieces of porcelains over a span of 80 years. Besides the Dutch East India Company, China also exported ceramics via Chinese, Arab, British, Japanese, Indian, Portuguese and Southeast Asian trading groups.

Complementing Dr Tan's historical work on maritime trade during Zheng He's era, readers learnt from Dr **Tai Yew Seng** that there was a precedent for official maritime trade in the period immediately preceding the Ming dynasty. Dr Tai indicated that, in the Yuan Dynasty, private trading in overseas was allowed from 1323. Private maritime trading flourished until the late 14th century in the early Ming Dynasty when the famous Ming Ban stopped all private maritime trading again. Importantly, Dr Tai pointed out that the difference between the sea bans of the Yuan and Ming dynasties are: the Yuan dynasty emperors used the sea ban and Official Capital Ships to monopolize maritime trade and maximize profits for the imperial coffers, but Ming dynasty emperors used the sea ban on maritime trading and the tributary system to manage and fend off neighboring countries involved in piracy. During the Ming Ban, Zheng He's (郑和 1371–1433) expeditions to East Africa can be considered as the natural progression of Yang Shu's voyages to Persian Gulf.

Sticking to this chronological historical narrative, Tan argued that from the 16th century to the modern age, in an age of colonialism and imperialism, Western powers armed with excellent and advanced weapons began to show their mighty hard power in harnessing natural resources in Asia and Africa. In the Cold War, Soviet Union and the United States of America became superpowers due to the possession of nuclear weapon. They dominated the world and divided the world into two camps, communist and democratic nations. Since the end of the Cold War, as a result of the disintegration of the Soviet Union, the US has since become the world's sole superpower.

Thus, the US pursued global justice and promoted western democracy, capitalist economic development and individualistic western lifestyle. The last decade of the 20th century and the first decade of the 21st century have enjoyed peace and yet the world has been full of smoke from gunpowder, conflicts and endless suicidal bomb explosions due to the ideological differences, struggles between major powers and clash of interest. Nowadays, international relations is still dominated by realist power politics and diplomacy. Contrasting with the age of colonialism, Tan argued that Cheng Ho's seven grand voyages brought about an era of political stability, economic prosperity and cultural harmony from China to East Africa. It gives a stark contrast to the war-torn region under the rules of Western colonial powers from the 16th to 20th centuries.

He then concluded that Zheng He or Cheng Ho's approach can be considered as an "Art of Collaboration". Tan then advocated that Cheng Ho's Art of Collaboration is certainly relevant and practical in today's international relations and politics. Confucian teachings aimed to build an orderly society, a government ruled by virtue and a harmonious world order. In the international stage, Cheng Ho fostered tolerant international relations with humanistic spirit of benevolence and racial equality so as to achieve a great unity among nations on win–win footing. Therefore, this Cheng Ho spirit could be a model for contemporary international relations and foreign relations. Reliving Cheng Ho's spirit in international relations based on mutual-respect, non-invasion, non-intervention and fostering good relationships with foreign states will result in the creation of a world order where multipolar powers are in a partnership to achieve world peace, universal harmony and equality.

In Section C, **Lim Tai Wei** noted that narratives of Zheng He may become part of the updated discourse on Chinese plans to revive the Maritime Silk Road which covers the span of trading cities from Fuzhou to Italy (the "one road" component of the "one belt one road" concept (known as Belt and Roads initiative in official Chinese terminology). Other interpretations see the Maritime Silk Road ending in Antwerp, Belgium, at the European end of the Maritime Silk Road. Mitigating Tan's unproblematic and optimistic assessment of the Zheng He (Cheng Ho) voyages, Lim argued that academic and historical studies are more circumspect with their comments about Zheng He's voyages, indicating Zheng's voyages as mainly an important trade catalyst for the region. Lynn Pan associated Zheng He's voyages with regional trade stimulus. Her edited volume featured renowned Southeast Asian scholar Anthony Reid who highlighted the following passage:

> The Zheng He expeditions marked the starting point of Southeast Asia's 'age of commerce'. His fleets stimulated the production of pepper, clove, nutmeg and sappanwood, and the distribution networks that brought these items to the major entrepots and took cloth, rice and manufactured goods in exchange to the production centres. Demand for Southeast Asian products in China leapt, with pepper and sappanwood becoming for the first time items of mass consumption in the 15th century.[1]

There are points of commonalities between these narratives on trade related to Zheng He's voyages. First, they offer center–periphery perspectives. In Tan and Pan's narratives, the periphery of Southeast Asia (in the Sinocentric world view) or overseas Chinese benefited from Zheng's role in opening up maritime routes and facilitating trade with China. Second, this exchange of goods is an incentive for Chinese traders to settle in Southeast Asia and become intermediaries between the Ming regime and the local rulers of kingdoms in the region. These Chinese traders became the seeds of settler communities throughout the region, including the Peranakans.

---

[1] Reid, Anthony, "Chinese and Southeast Asian interactions" in *The Encyclopedia of the Chinese Overseas* edited by Lynn Pan. Singapore: Chinese Heritage Center/Archipelago Press/Landmark Books, 1998, 50.

Third, it supports the idea of a vassal system, whereby local rulers can maintain these vigorous trade links by partaking in a tributary system where China is acknowledged (at least in the symbolic manner) as the center of the Sino-centric world order.

On the other hand, it is possible not to exceptionalize Zheng He's voyages. Wang's seminal work on the Nanhai trade reminds us that regional trade had been alive well before Zheng He's voyages, starting from coastal trade and eventually expanding to regional and then inter-regional trade. Seen in this context, with the participation of the Arab, Malay, Southeast Asian and Persian traders before the onset of Yuan or Ming dynasties, the seas around Southeast Asia had already become a regional trading lake. The regional order therefore is predicated over reciprocal trade between willing kingdoms rather than conceptualizing it as a hegemonic center with a distant reactive periphery. As merchants from large trading units reach out for trade, they need to find willing partners in the recipient smaller kingdoms for reciprocity, regardless of motivations (religious, profit-making or diplomatic reasons).

Along the same line of the amorphousness of interpretations of terms like the One Belt One Road (OBOR) or Maritime Silk Road, **Lim Wen Xin** noted that, given the broad scope of the OBOR plan, there is no unilateral interpretation on the OBOR initiative. Most of the writings she examined associated the OBOR with the economic, political and military outreach of China against the backdrop of globalization and regional integration and connection. Chinese sources routinely deny and reject the criticisms about China's clandestine agenda to influence, confine, dominate, intimidate, or generally leverage or manipulate other states involved in the undertaking. Chinese nearly altruistic goals in the OBOR are likely to be questioned by various parties and face multifarious challenges including regional instability, investment and credit risks, geopolitical influence of major powers and suspicion and mistrust from other states.

Countries will assess their national interests according to conditions for using the OBOR funding facilities, geopolitical priorities, domestic political situations, external factors and national resources and how the Belt and Road Initiative + Asian Infrastructure Investment Bank (AIIB) + Brazil, Russia, India, China and South Africa (BRICS) Bank *vis-à-vis* current existing established institutions like Asian Development Bank (ADB) best serve their needs. The success or failure of the OBOR concept will depend on the resources that Beijing is willing and able to devote to it, the adroitness of China's leaders and entrepreneurs in maneuvering in the international market and system, and the ability of China in shaping the regional preference.

Katherine Tseng Hui-Yi argues that China's nine-dash line claim serves dual functions, as it denotes a way to confirm a maritime boundary, so that Chinese sovereignty covered any structural feature, and arguably, waters situated within and therefore sovereignty over them should not be questioned. Tseng pointed out that protecting self-interest is demonstrated in significant developments in improving maritime capabilities among certain ASEAN claimants in the second half of 2015 at the point of writing. Realism and strategic expediency are also largely seen through the engagement of some extra-regional, non-claimant countries in the South China Sea, such as the US. Their stakes in the South China Sea vary, so do their involvements and prospects. The large number of players further complicates matters.

In her final analysis, Tseng pointed out that the key to China's claims in the Maritime Silk Road will be, how the Road plan, with the essence of cooperation and coprosperity, help transform and refine China's South China Sea claim, not treating the sea as an obstacle, but an aid to the realization of the Road plan. If China fails to reconcile between its South China Sea claim and the Road plan and ensure that the Road plan was able to attract ASEAN claimants' participation despite the South China Sea dispute, implications can be problematic. China may lose the credentials needed in its transition of its role as a regional great power, with great development potential and an outlook of promoting coprosperity among neighboring countries via the Road plan.

Moving on to the Overland Silk Road in Section D, **Lim Tai Wei** then wrapped up his studies of contemporary OBOR, Maritime Silk Road and Silk Road narratives by contextualizing them in recent concrete developments. Lim noted that, aside from discussions about the Maritime Silk Road, origins of the contemporary Overland Silk Road plan according to international media sources arose in 2011 when the first direct train from Chongqing to Duisburg Germany began and visions of the maritime route began from

Chinese port locations to Antwerp, Belgium.[2] Others consider the genesis of this reinterpreted Silk Road to be on 18 November 2014 when a train carrying 82 freight containers of 1,000 tons of export-made items departed from a large warehousing facility in Yiwu (Zhejiang 300 km south of Shanghai) to Madrid, when it arrived on 9 December 2014.[3]

The far end of this railway system may eventually be Rotterdam, Duisburg and Berlin.[4] *The Economist* is even more explicit in its economic analysis (as opposed to media observers keen on discussing geopolitical implications) of the Chinese Belt and Road Initiative): "As Chinese manufacturers move inland, getting their products to European markets has become more complicated. The journey back to the coast and halfway around the world by sea takes up to 60 days — an eternity for the latest iPads and other "fast fashion" products. Kazakhstan offers a backdoor route. Trains from Chongqing in south-west China to Duisburg in Germany, 10,800 km (6,700 miles) via Kazakhstan, Russia, Belarus and Poland, supposedly take just 14 days."[5]

To fund this ambitious overhaul of railway systems on a global scale, **Henry Chan Hing Lee**'s analysis on the funding source for OBOR indicates that China does possess sufficient financial resources, at the moment, to support its OBOR initiative. China already gained certain level of expertise in the infrastructure export through the State-owoned enterprises (SOEs) such as China Communication Construction Corporation (CCC), China Railway Group (CRG), China Railway Rolling Stock Corporation (CRRC), etc. They have obtained good overseas contract opportunities and the policy bank support have brought many of these opportunities to actual project implementation.

---

[2] Goh, Brenda, China Pays Big to Expand its Clout Along the New Silk Road, dated 10 November 2014 in the *Reuters* website [downloaded on 18 December 2014], available at http://www.reuters.com/article/2014/11/10/us-china-silkroad-idUSKCN0IU27R20141110.

[3] Escobar, Pepe, China is Building a New Silk Road to Europe, And it's Leaving America Behind, dated 16 December 2014 in *Mother Jones* website [downloaded on 18 December 2014], available at http://www.motherjones.com/politics/2014/12/chinas-new-silk-road-europe-will-leave-america-behind.

[4] *Ibid.*

[5] *The Economist*, The New Silk Road Hardly an Oasis, dated 15 November 2014 in *The Economist* [downloaded on 18 December 2014], available at http://www.economist.com/news/asia/21632595-kazakhstan-turns-geography-advantage-china-builds-new-silk-road-hardly-oasis.

China is running an annual current account surplus of around US$300 billion, committing such amounts of funding to OBOR financing is not going to hurt China's credit standing and financial system stability. Of course, we should note that OBOR is probably the most ambitious cross-border infrastructure initiative ever launched, scaling up earlier bilateral working model between China and the recipient country might not be a simple extension of modeling. The issue of country affordability, loan credit worthiness, long-term political stability and many more risk factors will be coming into the picture.

The Chinese government had set a deadline of 30 October 2015 in its solicitation of provincial inputs on the finalization of OBOR plan, how the plan is laid out will allow a more detailed analysis and lookout for its future prospect. Even in the absence of an integrated plan, Chinese overseas contract wins and execution are already at a high note, whether there is a need to overhaul the system or keep the existing system with a small twist are topics that observers are keenly looking into.

Going into technical details and cost-benefit analysis, **Henry Chan Hing Lee**'s chapter on railway diplomacy highlights the centrality of rail connectivity in the OBOR initiative. Chan argues that China is linking the proposed Euro–China High-Speed Railway (HSR) and Central Asia–China HSR to the Silk Road initiative. The proposed Pan-Asia HSR system is supplementing the Maritime Silk Road linkage between Southeast Asia and China. China's Silk Road initiative is connected to the "Rail Diplomacy". Chinese leaders' confidence in pushing "Rail Diplomacy" lies in its existing HSR network which has demonstrated world leading cost efficiency, technology and reliability. The safety of the system is also world class.

Many countries have noted the contribution of HSR to China's regional economic development, urbanization and industrial upgrading. Surprisingly strong economic agglomeration benefits from a cost-effective HSR had convinced many countries to consider railway investment as the preferred land transport system backbone in lieu of the post WW II conventional highway system. China is the only country building a HSR and rail base national transportation backbone. Though a latecomer in HSR, it had successfully build an indigenous industry after absorbing imported rolling stock and signaling technology. It is the only country that can offer complete Engineering, Procurement & Construction (EPC) solution under all weather & environment conditions in the world.

Cost analysis done by World Bank shows that China HSR projects was completed at cost which is at most 2/3 of that in the rest of the world. China has a commanding cost advantage in HSR construction. Two of the main reasons are (1) the standardization of design of various construction elements which significantly enhances construction efficiency and (2) development of innovative and competitive capacity for manufacture of equipment.

China embarked on six rounds of speed upgrade to its rail system between 1997 and 2007. It has achieved maximum speed of 250 km/h on upgraded conventional rail track prior to introduction of HSR in 2008. It is the only country with working experience in rail speeding up through existing conventional rail line upgrade. This is an attractive proposition to many developing countries with pre-WW II legacy rail system. HSR spillover technology in sub-high speed conventional railway and Rapid Transit Vehicle spearheaded the export of Chinese railway equipment and construction. New Greenfield projects approved under "Rail Diplomacy" in Kenya and Thailand are sub-high speed line using Chinese rail standards.

Passenger dedicated line in the HSR system had released a lot of freight capacity in the replaced traditional track. China Railway Corporation (CRC) is utilizing those capacity and moving to supplement its freight cargo business from traditional black (coal), bulk goods centric model with high value express cargo of white goods from e-commerce. CRC's success will enhance the export attractiveness of the Chinese railway business model. Combo passenger/freight model can meaningfully help the economic justification of a high initial fixed cost rail investment over a passenger dedicated line.

China complements highest level "Rail Diplomacy" with attractive bilateral financial support to developing countries interested in its HSR or rail system. China's offer is attractive and there are a good number of developing countries negotiating. "Rail Diplomacy" holds significant economic as well as geopolitical benefit to China. An efficient high technology transport backbone is a high profile project in enhancing the builder's national image as well as decades of future maintenance business relationship. Strength, Weakness, Opportunities & Threat (SWOT) analysis indicated that China enjoyed significant comparative advantage over its competitors on rail export contract. However, prospect of "Rail Diplomacy" also depends on geopolitical factors and domestic politics of the interested country. The just canceled Mexico HSR is supposedly the first complete export HSR project of China in HSR.

Besides railway development, another major theme in this publication is highlighting the connection between the Silk Road and China's Go-West policy, relocating manufacturers from expensive first-tier Eastern coastal cities inwards to the West where labor costs are cheaper. It also highlights the narrative that European markets (and, along the way, Middle Eastern, Central Asian and South Asian markets) will become increasingly important for Chinese exports. Thus, the rationale for the Belt and Road Initiative. On 8 November 2014, the Chinese promised to dispense funds amounting to a US$40 billion Silk Road fund with the broad objective of improving transport and trade links, in addition to the US$50 billion already allocated to the Beijing-initiated AIIB and the BRICS Bank. The BRICS Development Bank funds energy, telecommunications and transportation infrastructure with a starting capital of US$50 billion and China/India as its major shareholder.[6]

Connected with the emergence of these funding institutions, a major question discussed in this writing therefore is how China will disperse its funds. The key word that is mentioned in the international media, top leaders and policymakers' statements as well as the scholarly conferences and seminars that I attended was "connectivity" — how to link up the entire belt of countries along both overland and Maritime Silk Road so that trade can be stimulated. Up till December 2014, details were not forthcoming from Chinese sources on how their Silk Road-related budget will be utilized. Along with observers and the international media, this began to cause some countries located along both the overland as well as the Maritime Silk Road to seek more details about the initiative.

In seeking this reaction from the Chinese government, the immediate response can be divided into three ways:

(1) To use official and track II channels to ask for more details so that states in the designated regions of the Silk Road initiative can react accordingly to maximize their economic benefits from the scheme;

[6] Escobar, Pepe, China is Building a New Silk Road to Europe, And It's Leaving America Behind, dated 16 December 2014 in *Mother Jones* website [downloaded on 18 December 2014], available at http://www.motherjones.com/politics/2014/12/chinas-new-silk-road-europe-will-leave-america-behind.

(2) To preempt any issues incompatible with national interests by first opposing the institutions associated (or perceived to be associated) with the scheme such as opposition to the AIIB;
(3) Regardless of the shape and form of the Silk Road initiative which is expected to be organic and dynamic both in implementation and development, to persuade Beijing to be more transparent and conform to international norms by integrating with the international community, e.g. the early persuasion to Beijing to locate the headquarters of the AIIB in Seoul, Singapore, Jakarta and perhaps even the semi-autonomous Hong Kong rather than Shanghai or Beijing. These questions are pondered internally within China as well, between an internationalist faction keen to see the Silk Road initiatives as part of China's opening up with greater transparency and harmonization with international norms vs. those keen to construct an international trade and commerce system with firmer Beijing control.

Utilizing an international political economic approach and viewing the issue through a Chinese perspective, **Zhang Huang and Li Jie** dispenses policy recommendations for SOEs' stakeholders in such projects. He argued that, for neighboring countries of China, in order to build networks of HSR starting from China, Chinese companies and the state should not only avoid the traditional "tributary system" and civilization mentality, but also avoid cross-cultural barriers faced in exporting HSR systems by maintaining an inclusive and open attitude, and to carry out cooperation in HSR construction under equal terms and conditions with an understanding of the cultural identity of destination markets. Marketing Chinese HSR to the world may also trigger a new round of the "China threat theory".

In line with deliberate interpretations by some foreign media, Chinese internationalization attempt in the field of building railway traffic through constructing a HSR network, which radiates outwards to surrounding countries, and building traffic arteries across the South American continent, is directly related to its intentions and national interests in politics, economy, strategy and so on. For countries that are suspicious about the Chinese HSR, especially neighboring countries around China, China should be more proactive and patiently explain its peaceful development intention.

In essence, Zhang points out that the sale and exportation of Chinese HSR systems is a normative economic activity regulated by the market mechanism against the backdrop of globalization, just like other products and commodities made in China. China should express its cooperative, win–win intentions clearly, at the same time, attract a wide range of local technical elites, administrative elites and labor force in carrying out HSR design projects, operation and maintenance. China and others countries can work together to share the bigger economic cake of exporting HSR, while the presence of HSR benefits local communities and peoples.

In Section E, **Winglok Hung**'s short chapter argues that OBOR is a new economic strategy. The financial crisis in 2008 further exposed existing global economic problems and still requires a new international order to maintain peace. OBOR was established under this international context. There are many papers focusing on China's relations with emerging countries under the framework of OBOR. Hung admits that China's relations with emerging countries are important, but only China's successful interactions with Europe will transform the existing international order. Europe is important as it has always been the center of the world, particularly since 19th century.

Meanwhile, there are world leading business companies in Europe. As mentioned before, three components of the world international order system including international actors, international configuration and international norms are expected to change if OBOR is successfully practised. After the global financial crisis in 2008, senior scholars, foreign policy advisors and experts such as Henry Kissinger have been searching for a new global order. Hung believes that China, Southeast Asian countries, the Middle East regions and the African continent all take a role in OBOR and Europe is particularly crucial in this transformation.

Moving Eastwards from Europe to Central Asia, Lim Tai Wei argued that Central Asian actors have to thread between Beijing, Russian and also US interests carefully when interacting with China's OBOR initiative. The support or responses that they give to Beijing's OBOR initiatives are not entirely unqualified and without caveats. Meanwhile, other than Russia, India also wants a role in the region. P Stobdan, a former Indian ambassador to Central Asia, argued that the Central Asian region is undergoing a process of "de-Europeanization"; transnational forces like the Islamic State is moving into the region and China has challenged Russian regional monopoly to control trade in the region.[7] From such narratives, it appears India is also interested in projecting its geopolitical influence to Central Asia. To avoid being embroiled in geopolitical rivalries with Russia and India, China would do well to stick to the economic agenda that is in common with those of Central Asian states. Kazakhstan and Turkmenistan are relatively more developed than the other Central Asian states but they have commonalities of poverty, unemployment, unindustrialized economies and income gaps.[8]

Similarly in South Asia, **Lim Tai Wei** argues that Pakistan may be bandwagoning with China economically, while maintaining a good relationship with the United States at the state level. It may also be balancing against re-energized bilateral relationship between India and the United States. However the overall impact of the Chinese–Pakistani outreach is a potentially win–win situation for all, if the projects are transparent, if China negotiates successfully through the complex geopolitics and domestic politics of the South and Central Asian regions and if infrastructural connectivity promotes trade and commerce for the regions.

The balancing game seems to be applicable to Maritime Southeast Asian states like Malaysia as well. **Kong Tuan Yuen** argues that Malaysia will consistently keep a two-handed strategy as the best way to deal with China. In economic hand, Malaysia will make efforts to establish deeper and broader partnership with China through the OBOR initiatives, in order not to harm US interests in the Asia Pacific. In the political arena, Malaysia will echo the ASEAN countries' sovereignty claims in the South China Sea against China's maritime expansion. Malaysia will repeatedly try to maximize its economic interests subjected to comprehensive political considerations and priorities (both domestic and international).

Other than Malaysia, President Xi Jinping's November 2015 Vietnam visit appears to be part of charm diplomacy to smoothen out OBOR outreaches to Southeast Asian states. Like Japan, China was at the same

---

[7] Stobdan, P, IDSA COMMENT Modi's Visit to Central Asia, dated 6 July 2015 in the Institute for Defence Studies and Analyses (IDSA) [downloaded on 1 July 2015], available at http://www.idsa.in/idsacomments/ModisVisittoCentralAsia_pstobdan_060715.html.

[8] Wong, John, China's New Silk Road Initiatives and Central Asia Development, dated 28 June 2015–2 July 2015 in The Seminar on the Silk Road and Nazarbayev Theory of Peace. (Astana, Kazakhstan: Unpublished), 2015, 15.

Association of Southeast Asian Nations (ASEAN) and Asia-Pacific Economic Cooperation (APEC) meetings in end 2015. At the point of concluding this writing, Chinese President Xi conducted some charm diplomacy on the back of ASEAN and APEC meetings. Vietnam which the Chinese President Xi Jinping visited in November 2015 saw a mildly cold summit destination reception with a small anti-Chinese protest tolerated by the authorities taking place.

Xi is the first Chinese top leader to visit Vietnam in a decade. While relations are sometimes couched in terms of Communist brotherhood and fraternity especially due to Chinese help rendered during the Vietnam War against the Americans, they are juxtaposed with some frostiness and chilly encounters in reality. Relations reached a low point in May 2014 when Beijing positioned an oil rig in the disputed South China Sea. On another occasion, China also had to evacuate its citizens after anti-Chinese riots broke out and three Chinese nationals were killed in the turmoil.

Xi wanted to bring temperatures down by meeting the Vietnamese triumvirate of power brokers, the Communist Party Chief, President and Prime Minister. Contentious issues were discussed in the meeting including maritime disputes but so was cooperation in the usual economic realm, including trade and educational exchanges. For the Chinese side, perhaps infrastructure development was the most important item discussed due to the OBOR policy which emphasizes connectivity. Connectivity is not just about the physical transportation networks of highways, railways, ports and shipping lines. It is also more than the economic integration based on trade and finance. In the long run, connectivity is also concerned with people-to-people connection, social interaction and cultural exchange.

Ultimately, the end objective of any connectivity is not just for the partner states to take advantage of China's economic growth and its vast domestic markets by becoming more integrated with the Chinese economy. In addition, China is also trying to link up the Central Asian region with East Asia as the long-term goal of the new OBOR initiative. Vietnam falls within the Maritime Silk Road. Further down the road, if the OBOR is taken to its logical next step, one can even visualize the eventual integration of the Overland Silk Road with the Maritime Silk Road.

This will in turn bring Central Asia not just to China and East Asia but also the territories beyond the Western Pacific, i.e. the possibility of integrating all the regions in Asia. China's funding agencies like the AIIB, Silk Road Fund and other funding agencies offer the prospects of much-needed infrastructure loans and most importantly, Chinese investments and loans have comparatively less strings attached than their Western counterparts. In the case of Vietnam, there is potential for the Chinese one-party authoritarian state to speak in the same language as Vietnam's authoritarian government.

In general, China's charm offensive is historically associated with continental power and its maritime outreach is mainly commercial as in the Southern Sung dynasty regional trade network. It only briefly displayed naval ambitions during Admiral Zheng He's voyages in Ming dynasty. Vietnam is playing a game of caution in such outreach. Its Communist Party Secretary General Nguyen Phu Trong visited the US in July 2015 to forge closer ties. US has a strategy of pivoting back to East Asia. Vietnam is also a signatory to the Trans-Pacific Partnership (TPP) agreement involving 12 countries but not including China. Both US visit and TPP agreement are seen by some as an attempt to hedge against Beijing. While Xi was touring Vietnam, Japanese Defense Minister was concurrently touring an important military naval base in Vietnam. Japan is engaged in a close alliance with the US. There are also recent historical issues that affect bilateral ties such as the 1979 Chinese brief invasion of Vietnam in retaliation for Vietnam's own annexation of Cambodia (a Chinese ally).

After a successful thawing visit to Vietnam, Xi is trying to heal another wound in Manila during the 18–19 November 2015 APEC meeting. China is laying the ground for the presidential meeting by sending out signals that Beijing is unwilling to talk about the maritime island dispute in South China Sea. (Presidents Xi and Aquino had not met since a brief encounter in APEC Beijing 2014.) The mission of conveying this message fell upon Chinese Foreign Minister Wang Yi who flew in earlier into Manila for the groundwork.

At the point of this writing, Manila's bilateral chilly relations with Beijing is also showing some thawing signs as Foreign Secretary Albert del Rosario tries to separate the maritime disputes issues from overall relations so that bilateral relations can move ahead. This is yet another example of recent series of ice-thawing missions occurring throughout East Asia. And also possible indications of Filipino pragmatism in keeping the talks focused on economic cooperation and avoiding political issues. The Filipino President assured Beijing of their warm hospitality during Xi's visit. President Aquino mentioned that it was in Filipino culture to do so. Overall, the APEC Manila trip witnessed the successful wrap-up of an ice-thawing trip to Vietnam and an all-smiles diplomacy in Manila.

Finally, **Lim Tai Wei** studies Japanese reactions to the OBOR developments. He observed that what Japan ultimately offers is experience. Japan's overseas development assistance, loans, aids and investments contributed to the post-war industrialization of Southeast Asia and China and set up production networking in these countries. It has accumulated a wealth of experience in this regard. Japan therefore has the capacity to contribute its experience to developing Central Asia, along with other large economies like China and Russia. Political scientists may call the Japanese entrance into Central Asia "hedging" against Russian and Chinese dominance, while economists may consider it as a latecomer catch-up economic decision. Ultimately, regardless of perspective, Lim argues that the Central Asian developmental pie will be big enough to accommodate all big players, Japan, China and Russia.

Lim's chapter also pointed out that, in the economic realm, realizing the significance of a combined 600 million-strong consumer market, a young workforce, increasing foreign direct investments, greater net connectivity and tourist arrivals, and the Asia's third largest economy, Japan which has production networks in the region for decades is working with ASEAN partners to strengthen cooperation. By the end of 2015, the ASEAN Economic Community (AEC) will be set up, an important step that is the start of a long journey to forming a regional economic community. Japanese investments and aid/loans can help the AEC harmonize its standards for a smoother transition to become a regional organization. Likewise, China will also seize on such opportunities to have closer economic ties with the AEC.

Epilogue: Conferences and discussions

The Chinese Track II and academic institutions held major conferences in Istanbul and Hong Kong to discuss plans about the Beijing-led Belt and Road Initiatives in mid-December 2014. These conferences reveal several nuggets of information. First, there is some emphasis on lifting the living standards of countries (including those with per capita gross national income that is 46.4% of the international average standards) in the Eurasian

Zone-Road sections of the Silk Road.[9] *Xinhuanet* featured support from government ministers for the scheme from Balkan states like Montenegro and Serbia.[10] Maritime countries like Malaysia have also stated more concrete intentions to construct infrastructure for tapping into the Maritime Silk Road.

> "We are in the process of developing port cities collaboration between Qinzhou Port (of China) and the Kuantan Port (of Malaysia)," former Malaysian ambassador to China Abdul Majid Ahamad Khan said at a forum on ASEAN development on 13 December 2014, reported by China's Xinhua news agency.[11]

These revelations indicated that the Maritime Silk Road fund could possibly target underperforming economies, help them construct infrastructure, and also enhance connectivity with middle-income economies like Malaysia through cooperation in port facilities.

Operating philosophy

The manner or operating philosophy in which these funds would be managed and dispensed were also revealed by Chinese President Xi Jinping on 7 September 2013 at the Nazarbayev University in Astana, Kazakhstan. He mentioned that China and other countries like those in Central Asia can first compare their plans on economic development while infrastructure links can be enhanced with the guiding philosophy that China "respects the development paths and policies chosen by the peoples of regional countries, and will never interfere in the domestic affairs of

[9] *Xinhuanet*, Silk Roads Initiatives Enters New Phase: Think Tank, dated 15 December 2014 in Xinhuanet.com website [downloaded on 18 December 2014], available at http://news.xinhuanet.com/english/china/2014-12/15/c_133856803.htm.

[10] *Ibid.*

[11] *Xinhuanet*, Malaysia Ready for Greater Cooperation with China in Maritime Silk Road: Former Ambassador, dated 13 December 2014 in the *Xinhuanet* website [downloaded on 13 December 2014], available at http://news.xinhuanet.com/english/china/2014-12/13/c_133852521.htm.

Central Asian nations".[12] This pronouncement resembled Chinese past practices in which they dispensed aid without strict pre-conditions, that both led to praise amongst African leaders for the Chinese role in uplifting the continent economically and also criticisms from human rights groups for dispensing aid to brutal regimes or economies unprepared for economic take-off without proper accounting oversight and procedures. In other words, there are mixed reactions to the Chinese model of infrastructure investment strategies.

"China will never seek a dominant role in regional affairs, nor try to nurture a sphere of influence", he added.[13] This is again a familiar format that has dynamically evolved and eclectically incorporated the non-hegemony promise, vision of a multipolar world, peaceful rise of China and the in-vogue idea of doing what is necessary for China's national interest without infringing upon others. There are those who support and oppose this worldview. Those who support see this consensus as one that opens up an alternative developmental path for those who choose to place growth above political liberalization and competitive politics or system that have been time-tested by developed economies.

With regard to the BRICS Bank, both India and China declared broad and ambiguous terms of "justice, equity and transparency" to be conditions for their loan dispensing.[14] For most countries, the Chinese vision and more established developmental paths of the developed economies are not mutually exclusive, there are overlaps between these two choices. It provides more diversity of choices for funding and infrastructure development. For the critics, the problems they see with this range from challenging the status quo of the prevailing world order of trade and politics to the shadow of neo-Colonialism in resource extraction.

---

[12] *Xinhuanet*, Xi Suggests China, C. Asia Build Silk Road Economic Belt, dated 7 September 2013 in the *Xinhuanet* website [downloaded on 18 December 2014], available at http://news.xinhuanet.com/english/china/2013-09/07/c_132700695.htm.

[13] *Ibid.*

[14] Escobar, Pepe, China is Building a New Silk Road to Europe, And it's Leaving America Behind, dated 16 December 2014 in *Mother Jones* website [downloaded on 18 December 2014], available at http://www.motherjones.com/politics/2014/12/chinas-new-silk-road-europe-will-leave-america-behind.

Implementation

In terms of implementation priorities, some argue that China's main target is Central Asia and eventually proliferate to other regions that will not only include train infrastructure but also ports and eventually energy pipelines.[15] The evidence for this, according to this school of thought, is the direction of Chinese capital flow. China's capital flow to Central Asia: US$30 billion in contracts with Kazakhstan; US$15 billion with Uzbekistan; US$8 billion for Turkmenistan and US$1 billion to Tajikistan.[16] Chinese close relations with Putin's Russia is another evidence: the trans-Siberian high-speed rail remix reduces transit time between Beijing and Moscow from 6 1/2 days to only 33 hours.[17] These evidences further point to the narrative that the landed routes will eventually pare down the volumes carried on the maritime routes.

The process of achieving equilibrium in constant negotiations between the different views of constructing in setting an economic world or regional orders is a natural outcome of any ambitious regional initiative and such debates have taken place in the past for other initiatives as well. Witness the past debates over Fortress Europe when a pan-European economy was establishing, the production networks set up by Japan in East Asia, Soviet bloc of collectivization economies, Organization of the Petroleum Exporting Countries (OPEC) unity in the face of geopolitical crises. All of them were seen as challengers to prevailing world orders and were eventually harmonized or integrated into the world order. There are no indications thus far that the Chinese have intentions to overturn or replace the current international economic system. And there are also signs of outreach from perceived or imagined rival institutions. The ADB President may not agree with the AIIB idea, for example, but have belatedly welcomed cooperation between the two.

Thus far, the Chinese Silk Road initiatives also does not seem to be incompatible with APEC, WTO, TPP, Free Trade Area of the Asian-Pacific (FTAAP), Regional Comprehensive Economic Partnership (RCEP) organizations. In fact, the Chinese appear to harmonize or complement with at least some of these institutions. It is necessary to mention some concerns about these Silk Road initiatives by other stakeholders before discussing

---

[15] *Ibid.*

[16] *Ibid.*

[17] *Ibid.*

some of the positive features and concrete measures of the initiative at this early stage. Some of these narratives may be perceptions but perceptions are sometimes as important as concrete developments in issues related to international relations, geopolitics and economic competition. According to some journalistic writings, Beijing intends to pare down the 90% of world trade that still travels by maritime routes by increasing freight transportation overland through HSRs.[18]

The Economist lend possible indirect support for this argument: "Most containers still travel by sea, which is considerably cheaper — about $4,000 each rather than $9,000. But the gap is narrowing as European manufacturers start filling the empty carriages going back to China with high-priced products such as luxury cars."[19] The equilibrium or balance between overland and maritime trade routes in Chinese initiatives has already been highlighted in the international media. Such a prospect if not properly explained or managed may put maritime trading nations on their toes. Some observers see the AIIB institution as a challenge to the ADB. ADB is an institution established by and traditionally associated with US–Japan initiatives with a combined 31% contribution of the bank's capital and 25% of its voting power.[20] Rivalry with US–Japanese institutions is extended to the geopolitical sphere, according other observers.

Veteran contemporary China sinologist and economist John Wong highlighted the smart features of the Belt and Road Initiative and provided a balanced analysis with some concerns as well: "China is essentially leveraging its geo-economic power in order to achieve larger geo-political objectives ... In the case of the Overland Silk Road, China's efforts run the risk of creating suspicion and conflict with Russia. Many Central Asian states fall into Russia's traditional sphere of influence. As for the Maritime Silk Road, China's immediate diplomatic challenge is obviously how to untangle its

[18] *Ibid.*

[19] *The Economist*, The New Silk Road Hardly an Oasis, dated 15 November 2014 in *The Economist* [downloaded on 18 December 2014], available at http://www.economist.com/news/asia/21632595-kazakhstan-turns-geography-advantage-china-builds-new-silk-road-hardly-oasis.

[20] Escobar, Pepe, China is Building a New Silk Road to Europe, And it's Leaving America Behind, dated 16 December 2014 in *Mother Jones* website [downloaded on 18 December 2014], available at http://www.motherjones.com/politics/2014/12/chinas-new-silk-road-europe-will-leave-america-behind.

deep-rooted territorial disputes with neighbors such as Japan, Vietnam and the Philippines."[21] This is a succinct, timely, well couched, balanced and important reminder of China's vulnerabilities and weak points when it comes to the geopolitical feature of the Belt and Road Initiative.

Bloomberg's report on the Belt and Road Initiative also expressed similar concerns by some experts within Russia: "So far, China has understood Russia's sensitivities and has not challenged Moscow on political and security issues ... China, for the first time in 200 years or so, has become a more powerful and dynamic country than Russia ... I expect the Chinese to be smart and clever when dealing with Russia, without provoking it unnecessarily ... Should they, however, suddenly become abrasive and aggressive instead, a rupture in relations will follow." said Mr Dmitri Trenin, director of the Moscow Center at Carnegie Endowment for International Peace, he said.[22]

Essentially, it is quite well understood that Beijing is yielding the dividends from Russia's fallout with Washington and European majors, particularly after the Crimea issue. Beijing will have to deepen the bilateral relationship further to prevent any flip-flops or frictions in the future which are bound to occur between neighbors and also institute measures that will bring the bilateral relations into the post-Putin era. Beijing's collective leadership will have to cope with a political elite power structures in the Kremlin. Beijing also understands that the Kremlin was a pioneer and forerunner in Eurasian regionalism.

As *The Economist* pointed out, in 2011, Kazakhstan, along with Russia and Belarus, formed a customs union, which is scheduled to become the Eurasian Union in January 2015.[23] Besides Russian presence, *The Economist*

[21] Wong, John, Reviving the Ancient Silk Road: China's New Economic Diplomacy, dated 9 July 2014 in the *Straits Times* [downloaded on 18 December 2014], available at http://www.straitstimes.com/news/opinion/invitation/story/reviving-the-ancient-silk-road-chinas-new-economic-diplomacy-20140709.

[22] *Bloomberg*, Chinese Premier's Silk Road Trip Marks Advance on Russia's patch, dated 16 December 2014 in *Todayonline* website [downloaded on 18 December 2014], available at http://www.todayonline.com/chinaindia/china/chinese-premiers-silk-road-trip-marks-advance-russias-patch.

[23] *The Economist*, The New Silk Road Hardly an Oasis, dated 15 November 2014 in *The Economist* [downloaded on 18 December 2014], available at http://www.economist.com/news/asia/21632595-kazakhstan-turns-geography-advantage-china-builds-new-silk-road-hardly-oasis.

also pointed out other challenges in the Eurasian region. They include Russian swaggering (Ukraine, recent mobilization of troops near its border with Kazakhstan, European reluctance to trade with Russia, Russian obstacles to goods traveling to Europe at times of bad relations, domestic problems like corruption in Central Asia, elitist dominance of wealth creation, susceptibility to commodity fluctuations, criminal groups, etc.[24]

Self-interest

Ultimately, pragmatism may turn out to the deciding factor in the Belt and Road Initiative's shape, form and outcome. The Initiative is comparable to the analogy of choice offering based on individual assessment of national interests at this moment. The ultimate adjudicating factor is in the details, how each individual economy or state will assess the national interests according to conditionalities, geopolitical priorities, domestic political situations, external factors and national resources and how the Belt and Road Initiative + AIIB + BRICS Bank *vis-à-vis* current existing established institutions like ADB best serve their needs. Take for example the foreign policy strategy of a central player and stakeholder in the Belt and Road Initiative, Kazakhstan's position is reflective of such sentiments. *Bloomberg* reported on 16 December 2014 that Kazakhstan says it wants "to be on good terms with all the major powers like China, the United States and the European Union, as well as Russia, a nation with which it has long-standing historical, economic and political ties".[25]

---

[24] *Ibid.*

[25] Bloomberg, Chinese Premier's Silk Road trip marks Advance on Russia's Patch, dated 16 December 2014 in *Todayonline* website [downloaded on 18 December 2014], available at http://www.todayonline.com/chinaindia/china/chinese-premiers-silk-road-trip-marks-advance-russias-patch.

Index

F

G

H

I

J

K

L

M

N

X

Y

Z

Printed in the United States
by Bookmasters

Printed in the United States
By Bookmasters